Editor's Notes

In hopes of casting his readers into the era of the events that transpire the author has used the vocabulary of the period. The spellings of the day were used as well. Street and Avenue were not capitalized for example. Several words such as streetcar and backstop had hyphens. People stopped at hotels they didn't stay at them. Many of the expressions of the 1880's are no longer in use. He tried some hippodrome business makes no sense anymore, we'd say he tried to throw the game, and no one has the collywobbles either, we're just anxious. Nobody today is in high cotton, they're delighted, and we wouldn't say someone doesn't care a continental, we'd say he was indifferent. Now no one has a wire-edge on now, they're disgruntled or resentful.

Baseball was still base ball. A member of a team was said to play in the nine, not for the nine. A substitute catcher was a change-catcher. A pitcher, or twirler, was positioned between the points, or in the pitching box, not on the mound, there was no mound. And there were no dugouts, just a bench that the two teams shared. Teams rarely had more than ten players. The people in attendance were referred to as rooters, boosters, or cranks, not fans. The crowd was an audience of spectators.

"There's just one mistake in what your Pinkerton man reported. T'was whiskey, I've never had lemonade at that hour in me life."

Mike "King" Kelly

THE
#
BEAUTY

———

Copyright © 2025
W. G. Braund / Out of the Park
All Rights Reserved

———

ISBN: 978-1-967254-07-1 - *hardcover*
ISBN: 978-1-967254-08-8 - *softcover*
ISBN: 978-1-967254-09-5 - *e-book*

———

Book Design & Production
timmyroland.com

THE
$10,000
BEAUTY

W. G. Braund

OUT OF THE PARK

WORLDWIDE

THE
$10,000
BEAUTY

"No matter. I'm going to sign Kelly anyway."

Broad-shouldered, blue-eyed, full of ginger Mike Kelly needed to find a new place. He'd tried some of the Port Jervis boarding-houses but he was eighteen now and they had a lot of rules.

"Close, that door, you'll let the flies in," was all the woman at the first place seemed able to say before turning him out on the street for stealing ice for his beer from her ice box. The mistress of the second boarding house had evicted him for smoking cigarettes in his tiny bed. The shrew at the last house had caught him with something *worse* in his bed, a cash-girl from the apothecary.

The Delaware House was out of the question, its rooms went for $2 a night. That left the Three-States Hotel, the Globe, the Exchange, and the Crissman House. Mike ended up choosing the Globe, its advertisement in the town's *Evening Gazette* announced: "Refurbished throughout. Transient patronage solicited. Terms moderate. Wines, Liquors, Ales, and Cigars."

After he checked in Mike spent some of his first pay buying a pair of pebble goat button boots at Higby's on Pike street. He walked carefully in them, the town's streets were covered in horse droppings. He stopped for a glass of Milwaukee lager at Wyker's saloon in the Opera House block. He got a lot of looks from the other patrons, curious to know who the new young man in town might be. When he went back to his hotel he stepped out the back door to smoke a cigarette.

"Shite!" he exclaimed. His new boots had been treated to more droppings, this time from the hens that provided eggs for the Globe's dining room. At least the smoke from his cigarette helped mitigate the aroma wafting from the hotel's livery stable.

At one p.m. on June 12 the Delawares boarded train No. One and headed to Susquehannah for a four o'clock game against the Stars of that place. *The Gazette* reported that: "The boys started off in good spirits and if the wishes of their many friends avail aught they will show a good record for themselves and the village which sends them forth on the trial for the championship of Western New York."

The Delawares led 9-0 after three innings and held on for an 11-8 win. "Kelley, the catcher of the Delawares" according to *The Port Jervis Evening Gazette*, went hitless but "tried some hippodrome business in the ninth inning, taking a foul bound while on his back."

On Saturday nights Mike and the other unmarried players went to the Empire Music Hall to play shuffle-board, billiards, air gun, and pin pool and to drink beer and smoke.

"Have you taken a fancy to any uv the local girls then, Michael?" asked Marooney, who played third base for the Delawares and batted second in the order behind Kelly. He was the only one drinking whiskey. A glass here was ten cents instead of the usual fifteen.

"I've not," said Mike, whose Irish accent was almost as broad as Marooney's. "Most of them are as plain as porridge and as alluring as school marms."

On the Fourth of July against the Alaska nine from Staten Island Kelly made a base hit to right field to lead off the game. He had another one to lead off the third but was overzealous and got thrown out at the plate trying to score on a passed ball. He had a third base hit in the fifth but was stranded at third when Ingram struck out. The Alaskas scored their last run in a 4-1 win when Quilty ran home on a passed ball by Kelly. The next day against the Keystones of New York, a 5-4 loss, Kelly made two hits and "a beautiful one-handed jumping catch of a foul tip."

In the July 9 game "Kelley of the Delawares did well behind the bat and invariably caught his man on second." After his team had secured the lucky side of the coin and the captain had elected to have

the first swings at the crisp new ball, Mike led off the game with a base hit, made second on an error, reached third on a hit by Ingram, and scored on a passed ball.

Kelly had a base hit in the fourth and crossed the home plate on another passed ball. He made another base hit in the fourth. And scored on yet another ball that eluded the catcher's hands.

With no base ball on Sunday, Mike headed back to Paterson to see his mother and to spend a little time with Agnus Headifen, who he had to admit wasn't much prettier than the girls in Delaware. She made fancy trims for ladies' hats at the mill where Mike had worked. Aggie was hardly "his girl" they just went for walks or to the fair. This time he took her out to the countryside for a basket picnic. Nothing untoward happened, Agnus was much too prim and proper for that.

Unlike Mike she read a lot. He liked hearing her talk about the Vikings and the Romans and about their Irish forefathers. He was fascinated when she told him how Irish men had played a stick and ball game called hurling. Mike wondered if the large number of Irish ball players in the major leagues might be explained by the hand-eye coordination and knack for smacking a ball a long way they were likely to have inherited.

The July 14, 1877 edition of *The Port Jervis Evening Gazette* stated that the previous day's game between a nine from Philadelphia and the Delawares was the best game of base ball ever witnessed in the town. "Ingram's pitching was effective and Kelley supported him in a manner that elicited considerable praise." Mike, the catcher and leadoff striker, was put out on a fly in each of his first three times at the bat but he made a three-base hit in the seventh and scored the game's first run on Ingram's base hit. He batted Gilmartin home with a two-baser in the 8th as his club coasted to a 10-0 win.

The Delawares had a day off and the town's other nine, the Butter-Fingers, hosted a team from Monticello that had come in on the Port Jervis & Monticello railroad that morning. Kelly and a couple of his teammates took in the game and drank beer and chuckled throughout as the visitors managed to outmuff the But-

ter-Fingers and lose 23-20.

Mike received an offer to play for the Springfield, Ohio nine but the Port Jervis club offered to raise his pay to $70 a month if he stayed with them so he did.

On August 7 *The Port Jervis Gazette* reported that Kelly had gone to Columbus, where he'd secured a position as right fielder and change-catcher with the famous Buckeye club of the International Association. Their catcher Billy Barnie was unable to play owing to a broken finger. Mike arrived at the newly rebuilt Union Station where he was met by his good friend James McCormick. With a name like McCormick most people assumed that James was Scottish, but Mike knew Jim was the son of James McCormick and Rosa Lawry who were born in Ireland but moved to Scotland in search of a better life.

"Welcome to Columbus, Michael J. Kelly," said James.

"Thanks for recommendin' me fer the job, me friend," said Mike.

"You didn't come by way of Ashtabula I hope."

Kel shuddered at the thought. "Jesus, Mary, and Joseph! No. And we didn't have any bridges give out underneath us."

Eight months before, an experimental Howe Truss design bridge over the Ashtabula River had collapsed as a Lake Shore and Michigan Southern Railway train carrying 160 passengers passed over it. All but the lead locomotive had plunged into the river. The train's oil lanterns and coal-fired heating stoves had set the wooden cars on fire. Rescuers pulled individuals from the wreck rather than extinguish the blaze and many who survived the crash burned to death. The accident had killed almost 100 people.

"Well let's get you squared away, we've a game tomorrow."

"So you've taken Blondie's spot in the box then, Jimsy?"

"I have."

"And Edward's playing in the Indianapolis nine uv the League Alliance?"

"Aye, and our old friend from Paterson is doing quite well for himself by all reports. In a game last month he held the Hartfords to one hit. Then he twirled five straight shutouts in a span of eight days."

"No wonder the cranks have taken to calling Ed "the Only" Nolan."

"That's not all, in the middle of March in New Orleans against the Robert E. Lee Club he pitched a six-inning game and not a single batsman managed so much as a foul ball."

"Have you got a mouth rubber, Mike? Billy Barnie says he's got one he hasn't used if you'll be needin' one."

Mike took his mouth rubber out of his pocket and showed McCormick.

"Are you wearing anything else?"

"What d'ya mean, a glove or one uv those silly masks?"

"Aye."

"No I am not, just this . . . and protection for me privates."

As they crossed East Broad street they jumped out of the way of a buggy.

"I've never seen so many buggies in me *life*," said Mike as he straightened his tie.

"The Columbus Buggy Company is turning the things out about a dozen an hour. At that rate before you know it this place'll be the buggy capitol off the world."

When they got to the ball grounds they were greeted by John Franklin "Chub" Sullivan in his broad New England accent. Chub, who was actually tall and as skinny as a string-bean, had learned to play ball on the Boston Commons.

"This is our captain, Mike," said Chub, pointing to a man with long side whiskers who was eight years' Mike's senior. "Charlie Pabor, our intrepid captain and left fielder." Kelly had to squelch a laugh, James had told him their captain's nickname was The Old Woman in the Red Cap.

Pabor shook Mike's hand. "Good to have you, Kelly, they say you're a good man to have behind the bat," said Pabor in a thick Brooklyn accent. "I'm told you and McCormick have played together."

"That we have, we grew up together . . . in Paterson."

Charlie indicated the player beside him, who looked to be around Mike's age and about the same weight, though like most of the players he wasn't as tall as Kelly. "This is our second baseman, George Strief. He's from Cincinnati."

Pabor looked at Mike, straight-faced. "I'm doing much better here than I did in '75."

Chub and James laughed. Mike gave them a blank look.

Chub explained. "Charlie captained the Brooklyn Atlantics that year."

"And?" asked Mike.

"They only won two games," chuckled Strief.

"Enough. Let's get to work," said Pabor. "We've a game in two hours."

On August 11, 1877, the *Wheeling Daily Intelligencer* reported that "the Buckeye club of Columbus, Ohio met the Standards at the Fair Grounds yesterday afternoon and demolished our boys by a score of 10 to 3. It was like shooting fish in a barrel. The Standards were unable to get the 'hang' of McCormick's down shoots, not a hit being made until the ninth inning. The Buckeyes' fielding was remarkably good,

The next day the Buckeyes were in Springfield. Kelly, batting fifth, made three one-base hits and a two-baser. Mike took Barnie's usual place behind the bat and was charged with two errors but threw out two Springfields who tried to steal second.

On August 14 the Buckeyes hosted the Alleghenys of the International League. Pud Galvin was "balled out of the diamond for the first time during the year." Kelly had the collywobbles and was hitless in five tries at the lively ball but his catching and that of his counterpart, the Pittsburgs' Ned Williamson, "was superb." The

Buckeyes won 8-7.

On Friday, August 17 several hundred amusement-loving people gathered at the base ball grounds at the corner of Rhode and Niagara streets in Buffalo to witness the game between the home club and the Buckeyes. Mike led off and was behind the bat for the Columbus nine. He began the game by sending a ball to right field for a hit. He stole second on an error by Buffalo catcher Fields and got to third on a bad throw by the same party.

With Sullivan at the plate little Larry Corcoran, the Bisons' hard-throwing twirler, unleashed a wild pitch which struck Field's left thumb, breaking the bones and driving the nail into the flesh. Kelly ran home on the play. He missed the ball three times and was out his next turn at the bat, was put out on a grounder to first his next try and took his seat on the bench the two teams shared after fouling out his last time at the bat. Jim McCormick held the Buffalos to two hits and the Buckeyes won 4-1.

After the game Kelly praised his friend's performance. "A measly two safe ones off uv you this time, Jimsy. Mighty fine twirlin' I'd say."

"It could have been none," grunted James.

"How's that then?"

"Where did each of them go?"

Mike thought for a moment. "Up the middle as I recall."

"And who had the best chance of getting them?"

Kelly thought again. "Strief."

"He could have had both of them, Kel. He's a damn record player."

"A record player?"

"Aye, George shirks hard plays because if the ball goes off or through his hands it'll be scored an error. That's what everyone likes about you, Kel, you don't give a damn about your fielding record. You go after any ball hit within a hundred feet."

In a game in Elmira, N.Y. the Steam Hollow Boys' Nathaniel

Banker hit his brother Addison with a pitch. An angry altercation ensued and they came to blows. The brothers were separated by the other players but Addison persisted in his violent treatment of Nathaniel, whereupon the latter resorted to the persuasive argument of mobocracies and fired a pistol shot into Addison's bowels. After walking a few steps and then falling down he was taken to the home of the boys' parents. A messenger was sent to fetch Doc Dayton who did all that he could but the boy died the next morning.

On August 26 against the Buffalo club Kelly made only one mistake - a bad return throw to McCormick that allowed the man on the third to score the only run of the game. On September 1 in Columbus the playing of Kelly, Strief, and Sullivan against the Rochesters was "very fine". Kelly was behind the bat and made no errors but had just one safe hit in five attempts.

On August 28 in Columbus the Buckeyes scored an unearned run in the first inning and none after that in a 3-1 loss to the St. Louis Browns. Sullivan, Kelly, who threw out two runners from behind the bat, and McCormick "did nice work" for the Bucks but Chub had their only hit off Tricky Nichols who'd struggled with the New Haven Elm Citys of the National Association but was doing better with the Browns.

On September 5th Sullivan, Kelly, McCormick, and Pabor did the best work for the Buckeyes in their 5-2 walk-away over the Louisvilles.

J. Wayne Neff, the president of the Cincinnati club, watched the game with John Chapman, who ran the Louisvilles. It was the first time he'd seen Kelly play.

"He catches without a mask," said Chapman.

"And does so rather well," said Nuff.

"He's as full of pluck as an egg is full of meat and he's one of the best catchers I've ever seen," said Chapman, I'd sure like him in my club."

Mike had one passed ball but did good work in a rather surprising 5-2 win over the Louisville Grays, one of the National League's best teams. They dominated the league but due to small turnouts their

finances had collapsed to the point that they couldn't make their payroll and their players had resorted to passing the hat after home games. Their uniforms were filthy. Kelly guessed they hadn't been laundered in a month.

The Buckeyes made seven errors, the Louisvilles an even dozen. "Slippery Elm" Nichols seemed to be muffing on purpose and Jim "Terror" Devlin, the Grays' twirler, was throwing wild pitches in key spots.

"Isn't Devlin's one uv the top pitchers in their league?" Mike asked George Strief.

"He is," said Strief. "At least he was until a couple of weeks ago."

"What do you mean?"

"His best pitch is a ground shoot. It's well nigh impossible to hit."

"The Terror's not throwin' us any ground shoots *today*."

"Two weeks ago the Louisvilles were in first place. They'd won twenty-seven games - of course Devlin pitches every game - and they'd lost just thirteen. They were four games up on St. Louis and four and a half ahead of Boston with twenty games to play."

"Sounds like a mighty safe lead for a team that good. Joe Gerhardt told me the club's managers had already dug a hole for the flagstaff that was gointa fly their whip pennant, but the Grays aren't in first anymore are they?" "They just lost nine league games in a row, and a few exhibition matches they should have won to boot."

"What the hell's happened to them?"

"Makes you wonder, doesn't it? We don't hit *anybody* else this well and we shouldn't be hittin' Devlin a lick." He thought a moment. "And they have only two runs. Their man Nichols shouldn't even be in the lineup, Bill Hague - Old Cientific - is their regular third baseman. I heard he'd suffered with boils but he's a picture of health now. George Hall led the league in home runs last year and he's hittin' like a little girl this afternoon. He's struck out twice and he *never does*. Seems like some of them don't *want* to beat us for some reason,

9

they're booting the ball around like it's a bloody soccer game . . . well everyone but Shafer and Gerhardt. Butcher Craver's been accused of bein' a tad shady and having no small part in a number of put-up-jobs."

"Who's the young fellow in the charcoal dress suit?"

"No idea."

"Well he's surely keepin' an eagle eye on their players."

Pabor had overheard what Mike and George were talking about. "That's John Haldeman, his father's the Grays' president."

Mike watched as Craver let a slow ground ball slip through his hands then looked at Haldeman. He was madly scribbling something in a note-pad.

The Louisvilles ended up losing the championship to Boston. They won six out of their last seven games, making their season record of 35-25 look respectable, but the wins came after Boston had clinched the pennant.

On the morning of August 31 the Grays Vice-President Charles E. Chase was eating breakfast at home when a telegram arrived from Hoboken. Who the sender was he never learned but the wire stated that Hartford was mysteriously favored over the Grays - 30 to 20 - in the local pools and that something was clearly wrong with the Louisville players. Sure enough, the Louisvilles lost the game that afternoon. He'd had suspicions of his own and Chase knew the best person to ask about the nine's play. Haldeman's son had followed the club closely during the season and he was well acquainted with how the players could and should have played.

"I'm surprised it took you so long to ask," said John. "I knew funny business had been going on during the last Eastern trip." He handed Chase his dog-eared note-book.

"What's this?"

"Take a look. I've been making notes on some of the players ever since the team started losing, certain players that all of a sudden didn't exactly play like the bunch of world beaters they had been. I figured there was some manner of chicanery afoot, I'd heard talk of

men placing wagers against their own team."

Chase's eyes widened as he read one account of sloppy or indifferent play after another. The next morning he started an investigation. On October 4, the entire team was gathered together and Chase demanded that they turn over their telegrams. Every player except Craver complied. Chase contacted Western Union and obtained damning telegrams that had been sent to Craver. Nichols handed over a wire from a pool-seller from Brooklyn named Williams asking why Nichols hadn't contacted him and if 'arrangements' were in place. The telegrams linked Craver and Nichols as well as Devlin and Hall to a New York gambler named McLeod. Hall implicated Nichols, stating he was the contact man with McLeod as well as Williams and other gamblers. Devlin and Hall confessed to throwing several exhibition games late in the season with Devlin receiving up to a whopping $100 per game.

Craver, Devlin, Hall, and Nichols were expelled from the club. One of the major reasons the National League had been formed the year before was to rid the game of its associations with gamblers. On December 4 its president William Hulbert banned the four men from professional baseball for life.

The Buckeyes disbanded on September 15. Kelly had just 15 hits in 96 times for a batting average of .156 when they did. Sullivan, who'd batted .310, one of only three men to top .200, was recruited to play for Cincinnati of the National League. When he got there he told President Nuff about Kelly.

"I've seen him play, Sullivan, he's the genuine article. I asked around and I heard good things about him, especially that he seems to have an intuitive sense of what an opposing player is going to do and he generally outwits him. But I was also told of his unfortunate tendency to fall down at critical moments without apparent cause, his feet becoming panicky when he is about to catch a ball."

"Well, he does . . . "

Nuff raised a hand. "No matter. I'm going to sign Kelly anyway."

Mike was offered a $125 a month contract to play for the Red

Caps, who knew they needed a much stronger nine in '78. They'd placed 6th in the six-team National League with a 15-42 record. One of their pitchers, Bobby Mitchell, a local boy, was a left-hander. Kelly didn't want the team to know that he'd never caught a southpaw. Over the winter he'd find one to pitch to him.

2

"Make sure you lock your door!"

The 1878 Reds would feature just three carry-overs, 21-year-old Mitchell, Chub Sullivan, and speedy Lipman "the Iron Batter" Pike. He'd beaten a racehorse in a well-publicized 100-yard dash five years before but was slowing down at the ripe old age of 33. Though a left-hander, Pike played some second base, but he generally plied center field. Base ball's only Jewish player, Lip hit for power. Playing for the Philadelphia Athletics in 1866 he'd belted six home runs against the Alert club one afternoon though he wasn't the only batsman to feast on the Alert twirler. The final score was 67-25.

Billy Geer, who'd made his professional baseball debut for the New York Mutuals of the National Association at the age of 15 in '75 would be the Cincinnatis' shortstop and jocular, hard-hitting Charlie Jones would tend left field. Mike thought Charlie looked like a riverboat gambler. Second baseman Joe Gerhardt had played for the Washington Blue Legs, the Baltimore Canaries, and the New York Mutuals in the National Association and then two years with the Louisville Grays. Joe knew he was damned fortunate not to have been banished from base ball for failing to report the actions of his teammates. So was Orator Shafer. The fact that the two had been the Grays' leading batsmen and steadiest fielders throughout the season had relieved them of any likelihood of being involved in the throwing of games.

The Red Caps' biggest need was a new battery. Candy Cummings had won just five games in '77, Mitchell had won 6 and lost 5, and their other change-pitcher Mathews had won just three. The catcher, Scott Hastings, had fielded miserably and batted an anemic .154.

In November, rumors had made the circuit that the White brothers would sign with Cincinnati. In 1872 *The New York Clipper* said of Jim White, "We have never known him to growl at an umpire and his record for integrity is untarnished by even a hint of suspicion." But despite being one of the top players in the country and perhaps the best catcher in the game, White decided to retire. He went back to his farm in Steuben County, New York. In a letter to the *Clipper*, captain Harry Wright said, "James White has not arrived. He has been converted to religion and thinks at present that he would not be doing right if he should play base ball."

White had a change of heart and, in addition to teaching Sunday-school, he batted .392 which was good for third in the league list. On defense he led all catchers in putouts and double plays. *The Clipper* called him "as agile in his movements as a cat and as plucky withal as a bulldog." Jim batted .376, .343, and .387 from 1875 to '77.

Considered a silver-tongued orator, White was starting to be called "The Deacon" by his peers. His brother Will, who'd just married 16-year-old Harriet Holmes, had developed a sharp-breaking curveball while pitching for the Lynn, Massachusetts Live Oaks, one of the strongest amateur clubs in the country. Jim convinced the Boston Red Stockings to give Will a three-game tryout. He proved he could pitch, winning two of the games including a shutout. He also became the first major leaguer ever to play while wearing eyeglasses. With his thin frame, receding hairline and wire-rimmed spectacles Kelly thought he looked more like a college professor than a ball tosser. The White brothers were the only Reds who didn't swear, due to their strict religious beliefs.

One day in the dressing-room Kelly said to Deacon White, "Jim, is it true you believe the world to be flat?"

"It is, Michael."

"How can you be so sure?"

"The Bible tells us how Jesus would send the angels out to the four corners of the earth to gather God's chosen people from one end of the world to the other."

"Of course," said Kelly, "why have I been thinking it's round me whole life? Pshaw, those teachers didn't know what they were talkin' about. I'll bet Columbus really had *five* ships and two of them sailed over the edge of the earth."

Calvin McVey would play third base and serve as the club's captain, replacing Lew Pike in the role. Cal had been a first baseman when the Chicagos acquired him from the Bostons, but in '77 he'd been behind the plate and he hadn't liked it there. He was glad Kelly would be the Cincinnatis' change-catcher, his hands were much too soft for the job. Mac had worn brick-layer's gloves with the fingers cut out, but they didn't protect against foul tips.

As a teenager McVey had been a student at North Western Christian University, a piano maker for the Indianapolis Piano Manufacturing Company, and a capable bare-knuckle pugilist. Mac was introduced to base ball and played for two different amateur clubs, the Indianapolis Actives and the Westerns. In 1867 the Westerns took on the powerful Nationals of Washington, D.C. in a highly publicized match of one of the best teams in the East against the best of the West. McVey's team lost, but the teenager earned a national reputation as a talented base-ballist.

In 1869 A.B. Champion formed the nation's first club of professional players - the Cincinnati Red Stockings. They were the first nine to all wear knickerbockers instead of full-length pants to avoid tripping. Most of Champion's players were imported from the East, with only one of them a native of Cincinnati, Harry Wright, who'd been a member of the famous Knickerbockers of New York. He'd gone to Cincinnati to play cricket but Champion named him manager of the Red Stockings. Wright had heard about the exploits of the youngster with the Indianapolis Westerns and signed McVey to a contract. Calvin became the first professional born west of the Mississippi River.

After two seasons in Boston, McVey departed for Baltimore, where at the age of 22 he became the league's youngest captain. He spent only a year with the Lord Baltimores, or Canaries as they were sometimes called, before going back to Boston.

William Hulbert, a hard-driving coal merchant, was a competitive sort who viewed the revival of his White Stockings as a powerful metaphor for the renaissance of the city of Chicago, which was still struggling to rebuild after the disastrous fire of '71. But his club proved an embarrassment with its poor performance in 1874, especially during a month-long eastern trip in June. On the 15th, Philadelphia's Candy Cummings struck out a record six White Stockings in succession, a feat that made national headlines. Three days later, the Chicago nine traveled to Brooklyn and lost to the New York Mutuals by a score of 38 to 1.

Hulbert, who told people he would rather be a lamp-post in Chicago than a millionaire anywhere else, had no interest in building his team gradually. He intended to challenge Boston for the whip-pennant in '75 and the best way for him to do it was to raid the club he wanted to beat. He went to Boston and met with Albert Spalding who'd averaged 45 wins in his past five seasons with the Red Stockings.

"Spalding, you've no business playing here," Hulbert told the ace over dinner at the American House. "You're an Illinois boy, you belong in Chicago. I'll give you a $500 raise in salary and a 25 percent share of the gate receipts to pitch for and manage my White Stockings."

Spalding accepted. He knew that Boston's perennial domination of the league - due in large part to his own excellence between the points - was killing interest in the game. He was open to the challenge of returning to the Midwest and building another championship team. He began helping Hulbert by rounding up other players. On Hulbert's behalf, Spalding made generous offers to three of Boston's biggest stars - catcher "Deacon" White, first baseman Cal McVey, and second baseman Ross Barnes. Hulbert agreed to pay them handsome salaries the parsimonious Boston Triumvir of Charles Soden, J.B. Billings, and William Conant would not. As the Bostons dined after an exhibition game in Taunton, Massachusetts McVey said he would not be playing in the Red Stockings next season. Harry Wright took it as a joke but discussed it with White after

dinner. Jim admitted that they'd agreed to play in Chicago. In a letter to the *Boston Herald*, White said he had met with the president of the Boston club a month earlier before the team's Western trip and he'd told him the Red Stockings could not compete with the "fancy Western prices." All three men signed contracts to play for the White Stockings in 1876.

In late June, when Boston played two games in Philadelphia, Spalding obtained a similar agreement from the best player in the Athletics, Adrian Anson, whose heavy hitting had attracted the notice of William Hulbert as well.

But Adrian encountered an unexpected road-block. His decision to play in Chicago drew heated opposition from his fiancé Virginia. She didn't want to leave her family and friends to live in the West. She was so adamant about the matter that Adrian decided to try to free himself from his commitment to the White Stockings. He wrote a letter to Spalding and Hulbert requesting his release, but the Chicago team executives ignored it. He then made two trips to Chicago in late 1875 to plead with Spalding personally to let him out of his agreement but Spalding wouldn't budge. He wrote a letter to Anson threatening to expel him from the new league that was being planned by Hulbert if he didn't fulfill his obligations to Chicago.

The warning might have ended the matter but the Athletics had made a lucrative counter-offer and Adrian was not a man to give up easily. He decided to try one more time. He visited Hulbert's office and once again asked out of his agreement. When the determined owner turned him down Adrian pulled a large roll of bills out of his coat pocket and placed the money on Hulbert's desk.

"There's $ 1,000. I'll give you that for my release."

Hulbert nearly fell out of his chair in astonishment. Anson was offering to buy his freedom rather than break his word. Unfortunately, the offer had the opposite effect of what Adrian had hoped for, Hulbert decided then and there that Anson was just the kind of man that he wanted in the White Stockings. Anson's offer of $1,000 cemented his reputation for integrity but left Anson with no choice but to play

for the White Stockings or not play at all.

Kelly sat with McVey at breakfast one morning. "That was quite the nine you were in with the Bostons, Cal."

"You heard about us?"

"I was a base ball crank long before I started gettin' paid ta play. I used ta see your names in the sports pages when I delivered newspapers. I'd get out uv me bed at four every mornin' and take the train to New York to get the morning papers, then I'd bring them back and sell 'em in Paterson. I used to read about your championship club all the way home."

McVey set his fork down. "What a club *that* was."

Cal pointed to Jim White who was waving at the perky young waitress for a refill of coffee. She filled his cup and cast a provocative glance in Kelly's direction.

"We had Barnes and the Deacon, Jim O'Rourke, and the Wright brothers . . . "

"George and Harry," put in Mike.

"George at shortstop and his brother Harry our captain, who was going on forty, in the outfield. And of course our twirler was Al Spalding who was nigh onto unbeatable. We were together for all those championships before Spalding and Jim White and I went over to the Chicagos."

The Red Caps' line-up would feature base ball's first brother battery, Will White in the pitching box and his brother Deacon White behind the bat-along way behind the bat. It would be several years before catchers would crouch anywhere near the plate, even with runners on base. *The Chicago Tribune,* which had purchased one of the just-patented folding and pasting machines that replaced folding by hand and could crank out 15,000 newspapers an hour, cheerfully acknowledged the strength of the team but did not believe the talk in the Cincinnati newspapers about them "surely walking away with the pennant." The Reds certainly looked to have a hard-hitting team based on the League statistics from 1877 that listed Jim White at

.385, McVey at .322, Sullivan at .304, Gerhardt at .290, and Pike at .285. Kelly's minor league average of .156 looked paltry beside his new teammates' numbers and some of them wondered aloud whether he belonged.

When Mike got to Cincinnati he went shopping with Chub and ended up getting a dark blue flannel suit, a light brown duck vest, and a pair of tailored cassimere pants.

"Aren't you the handsome one?" chuckled Chub as Kelly admired himself in the mirror. "You'll be beating the ladies off with a stick."

During a pre-season practice in bone-chilling weather Mike sat and shivered beside Cal McVey as they waited for their turns to bat.

"It looks as though *this* league is going to last," said Cal.

"A little better run than the association was, is it?" asked Mike.

"When the National Association of Base Ball Players was organized in '71 the entry fee for a club was only $10 so any town the size of a postage stamp could get a nine into it. The clubs were on their own to schedule the dates of the matches and that often didn't go well. The home side had to hire an umpire and sometimes the gate'd be so small we couldn't afford the $2 they required so the tenth man from one of the two teams would umpire.

There were no owners or club directors so there were no payrolls, the players collected the admissions, a dime or sometimes a quarter, and the two clubs split the gate - which meant that a poor turnout resulted in a meager payday for us players. Having so many small towns pretty much guaranteed small turnouts and that made us easy targets for gamblers."

"Were *most* of the games on the level?" asked Mike.

"Whether there was hippodroming going on or there wasn't it was believed to be widespread. Hell, the integrity of the association games got so low sometimes when we got to the grounds the police had posted signs that said the game to be played that day shouldn't be trusted. Teams in the larger towns often reneged on their agreements to play in small towns, it was more profitable to stay at home

and play exhibition games. I remember we played the Hartfords one time and drew three thousand people. It's too bad my friend Tom Barlow wasn't still catching for them when we split *that* gate. They'd released him. He'd been picked up for petty larceny the last I heard.

But gambling wasn't the only problem with base ball. Alcohol flowed in the stands and all too often it spilled onto the field. Drunken brawls broke out and we couldn't afford to hire retired policemen so we often had to flea for our damned lives. It was lucky we had bats or we might have been skinned alive. Exciting times they were but no way to make a living. As the problems became more obvious, base ball enthusiasts began to lose interest. Attendance declined each and every year of the organization's existence.

The time was ripe for a stronger, centrally governed league so Hulbert set up a meeting at the Grand Central Hotel in New York City in February of '76 with representatives of seven other clubs. The meeting led to the formation of the National League of Professional Base Ball Clubs. Hulbert's signing of the Big Four and Cap Anson from the Athletics was a violation of the National Association's rules, and the players could have faced expulsion. The formation of the National League eliminated that possibility.

At the end of '76, the National League's inaugural season, the New York and Philadelphia clubs were expelled for failure to complete their schedules which left the infant league with no presence in the country's two largest cities. Reduced from eight to six clubs, the league was beset by the Grays' gambling scandal, which triggered exits by Louisville, St. Louis, and Hartford. That left only profitable Chicago and Boston and floundering Cincinnati out of the League's initial lineup. To fill the voids, new franchises were awarded to Milwaukee, Providence, and Indianapolis."

"But Hulbert didn't just want to get rid uv gambling, did he, Cal?"

"No, he wanted bums and booze out of his league, so he prohibited the sale of beer and alcohol at games and made all the clubs charge fifty cents admission."

"Which most people can't afford. And they said the games would

start at three-thirty, which was fine for businessmen, accountants, bankers, and lawyers who could duck out at three …"

"And for ladies who don't work."

"Aye, ladies who don't work could go too. But workin' men can't leave their sweatshops and train yards early. Which explains why the stands are always full uv well-heeled, fancily-dressed people."

"Laborers could go to Sunday games and they'd love to enjoy a couple of glasses of lager while they were there, but there's no chance of that, Hulbert put a stop to Sunday games too."

Cincinnati's Avenue Grounds was four miles from downtown. The Marietta Railroad built a station next to the park and transported passengers to the grounds and back downtown after a game for 15 cents. Next to the grounds were three pork packers. The smell emanating from them often wafted through the grounds. Kelly often held his nose between pitches. The field was oblong in shape, with deep left and center fields, but right field was so shallow a high wall was erected to keep lazy fly balls from exiting the park.

The Red Caps had spent $12,000 fitting up the grounds with a seating capacity of 7,000. The 50 cents admission to the grounds was lowered to 10 cents after the fifth inning. The ballpark's cuisine included hard-boiled eggs, ham sandwiches, and mineral water. Lemon peel and water drinks sold for 10 cents.

Of the Red Caps' season opener on May 1 *The Cincinnati Enquirer* said, "Bredburg of Chicago had been chosen Umpire by the Cincinnati management from the five names submitted by the Milwaukians but for some reason he was never notified of their choice. Chapman, the Grays' captain, took advantage of the privilege to choose an umpire and he put in Crandall, who acquitted himself quite well. The management had imported an official short-hand scorer from the East, a relative of the White brothers, and he was on hand for the game. When the game ended, he had no score at all. Will White had to sit with him after dinner to make sense of what he'd scribbled.

Before the days of turn-stiles the crowd would have gone down in newspaper history at about 3,500 but the turn-stiles counted 1,600

and two hundred more came in through the carriage-gate. About 300 spectators were in the grand stand, many of them ladies, a phalanx of taffeta and lace, hair spilling out from under elaborate bonnets, powder on their cheeks and a plethora of bows on their dresses.

Mike straightened his white cap, adjusted his red belt, and made sure his red necktie was tucked into his freshly washed white shirt with the distinctive *C* on the right breast.

A few rows up from the diamond a woman in a black and white summer frock with a rich-red poppy ornamenting a flare over her left ear peered through opera glasses at the players as they warmed up.

"Who is the new player, Willamena?" she asked a woman who was trussed up like a turkey.

"The one going to get a drink from the water-bucket?"

"Yes, him."

"I don't know, but I would certainly *like* to."

They were greatly impressed when Mike sent a hard one over the right fielder's head. He tore around first in front of them and made it to second easily. As he swiped dirt off his no longer white uniform he noticed the pair admiring him and nodded slightly. Embarrassed, they quickly looked away.

The Red Caps held a one-run lead going into the ninth but several of the visitors had found a bat that suited them and racked up a dozen hits off Will White. The visitors had won the toss and Chapman had elected that his men would bat last. Mike knew his club could use a run. He waited for something to hit and got nothing at the height he'd requested so he settled for his base on balls and then stole second. Will White cleaned his spectacles then sent a liner at the Milwaukees' big left fielder Abner Dalrymple.

When Kelly reached third he rounded the bag and then, thinking better of trying for home, dove back to the bag just as Dalrymple's throw smacked into Foley's hands. Mike prided himself on his daring base-running but he'd chosen wisely, he knew McVey was next

at the bat and he'd made three hits off Sam Weaver, the Milwaukees' new pitching terror. He made his fourth on Weaver's first delivery and Kelly jogged home with an insurance run."

"Hip, Hip, Hurray!" yelled the crowd. Mike tipped his cap to the ladies as he headed to the bench the two teams shared and beaming smiles were directed his way. The pair would be back . . . many times.

In a 6-2 win over the Grays the next day "Sully", Kelly, and the Whites did the best work for the Cincinnatis. Kelly batted eighth and hit a run-scoring single. Will White beat Weaver for a third time the next day and the Reds were off to a roaring start. Then the Chicagos came to town and Will bested Frank Larkin three straight. "The playing of the Reds is a guarantee that we have no slouch club here," said the delighted *Enquirer*.

But there were two pitchers White couldn't beat, Boston's Irish-born Tommy Bond and "the Only" Nolan, the Indianapolis twirler whose blistering speed and killer downshoots had made him famous throughout the base ball world and had persuaded the National League to import the entire Indianapolis club.

May 9 was a beautiful day for a game. *The Enquirer* said, "The grand-stand was comfortably filled and more than a hundred carriages and turnouts filled the space beyond the railings. Several score of youths who had no money to pay admittance grouped together on a knoll west of the grounds where they could look through the carriage-gate like lost souls peering into paradise.

Base hits by Jim White and Gerhardt, a sacrifice by Sullivan, and a 'darling' over short by Kelly earned two runs in the second inning. In the fifth, Hankinson hit a drive to right-center field "upon which Harbridge thought he read a title to score but Pike and Gerhardt's quick handling of the ball crushed his aim and as Jim White shoved the ball up against Harbridge's belt the spectators howled their delight. Kelly relieved his pent-up soul by flip-flopping a back-somersault in the air and alighting squarely on his feet with the grace of a tumbler." The Reds won their fifth in a row, getting the grand bounce by the score of 9-1."

"We waxed 'em that time, boys," said Kelly.

On the 14th the Red Caps got their first dose of defeat, a 5-3 loss in Milwaukee. Kelly, with four hits in his first twenty-two at bats, was the second worst batsman on the club and he'd scored only three runs in seven games. Of course often being last in the batting order wasn't helping.

On May 20 the club took a Chicago, Milwaukee, and St. Paul Railroad train from Milwaukee to Chicago, a city now five times the population of Milwaukee and already twice as populous as Cincinnati. The train sped toward the hazy outline of the growing metropolis past little houses of new wood already covered with soot as lines of ugly telegraph-poles, their arms hung with thick wires, flashed by. They went by stock-yards and a factory that was assembling shiny Pullman cars. Sidetracks became more and more numerous and as they went through the sprawling train-yard and approached the depot Mike saw freight cars by the hundreds from all over the country. He'd heard that thirty railroads terminated here.

The car-wheels squeaked and the train stopped to let a bridge swing open so boats could pass underneath. A pair of dirty-faced urchins hopped onto the cow-catcher for a ride.

"What's that *smell?*" asked Mike.

"It's the river," said Cal. "Fragrant, ain't it."

Kel looked down to see puttering tugs chugging along in the black, oily water. Tall piles of coal and enormous grain-elevators dotted the shores. A group of stevedores idled on the bank of a lumber-yard whose wall skirted the water. Mike could tell by their red shirt-sleeves, suspenders, and swarthy complexions that they were Irish. Each man had a short pipe stuck in his mouth.

"There but for the Grace uv God and me throwin' arm is what I would be doin'," Kelly said to himself.

The train's bell rang and they shunted to a start. At bustling grade-crossings street-cars rambled past while muddy-wheeled buggies waited on the unpaved streets. Well-dressed shoppers walked alone or in fashionable pairs along stretches of boards laid along the streets.

The team took a street-car to their hotel, the Sherman House, at Clark and Randolph streets. The gray sandstone version had replaced the one that had been destroyed by fire six years earlier.

When they were checking in McVey called Mike aside.

"Make sure you lock your door when we leave for the grounds tomorrow."

"Any reason in particular, captain?"

"In '75 Geer was in the New Haven Elm Cities club. They played a series of exhibitions in Canada and when the team was in London, Ontario they stopped at the Tecumseh House. When the players checked out, the hotel's owners noticed that Geer and his roommate Harry Luff happened to have more luggage than they'd had when they checked in. An investigation revealed that several valuable items of clothing including a fur coat were missing and when the hotel contacted the New Haven team they turned the matter over to the police. The stolen items were discovered in Luff and Geer's room in a New Haven boarding house. Both of them were arrested and released from their contracts by the Elm Citys. Luff claimed Geer had taken the things and he had no knowledge of the thefts. After the arrests, stolen items from a hotel in Scranton where the club had stayed were found in Geer's room."

"*Now* I see why you think I should lock me door."

THE
$10,000
BEAUTY

"A young man who cannot be spared from the nine."

On May 21st, Kelly made the catch of the day in the fourth inning and later threw Adrian Anson out on a close play at first. It was dollars to cents the White Stockings' bellicose captain would kick and he surprised no one including the grounds-keepers when he fumed and called Umpire Walsh names that shocked the matrons in the Ladies section.

"His batting figures are like his family jewels," McVey told Mike. "Everybody knows he's the beneficiary of twenty or more extra hits every year thanks to the Chicago score-keeper. Anson scares the shit out of the poor little fellow. If you fumble a ball Anson hits your way you can be sure it'll be a hit for him and not an error for you."

The Red Caps gave the White Stockings a terrible whipping. The Chicagos had butter on their fingers and made twelve errors that led to thirteen runs while they tallied only two.

The Chicagos had local boy Laurie Reis between the points on May 25. He'd allowed just three earned runs in his four complete games in 1877 but his right arm had lost its cunning and he was batted hard by the Reds. Kelly made four base hits in a 10-8 win.

Mike wished he could bat against Ries every day. "He looks as though he could use a tall glass uv Cincinnati beer," he chuckled after his last hit.

The men from Southern Ohio were in high cotton. Their sweep of the White Stockings moved them three games ahead of second-place Boston.

The "free, easy batting of Kelly" was the prominent feature of a 4-1 win over Indianapolis on the last day of the month. The Blues had sent his old friend James McCormick to the pitching box to give a rest to The Only Nolan, who was on his way to a dismal 13-22 record. Ned Williamson and Frank Flint were among the Indianapolis players that would be Kelly's teammates the following season but it would be a while before Mike and Jim played in the same nine. Mike won "general and generous applause" that sang in his ears. He made two errors in right field but threw out two base-runners.

Kelly played long catch with Chub Sullivan before the game with Indianapolis the next day.

"McVey's putting Mitchell between the points today," Chub told Mike.

Kelly chuckled. "I guess Cal hasn't heard."

"Heard what?"

"Mitchell and Buttercup spent last night at Charles Martin's saloon and ended up at a house of ill-fame on Smith street."

Will White had struck out Russ McKelvey four times in the last two games but McKelvey hit a home run over Jones' head off Mitchell and Indianapolis won 6-5. Kelly was hitless in four chances and while he threw out two runners he dropped two fly balls. But it was Gerhardt who wore the goat horns, his error in the ninth allowed the winning run to score.

The Cincinnati nine hammered the Blues 11-4 in Indianapolis on June 6. Nolan was between the points and he was as erratic as a comet. He and Kelly had hoisted a few the night before. Mike took the curve out of him and made two long hits.

The only dustup of the game came when Cal McVey hit Orator Shafer in the side of the head on a swift throw to get him at second base. Shafer, whose ear was severely hurt, was certain McVey had hit him on purpose as the throw was nowhere near Gerhardt's hands.

The Orator, who was so dizzy he couldn't judge flyballs, had plenty to say about it.

Mike perished at first on a weak grounder in the first inning but reached base in the third on Flint's muff of a third strike. He went to second and then on to third when the blond-haired catcher made a wild throw to catch him stealing. Kelly went home on McVey's grounder past short, which Nelson dodged to avoid trouble to his hands. In the sixth inning Michael reached base on a doubtful judgment of Umpire McLean. Pike carried him to third on a stinging grounder to Nelson. He'd wanted no part of that one either. Shafer made a square muff of McVey's fly and Kelly ran home again.

Kelly sat down beside Cal McVey when the team departed for Providence. A whistle blew and with a jolt the train left the station. Out his window Mike saw a young luggage-boy teetering under suitcases. Kelly was afraid Cal might be in a sour mood, *The Cincinnati Times* had decided that third-base was the Reds' weakest point and opined that if McVey would pay more attention to the game and less to his outside business he might get along a great deal better. The journal felt McVey had too many things on a string. Or maybe they'd said he had too many irons in the fire, Mike couldn't recall. At least *The Times* had decided that when McVey had hit Shafer in the ear it had been an accident. But Cal was in fine spirits. The only thing in the newspaper that seemed to upset him was the news that while the club was on the road they'd miss the Grand Opening of the Schooner Saloon on Vine street.

Kelly enjoyed spending time with McVey, he liked hearing him talk about his early days.

"Did you ever stop to think why we call the home base home plate, Mike?"

"Can't say as I have. Why?"

"In the early days it was a round disc buried in the dirt."

"So it was the shape of a dinner *plate*."

"That's right, and it was the only base stuck into the ground instead of sitting on top like the others. The first plates were metal, it was just last year that the league decreed they must be stone or marble, nor more iron or wooden ones to tear your legs and stockings on."

Just as fascinating to hear about was his time in the 1869 Cincinnati Red Stockings. After a game in Washington in which they'd routed the Nationals the club had been invited to the White House. It was quite a thrill for the 18-year-old Iowa farm boy to meet President Grant. After defeating all the best teams in the East and the Midwest the Red Stockings had headed for the West Coast. They took a stagecoach from St. Louis to Omaha with Cal and the manager's brother George Wright sitting next to the driver. Then they boarded a train for San Francisco, the first ballclub ever to travel on the new transcontinental railroad.

At the midway point of June Kelly ranked sixth among the Reds in runs scored and runners thrown out, eighth in total bases, and last in hits made. He heard how everyone was raving about young Dalrymple of the Milwaukees and his astounding .419 batting average and wished he were doing half that well.

The Globe scribe waxed eloquent over the June 17 game. "Fully 6,000 Bostonians filled the West End Grounds including many ladies perched decorously in the grand-stand. In the full blaze of the brilliant sun they presented an absolute carnival of color. To depict it as an artist's pallet would not do it justice, it was that rich in the varied hues of shawls, gay dresses, startling parasols, and fluttering fans."

Mike had never seen so many beautifully dressed women, nor had they ever seen such a handsome ball player.

"Who is your new right fielder?" a lady in the front row called down to McVey, whom she knew from his time in Boston.

"A mid-west semi-pro by the name of Mike Kelly," Cal told her. "Why do you ask, Lydia?"

"Oh, no reason."

Cal smiled. He knew the reason.

The Red Caps, about whom the Cincinnati newspapers had done so much blowing and puffing in May, lost 4-2 and then 5-0 three days later. Pike, who'd boasted that he'd knock Tommy Bond all over the fucking field, took the little end of the horn with just one hit in eight tries. He struck out four times, just three times less than Kelly would the entire season.

On the 21st the Red Stockings, the Red Caps, and the Blues boarded the Tunnel Line train and headed West. When the weary Cincinnatis reached Indianapolis they checked into the National Hotel across from Union Depot. They managed just one hit off James McCormick in the first eight innings in the first game at South Street Park, a 5-1 loss. Kelly manhandled a bounder in the seventh then compounded his error with a wild throw to the plate.

He started in to catch the second game but a damaged thumb sent him back to right field in the third inning. He was held hitless by his boyhood pal just as he had been the day before. The Hoosiers won 7-3 and the gamblers who'd gone with the favorites were happy.

"I'm glad ta see you out uv yer base ball suit, Jimsy," Mike told McCormick the next day, "if I kept goin' up against the likes uv you me battin' score would right be down around where it was in Columbus."

He got one of his bats and took a few practice swings. "Remember when we decided to make a theater and stage a play in your basement?"

Chub Sullivan came over and sat down to listen.

"It was so big we managed to get forty-five kids in to watch," said James. "A penny each for admission ... and we had to turn some away."

"I wanted us ta put on Dick Turpin and then I lost the starring role to you and we ended up doin' Jack Sheppard."

"Why was that?" asked Chub.

"His father owned the theatre," chuckled Mike.

"How did it turn out?"

"The play had a run uv exactly only one performance. In the final scene Jack Sheppard was to be hanged. As the curtain closed, the block upon which Mac stood with a rope around his neck was kicked away leading the audience to believe the hanging was actually takin' place. It was." Mike suppressed a laugh and looked at James. "Mac here turned blue in the face and only the arrival uv his father to cut him down saved his life. So me theatrical career was cut short and I was forced ta play ball instead."

Nolan was between the points. It was a secret to no one that "the Only" was close to invincible with a mush ball but struggled with a hard one. In his last game the new ball had mysteriously vanished after the first inning in which Nolan had been hit hard. A softer one had appeared in its place. Nobody could account for it but the milk in the cocoanut was that a soft ball had been run in by one of Nolan's teammates. He was unhittable thereafter so now the umpire took possession of the ball at the end of each inning and put it back into play only when the twirler was back in the pitcher's box.

Kelly got to Nolan for three hits but Will White was still worn out from the long train ride and his work the previous two days. He allowed 18 hits and lost 9-5.

On Saturday the blue-hosed hosts gathered in another win over the Cincinnatis. Mitchell was put in to pitch and Kelly to catch and the result was a disaster for the visitors, a stinging 10-2 loss that dropped the Red Caps two games behind Boston. The game was called in the 8th so the two clubs could catch their train back to Cincinnati.

At the end of June the *Cincinnati Star* informed its subscribers that, "Jones leads the Red Cap batsmen with an average of .333, Pike is second at .327, Gerhardt stands third with a mark of .327, McVey is fourth at .270, and Kelly is in the fifth place at .239. Geer, who hasn't hit a lick in weeks, is at .173 and Sullivan is batting at the brisk clip of .167."

Kelly's astounding running catches and line throws to first and to the home plate on July the 2nd were remarkable specimens of their kind and excelled any right fielding ever done on the grounds. His catching on the Fourth of July "was more than perfection" and his support of Specky White fully verified Jim's assertion that Kelly

could catch his brother as well if not better than he could. Jim certainly knew the virile 20-year-old *threw* much better than he did.

There was no shortage of places to spend a summer evening in Cincinnati, the business directory listed 1,300 saloons. The great majority of them were unassuming beer halls devoted to pouring sudsy lager into schooners or pails. The sophisticated tippler had to hunt for something a little more upscale than what the standard saloon offered. *The Cincinnati Enquirer* published a guide to "Cock-Tail Slingers" as well as a list of "fashionable drinking resorts" and observed that,

"Notwithstanding all of the puritanical pow-wow of the Evangelical Know-Nothings about the alarming wickedness of Cincinnati, most rational minded and moderately informed persons are well aware that there are far fewer inducements to hard drinking and much less drunkenness in this city of ours, comparatively speaking, than in any other of the great Western burgs."

The better bars were usually hidden away inside hotels or restaurants and even cigar stores. With few exceptions, the "interiorly elegant" bars were clustered along Fourth street between Main and Elm and along Vine street between Sixth and Seventh. Schultz's Restaurant on Fourth near Race catered to the artistic crowd.

The players avoided the St. Joe restaurant on Vine street, which was frequented by "journalists and men of irreproachable morals" and the nearby Club House run by Jacob Aug which was "patronized by popular politicians and society's most brilliant intellects."

They favored Dave Kendall's Billiard Parlor and the Atlantic Garden on Vine near Sixth which was the "favorite summer evening resort of a mixed multitude."

Across the street from *The Enquirer* building was The Post Office. It was the "favorite resort of frisky young bloods who liked their bourbon straight." It was christened The Post Office "wholly with the wicked object of deceiving gentlemen's sternly-moral spouses as to the nature of their husband's twilight wanderings."

Kelly, Sullivan, Gerhardt, and Dickerson sat by the window at the Atlantic Garden on Saturday night. Jones wasn't with them this time, he was meeting a friend somewhere - they suspected it was a lady friend. The White brothers were at a Knights of Columbus meeting. Nobody knew what Geer was up to and no one cared. He was like a red-headed step-child, none of the players could abide him, not even Kelly.

Mike sipped whiskey, the others drank amber lager and wolfed down salty peanuts. New beers had emerged in response to consumer demand, pale ones that were drier and lighter than Pilseners.

"They add starch to the malted barley," said Gerhardt. His father had been in the restaurant business in Prussia, Joe knew his beers. "Pabst and most of the other brewers prefer corn but Anheuser Busch uses rice." He held up his glass and examined the contents. "It's what gives Budweiser its snappiness."

Mike narrowly avoided fights when men caught their wives making eyes at him. He did his best not to return their stolen glances.

"Looks like you'll be playin' center from here on in," Kelly told Buttercup.

"Why?" asked Dickerson. "What's happened to Pike?"

"Remember how he had a row with McVey after the game."

"Of course, they nearly came to blows. Is Lew *still* mad they made Cal captain?"

"I don't know about that, but he asked for his release and President Neff gave it to him. Neff said Pike's been a disturbing element in our nine all season."

"Well he could've said good-bye," said Chub.

"He's on a train back home to New York," said Mike.

"Pike's no spring chicken but I hope he catches on with another club," said Joe, wiping suds from his drooping mustache. "Any of the eastern clubs would be a lot closer to home for him."

"I guess I'll be the one picking up after your muffs now, Kel,"

34

said Dickerson.

"You'd best call it a night soon then, Heaven knows there'll be plenty uv *them*."

On Tuesday the 9th the Providence club booked rooms at the Grand Hotel for a three-game series. "Cherokee" Fisher, who in Mike's opinion bore no resemblance to an Indian, made his only appearance of the season for the Grays. He was struck amidships and surrendered thirteen hits and a dozen runs. His battery mate Lew Brown, who'd led the League in most times striking out in 1877, a whopping 33, wasn't much help to Cherokee. Brown made eight of the Grays' 19 errors. He'd just gotten out of jail, having been arrested for debt.

Fisher had to call time in the seventh when Brown was overcome by the heat. The Grays were accustomed to the cool breezes of their sea-shore home. Kelly was looking forward to another series in Providence at the end of the month.

In a 13-9 win over Providence on July 15 Kelly scored three times and knocked in four runs. The team made fourteen errors and surprisingly Kelly was responsible for none of them.

The next day the Reds' batsmen had eyes as big as doughnuts and laid it down fine to Boston, "the model club", with fourteen hits off Tommy Bond. Mike had chuckled when he heard that in the offseason Bond worked in a grocery store. He pictured him firing items into paper bags. Tricky Tommy lived at the edge of the rule against pitching overhand, throwing sidearm with tremendous speed, but Mike caught on to his delivery and made three safe hits.

By the middle of the month the Red Caps, who'd fallen suddenly to the rear a few weeks back, had gotten back to work again. Of their comeback win on July 16 over the Bostons, who were showing signs of breaking up, *The Cincinnati Enquirer* man melodramatically wrote, "Last night at the Burnet House Harry Wright issued orders to the Boston club that they must win the next day's game and then he sent them to their beds. Today he came away from the Cincinnati Ball Park a broken-hearted man whose life had been blighted in

one short hour. At four o'clock and twenty minutes the white-beard-ed manager was happy as a lark and fat as a plum-pudding; at five o'clock and thirty minutes he was but a wreck of his former self. The home team collared Bond from the start and pounded him unmerci-fully. The extension of the pitching distance by five feet has been the death of his arm. Kelly's base running took the cake."

In the second inning Manning's liner was finely caught by Ger-hardt and Geer cared for Burdock's fly back of the base-path. Sut-ton batted a rising hit to right field that brought calamity to Kelly. He let it get over his head and Buttercup took off running after it. Morrill sent Sutton home a minute later by a hit to Dickerson, who was still panting. Dickerson was sure-handed but he had a terribly weak throwing arm, enemy baserunners liked taking chances on hits his way. Buttercup would throw out only one base runner all season. Morrill trotted home as Buttercup's throw fell twenty feet short of the plate.

Kelly the rookie learned a valuable lesson the next inning. Tom-my Bond's arm was limp and Gerhardt smashed his first pitch for a hit. McVey, Will White, and Kelly followed with clean, cracking hits of their own that tied the score. Sullivan reached on an error by Burdock that sent Kelly to third. Sullivan started for second to make Snyder throw.

Snyder did, but not to second base. He threw instead to shortstop George Wright. Kelly hadn't noticed that he was playing shallow, well inside the diamond. Wright fired the ball back to Snyder and Mike was out at the plate by ten feet. He vowed he would pull the same trick himself but he'd never again have it played on him.

As it turned out his foolhardiness didn't cost his team the game. Jones hit a terrific drive to center for three bases and came home when Kelly's flyball dropped safely between Murdock and O'Ro-urke. The exciting affair ended 5-3. The Boston players were star-tled when Harry Wright snapped his walking stick in half and very nearly cussed.

There was a war going on over the right to post inning-by-inning scores. The Cincinnati management's first move was to ban the post-ing of game and inning-by-inning scores in billiard parlors, gaming houses, and other establishments where cranks and gamblers who hadn't paid to witness the game gathered. Their next move was to prevent Western Union from telegraphing the results. The press countered by using Western Union's rival, the Atlantic and Pacific Telegraphy Company. A messenger would carry the results from in-side the grounds to an outside operator, who would wire the vital info to all and sundry so President Neff banned the messenger from the park. The pool runners retaliated by putting a spectator in "a bought and paid for" reserved seat. The spectator scribbled the ac-tion of each inning on a slip of paper, waddled it up into a ball, and tossed it over the fence to a waiting messenger. Management then ordered the "spectator" to change his seat. He did, sitting where he could signal his crony outside with his fingers how many runs had been scored by each side.

It was thought that the Red Caps were working in better accord since the release of their former captain Pike. Two bosses in a nine were one too many. Mike had known that either Pike or McVey had to go and he was glad management had chosen Pike. It was more fun to come to work now that he and the others didn't have to listen to Lew and Cal natter away at one another.

On July 18 in Cincinnati the home team collared Tommy Bond from the start and pounded him terribly. Kelly opened the sixth inning with a two-bagger to right center and went to third on Sul-livan's single. Will White's dribbler was fielded out by Bond but off Geer's long fly to center Mike scored what turned out to be the winning run. His club now trailed the first place Bostons by just a game and a half.

'Specks' White lost a heart-breaker on Saturday. With Manning on base via one of the Bostons' only three hits of the day, Burdock sent a high pop fly up between first base and the pitching box. The sun was in White's peepers and the eyes of Chub Sullivan as well and the grey ball landed between them. As lead-footed Burdock started to run to second Deacon White foolishly threw to Gerhardt. The ball sailed over his head letting Manning score the game's only run.

The Reds' July 25 game at Boston was "chock-full of enthusiasm." It was another rare bad outing for Bond. The Cincinnatis amused themselves by teasing James O'Rourke. The Bostons had played an exhibition in Lowell the day before. "Lady killer" O'Rourke was playing center field near the carriages and had eyes only for a lovely girl sitting in a barouche. While intent on his mash a Lowellite hit a ball over Jim's head and got to third base before the astonished fielder knew what was happening.

Kelly was presented as catcher. *The Enquirer* said, "A word of praise and encouragement is due the lad for his exertions, which fairly deserve to be called heroic. From the start his hands were not in the best condition and long before the last inning was played he plainly suffered greatly. The presence of a number of ladies in voluminous skirts graced the game. Miss Rea Gray of Columbus, Miss Marnie Jones, and Miss Mamie Caldwell were among the attractive young ladies spotted in the grand-stand. A buzz went though the audience whenever Mike Kelly came to the bat or made a play in the field."

Before the game Bond had told his teammates, "Wait till Kelly tries to steal, I'll kill him sure before he reaches the base."

After Kelly managed a scratch hit, Pop Snyder, the Red Stockings' crack catcher who was teased mercilessly because he wore a mask, took it off and yelled out, "You're going to steal it, are you?"

The infielders laughed loud enough that the crowd could hear them. When Mike took off for second and Snyder threw him out the spectators all laughed.

Mike had three clean hits but he was dreadful behind the bat with a three-strikes muff, a foul muff, and three passed balls that contributed to the Bostons' 10-9 win. That made it three straight over the Cincinnatis, who were suddenly 5½ games behind.

Kelly felt bad that night, but a lot better the next day when the Cincinnatis edged the Red Stockings 3-2 and he made three more safe hits. He stole second after his first hit and again after his third. Snyder snarled at him and Mike chuckled to second baseman Jack

Burdock, "Looks like I've got Pop's goat now."

"Aye, that you do," said Burdock.

Snyder glared at Kelly and lobbed the ball to Bond and Kelly was off in a flash. Bond was stunned. He whirled and threw to Ezra Sutton.

After applying the touch to Mike too late Sutton said, "You're a *sneaky* bastard, Kelly."

The crowd was impressed with Kelly's nerve. "That fellow's one to watch," a man in a striped cassimere suit told his friend.

The Indianapolis Club announced that "the Only" Nolan would be released as soon as it was verified that the cock-and-bull story he'd given them for missing a game was a bald-faced lie. Ed had claimed that his brother had just died in Paterson. Kel was pretty sure Nolan's brother was just fine. He had a chuckle when it turned out Ed had spent the afternoon in question with a prostitute.

Holbert, the Milwaukees' catcher, was hit in the groin by a foul bound and disabled on August 17. Bennett had a swollen thumb as big as a young pup and Bennett's hands had given out in Wednesday's game. Manager Chapman telegraphed Milwaukee for Khowdell but he was fishing and didn't get the wire until it was too late to get to Cincinnati so Al Jennings, an amateur, was thrown into the breach to catch hard-throwing Golden. The result was a rip-roaring circus. No one who went to the game would have missed it for a small cow.

Jennings had played with the boys down in Millcreek and he looked so big Chapman was mashed and straightaway engaged him and clinched the bargain with a grand dinner. When Al pulled on his sole-leather gloves at 3 p.m. the crowd scarcely breathed. Zip came the ball from Golden's hand and BANG it went against the back-stop. Jennings did stop a ball once in a while, but the low comedy came when he went up close behind the bat with Cincinnatis on base. All a Cincinnati man had to do was get himself on base and skirmish around to third without danger of a throw from Jennings, as he'd already sent two balls soaring into center field, and then come home on a passed ball. Gerhardt, McVey, Dicker-

son, and Sullivan each did it twice.

"What's Jennings' first name?" Kelly, who'd raised the spectators to their feet by throwing two Grays out at third, asked McVey.

"Al. It's short for Albert, but they call him Alamazoo."

"How many's *that* he's let by?"

"Eight I think."

"Think he'll hit double digits?"

"He just might."

Jennings did. He had four errors and ten passed balls in the Red Caps' 2-hour, 35-minute 13-2 win. Julian's umpiring was square up. He was as honest as gold and generally gave satisfaction.

The Enquirer lashed out at Joe Gerhardt on the 23rd. "Gerhardt's playing yesterday was very good, as we have fairly given credit. That of Wednesday was very bad as we declared yesterday in a spirit of friendly criticism just as we have from time to time spoken of bad playing by McVey, Jones, Kelly, and Geer. They have always taken severe criticism good-naturedly like gentlemen. But Gerhardt took offense at what we said and was loud in his boasts that he would 'break the Enquirer reporter's G_d d____ed head for it.' Afterward he bragged that he had frightened the reporter so badly that he was sure to 'go slow' in future.

Maybe Gerhardt could physically overcome our reporter since he has the advantage of brute force on his side at about two to one, but the way to whip a reporter is to whip him and not advertise it first. Mr. Gerhardt has certainly made an exhibition of himself. He himself said after Wednesday's game, 'Well I lost the game and I don't give a G_d d__n,' so why should he find fault with newspaper criticism. No loud threats or physical revenge will sway our Base-Ball Department one jot or tittle.'"

At The *Buffalo Commercial's* office on August 28 their sports reporter, who always talked out loud with a cigarette dangling from his lips as he typed, was working late. The lamp on his desk was almost out of kerosene. He thought for a moment and returned to his writ-

ing. "The day was all that could be desired for and a fine audience graced it with their presence, including a number of ladies, many of whom had their eyes on Michael Kelly the whole time. Poor Kel looked awfully unhappy when Gilliam decided him out at first in the eighth inning. He worked hard all through the game, even as to coaching. Kel the enthusiast always wants the boys to run and make the other team throw the ball."

The Cincinnatis whitewashed the Bostons 3-0 on Tuesday, September 3, though New England croakers regarded it a lucky win. The Red Caps downed the Red Stockings 6-1 on Saturday in their last home game of the season in front of a tiny audience. It was their seventh straight win and it moved them within four games of the Bostons but only three games remained on the schedule.

The Cincinnatis went out in a blaze of glory. A band played and a photographer was there with his instruments to photograph the nine. They sat or stood as stock-still as they could manage as their image was slowly soaked up and burned onto the plate for posterity.

The team hurried off to close out the season in Chicago. They'd expected it to be a crucial series but the Bostons had reeled off four straight wins to dash their hopes of a championship. The Red Caps' six straight losses in the last half of June had ruined them.

Dickerson had signed back on with the Reds and McVey came home on Sunday with a contract with Foley's name attached to it. The White brothers were staying with the Reds and Gerhardt, who'd been in poor health most of the season, though it had been kept a secret, promised to play with the Cincinnatis if he played anywhere. Geer wouldn't play ball so a new shortstop would be needed. Sullivan had received offers from Boston and Providence and since he hailed from Beantown the former was the more tempting one. Mitchell would be the Red Caps' change-pitcher again and Kelly would likely be retained as change-catcher even though his rookie year had been anything but a triumph. The Syracuse Stars, who'd captured second place in the International Association, were recruited by the National League as they were one of the best nines not already in the League.

The Stars and the Buffalos would replace the teams from Milwaukee and Indianapolis. Troy and Cleveland got teams to make the NL an eight-team league again for the first time since 1876.

On October 10 the *Enquirer* told its readers what some of the players were doing. "Will White left for home last night, Jim leaves tonight. Geer and Gerhardt will ship out for Syracuse and Washington respectively next week and Dickerson for Baltimore. McVey, Kelly, Sullivan, and Mitchell will winter here. Sullivan is looking for work, he has had a large experience with the book and periodical business."

During the league meetings in December, Nolan's appeal for reinstatement was denied. Ed was allowed to return to the league in 1881, but the league would adopt a blacklist of players who were barred from playing for or against any League teams until they were removed by unanimous vote of the league clubs. Nolan was one of the ten blacklisted for "confirmed dissipation and general insubordination." The other nine included Lip Pike and Buttercup Dickerson.

The *Enquirer* had the pleasure of laying before its readers the full club as chosen for 1879. "The ten men under contract are: W. White, p; J. White c; Sullivan, 1b; Barnes, 2b; Burke, ss; Gerhardt 3b; Dickerson lf; Hotaling mf; Kelly rf; Foley, sub.

"We challenge the country to show a more promising nine and it is predicted right here that any League club which beats the Cincinnatis of 1879 out of first place honors will have to play a mighty lively game of ball. Barnes is recognized as a 'big card' and the management had to pay no small or medium amount to secure him. The health which deserted him briefly during 1877 has been fully restored and people here may expect to see Ross play second base next season as in days gone by when he had no equal in the position. Hotaling comes highly recommended by Jim White and other players who think him a highly talented center-fielder. There may be better right-fielders than Kelly, but none more honest, earnest, and conscientious. He is a young man who cannot be spared from the nine."

"Voulez-vous couchez avec moi?"

For 1879, the eight-team schedule was expanded from 60 games to 84. Kelly was looking forward to playing with Pete Hotaling. He'd played in the Syracuse club of the International Association in 1877 and '88. Before that he'd been the Ilion Clippers' catcher. He'd suffered an eye injury when hit by a foul tip and was out of the lineup for a month. When he returned to duty he had on a mask he'd had commissioned by the Remington Arms Company. He became the first professional ballplayer to use one but wearing the "cage" caused him to be labeled "Monkey."

The Cincinnati Enquirer heaped praise on him. "Hotaling, the new center fielder, will prove a talking card. He is a broad-shouldered, heavily-built fellow who does everything with a manner that bespeaks confidence. He hits left-handed hard and beautifully."

Buttercup Dickerson took his weak arm over to left field, Charley Jones had gone off to patrol left field for the Boston Red Stockings. Kelly was moved to third base. Deacon White would manage the team on the field - but not for long.

Kelly sat with Cal McVey at breakfast one morning before a practice session in April. He pointed to Ross Barnes, who was trying to extract something from his bushy walrus mustache. Barnes had dark eyes, hair as black as a crow's shadow, and a dark, aristocratic countenance to match. Mike thought he was a bit too high on his horse.

"Barnes led the league in everything in '76," said McVey, "batting average, .429 as I recall, runs tallied, hits, two-basers, and three-basers. The trick he used was to cricket the ball with a hard swing

so it'd land fair and then bound off into foul territory. The fair-foul was almost impossible to defend against and few batsmen could hit them like Ross did. When the League banned them at the start of last season I knew it would hurt Barnes worse than anyone.

He left the White Stockings in mid-May. He was suffering from some mysterious debilitating ailment and wasn't able to exert himself in the least. He went home to Rockford to recover and we expected him back in June."

A look of contempt came over McKey's face. "*The Chicago Times* said Ross was fabricating his illness and should be released - which we all knew was scandalous and utterly unfounded. Ross seldom left the house and was growing weaker every day."

McVey stuck a piece of bacon in his mouth and carried on. "When Barnes showed up at the Twenty-Third Street Grounds in early August the crowd gave him a hearty round of applause but he was a shadow of his former self. He'd lost all his vim and he played without energy or life. Turned out he was suffering with an ague that caused fevers, chills, debilitating muscle aches, and terrible pains."

"What did the team do if he wasn't able ta play?" asked Mike.

"Hulbert deducted a thousand dollars from his salary."

"How much was he making?"

"Twenty-five hundred I believe. His contract - like every other player's - stipulated that he assumed all risk of accident or injury in play or otherwise and illness from whatever cause. They claimed that while he was sitting out he wasn't entitled to his wages. Barnes sued the club anyway."

"What happened?"

"The Cook County Court sided with the owners. The judge said they needn't pay for services they'd never received. The Chicagos didn't offer Ross a contract for this season, that's how he ended up here."

In his account of a game between the Cincinnatis and a Picked Nine in late April a reporter said the batting of the professionals was

something at which to marvel. "Dickerson was all wool and a yard wide and put the other batsmen's efforts in the shade, but the Cincinnatis need to do better work with their hands." He added that, "Spalding needs to do something to make the League ball so it can be distinguished from a stone. A roller weighing about a ton went over one of the balls without making the least impression on it."

In the season opener on May Day, in front of a disappointing crowd of just 1,200 due to the foul weather, the Cincinnatis prevailed over the Troy Cities by a score of 7-5. The Troy players, whom the *Enquirer* man described as "young, athletic, and earnest," were nicknamed Trojans like the residents of Troy in Homer's Odyssey but were sometimes called the Troy Cities or the Haymakers. The team would struggle badly in its first season, finishing dead last with a record of 19-56. Dan Brouthers was the club's premier batsman and the only Trojan to hit any home runs with a total of four. Their "ace", curly-haired George Washington Bradley, was saddled with forty of their losses.

Kelly hit one of Bradley's soft ones to the carriage-gate in center in the fourth and circled the bases for a home run. *The Cincinnati Enquirer* had promised a special bat ordered from the A.G. Spalding & Bros. Co. to the man who batted the first home run of the season on the home grounds and hadn't imagined it would come in the very first game. The paper said, "It could not gratify The Enquirer more to give it to any other player in the League." The good folks of Paterson passed the bat every day. The owner of the dry goods store had learned of it and Kelly had given it to him to display.

Kelly missed the second game of the season due to a lame leg. Foley took his place in right field. Mike wasn't missed, the Reds Caps hammered the Troy club 10-1. The Cincinnatis outlasted the Trojans in a 13-12 marathon on Saturday. On May 6 they nosed out the Syracuse Stars 7-6, the winning run coming in on Kelly's legs in the ninth inning. Mike was a happy man when he crossed the plate, he'd made a pair of palpable muffs that had led to most of the Syracuse runs.

The Bostons arrived on Tuesday, May 13th. The Cincinnatis outbatted them but the umpire was dead against them and was hissed

repeatedly by the partisan crowd. The visitors had proposed Stam-
baugh, Bredburg, Walsh, or Wilbur to call the game but the Red
Caps failed to have any of them on the grounds so Harry Wright
picked his old friend Brockway out of the crowd. He ruled the Cincinnati men out on the bases when there was no one near them and
wouldn't give outs that were fairly made against the Bostons. Kelly
was hit in the head and knocked down by a pitch from the hand of
Tommy Bond. He wasn't surprised, everyone knew Bond purposely
threw at enemy batsmen. Kelly was deluged by water from the team
bucket and cheered by the crowd. His head was proof and it stood
the pressure.

Kelly got in a hit in the third but was thrown out when he tried to
stretch it into a two-baser. He batted in Will White in the ninth with
his second baser of the day to tie the game at two each and the Red
Caps won a 3-2 victory by another run in their half of the inning on
Burke's wide throw. *The Enquirer* reported the name of the umpire
as "A Fraud."

Four days later *The Enquirer* reported that, "Chicago's black cat
Champion had kittens last week, six in number and all black ones
too. The Buffalos and the Clevelands will have a tough time if the
'black brigade' can be induced to march across the field while the
games are being played." It also remarked that, "Some of the unmarried Cincinnati players should be corralled somewhere. If they can't
take care of themselves a keeper should be appointed."

In the last game of their first home stand the once red-hot Red
Caps fell to 6-6 with a humiliating 17-1 loss to Providence. *The Cincinnati Commercial* said Harry Wheeler was to blame for the horrible defeat, which was something of an understatement. In his one
inning of work he gave up ten runs. "The spectators, down-hearted
at first, finally got the spirit of the affair and found the Reds' play
hilarious entertainment. As runner after runner came in each was
cheered uproariously. The Providence men went around the bases so
fast Wheeler thought he was the center-post of a flying Dutchman."

At the train station that night the Reds' Vice-President Johnson
read the players The Riot Act. He told them they had been hired to

play ball, not for the purpose of seeing how much bumming around they could do. He threatened that the next man caught violating the club's rules would be discharged.

The chastened Cincinnatis embarked upon their first road trip of the season. Their first stop was in faraway Troy, New York. Iron, steel, and textiles had swelled the city's population to 57,000. Its rapid growth had convinced the League to invite Troy to set up a professional baseball club, though Hulbert had needed to twist the arms of the other club owners to admit Troy since the minimum population for a League club was 75,000.

"Seems like a nice enough burg," said Joe Gerhardt, as he saw one newly-built freshly painted house after another.

"The houses are all new on account uv the fire," said Mike.

"How would you know about that?"

"I was *born* here. We moved away after our whole neighborhood burned to the ground. I was just a wee tyke but me muther told me about it later. Me dad was off fightin' in the Union Army. The fire started in the covered wooden bridge that crossed the Hudson. There was a furious gale blowin' and the supports uv the bridge were carried in so many directions the fire department couldn't do anything and the wind kept continuing to spread the flames. Close to six hundred homes went up in the inferno."

The Reds checked into the Troy House at the corner of First and River streets. All the rooms were $2 and the meals 50 cents. The players liked it because it had a billiard room and the dining room served a mouth-watering tripe in white sauce. Mike shared a room and a bed with Buttercup Dickerson. He was glad Buttercup didn't snore but he left his clothes hanging all over the place and never once put his tooth powder way.

The next day *The Enquirer* man thought that when they read the evening papers the Cincinnatis' rooters must have wondered how the calamity of the afternoon could have befallen their nine. When the Red Caps went to bat in the fourth inning the score-board blared 10-0 for the home side. "From that time out the Ohio men went

down rapidly and the Troy boys were bigger than the nine elephants of a circus. Will White is sick with neuralgia and one side of his face is swelled up fearfully. It was a wonder he played at all.

I know Cincinnati boosters will turn up their noses and sneer at any report from me which pleads hard luck for their club in their 20-6 loss on the Putnam Grounds," he declared, "yet hard luck was accountable for much of the result. Sixteen of the Troys' runs were scored after two hands were out and the Cincinnatis' five errors cost them fourteen runs. Clapp's three-baser to the fence was made with his eyes shut trying to dodge a ball close into his head. With two out in the third Bradley's three-bagger and Doescher's single gave the Troys a run then Burke gave them life by an error on a slowly hit ball batted toward second and Kelly's muff together with a hit by Reilly let in three more unearned runs.

The run in the sixth was off Clapp's hit, Kelly's south of Ireland throw, and Jim White's accomplished muff at home plate after the ball rolled through Barnes' legs. After two were taken care of in the seventh Munsell should have been retired at first on his grounder to Barnes but he dropped the ball like a slippery piece of soap. Then three successive hits scored as many runs. With two in the eighth two runs were made off Kelly's second muff fly, which he accomplished with all the grace of Chesterfield. Two wild throws completed his work for the day.

After the visitors had put two men out in the ninth Will White muffed a fly ball with his chin in the charming manner he has of doing so and three more base-hits brought in the final three runs. Barnes and Kelly's offishness was abominable. Both are said to be considering a nunnery on the Hudson River. From what I hear the tenth place on the club lies between Mike Burke and Mike Kelly with Kelly holding a slight edge at this juncture."

The team travelled to Syracuse and got shellacked again. They scored just five runs in the three games and gave up twenty-five. Deacon White telegraphed President Neff of his desire to relinquish the captaincy forthwith. He'd taken on the position under the understanding that he would have sole control over the club but had

quickly discovered that he was being used as the cat's paw of the President.

Neff responded with a letter to the players that said the first man who didn't play ball to suit would get twenty days' notice and be released. He added that he had three new players ready to step into any such vacancy. White chose not to share the letter with the team and when Neff arrived in Syracuse in person Jim admitted he hadn't read the letter to the players. Neff hauled them up on the hotel carpet in front of several startled patrons and hung them on tender hooks.

The Enquirer said, "The course of the President in thus driving the nine by threats has led more toward the team's demoralization than anything else. There is not a man in the club who has a kind word to say about Neff and most of them are open and bitter in their condemnation of the man."

On June 10 in Providence Kelly gave the home club three runs in their 6-1 win. McGeary's safe hit was thrown wild by Mike. A good throw would have doubled up McGeary and Hines but the atrociously wide one let Hines trot home instead. It wasn't Kelly's only bad throw of the day.

"I suppose one uv those three men Neff was talkin' about'll be taking me place in the nine soon enough," Mike told Chub after the game.

On the 13th a remarkable feature of Cincinnati's playing was Kelly's inability to bat. He got served some humble pie, striking out three times in five tries at the bat, more than he usually did in a month. He'd gotten in around 4 a.m. with a fine jag on and he had a hell of a time following the flight of the ball.

Kelly received special attention from the crowd his last time up. He took a considerably long time to choose a bat from the bag.

"Don't imagine where it'll make much of a doggone difference," called out a crank in a soft felt hat that was twisted and pulled out of shape.

"Why not take the whole *bag*," yelled another.

"You might get a piece of the ball if you use the *bench*," sug-

gested another.

Burke took over for Kelly in right field the next day.

It was felt that some of the Cincinnatis had speed on the bases but lacked judgement and others the reverse. Some had neither. Burke was quick enough but he had a serious fault, namely in not running to first base fast when he thought it useless because he couldn't beat the ball there. The fault not only lost many a run but sat badly with the audience. Contrarily, Kelly often caused an error by his effort at running hard which would not have been made by the baseman if he had not.

Heavy batting was the rule of the day on July 2 on the White Stockings' grounds. Kelly got a feather in his red cap with three hits. He batted home a run in the first by a sacrifice fly to Shafer, who had to interrupt the speech he was making to the people in the beaching-boards to catch it. A run was made in the fifth due to a base-hit by Hotaling, a long fly for two bags by Barnes, a fumble by Shafer, and a two-baser by Kelly. The ninth opened with Kelly at the bat. He hit safely, made a blatant theft of second base, and scored when McVey corked a liner between left and center field.

Ned Williamson and Jim White, who was in a foul mood due to a carbuncle on his shoulder, were both fined $10 for chinning Umpire McLean. He finally retired from the field when the bull-dozing wouldn't stop. Chicago team president William Hulbert persuaded McLean to return by assuring him that he was sustained in his decisions by all of the *decent* people in attendance. After the game McLean told reporters that the rumor going round that the light flannel suits he wore were given to him by President Hulbert was 'bosh.' He pointed out that he had begun wearing them before he even met Hulbert.

The Enquirer held that Billy McLean was the most useful umpire in the profession. "As most players are aware that McLean is a former pugilist his decisions are rarely questioned. The players like him, he hops around lively and makes himself useful fielding in foul balls."

McLean had become the League's first travelling umpire, until now the arbiters had all been local men. In the 1870's umpires had been respected officials with a greater knowledge of the rules than the players and spectators. By the 80's he was just a member of the cast of characters in the show and was often considered to be playing the part of a villainous buffoon. Omnipotent no more, umpires were abused and even mobbed and ridiculed and slandered in the newspapers as a team's mortal enemy. As gate receipts were of paramount importance to the owners they rarely did much to protect the umpires, the rowdy behavior of their players added to the drama and excitement of a game. But thanks to constant kickers like Anson an umpire could now levy fines to players when their conduct became outrageous and humiliating.

The Cincinnati Enquirer reporter said of the Reds' 6-1 loss to the lowly Stars on July 8 that "Neagle, the new change pitcher Billy Geer dug out of the New York sand country, went to the box and Will White took up a position at the carriage gate to watch his fill-in. Neagle may be a fine little gentleman but if he has a talent for any other occupation he would be wise to clinch to it quick. He pitched without judgment, fielded like a member of a female ball-club, and if he has any batting ability he reserved it for another occasion."

On Friday, July 11 the Red Stockings hammered the Red Caps 11-2. *The Enquirer* said, "The Bostons went helter-skelter, knocking the ball to the extremes of the grounds and stealing bases with the greatest impunity. After sundry errors the audience began to guy the players and hooted and laughed at the boys in red and white until they wished they were wood cutters instead of ball players. Behind the bat Kelly was never so weak as he was to-day. He neither held the ball, threw to bases, or had the ability to catch fly-balls or thrown ones. He wound up with five errors and three passed balls. Kelly is a valuable man to relieve, a good batter, and one of the best base runners on the team, but he is far from steady in the catcher's position."

Kelly went to talk with Boston's Charlie "Pop" Snyder after the game ended. He was the same age as Kelly but he'd been playing in the major league since '73. He didn't handle a bat very well but he did well behind one. Mike always watched him to see how he handled pitchers.

"Rough game," said Snyder when he saw who'd tapped him on the shoulder.

"They'd uv done better to put a monkey behind the bat, Pop," groaned Kelly.

"You shouldn't lunge for the ball, Michael. You need to wait and see how and where it's going to land. And when it's catchable, don't reach for it. Let it fall into your hands."

"Makes sense, I guess I'm just tryin' too hard."

"You are, I did at first too. Say, what are your club's owners like?"

"They don't like to drink with the players."

Snyder laughed. "No. I mean are they cheap?"

"Well the club's on the verge of foldin' so they aren't exactly spendin' money like drunken sailors on shore leave, but I wouldn't call 'em cheap. Why?"

"Soden cut our damn meal money and it wasn't much to begin with. We travel on the oldest, slowest, most rickety and dangerous railroads, and he books us into flea bag hotels you wouldn't take the loosest woman in town to. We have to man the turnstiles, cut the grounds and wrestle fans for foul balls. Do you fellows have to pay for having your uniform cleaned?"

"At home we do. Not when we're on the road."

"Well we do. Soden's so cheap he offers us an incentive if we make our shoelaces last for two years instead of one. Anyone who manages to do it gets his fare paid on the horse cars either to or from the ball grounds."

On July 16th 472 people passed through the turnstiles which, with the boys in the bull-pen, probably footed up a total of five hundred persons. The blue-ribbon twirling of Will White, the pretty fielding of Barnes and McVey, and the heavy batting of Kelly which earned the Cincinnatis their three runs, were the brilliant points of the game. In the second inning Hotaling hit a liner that Hague par-

tially stopped with one bound but couldn't field. Kelly fell upon the ball for a two-base hit to center on which Pete came home. McVey batted Kelly home by a safe bounder over second.

During the sixth inning two of Billy McLean's decisions turned the tide of the game. There was considerable growling about his calls, especially by the betting class. Kelly had led off the frame with a two-baser to center. He got past McGeary without being touched but McLean decided him out. He later claimed Kelly had run out of the base line but he hadn't. He then ruled McVey out at first even though O'Rourke had taken his foot off the bag. The calls so incensed the crowd that cries of "Put him out!" resounded through the stands. Billy turned to the crowd and said, "Maybe one of you'd like to come down *here* and put me out." No one dared.

The eighth inning was a blinder. Mike opened the ninth with a ferocious belt to left. The bullet hit the ground near York and bounded over him. Before York could get to it Kelly had done a great sprint act and crossed the rubber in splendid style. He was compelled to lift his cap in acknowledgement of the crowd's cheers. The blast brought the Reds within a run of the Grays but Providence added an insurance run on a bad throw by McVey in their half of the inning. *The Enquirer* claimed the Marquis of Kelly was "a man who 'its 'em 'ard."

On July 19 Mike made three hits and scored three times in his club's eleven inning 7-6 win over the Troys. The Cincinnatis had a much easier time with the Trojans after the obligatory Sunday of rest, clobbering Bradley 10-0. It being wash day, the crowd was small but the fieldwork of the Red Caps won them hearty huzzahs. Kelly went to third again and his play there was a model of its kind seldom seen as he made five glowing stops and throws.

Mike Burke had gotten full of beer that morning and decided to visit President Nuff's office. Nuff sent word to McVey to lay Burke off and play Neagle. After the Cincinnatis were in uniform Burke walked onto the field and began calling McVey foul names and accused him of telling Nuff he was drunk. Mac told him to go away and Burke assaulted him. Kelly rushed up and held Burke until a

policeman came and dragged him off the grounds. At the gate the vanquished player attacked Manager Howe. His release had not yet been drawn up but it was likely he'd be expelled.

On July 26th the audience was smaller than usual for a Saturday in Chicago due to the race activities at the Jockey Club Park. The White Stockings' change pitcher Frank Hankerson "was pie for the Porkopolis nine, who batted him too deucedly for those who'd hoped for a home nine win. The bejangled umpiring was the worst seen in Chicago in some time. Mr. Houtz seemed to have no conception of the difference between balls and strikes and frequently mistook the one for the other," chided *The Chicago Tribune*.

Kelly, who ranked eighth in the League in batting with a .331 average and stood tenth in times touching the plate, singled and scurried home at a 2:12 ½ pace when Dickerson hit for a couple of bags in the second and he singled twice more in the Reds' 11-8 win.

Two days later the Cincinnatis hit Larkin all over the grounds and played superbly in the field. Deacon White had two passed balls and made a wild throw to third that resulted in the Chicagos' only runs while Kelly played third base flawlessly.

The flip of the copper sent the Chicagos to bat and Dalrymple, Peters, and Williamson never reached first base. The Red Caps were more fortunate. Hotaling led off with a strike out. Kelly fouled a ball off a policeman's headgear, apologized, then sent the dented ball far out into the left field. Dalrymple should have got it but grossly misjudged it instead. He made a feeble struggle to get the ball but Kelly had reached third in the meantime and McVey brought him home on a two-baser.

After Hotaling went out again in the third Kelly got first on Peters' muff, second on a wild pitch, third on a wild throw by Flint to catch him stealing, and home when Flint and Williamson were trying to put him out between third and the plate and Flint dropped the ball. The fifth was barren of tallies but the red-legged and under-shirted players did get in some licks, Kelly and McVey securing base hits.

With Larkin on first in the ninth Gore sent one just over the head of second baseman Barnes. Both runners believed the ball would drop in for a hit and took their time but Kelly by a hard run made a brilliant catch and kept bowling right along to second base where he handed the ball to a startled Ross Barnes who touched Larkin for the out.

The Reds had a day off after the series so Kelly decided to go to Haverly's Theatre to see "The Banker's Daughter." He'd heard good things about the farce and even better things about its star, Miss Sarah Cowell. After the show he went backstage. He looked around and found a stagehand he'd seen at White Stockings' games and asked if he could direct him to Cowell's dressing-room.

When Mike knocked lightly the lovely actress opened the door. Sarah had a Cupid's mouth with a faint air of amusement on her lips, a graceful neck, and a lovely, modeled face. She'd taken off her blouse but seemed completely unflustered that a man was seeing her in a state of undress. She motioned him inside, sat down at her dressing-table, and pulled on a pair of silk stockings. Trying not to stare at her shapely legs, Mike looked around the room, which was a riot of silks, satins, scarves, hair ornaments, and perfume bottles. Sarah picked up a brush and combed her long, chestnut-brown hair.

"I'm Mike Kelly, Miss Cowell, I wanted to tell you how much I enjoyed your performance."

Sarah looked Kelly up and down. "Kind of you to say. Are you an actor, I don't recognize you but you are certainly *handsome* enough to be one."

"I'm no artist, I'm a base ball player."

"A base ball player? With a lovely Irish accent and lovely blue eyes to match. I would invite you to sit down but as you can see there is only one chair."

"I'll let you finish dressing then."

"Did you eat before the show, Mike Kelly?"

"I did not."

"Nor did I."

"Do you like oysters? What about Rector's?

"There are always show people there. I don't feel like talking shop tonight."

"Have you been to the Palmer House, Miss . . . "

"Call me Sarah. No, I've not. I'm afraid our manager won't spend the money to have our company stop there."

"Well they have three dining rooms so I'm pretty sure we can get into one of them without a reservation."

"I'm starving. I'll be dressed and ready in ten minutes."

Sarah had a good appetite. She had smoked tongue and turkey wings with stewed tomatoes for an appetizer, then poached salmon with breaded rice and fried parsnips. She polished it off with a carafe of red wine and then asked if she could have a glass of the whiskey Mike was drinking.

"Have you been to Schlogl's?" Kelly asked her as she was finishing her dessert.

"The saloon next to the Daily News building?"

"That's right, on Wells Street." He took out his watch and opened it up. It's after eleven. Do you need to get back to your hotel?"

"I generally sleep until noon so I don't think a couple of more drinks will be a problem."

There were several reporters drinking at a table in the corner when they went in.

"Isn't that Sarah Cowell?" Mike heard one of them ask the others.

"It is," said *The Tribune* base ball man. "And that's Kelly from the Cincinnatis she's with."

"You're right. Pretty cocky for a young Irish ball tosser to be stepping out with an actress," said *The Daily News* reporter.

"If I had Kelly's looks I'd be stepping out with actresses too," said *The Inter-Ocean* man.

Sarah put her hand on Mike's and when she leaned closer to him he breathed in the fragrance of her perfume. She whispered in his ear. "Voulez-vous couchez avec moi ce soir?"

She got back to the hotel at 1 but it was *Mike's* hotel. Not hers. Buttercup had to sleep in the hall."

THE
$10,000
BEAUTY

"I think they figure we're stage-coach robbers."

On August 9 the fielding by the White Stockings was the most lamentable ever seen on the Cincinnati grounds. Flint suffered an injured thumb in the opening inning and Williamson relieved him. Shafer took his place at third base and was constantly employed as the home side did their best to send balls his way. He failed wretchedly, muffing all but one of them. The Chicago players' most costly display of blunders came in the fourth when Remsen and Peters reaped a whirlwind that manifested itself in six runs.

In the eighth Kelly, who was at the top of the League ladder with a .352 average and feeling like he could make a hit whenever he wielded the willow, batted one into the middle field. He thought it merited two bases and ran with all his speed, making a wide turn rounding first. The throw came into Anson who had to step back to take it but remained on the basepath. The width of Kelly's turn pulled him off the path and Anson couldn't reach far enough to touch him. He claimed an out but Houtz refused to allow it. Anson intimated loudly to Umpire Houtz that he was now playing the game under protest.

In the midst of the squabble Kelly ran from the wrangling players and scored, nobody in the field being able to intercept him but Larkin, who muffed the ball when it was finally thrown home.

Anson turned to the Chicagos around him. "Did you see that? We'd best keep an eye on *that* bog jumper."

On August 14 the Cincinnati club, numbering ten men in the charge of Secretary Howe in addition to the White brothers' prim wives travelled to Buffalo. They reached the city early in the after-

noon and proceeded directly to Pierre Pierce's Hotel. They'd left home late the night before and as no sleeping-car had been available the players had been forced to sleep in their seats.

"I'm afraid the dining-car is closed for the night, ladies and gentlemen," the conductor announced.

"Well doesn't that take the biscuit," said Kelly. He turned to Howe. "How about you try and book us on another railroad next time we come this way."

Howe felt bad. When the train stopped for water he hurried into the hotel nearby and came back with ham sandwiches, boiled eggs, and coffee for the men.

"What, no beer?" asked Gerhardt.

"Sorry, Joe, apparently this is a dry county."

When they reached Buffalo the team checked into the Invalids' and Tourists' Hotel at Porter and Prospect avenues. The hotel featured bath appliances, a steam elevator, and a fully furnished gymnasium as well as stunning views of the Niagara River from its piazzas and grand porches. The players were too tired to enjoy the view or use the gymnasium. They felt more like going to bed than playing ball.

Pete Hotaling was the first to call for his key. Before going aloft he asked to be awoken at six and then told a bystander that he was thankful a certain Cincinnati newspaper man was not in their party as he might chronicle the doings of the players which they didn't care to have given to the world. Barnes took to his virtuous couch. Jim White and his saintly wife enjoyed a friendly chat with two Directors of the Buffalo club on the porch. Kelly, who'd slept like a baby on the train after a number of sips from his flask, waited until the rain let up and then strolled out of the hotel, presumably to sketch some scenery.

After another rainy day the skies finally cleared on Friday. Mike had two hits and was sharp at third base once again even though the grounds were damp and a strong wind blew. The other Red Caps

were overly generous, giving the Bisons eight unearned runs in a 10-9 loss.

The Reds had a picnic with "Pud" Galvin on August 25. He'd been given his nickname by teammates who said he reduced enemy batters to pudding. His tiny head seemed out of proportion to his massive shoulders, it looked like a turtle sticking its head out of its shell. Galvin's tiny hands were too small to allow him to throw a curveball so he relied on the speed and accuracy of his shoots and his deadly change-up made them seem that much quicker.

Pud was born and raised in the Irish slum in St. Louis known as "Kerry Patch" and his personal habits left much to be desired. He wore only flannel shirts and preferred to eat with his fingers. His teammates often insisted that he eat by himself in the kitchen rather than dine with them. Galvin was full of the jiggery-pokery, Kel knew he had to keep his wits about him when he was on base, Pud had no qualms about bending the rules to pick off a runner.

Kelly had a baser and scored in an 8-run second and singled and scored again in the sixth in a 10-2 roundup of the horned cattle.

The Enquirer chastised the people who were calling for League teams to reduce their admission prices from 50 to 25 cents. If clubs were struggling to make a profit they believed the solution was to reduce the salaries of their older players. "Two thousand dollars for six months work is entirely too much. Let them sign contracts for salaries which come to the level of the younger players or step aside and let more young men have a chance. Take the Cincinnati team as an instance, three men in the team - Jim White, McVey and Barnes - are drawing $6,250. Will White, Kelly, and Hotaling together do not receive as much as $2,000 and yet when the season ends and their work at the bat and in the field is summed up the balance will be to their credit."

Two days later the Cincinnati boys had matters their own way in a 15-4 win in Cleveland. The Blues were attired in white caps and trousers and white tunics with a C on the left breast and blue neckties and stockings. The Kennard Street Grounds were small. The right-

field fence wasn't much further back of first base than the base was from home-plate. Kelly played with his back almost against the fence and on most hard hits he got the ball on the rebound as boys do by throwing a ball against the gable end of a schoolhouse.

He noticed that the Blues' first baseman Bill Phillips was sporting a fine pair of black eyes. Phillips told people they were the result of an encounter with a buggy at Rocky River. James McCormick, the Cleveland captain, was asked about the goings-on of his players of late and with as straight a face as he could muster he swore they'd been doing nothing worse than attending Sunday-school since Saturday.

Kelly, McVey, and Jim White led the way with their bats. Kelly ripped a pair of stingers off his friend, a regular cowslip-bruiser at shortstop Carey and a finger-burner to "Pebbly Jack" Glasscock, so-named for his habit of picking up pebbles along with the ball and firing the lot to first. *The Buffalo Commercial*, which was still spelling Mike's name Kelley, reported that he wielded the willow most effectively. He had six chances at third base and accepted five of them. In the second inning he made a one-handed stop of a line hit that elicited prolonged demonstrations of approval.

The Cleveland Leader called it "the dirtiest, noisiest game played in Cleveland this year. "There were only two red-legs not making abusive sounds, Whoop-La White and his brother Deacon, due to their religious dispositions. Gerhardt talked back to Umpire Pratt and the indulgence cost him $30. Whenever a Cleveland player batted a ball into the air eight captains yelled the name of the player who was to catch it.

The visitors gained a one run lead in the sixth inning, scoring three times to capture a 5-4 lead. It looked like their day, but Tom Carey clubbed a clutch two-bagger that sent McCormick trotting home with the run that sent the game into extra frames.

George Strief led off the bottom of the 11th by popping out then McCormick launched the ball high into the infield air. Barnes settled under it but let it slip through his fingers when it finally returned to

earth. The game had now lasted just over four and a half hours. Kelly groaned. He was thirsty, and not for water. Phillips singled and Mike watched James jog into scoring position. Charlie Eden got a good pitch and turned it into another single and McCormick came around and stomped on the plate with the winning run. According to the rules, three outs needed to be recorded before the game could be counted as an official one. Thankfully, Warner and Glasscock obliged in short order.

The Enquirer man, who signed his scribblings 'Dennis', believed that too little importance was attached to a player's baserunning ability. "The only questions asked are Can he bat? and Can he field? When Wright or York secure a base hit they stand still until they are batted home or are caught asleep off a base. When Kelly, who stands first in batting average, second in hits, second in runs batted in, and second in base-running, reaches base it's one to two he'll cross the plate."

The September 11 game with Troy was a 10-1 walkover for the Cincinnatis. Kelly started the ball rolling when he got in a safe drop fly over second in the fourth. He shot a high-flyer over third base in the sixth that sent Hotaling across the plate and he knocked the daylights out of the ball and made it home on McVey's safe hit to right in the eighth. Behind the bat Kelly made no errors and let no balls get past him. He was as happy as a clam in high water.

"I'm not one ta blow me own horn or sing me own praises, Sully," he said to Chub, "but I think I might just stick in this league after all. Maybe it's not just a pipe dream uv mine."

"I'll wager you'll do a lot more than just stick, Kel."

Mike's Troy counterpart John Kelly had a dreadful day with three errors and four passed balls. After an understandably brief playing career, John - later "Honest John" Kelly - would go on to be the League's most respected umpire and would one day go into business with Mike.

There was news out of Syracuse on September 11. After falling $2,500 in debt the Stars were disbanded for want of spectators and

funds. They forfeited the rest of their games, finishing their NL life with a 22-48 record. Having played Troy only 6 times, the official NL standings were adjusted so that only the first 6 games of the number each team played versus Syracuse would count. The Stars would be replaced by the Worchester Ruby Legs for the start of the 1880 season.

Kelly had dinner with Charlie Jones and Chub Sullivan that night. As he pushed away his empty plate Charlie turned to Mike, who was lighting a cigarette. "What did you do before you tried earning a living playing ball?"

"I had a job at the Murray Silk Mill in Paterson. It made cords, gimps, braids and tassels, fancy headgear, false curls, neckwear, articles for theatrical costumes, and trimmings for use by carriage makers, tailors, undertakers, and hatters."

"What did *you* do?" asked Chub.

Mike exhaled a puff of smoke. "My job was ta carry baskets uv coal up from the basement to the top floor. The clatter of the weaving and embroidery machines was deafening. Sometimes I wouldn't wait until all the coal bags had been hauled up. My boss caught me jumpin' out uv a second story window to skive away for a ball game one time and it nearly cost me my job. Then I was given the far more important position of turning the crank that kept the mill's power going. When I took a water break the whole mill stopped until I returned. That job lasted two days."

"Two *days*? Why?"

Mike laughed. "Too many water breaks."

"How did you get into base ball?"

"I was pretty strong from liftin' all those baskets of coal and when I was fifteen I was good enough to be recruited to play on Paterson's top base ball club, the Keystones. The nine was captained by Blondie Purcell and me best friend Jim McCormick was the team's pitcher. I was his catcher, just like when we were kids on the sandlot. We dominated all uv the local competition. Jim and I did a stint with the Pa-

terson Olympics at the end of the 1875 season and I did well enough to earn a full-time spot with the city's top club for '76. I played in Port Jervis, New Jersey for a couple uv months in the Delawares. They were captained by Blondie Purcell. Blondie went off to play in Columbus and around the end uv July he wired me to join him in the Buckeyes."

"And you played with Chub in Columbus and he was the one that recommended you to the Cincinnatis."

"He was. Otherwise the two uv yas would be dining alone."

Kelly's work in the second week of September "was worthy of a gold frame with a silver background." He went to the bat 22 times and reached base on sixteen of them. Out of 30 chances offered to him at third base he missed just two.

On September 23 a Special in *The Tribune* said, "For some time past your correspondent has been aware of serious trouble among the stockholders and officers of the Cincinnati Club and that it was not improbable that the close of the present season would witness the death of the organization. This year's team has been a ramshackle affair from the start and instead of growing better it has steadily deteriorated and at present it is about as demoralized a concern as could be found. The current management is heartily disgusted with base ball in general and Cincinnati base ball in particular. Mr. Neff is a very pleasant gentleman but as the head of a ball club he is more distinguished for failure than success.

At the end of last season he resolved to secure a nine for 1879 on the regardless-of-expense plan. It is one of the easiest things in the world to do if your bank account is robust. He expended funds with princely liberality in signing as fine a lot of duffers as was ever gathered together but they turned out to be of the easily dispirited and fault-finding variety and some of them were also afflicted with what is known as 'the big head.'

Jim White was installed as manager after McVey proved a failure in 1878 and it naturally riled Mac's friends who set to work to make things as unpleasant as possible for the Deacon. The team contained so many elements of discord that anything like harmony was out of the question. White inaugurated his brief career by releasing Mitchell, an excellent change pitcher, so that 'brother Will' might have full sway between the points and then he imported a brother-in-law from the wilds of Corning, N.Y. and installed him as score-keeper. The move brought upon the club the hostility of The Enquirer whose amateur base ball reporter had unsuccessfully applied for the position.

One of The Enquirer's pets was Burke, who had been engaged to play shortstop but was forced out to make room for Barnes, a high-priced ornament with whom the Chicago organization had such an unpleasant experience in '77. Gerhardt, who had played second base in a very acceptable manner was shifted around to make room for Barnes who can't hold onto Kelly's throws to second no matter how 'on the money' they are. Then two members in the nine began to drink heavily and Jim White was unable to control or direct them. Things got so bad that during the team's first Eastern trip the directors held a meeting and removed White, replacing him with McVey. Since then, the record of the team has been so disgraceful it cannot draw a paying audience at home or abroad and the club has lost over $10,000 over the season.

By the start of September Mr. Nuff was quite willing to retire if anybody would kindly provide him with a hole to crawl into. His first move was to give the men notice that after Oct. 1 their services would no longer be required. This was the first intimation of the club's collapse."

The Cincinnatis won six of their last seven games to finish fifth with a record of 43 and 37. They could hardly blame their disappointing season on Mike Kelly. He'd improved defensively from his dismal start and he'd had a terrific year with the willow. Batting third in the last game of the season Kelly made two hits to finish with a .348 average though the League wouldn't release the actual numbers for some time. When they did, Mike would finish second in Batting Average; third in hits, three-basers, and Slugging; and fourth

in times on base and runs scored. In many of their games Kelly had driven in every one of the Cincinnatis' runs.

At the end of the season Robert Miles of the Grand Opera House of Cincinnati made arrangements for the Cincinnati club to make a barnstorming trip to California. Kelly, McVey, Hotaling, and Purcell were the only Red Caps who signed on even though Miles promised the players they would make "a pile of money" so he added John Clapp, Davy Force, Jack Rowe, and Pud Galvin of the Buffalos. Their opposition would be local California nines and the Chicago club which was also heading west.

Miles and the players boarded the "Tunnel Line" train and left Cincinnati for the West Coast on the evening of October 5. They arrived in San Francisco on Saturday, October 11 and checked into the Baldwin, a luxury hotel built by millionaire Comstock Lode and "Lucky" Baldwin, a notorious gambler, on Powell street near Union Square.

On the train the players had read about the Palace Hotel but they knew $3 a night was out of the question, the Baldwin's $2.50 rate was dear enough. When they arrived, Mike, Cal and Hotaling approached the clean-shaven clerk at the front desk. Cal asked where he might find some fine cigars. Mike and Pete were more interested to know if he might be able to recommend some places of amusement.

The clerk leaned over the counter. "It might be of interest to you men, if I may be so bold, that San Francisco has devoted a considerable share of her attention to the pursuit of pleasure."

"Smooth cigars are fine," said Pete, "coquettish women are finer."

"We wouldn't mind procurin' a few libations for our rooms," said Kelly.

"I would recommend Sherwood and Sherwood. They feature Bank's Scotch and Irish whiskies," said the clerk. "You can walk or call a cab. The telephone number is there." He pointed to a sign at the end of the counter that read, "City Cab and Carriage Company,

prompt attendance to theatres and balls, telephone 1422."

The hotel was busy and the city was busy too. There were still a lot of horse-drawn trolleys but street railway companies had started to hustle people along the congested streets that were being paved with cobblestones. Kelly thought San Francisco's streetlights were attractive but the telephone poles were eyesores.

On Sunday, the Cincinnatis took a boat to Oakland and shut out the town's nine at the Oakland Grounds before a crowd of 2,000. After the game Kelly talked with the team's captain. "Most uv the players in our league have ta work at sumthin' in the winter ta make ends meet, how about you lot?" he asked.

"We're paid about half of what I hear you fellows pull in. We *all* have jobs in the off season." He looked around at his teammates. "Let's see, we've got a box-maker, a harness cleaner, a drayman, an iron-ruffer, a cooper, a car conductor, a gripman, a hostler, and a hackman."

Kelly chuckled. "You've got everything but a butcher, a baker, and a candle-stick maker." He laughed at his own joke and then asked the captain, "Do ya know how to poison an enemy ball player at the end uv an inning?"

"How?" asked the captain.

"With strike-nine."

"They told me you were quite the kidder, Kelly. Thanks for the drubbing."

The Easterners spent most of their evenings at the California Theatre, though the Baldwin had its own. They didn't frequent their hotel's bar either, it specialized in wine. They drank at the Colosseum Liquor Saloon a few blocks down Market street instead. The bar-tender, Edward Collins, told Kelly and Blondie Purcell that he'd almost been run over by a carriage on his to work from way his place on Howard street.

"Say, me hair's gettin' a wee bit long. Would ya happen ta know a good barber?"

"My brother Edward's a barber, he has a shop a few blocks from here."

"What time does he open?"

"Eight o'clock."

"Great. Say, the boys are lookin' for some fun while we're here and the fella at the hotel made it sound like there's a pretty good chance we can find some. Are there any other spots on Market street we could try?"

"Not really. You can find whatever strikes your fancy on Pacific avenue between Kearny and Montgomery. There's everything there, melodeons, concert saloons, gambling dens, dance halls, and brothels. Hell, even the restaurants have bawdy shows going on."

Blondie Purcell wiped the beer suds from his mustache and said, "I believe we'd enjoy the dance halls."

Everyone burst into laughter.

The bar-tender continued. "The Coast is a whole lot safer than it used to be, the authorities have cleaned it up some. It used to be nuthin' but thugs and crimps, pickpockets and cutthroats, whoremongers and opium dens. Crimps used to shanghai fellas. They'd spike their drink, kidnap 'em and put them on a ship for forced labor. Some bars even had a trap door in the floor for easy pickings. The Bull Run Saloon was the worst. Police officers didn't *dare* to patrol the district by themselves and a night rarely passed without at least one murder.

Now it's the *waiter* girls you to need to be careful with. They're pretty and scantily-clad and they're paid to seduce and exploit their customers. Keep in mind there are still far more men than women here and a lot of the men in San Francisco make a killing on the mines or in speculation and it's often gone in one night on Pacific avenue."

"*I'd* settle for a waiter girl or two," sighed Blondie. "It's been a month or more since I've been with a woman. The last time, the gal had hardly finished unbuttoning my fly when I spilled my load."

The club defeated the Californias 13-0, the Athletics 8-2, and the Mutuals 23-0 and 11-1. The Chicago club played two games on Saturday, October 25, trouncing the Mutuals 11–1 and, with Corcoran, the change pitcher they'd brought with them between the points, they shut out the Oaklands 18-0. The Cincinnati and Buffalo nine punished Corcoran's pitching on November 1 and pummeled the Chicagos 12-5.

The following day, Cincinnati again prevailed, 5-1 this time. On Saturday, November 8, Chicago scored the deciding run in the ninth inning, edging Cincinnati 3-2. The California fans loved Mike's bantering on the field and his kicking.

Anson watched Kelly catch for the "all-stars" and almost single-handedly lead them to a victory over his club and the Hop Bitters, the best barn-storming team in the country. He'd watched Kelly whenever the Chicagos played the Cincinnatis. He knew Mike was intuitive and took in everything he saw on the field and stored it away for future use - a baserunner's speed, a batter's fear of inside shoots, a fielder's arm and how quickly he could get a throw on its way. Anson sent a four-word wire to A.G. Spalding that night. *"Must sign Mike Kelly."*

Back east, the League owners were meeting in Buffalo. Neff failed to appear, he told people he was getting out of base ball. President Hulbert telegraphed him as to which five of the Cincinnati players should be reserved for the next season. Neff replied that Hulbert had his proxy to act on his behalf in the matter. Hulbert was sure the five players the Cincinnatis would most desire to protect were the Whites, Kelly, McVey, and Hotaling. Shortly after the meeting adjourned notice was received of the absolute release of the players in the Cincinnati Club, which abrogated any reserves. Hulbert felt entitled to agree to Anson's urgent request.

When Anson asked him to join the Chicago club Kelly was surprised, he'd heard how little the Chicago captain thought of Irishmen. Mike wanted $100 more than Anson was offering and he held out until Anson finally and reluctantly relented.

Kelly, Hotaling, Purcell, Smith, and Reilly arrived at Council Bluffs Christmas night in a blinding snowstorm and were compelled to stop over at the Ogden Hotel. They were quite a sight. Their faces hadn't met a razor for many days and they all wore flannel shirts they'd bought to stay warm on the poorly heated train. The proprietor was taken aback but he invited them to a dance that was about to begin in the big dining room.

They went to their rooms and got decked out in blue shirts and black ties but the ladies and gentlemen were frightened half to death.

"I think they figure we're stage-coach robbers or the like," said Blondie.

After everyone had helped themselves to the punch the Council Bluffs denizens forgot about the players' strange apparel and made them lions for the night. They danced until 6 in the morning.

When Mike arrived back in Paterson on New Year's night he went straight to another dance and was at that one all night.

THE
$10,000
BEAUTY

"You bet your bustle I would."

Kelly was known as a fashion plate and a dasher among the girls. With a little money in his pocket, he dressed in pointed, patent leather, high-button shoes and wore a high silk hat, jauntily cocked off to one side.

When he got to Chicago in March he booked himself a room at the seven-story Palmer House at State and Monroe, a short walk to the ball grounds. Rooms went for $3 dollars a night and suites for as much as $5 but renting a room by the month wasn't as expensive. Every time Mike had been in Chicago he'd heard people describe a point in the city as being so many blocks from the Palmer House. That was the place for Kelly.

Constructed of brick, the glamorous hotel claimed to be the first wholly fireproof hotel in America. Its builder Potter Palmer liked to bet his friends that if they started a fire in any of the guest rooms it wouldn't spread to any of the other rooms because of the thick plaster walls. No one had ever taken him up on it. Outdoing the city's other grand hotels, the Great Northern and the Tremont, the Palmer was the first in Chicago to be equipped with electric light bulbs, telephones, and two elevators that ran day and night.

The walls were adorned with paintings by Louis Pierre Rigal and other French painters Mike had never heard of and impressionist art the likes of which he'd never seen. The Palmer was bedecked with garnet-draped chandeliers, Louis Comfort Tiffany masterpieces, and a breathtaking ceiling fresco.

The hotel's amenities included massive rooms, luxurious decor,

and sumptuous meals served in grand style. Its three lavish dining rooms were cloaked with enormous garnet-draped chandeliers, thick pile carpet, and stone pillars that reached up to a high gold-leaf ceiling. Kelly loved hearing the clink of polished silver on fine China when he ate in one of them. The cuisine avoided the French and Italian food served in Chicago's other fine restaurants, which was fine with Kelly. They offered appetizers of spiced oysters, smoked tongue and corned beef, and a diner could choose from venison steak with currant jelly, breaded turkey wings with green peas, or macaroni with cheese. Side dishes included stewed tomatoes, boiled potatoes, boiled rice and fried parsnips.

Guests incurred extra charges for private parlors, room service, fires in private fireplaces, and desserts taken to one's room from the dinner table. For their further convenience the Palmer House had its own stable. Leroy Payne's Livery housed 200 horses and more than 100 different vehicles from the latest styles of carriages to six-horse tally ho coaches that could carry forty people. Payne employed 115 men including drivers, groomers, and blacksmiths.

The hotel offered guided tours for those who couldn't afford to stay there, a lot of people wanted to see where the rich and famous stayed. Aware that ball-players weren't handsomely rewarded for plying their trade, guests and visitors who happened to be base-ball enthusiasts were always shocked to see Mike Kelly having his dinner or waiting for an elevator.

Mike chuckled when he got his morning shave in the sumptuous barber shop. Its floor was tiled with silver dollars. He wasn't the only guest that remarked upon it. Rudyard Kipling and Oscar Wilde had commented in their writing about the barber shop's floor. Mike whistled when Giuseppe, his favorite barber, told him the furnishings of the shop alone had cost $23,000.

Kelly, who was far less wealthy than most of the hotel's guests, often took his meals in the Café or the circular restaurant decorated with marble and mirrors. Without turning around Kelly could watch masters of industry and beautiful women pass by. Women, beautiful or otherwise, were almost never seen unescorted. Women traveling

alone presented a serious problem for hotel keepers. Immorality on a lone woman's part could sully an inn's reputation. Hotel keepers needed to assure their refined clientele that female guests were entirely respectable. If not, the establishment risked degenerating into a common assignment house. Kelly would have been shocked to see a woman by herself.

A proper lady bypassed the bustling lobby to avoid stares from men gathered there. She entered by the segregated Ladies' Entrance and checked in at the separate registration desk located on the second floor where there was a tearoom and a parlor exclusively for women.

It was common to spot someone often seen on the front page of a newspaper in one of the dining rooms of the Palmer House. At breakfast one morning Mike's chatty and effeminate waiter excitedly told him in his high-pitched voice about some of the hotel's famous visitors. "James Garfield and Grover Cleveland have stopped here ... not at the same time of course . . . and Ulysses S. Grant was here. All he did was sit by himself in that corner table drinking whiskey and smoking big cigars. Buffalo Bill put on a little show in the lobby for the guests when he was here. Charles Dickens stayed here, but that was before my time. They said he was hard to please, he doesn't like American food. Mark Twain, I mean Samuel Clemens, was working on a book I think he said he was going to call A Tramp Abroad when he was here last year. I'm told Oscar Wilde's coming next year. I love his poems, they're absolutely divine. And Wilde is so attractive. Sarah Bernhardt's coming here next fall. I hear she keeps a satin-lined coffin in her bedroom and sometimes lies in it to practice for roles. Apparently she doesn't take it with her when she travels ... at least I hope she doesn't, she'd scare the chamber-maids half to death."

The waiter pointed to an attractive woman in a cambric dress with a blue velvet spencer at a table nearby eating with another woman. "That's Eleanora Duse - she's appearing in something at Haverly's Theatre." Mike remembered seeing the Italian actress' name in the newspapers.

The waiter looked around to see if any of the other diners could hear. "They say she's having an affair with a journalist named Martino Cafiero and there are rumors she's carrying his child."

"Who's that she's with?" asked Mike.

"Louise Hagemann, the costume designer."

"I wonder if she's having her make gowns to hide her belly."

"Oh, I hadn't thought, you may be right. So you're having pancakes and sausages?"

"Yes."

The waiter turned to leave.

"Wait, me new captain wants me ta lose twenty pounds, you'd better cancel the pancakes and sausages and bring me some egg whites and half uva grapefruit instead."

Mike crossed Monroe street after breakfast and bought a diamond stick-pin at Rowe & Brothers Jewelry and then a fountain pen at Maxwell's Stationery a block north on Wabash. Then he bought cigarettes at O'Connor the Tobacconist's shop on Clarke street. He took a look inside Edwin Kelsh's millinery store thinking he might find a new hat, but Kelsh carried only cravats and ascots for men. His stylish hats were for ladies, so Kelly walked two blocks down Monroe street to Charles P. Kellogg's and then Henry W. King's clothing stores and found some items he'd buy when he got his first pay on May 1st.

When Mike woke up in his fine bed-room the next morning it took him a moment to realize where he was. He went to the window and pulled opened the shades. He looked up and down State street at the passing carriages and heard the clop clop of their horses and then a newsboy yelling out, "Wabash first city illuminated by electric lighting!"

He noticed there was a note under his door. It said his uniform had been cleaned. He opened the door and there was his uniform, as white as when he'd bought it. "I hope they do as well with lipstick on me collars," he said to himself.

He opened the valise he hadn't entirely unpacked, looked inside and made a mental note to buy mustache wax and then took his mustache brush out of the case and set it on the richly polished dresser.

He got washed in the finely decorated bath-room he could hardly believe he had all too himself - in addition to not having to share a bed with a teammate - though he'd still have to on road trips - and then got dressed. He attached a new collar to his shirt, fastened his pearl cuff-links to his sleeves, then double-checked that all of the buttons on his fly were fastened. He popped a peppermint into his mouth, checked the time on his watch and slipped it back into his vest pocket. On his way out the door he looked in the mirror to see that his hat was tipped at its usually dapper angle then headed to the elevator.

On his way he saw a pretty chamber-maid coming out of another room. She had sparkling green eyes, a dainty chin, and rosebud lips. She wore a starched white apron that looped around her white neck and was tied in the small of her spine with a perfect crisp bow. She looked up at him and smiled. Mike looked her up and down, admiring her form. "And what might your name be?" he asked.

"I'm Colleen. Would I be able to clean your room now?"

"Aye, I'll not be back 'til late this afternoon."

"Very well then. How many nights will you be with us, Mr. Kelly?" she asked, a charming lilt in her voice.

"I'll be here until the end uv September."

She picked up a curl of hair, pulled at it playfully, then let go. It bounced as it settled back into place. "I'm glad to hear uv it," she said with a saucy smile. "Let me know if there's anything ... special I can do for you."

The addition of four members of the disbanded Indianapolis Blues - catcher Silver Flint, second baseman Joe Quest, third baseman Ned Williamson, and right fielder Orator Shafer - at the start of the 1879 season had greatly strengthened the White Stockings, who'd placed fourth in '78. The club had been tied for first on August

15 in '79 but nine straight losses in September knocked them out of contention.

Kelly would be taking the Orator's place. He'd heard that Flint and Shafer had left Indianapolis with some unpaid debts. When the White Stockings traveled there to play an exhibition game in June the local sheriff was waiting for them. After the game the two escaped from the ballpark in a horse-drawn carriage and Cap Anson was taken to jail.

The only first year player in the club was 23-year-old Tom Burns, who hailed from Honesdale, Pennsylvania. He showed cleverness in pick-ups and throws from short field and threw on a dead line with a quick turn of the wrist, though he had a tendency to throw wild on occasion. Tom drew more than his share of walks so he was an ideal leadoff hitter. Kelly thought Burns was as spry as a Scotch terrier with a rat in sight.

Joe Quest played second base in a manner in which it had never been played in Chicago. He knew he had to do good work with his hands, he was awful with a bat. He'd hit .205 for Indianapolis in 1878 and Anson had put up with his .207 average in '79 only because Joe led the League in assists and fielding percentage.

The White Stockings had picked up hard-hitting left fielder Abner Dalrymple from the Milwaukees. In his teens he'd been hired as a brakeman for the Illinois Railroad, but they really wanted him to play in their base ball nine. Finding the competition lacking he signed on with the Janesville Mutuals and then in 1877 the Milwaukee club in the short-lived League Alliance. The team was managed by Jack "Death to Flying Things" Chapman and their "sharp style and strong home town support" earned them a place in the National League in '78. Abner led the team in doubles, runs, and slugging and was second in the entire League in batting with a .354 average.

In center field was George "Piano Legs" Gore, so named because of his powerful calf muscles. In his youth he was a big, awkward country boy but he could run like a deer and hit a ball like a trip hammer. Gore signed with the New Bedfords for $50 a month but didn't stay with them long, his splendid batting attracted the attention of the entire baseball world. While the Chicagos were in Boston Hulbert ran up to New Bedford to have a look at George. Luck was with him, he made three home runs in the game. Before Hulbert left New Bedford he had Gore's name on a contract to play in Chicago in 1879 at $150 a month.

The Chicagos would be tough to beat with such a lineup but Spalding and Anson knew they had to improve upon Larkin, whose arm had a habit of going lame in the middle of a game, and mild-mannered Hankinson, who'd been on the shelf a while due to attacks of diarrhea. Both had fallen apart in the stretch drive.

Five foot three Lawrence Corcoran was born in Brooklyn on August 10, 1859 to William and Ann Corcoran, Irish immigrants. As a boy in his back-yard he used to throw balls at bedsheets on a clothesline horse to gain control of his curves. The horizontal bar across the horse was supposed to represent the height of a batter's waist. Larry practiced curving the ball around the support sticks.

Corcoran joined the Springfield club in 1878. In August he moved to the Buffalo Bisons, an independent team. He returned to Springfield in 1879 because no catcher in Buffalo could be found who could handle his pitching. The Springfield Club disbanded in September of 1879 and Corcoran was asked to join the White Stockings on their trip to California in October.

Spalding had seen Corcoran pitch in exhibition games and he'd been impressed, but Larry's sour disposition was off-putting and Hulbert was a trifle loathe to take him. He asked Flint about him.

"Get him," said Frank, "I'll do the rest."

"Flint could make a silk purse out of a sow's ear," Anson told Spalding and Hubert. "He'll make a diamond out of Corcoran."

Hulbert signed Corcoran then Spalding called him in for a talk. "Look here," he said, pointing to Flint, "That fellow is your boss. You do everything that he tells you to. Disobey and I'll fire you right off the reel."

For such a little fellow Corcoran possessed an unusual amount of speed. He excelled in keeping base runners honest and he had the endurance of an Indian pony. His phenomenally swift delivery made him "the terror of batsmen." He threw a double shoot, a "Chicago snake ball", and Kelly was glad he wouldn't have to face him. Corcoran grasped the ball hard and imparted a twist to it that caused the ball to curve to the right until it was ten or twelve feet from the plate, at which point it took a sudden dive to the left.

As a batter he was only fair, but as a fielder of his position he was remarkable, quick and as plucky as could be. He shifted his chaw of tobacco from his right cheek to his left when he wanted to throw a curve, then waited to see if Flint approved. Off the field Corcoran, who spoke with a Brooklyn accent, always wore a gray waist coat and a black vest.

Hulbert and Spalding were going to try the novel experiment of using a two-man pitching rotation instead of a workhorse and a change pitcher who was used sparingly. The other half of the rotation was going to be Fred Goldsmith who'd won just two of his six starts in his rookie season with the Troy Cities. Anson knew most of the runs he'd given up had been due to the Trojans' atrocious fielding. Fred wasn't one of the five players the Troys elected to protect so he signed with the White Stockings for 1880.

As a teenager, Goldsmith spent a lot of his time tagging along with Yale University's base ball nine and he became acquainted with Charles Hammond "Ham" Avery, the star pitcher of the Elis in the early 1870s. Avery was the first college hurler to throw a curveball successfully and he made national headlines when he used the trick pitch to shut out Harvard in '74. Fred was fascinated by the curveball and though he'd trained as a bookkeeper he was more interested in mastering the elusive pitch.

Goldsmith played semi-pro ball in and around New Haven for several years, making a name for himself with his curve pitches. They made him a desirable property and in early 1876 Fred received a handsome offer of $300 a month to pitch for the Tecumseh club of London, Ontario. His father had expected him to take over the family printing business but Fred couldn't resist the lure of the diamond.

With Fred recording a 41-5 record the Tecumsehs won the Canadian championship. The team joined the International Association and took the '77 pennant. On two occasions Goldsmith had dominated the White Stockings, prompting Spalding to file his name away for future reference.

In Goldsmith and Corcoran, whom Hulbert called "a slight, natty little chap," the Chicagos had the best pair of curvers in the League. On April 16 *The Chicago Tribune* opined that, "The general verdict is that this year's team is a marked improvement over the ones that played at Lakefront Park in '78 and '79. The two pitchers are as yet untried against League batsman but both are known to be exceptionally effective and there is no doubt that they will give excellent satisfaction.

In every other position the changes have been for the better. The infield will prove to have been strengthened by the placing of Burns at shortstop. He is a lithe, active player, a fine, straight thrower and a clear hitter of ground balls. In right field is found Kelly of last year's Cincinnatis, a reliable fielder, one of the strongest batsmen and base runners in the League, a good third baseman when needed there and an excellent catcher. It is safe to predict that he will make hosts of friends in Chicago with his charming demeanor and earnest, skillful play. Being a fast runner and a sure pick-up and straight thrower, he should fill the bill excellently."

What the *Trib* man didn't know about the Chicago's new easy-going and good-natured right fielder was that Kelly was determined to be much better than he already was. Mike knew he wasn't a gifted fielder or a speedy runner or a batsman who regularly drove the ball great distances so he read the rule book from top to bottom, then he read it again. Then he read it once more, put it down, and said to himself, "Fine, that's what's there. Now what's *not* there?"

Winter conditions persisted well into the spring at bone-chilling, wind-whipped Lakefront Park. On April mornings the players sat on the bench shivering in their overcoats. When called upon to run they

sloshed around the bases through mud, slush, and sometimes snow. When they finished, they wrapped themselves in blankets in a sweltering room in the clubhouse that had been turned into a sweatbox. A reporter sent to study the operation entered a dark chamber and, straining to adjust his eyes, barely made out a makeshift bed on the floor. In it were "two motionless forms" that turned out to be Fred Goldsmith and Ned Williamson.

"There they are," Kelly informed the reporter with a wink, "all that's left of 'em. Rather more than a bunch of toothpicks, but not much."

Williamson, fattened up by his New Orleans trip, popped out from under the heavy covering, his face as red as a beet and swathed in perspiration, and Goldsmith poked out an equally moist and blooming countenance. In an adjoining room was a mammoth stove in full blast and a pile of wraps used for the operation, blankets, rugs, canvas-flaps and the like.

It was a primitive treatment but the ballplayers swore by its effectiveness in melting away flab and purging toxins from the bloodstream-mainly the residue of months of heavy whiskey drinking.

"So apart from this, what's the training regimen?" asked the reporter.

No one else piped up so Kelly answered his question. "It includes a light breakfast, morning calisthenics, and a mile walk. That's followed by a fifteen-mile dog trot. Anson leads the way and when he looks back you had better not be far behind. Then it's lunch at the hotel, an hour's rest, then off to the ballpark. We get on our uniforms and play inter-squad games with local amateurs filling in at the needed positions. You can bet yer life those games are hard fought ones, old man Anson'll tear inta anybody not playin' ta win."

Mike sat down beside Anson after a round of calisthenics. Both were sodden in sweat.

"Burns seems ta be the only man in the nine that steers clear uv drink, Cap. But I don't see you taking much uv the stuff either."

"I was a rough-and-ready type in my early days, as full of unbri-

dled spirit as an unbroken colt and just as impatient of restraint. I drank until all hours in saloons, made sizable wagers when I played billiards – though I nearly always won - and, after taking boxing lessons from a local prizefighter, challenged many a man to fight."

"What made you give it up?"

"One night, when the beer was in and the wit was out, I decided to test my pugilistic skills against a policeman."

Mike chuckled. "Who won?"

"Neither of us, there were other cops with him, they hauled me off to jail."

"That's why you gave it all up."

"No. The club owner was a police commissioner so I got off, but as I was reeling along the street a few hours later, still drunk as a lord, I ran smack into the girl I'd been seeing. She was mortified. It was bad enough for a girl to be stepping out with a ball-player but now he'd turned out to be a drunken brawler. She reminded me that her father owned a bar. She'd seen her share of drunken men, but she had no intention of *marrying* one. I was damned lucky she finally forgave me; I've rarely touched the stuff since that day."

"Maybe it's none of my business, but are you sure you should not be putting some of your wages away for a rainy day, Mike?" asked Cap. "I imagine it's costin' ya a pretty penny ta stay at the *Palmer House*."

"What's money for if not to make yourself happy?" asked Kelly.

"It's happy and broke you'll be soon enough at the rate you are going," harrumphed Anson.

The Chicago Tribune reported that, "The management of the Chicago club has very wisely decided that the skinny white uniform with tips of blue is not the best of its kind, that good taste dictates higher colors for the field, something that will bring out instead of dwarf the muscular developments of its wearer. The customary white flannel will be used for the body . . . in this respect they will all be alike, but each man will be furnished with an individual cap, short neck-tie, belt, and a band three inches wide around the thickest part of the calf. The players will wear white stockings. The colors have been selected, and Spalding Bros. are now at work upon the uniforms."

Spalding had cleverly cornered the market on baseballs. Prior to 1876 each home team had supplied the game balls, which varied slightly in weight and hardness. The Spalding ball contained one ounce of live rubber now not three-quarters of an ounce and it had a double cover with a woolen finish. They could be handled without the danger and errors that attended the use of the earlier cotton-finished ones. Kelly asked Anson why the League Secretary delivered the balls - wrapped in foil and placed inside red boxes - to the clubs in person.

"To make sure none of the cubs use balls with less bounce when they play hard-hitting nines like ours," he'd explained.

Spalding offered to supply the balls for free, they'd be uniform and lively enough to ensure plenty of hitting and - reasoning that young boys would flock to buy his company's official base balls-he not only supplied them for free, he *paid* the clubs a dollar for each box used."

Now Spalding began putting baseball *gloves* on the market. The first player to wear a glove - one made by a saddle maker - had been Doug Allison of the Cincinnati Red Stockings. In 1875 a first baseman named Waite donned one and took a terrible ribbing from spectators and players who yelled "Sissy." When Spalding moved over to play first base with the Chicagos he wore *two* of his company's gloves, one on each hand, black ones so the whole crowd could see them. He began selling pairs of the gloves from a dollar to $2.50. Sales took off, but it would be a while before most League players would wear them.

One of the first things Kelly discovered about his new team was that they travelled around on much better and safer trains that his old club. Travel conditions had improved a lot since he'd taken the train back and forth to New York to pick up newspapers. After spending the night sleeping in his seat on a train trip from Buffalo to Westfield George Pullman was inspired to design an improved passenger

railcar that contained sleeper berths for all its passengers. During the day the upper berth was folded up overhead. At night the upper berth folded down and the two facing seats below it folded over to make a comfortable lower berth. Curtains provided privacy and there were washrooms at each end of the car for men and women.

In 1863 trains running between Philadelphia and Baltimore had cars fitted with something new in railroading - an "eating bar." They had no kitchens, the food was cooked in restaurants and placed in steam boxes just before the train pulled out of the station. The cars were immediately popular and the B & O Railroad was the first to purchase them. They weren't profitable but they were the only alternative to stopping every few hours for the passengers to get off and eat. Railways were highly competitive and they were all keen to shave time off their trips. A few years later Pullman introduced a "hotel car" equipped with a kitchen for preparing and serving meals so passengers could live in it like they could in their home or a hotel.

After Spring workouts and exhibition matches, the White Stockings boarded the Cleveland, Cincinnati & Chicago train and headed to the Queen City to play the Red Stars at their new park, Bank Street Grounds. A large number of free masons, Knights of Pythias, and men from the Odd Fellows' Club were in the grand-stand, where the seats went for 75 cents. Less well-dressed spectators who could afford only 60 cents sat on the bleacher benches. People with even less of their pay to spend on a ball game paid the League minimum 50 cents for General Admission.

Mike went up to Blondie Purcell after warming up. "You've got some men I've never even seen before, not even when I was in the Buckeyes."

"It could be a very long year in Cincinnati, Kel. I hope they don't mind if we drink."

The Stars got off to a miserable start, a 6-26 record in their first 32 games which included losses of 20-7 and 15-1 to the White Stockings and 13-0 to the Worcesters. Cincinnati would never get it together. They had a mortgage on the tail-hold and would finish in last place in their only season, 44 games out of first.

Many of the spectators were members of the fairer sex who had come to see Mike in the new tight-fitting uniform.

"My, what a fine physique," a woman in a flowery bonnet observed to her friend.

"He is rather easy on the eyes, Gladys."

"I wonder if he'd come for tea one day."

"He's Irish, dear, I think we'd need to serve Mr. Kelly something a lot stronger than tea."

According to *The Enquirer*, "the Chicagos played a steady, strong game. Kelly made several bad errors but none were of such a character as to materially affect the score and his three pick-ups of apparently safe hits and fielding out of batters at first entitled him to considerable credit. He took particular pleasure in laying onto the sphere for three bases in the first inning off Will White, putting it clear over the left field where there was no one to stop it. The crowd showed evidence of delirium at the way Kelly punished his old companion. The ball rolled along the train tracks and was picked up by a brakeman who kindly threw the ball back over the fence. Unfortunately, it struck a handsomely dressed dowager in the back of her head.

The Enquirer stated, "Kelly can still play ball even if he *does* live in Chicago. Nor has he forgotten how to rally his teammates with his familiar 'Neow you're off!' as his did in the last inning."

Kelly made his second hit of the game in the fourth, but he was overanxious and when Smith captured Flint's fly he was touched out off second base. He was relieved when Burns and Corcoran scored in the ninth for a 4-3 win.

The Chicago Tribune believed the Chicago players were "engaged in a late-hour contest for supremacy in the matter of beer drinking." *The Cincinnati Enquirer* said the team "contains nine of the greatest drunkards in the league."

That night the usual gang went to Michael McGreevy's. The place was plain - there was no fancy marble wainscotting and the spittoons had been dented by scores of boots - and it was dark, not brightly lit like the city's German saloons. They stood at the bar. In Cincinnati's four hundred Irish saloons there were no tables. Mike didn't mind. He raised his glass and said, "The Irish believe that a man can down a greater volume of whisky if he is in an erect position."

Talk turned to superstitions. "I hear the antics the Baltimore players perform with a new ball are good enough for a stage act," said Dalrymple, who firmly believed that if he didn't strike at the first pitch thrown him he wouldn't make a base hit the whole game. "Houck gets it first and wipes it vigorously on the bottoms of his shoes. He then throws it to Manning who rubs the ball on the grass, spits on it and rubs it on his left elbow. Muldoon gets the ball next and wipes it on his cap after which he stains it with a piece of plug tobacco. At that point the ball is supposed to be in good enough condition to be passed to the pitcher."

"The Boston team devoutly believe in the benign influence of a white pigeon that hovers over the field," said Gore. "What they *really* need is a new pitcher and eight men who can hit a ball."

"Peters believes that if the first ball sent to him is properly handled the game can't be lost," said Frank. "Hines must have his uniform cleaned three times a week, dirty or not. Joe Start points his bat at the pitcher's nose. George Wright carries a straw in his mouth and thinks it's lucky to put the man with the most years of experience at the head of the batting list—even if he's as slow as an ice-wagon."

"You were in the Cincinnatis, Mike," Gore said to Kelly. "Were any of *them* superstitious?"

"McVey turned a somersault in the dressing-room before a game and one after as well if we won. Deacon White had a lucky copper he always wanted whoever was captain ta use for the toss uv the coin."

"Bradley of the Troys was presented with a twenty-dollar gold piece to toss for choice of in or out," said Flint. "He's afraid to take the thing on the road for fear someone'll nip it."

87

Williamson elbowed Dalrymple. "Abner here thinks it's good luck to see a steamboat come into port. On the days we have a game he haunts the Goodrich docks first thing he wakes up and looks for the Grand Haven to come in."

"You think it's bad luck to go through the Washington street tunnel the day of a game, don't you George," Abner said to Gore.

Flint turned to Ned. "You take a little bag of rosin on the field every game and place it under third base for luck."

"And you deal a deck of cards before each game," Williamson said to Flint. "Two hands and you play them at seven up. And the number of points in *your* hand is the number of hits you'll make that game."

"And it almost always is," said Flint. "Quest would sooner take the field bareheaded than wear his cap straight and Anson's little peculiarity is putting on his left shoe first when he dresses for a game. He's convinced we lost a game in Providence last year because he accidentally put his right shoe on first."

"What about the black cat?" asked Mike.

Flint explained. "On the day the team was called together last year - while we were getting instructions as to what was expected of us - a black cat sidled in. Every man felt it meant something - good luck or bad. The greatest pains were immediately taken to propitiate the cat. After we won our first game each man had a kind word for the puss and all of us made a fuss over it. We named him Champion as that's what we all hoped he would make us. When we went on the road we were going to take him with us but we decided the perils of such a journey would be too much for him so we left him in Finley's care. He wrote to us every week to let us know how Champion was doing. He disappeared one day and of course we lost. He came back again this year, we'll see how well we do."

Kelly chuckled as he thought of the Orator. "Shafer makes a speech to himself after every play he makes. George Shafer, you are one poor base-ball player or By all rights you should have had that one, George."

"Larkin's as mad as a hatter, I'm glad Spalding released him," said George. "He thought he'd only pitch well if he played a tune on his damned banjo before the game. We got mighty sick of hearing The Rocky Road to Dublin."

"Hecker says he wore sliding pads in three games and each time he failed to get a hit, said Frank. "He says pads are Jonahs."

"I suppose we all have *something* we think will bring us good luck," said Gore.

"What about you, Kel?"

Mike held up his glass of whiskey. "I've got it right here in me hand, Piano Legs."

After taking two out of three in Cincinnati the two clubs shared a train to Chicago for the White Stockings' home opener. The usual acrid, sweet smelling black clouds of coal smoke from the nearby railroad yards drifted above the grounds at Lakefront Park, dimming the afternoon sky. The field was alive with base runners at all times and the outfielders were engaged in a leather-hunting raid the whole afternoon.

Umpire Bradley shouted, "Striker up!" at 3:30 and at once the fun began. The men from Chicago took hold of Will White in the very first inning and batted him for no less than eleven total bases before the third hand was out. Purcell gave Dalrymple a life, allowing his drive to center field to fall for a two-baser and Gore and Williamson followed with base hits. Captain/managers weren't required to submit their lineups before the game. If neither of the first two Chicago batters reached base Anson would wait and bat in the second inning. Now he announced that he would hit next and grabbed his favorite bat. He hit a weak grounder to third but was spared by Leonard's muff. Kelly hit for three bases, sending home Gore, Williamson, and Anson. Then there was a running fire of passed balls, wild pitches, and wild throws and when the smoke cleared the visitors had rung up ten tallies.

In the bottom of the inning Hick Carpenter sent a stinging bounder to Kelly's hunting ground in right. He grabbed the ball with one

89

hand on the dead run and without stopping threw to first in time to make the out.

John Clapp was on the Cincinnatis' bench beside Blondie Purcell. "Did you see that?"

"Kelly throwing Hick out at first? I did."

"I've never seen a man thrown out at first from the outfield. Did you see the look on Hick's face when the ball reached first before he did?"

"Kelly tripped over his own feet and fumbled more than his fair share of flies when he was in the Cincinnatis," said Blondie, "but the man's as quick as a flash and he's got a hell of an arm."

The batsmen of the home team cut loose in terrible fashion again in the third. Kelly set the pattern with a two-baser and five more runs were scored.

The home nine whipped the visitors 20-7. After the game the beleaguered official score-keeper sent in a request for an assistant to fetch him more score-sheets and pencils.

The 13th was not a hoodoo for the Chicagos, they shut out the Bisons 6-0, but it was certainly an unlucky one for Al Hall. The Reds were at home to the Clevelands and the game opened with an awful accident. Manning was first at bat and he sent a high fly to center. He was a right-handed batter so Captain Pete Hotaling was playing well to the left of center. He and left fielder Al Hall both headed for the ball at breakneck speed. Hall always played with all his heart and he was known for making spectacular over-the-shoulder catches. He was determined to get to the ball.

"I've got it, Al," yelled Hotaling. Hall kept racing toward the ball.

"The center fielder takes priority on any ball he can reach, doesn't he," a teenaged boy with scrub brushy hair said to his father.

"Yes, he does son."

"But Hall isn't stopping."

"It's my ball, Ed!" yelled Hotaling.

It was evident that Hall was too focused to hear him. The two men met with full force and the spectators in the stands nearby gasped when they heard a sickening "Crack."

The two fielders had collided like locomotives. They lay motionless on the ground. Hotaling came to his senses, looked around, picked up the ball and threw it to third then looked down at Hall. His eyes widened as other players arrived on the scene.

Hotaling took off like a madman toward the bench. "Get a doctor! Now!"

Two of the bones in Hall's right leg had snapped in two. They protruded out between his knee and ankle. A woman in the front row clutched her bosom and fainted.

A doctor arrived and fashioned a makeshift splint and a lifter. "Take him to the clubhouse and call the man an ambulance," he instructed.

Mike heard about it the next day when he got to the ball grounds.

"Did Al have ta pay for the doctor?" Kel asked his new best friend Abner Dalrymple.

"He did. And his stay at the hospital."

Mike thought for a moment. "And the ambulance?"

"Of course. And the team suspended him and put a stop on his salary. At least when someone from the club went to pick up Hall's uniform at the hospital he gave him back the $12 he'd paid for it."

"Bluddy owners," said Mike. "Is Al still in the hospital?"

"He can't afford to stay another night. He's on his way back home to Oil City, Pennsylvania. He'll likely never play base ball again. John Evans, the owner of the Cleveland club, was at a champagne breakfast when he heard players are planning to play a benefit game to raise money for Hall. He said he *supposed* that would be allowed. On a related note, Anson says the National League has set up a new system of discipline with penalties for insubordination or misconduct. Cap says it's to deal with players of morally weak tendencies. What

do you think of that, Kel?"

Mike chuckled. "I'd best drink stronger whiskey . . . ta strengthen me tendencies."

On May 23 *The Chicago Tribune* thought the team had not disappointed a single expectation formed regarding it at the beginning of the season. "It has proved itself so far the strongest League nine in every essential particular - batting, base-running, fielding and earnest, harmonious play."

Mike went to Kelsh's to look around the next morning after breakfast. Two eye-catching women who seemed to be sisters were looking at petticoats and camisoles. Kelly stepped around a tall display out of sight so he could hear them talk.

"Did you see the man looking at ties, Mary?"

"I did, Collette, those *eyes* of his . . . "

"Forget the beautiful blue eyes, did you see his tanned skin, his chest and his shoulders? What a breath of fresh air after all those pale dreadfully effeminate popinjays we met in Europe. And those powerful hands."

Mary smiled. "It's been a while, hasn't it? Would you like those big hands all over you?"

"You bet your bustle I would."

"Through the skylight?"

According to *The Buffalo Morning Express*, on May 26, "Kelly ran the bases like a deer and gained his two runs by daring steals of third and home. There was no great amount of hallooing and uproar but Kelly and Anson kept their eyes open and when an opportunity was afforded they gave the 'word' and the man went to the best of his ability, letting the consequences fall upon the head of the coacher. The contrast presented by the Buffalos was almost ridiculous.

In the fourth Kelly hit a bounder to third base that was too hot for Richardson's hands and then showed his heels to all three Buffalo base tenders, making second on Flint's out, third on a wild pitch, and home on Burn's little baser. Corcoran allowed the heaviest batting club in the League just six safeties in his 4-2 win.

After the game Gore and Kelly went to Heilbronn's 15 Ball Pool & Billiards Parlor on Genesee. It served beer and spirits.

"Did you read what the Buffalo Morning Express said about you George?" Kelly asked Gore as the two played a game of 8-ball.

"I did not," said George as he sank the seven-ball ball in the corner pocket. Kelly watched as he did, noticing that while George always parted his hair in the middle, the part was never straight. "Something very *kind* I'd expect."

"Not all *that* kind," chuckled Mike. He set down his cue, went to get the newspaper he'd read earlier, and opened it to page 3. "They said that, taken all and all, you're not such a really bad fellow."

Now it was Gore's turn to chuckle. "But . . . "

"They said you've been tailored in the wrong school and believe that base ball playing consists of brutal assaults on basemen and general interference with opposing players, which might be the style Chicago people delight in but Easterners do not. So there. Wasn't that a fine how do ya do?"

"Fine. I'll be sure to run over a few more Buffalo men tomorrow."

Mike was about to set down the paper when he noticed a piece under *Base Ball Bits and Bites.* "Listen to this, the Worcesters will make their six weeks Western trip in the excursion car City of Worcester. They will take their own cook and porter with them and make the car their hotel during their excursion. The car has lavatories and ice lockers for preserving game at one end and drawing-room furniture and sleeping berths at the other. The cost of the trip will not be increased by this plan, but the comfort of the players will be promoted. The car has accommodations for all the players and the umpire assigned to the Worcesters' games. Well, I'll be a monkey's uncle. And we thought Hulbert was sendin' us around in style."

George chalked the end of his cue. "How much did Hulbert give when Pete Hotaling came around askin' for money to help out Al Hall?"

"A hundred. How about you?"

"Five dollars, same as everybody else. How much did Spalding kick in?"

"Spalding Brothers *store* gave Pete ten, I hope it doesn't put them under," Mike chuckled dryly.

Gore sank the eight-ball, grinned, and turned to Kelly, "Who was that voluptuous blonde I saw on your arm on Saturday night?"

"I went to Kelsh's after the game the other day, some fine-looking women shop there. She and her sister were looking at fancy underclothes. She recognized me and we struck up a conversation. They'd just returned from a European tour; their parents were hoping they'd meet some duke or baron but all the men they met went around with their noses in the air talking about their art collections. Turns

out she had no dinner plans so I took her to Wilson's. She was in the mood for romance after the oysters so she asked to see my room at the Palmer. When we got there she said she couldn't wait ta see me with me shirt off."

"What did you say?" asked George, smiling.

"I told her the feelin' was mutual."

"You mentioned a sister. What does *she* look like?"

"About as fine as her sister but a couple uv years older."

"I could forgive that."

Kelly smacked a ball down to left field in his first time at the bat in Boston on the 29th and the ball bounded high over John O'Rourke's head. Mike capered around to third base and Corcoran sent him home on a single. He swung the ash and hit safe in the third, stole third without malice aforethought, and came home on a passed ball. He hit the battered ball to the center field fence for three bases in his last try but the Bostons scored three runs in the eighth to beat the White Stockings 11-10.

Kelly was relieved that he'd managed to play the game, which lasted a staggering three hours and thirty-five minutes, without one miscue. His eleven errors and .694 fielding average were the worst on the team. Corcoran threw 205 pitches, 25 were called strikes, 36 were strikes missed, 19 were struck foul, and 125 were called balls. Anson had a case of the mollygrubs, he'd been fined $20 for talking back to the umpire.

Kelly stood over Anson after the game as he sat at the desk in the lobby of the St. James Hotel writing something. After a while Kelly squinted at Anson's paper then scratched his head.

"What the devil is that, Cap?" I thought I knew how ta read but I can't make out a single word uv what you just scribbled."

"I'm sending Spalding an outline of what I've got in mind for the team, who'll pitch against which teams, where I'm gunna position the fielders, the batting order I'll use . . . "

"But why can't I read it?"

"It's in cipher."

"Cipher?"

"That's right."

"Why?"

"It's in case any gamblers get a hold of the message."

"Aren't you the sneaky devil."

The White Stockings beat the Red Stockings 5-4 on June 2. The Boston cranks outdid themselves in trying to see how mean they could act, with all sorts of cat calls and names unworthy. It was the most Godforsaken crowd you could imagine, seeming like the boy who was after the woodchuck.

The Chicagos arrived at Union Station in Providence on June 7. They crossed the Providence Point street bridge once its 250-foot swing span had been shut to allow traffic to travel over it. They passed the Providence County Court House that had just been dedicated and the impressive City Hall that was nearing completion and checked into The Exchange Hotel on Main street. George Washington and General Lafayette had stayed at the nearly 100 years old hotel.

Construction on Messer Park had begun on April 1. The final nail was hammered five minutes before the opening game got underway on May 4th. The large grand-stand, which was covered by 7,000 feet of canvass, held 1,200 people though that would be an unusually high turnout in so small a city as Providence. In the rear it was raised 34 feet so spectators in the highest rows could see over people's hats. A platform 60 x 8 feet was erected for the reporters, scorers, and invited guests.

Two turn-stiles admitted patrons to the grounds and as each ticket holder passed through the gate he stepped on a raised platform and by a mechanical arrangement was registered. At the southeast corner there was a large gate to admit carriages to the park. The diamond was as level as constant rolling by heavy stone and iron rollers

could make it.

The Grays were the first team to install a backstop in their park. The large screen was installed directly behind the catcher, an area known as the "slaughter pens" for all the foul ball injuries that occurred there. A fence with gateways in front of the club rooms prevented the crowd from talking with the players. To the chagrin of the team management, just beyond the short left field lay a building where fans could sit on the roof and watch the game for a discounted rate of 25 cents.

Under the grand-stand were dressing-rooms fitted up with wardrobes. A wash-room supplied Pawtucket water. The Western Union Telegraph Company had a room, as did the stockholders, and there was a refreshment saloon managed by caterer Ardoene. In the opinion of Harry Wright, who'd seen as many ball grounds as anyone alive, the grounds were without doubt as fine as any in the country.

It was hard luck that kept the Chicagos from winning the extraordinary first game. Four gallons of ice water was the amount swilled down by the eighteen players during the marathon. Williamson led off the 17th inning with a 3-baser and with Anson, Kelly, and Corcoran to follow him to bat it was almost an absolute certainty that the winning run would be scored. But the Grays suddenly discovered that it was getting dark - though it was half an hour before sunset - and the umpire was persuaded in calling the game. *The Tribune* whined, "There is no help for such a deal in umpiring; it is simply Chicago's luck to get it on all critical occasions." Even Kelly rolled his eyes when he read *that*.

Though out-batted and out-fielded by the Grays on June 8 the Chicagos completed their chain of victories over the champions. Williamson scored the opening tally on his single, called balls to Gore, and Kelly's baser. Williamson singled again in the 3rd, Anson followed with a two-baser, Kelly singled, and, on and a fumble of Peters, Williamson ran home to put the finishing touch on the Chicagos' four-game sweep.

On the 11th in Troy the White Stockings kept their streak go-

ing with a 10-5 win that put them six and a half games ahead of Worcester. They were a jaw-dropping sight when they marched onto the field, their six-foot-tall players muscular, mean, mustachioed men. They were dressed in the best uniforms money could buy, with white silk stockings and crisp black knickers and jerseys, CHICAGO stitched in bold white letters on the fronts. Their smaller, shabbily attired opponents couldn't help feeling intimidated.

"They look like *murderers*," a Worcester man gasped when they went by.

Kelly heard him. He smiled and tapped Dalrymple on the shoulder. "We've got 'em whipped before we even throw a ball, Ab. We have the poor buggers scared half ta death. It's a case uv eat 'em up Jake."

Mike had three hits, scored three times, and drove in three runs. The players were relieved that they hadn't been going from Providence to Boston on the 11th. That foggy night the passenger steamer Narragansett collided with the steamer Stonington off Long Island Sound near Saybrook, Connecticut. While neither vessel sank, 30 people—mostly women and children—were killed as a result of the fire on board the Narragansett.

The Chicago nine won their first game in Worcester 7-6 on June 16. In the second game they scored in each of the first seven innings and won 8-7. Kelly hit two singles and two doubles and scored three times. They took the third game 11-8. Corcoran obeyed all of Flint's signals and everything went along fine until he threw one of his cranky fits. He stopped obeying the signals and crossed Silver up several times.

Flint went out to speak to the touchy pitcher. "Larry," he said quietly, his eyes snapping, "you either do what I say or you go straight into the clubhouse. I don't care a tinker's dam which you do. Now get to work."

Corcoran complied. Hulbert was sitting in the grandstand. After the last out he called the pitcher over to him. "Look here, Lawrence, didn't I tell you that Frank is your boss? If you let out another yip like

you did today you'll be fired so quick your head will swim."

Everyone had a good laugh when Dalrymple, who couldn't hit the side of a meeting house with left-hander Richmond in the box, switched around to the other side of the plate and batted from the right side. Kelly wouldn't have given an Indian-red cent for Dalrymple's chances of making a hit and he was shocked when he actually made contact. The crowd erupted when Abner took off at full speed—for third base.

The players had another good laugh on their tally-ho ride back to the hotel. Teamsters played a trick of driving in the tracks of the street railway with a tall load of hay. Ladies and gentlemen in fine raiment occupying seats in passing carriages and turnouts were showered with dust and hay-seed.

Mike looked around at his new teammates. Quest stood out among the group, his handle-bar mustache was hardly the only one on the team but it was the only red one. Flint was hard to recognize without a chaw of tobacco in either cheek. Big Ned Williamson had a lot in common with Mike, he liked to drink and he spent money like there was no tomorrow, but he let himself go more in the off-season that Kelly did. Burns was the only teetotaler in the Chicagos. He loved telling the other players what he'd just read in the newspapers.

Goldsmith was one of the married men. His pretty wife Rowena was a Canadian. Fred told Mike he'd met her while he was pitching for the Tecumsehs in Canada. She was a 19-year-old aspiring concert pianist. Her father had opposed the marriage, but Rowie decided to go against his wishes and give up her musical ambitions in exchange for a life with Fred.

Kelly liked Gore, who sometimes turned the brim of his cap to the back of his head to play the fool, but he teased him about his hypochondria. When he'd come up with yet another mysterious ailment Mike would say, "At death's door again, are ya, George? Wait! Look there. I see him comin' for ya, it's the grim reaper ta be sure."

"No, this time it's really serious, Kel," George would assure him.

"Hell, George, you spend more on doctors than I do on whiskey."

Frank Flint had just married Eva de la Motta, the ex-wife of a minstrel show performer. Mike thought he would probably start taking his new bride on road trips.

Kelly liked clean-shaven Dalrymple, another of the team's bachelors, but he was cheap. He could work out the cost of a cabbage and two onions quicker than an Aberdeen grocer. He always waited for someone else to buy a newspaper and then grabbed it off the table after he'd finished reading it. Mike had been shocked when Abner told him he'd dined at the Tremont House. On the days the team didn't have a game Dal usually went to one of the saloons that had started offering free lunches. It turned out he'd ordered the Tremont's new special, the Steak Hambourgeoise. Kelly was impressed until he realized it was just a hamburger.

It always got Kelly's dander up when Dalrymple would hold up and let a hard hit ball drop in front of him rather than going after it and risking an error. He was a 'record player' who cared more about his own statistics than how the team did—just like George Strief.

The White Stockings were given a hearty reception on June 22. Their uniforms showed plainly the kind of work they'd done in the East. Mike was lucky the Palmer House laundry did such a good job on his uniform. The other players' launderers struggled to get grass stains out of the knees and dirt out of the seats and their white stockings were often beige. Tobacco juice stains were a real challenge. But Kelly's uniform always looked as though he'd just bought it. There were no creases or scorch marks in his dress shirts and the collar wings were all pressed to exactly the same size - and they were getting out the lipstick stains as he'd hoped.

"Oh my! Isn't Michael Kelly a pet?" whispered a beautiful girl in the front row of the grand-stand to her brother.

The men could see what the wins had done to their place in the standings. A large white bulletin board had been erected on which the League standings and the inning-by-inning scores of the out-of-town games were posted.

The Troys were unable to get around home until the fourth inning

when they tallied once. They scored just one more time, in the ninth, when Evans batted an easy bounder to Williamson and he threw it six feet over Anson's head. Before Kelly could recover the ball from among the chairs Evans was sliding into third. He scored when Flint let the ball go between his legs. Clearly the men were tired, having gotten in early in the morning.

Dalrymple hit for three bases in the opening inning and the applause was tremendous. But when Gore followed with a two-bagger and Kelly, Williamson, and Anson each hit for a base the cheering was continued and deafening.

On the 24th against Troy, Silver Flint was behind the bat and his five passed balls would have been considered poor if not for the twelve that got by James Haley, who was informed of his release after the game, his second of the season and career. The fact that he was "useless with the stick" as well didn't help. Kelly was designated to the second base. In the fourth inning he essayed to muff Buttercup Dickerson's lazy fly for a double play but the umpire refused to see the point and gave it a catch.

The Tribune man considered the Monday, June 28 game against the Worcester nine to be "almost a model one" for up to the ninth inning not a single error had been made. *The Clipper* man made the absurd assertion that the Chicagos' games had grown so one-sided as to cause their backers to lose interest. Quite the contrary, whenever the team played Worcester, Boston, Cleveland, or Providence there need be no fear of light patronage on the home grounds—or theirs either for that matter.

In the opening inning Wood got around to third. Stovey, whose real name was Stow - he played under an assumed one to keep his less than respectable profession a secret from his mother—hit a short fly which Dalrymple ran in for and captured, holding him at third. When he undertook to make home on Irwin's grounder to Burns he was handsomely caught at the plate. Knight then sent a two-baser over Gore's head and the right kind of base-running would have taken Irwin all the way around but he stuck at third and both were left on their bases when Richmond struck out.

The Tribune's account of what happened next read, "There is not a man on the Chicago club who would not have tallied from first on such a hit. Such is the science of base-running and the taking of chances. No better illustration could be found than was forthwith furnished in Chicago's half of the inning. Kelly, having hit clean for two bases, was sent to third on a single by Williamson, who at once stole second. With the infielders playing well inside the base lines Williamson took long ground, actually getting two-thirds of the way to third base so that when Anson hit Corey a difficult bounder that he did not stop and send to first ahead of the striker he ran like a deer for home close behind Kelly and two earned runs were scored where ordinary base-running would have produced but one.

Chicago got in two in their half of the seventh. Corcoran hit for his base and was helped to third by Flint's two-baser over the right field fence. Bushong captured Quest's foul fly in his leather gloves, then Dalrymple went up to face Richmond. He'd begun to put on his toughest curves so the crowd called to Abner to change hands and strike in his usual way. His answer was a corking grounder through the middle that scored Corcoran. After Gore gave Knight an easy fly, Kelly, who had no trouble with left-handers, followed with a beauty that sent Dalrymple to third but Williamson left them both stranded when he gave Bushong a foul bound.

Corcoran held on for the win. Goldsmith had spent the afternoon in the counting room footing up stacks of quarters, dollars, and half-dollar coins.

Mike and Abner talked while they ate their dinner that night.

"What were you like as a boy, Mike?" asked Abner.

"Happy, I suppose. Me parents were fine people and me older bruther was always good to me. He and I used to play hide-and-seek, and mumblety peg, and prisoner's base before I took ta playin' ball mornin' noon and night. The big fire that claimed our house put me father out uv work so he joined the army. I can still see him marchin' off fer the war with the New York 165th Volunteer Regiment in his fine, fancy uniform with all those shiny buttons. When he got out

uv the service he moved the family to Washington cuz he'd got a job with the government. He died soon after and muther was left to take care uv us. She decided to move us to Paterson."

"And she let you do whatever you liked?"

"Pretty much. I spent most uv me time on the sandlots playin' ball. I was always the fastest player and I could throw. Blondie Purcell signed me to play in his amateur traveling team when I was fifteen."

"And then you joined the Buckeye club of Columbus?"

"Aye, that I did. That's where Chub Sullivan saw me play and recommended me to the Cincinnatis."

Tricky Nichols was in the pitching box for the Ruby Legs for the last game of the series. Corcoron opened the seventh with a base-hit, Dalrymple hit safely, and Kelly, who was behind the bat to give Flint's hands a rest, followed with a model liner that earned two runs. He took off for second on the first pitch to Anson. Ten feet from the bag he jumped into the air like a boy playing leap frog, dove directly for it, dug one of his spikes into the bag then swerved clear over on his side. George Creamer, the Worcesters' second baseman, never applied the touch. Kelly was safe.

When Creamer got back to the bench Chub Sullivan, the Ruby Legs' first baseman, asked Creamer why he hadn't tagged Kelly since the catcher's throw seemed to be in time to get him.

"It takes a lot more nerve than I've got to try to tag Kelly when he makes one of his hurricane dives and the only way to get him is to wade into his spikes with your face."

Two innings later Creamer was called out at the plate when it looked as though he'd be safe.

"Why you didn't touch home before Kelly tagged you?" asked Sullivan.

"I couldn't see the damned plate?" shrugged Creamer.

"Why not?"

"Kelly'd put his mask on top of it!"

Kel batted leadoff and hit a single and a two-baser in the Chica-gos' 3-1 win over the Worcesters the next day. The win moved them ten games ahead of the Grays. He was second in batting to Anson but a distant last in fielding with a dismal .694 percentage though it did need to be taken into account that Mike went after balls other players wouldn't even think about trying for.

Hulbert was delighted to read what *The Tribune* said of his club on July 4. "This newspaper has over and over again pointed out the plain fact that the Chicago team of 1880 is not of the fall-down vari-ety; a repetition of last year's disaster is absolutely impossible."

The Tribune had taken a new departure in compiling statistics on the club's work that was believed to be exceedingly valuable. They were tabulating the number of times each player batted home a run-ner. Anson led the way with 25 runners driven in, Burns and Gore had 18 each, and Kelly was fourth with 16. The paper soon stopped doing so after a number of readers complained that the practice was unfair to batsmen such as Dalrymple who led off and therefore went to the bat with no runners to drive in at least once a game and the men who hit in front of them the other times, the numbers eight and nine batsmen, were unlikely to be issued bases on balls or hit safely.

The game two days later was expected to be "a park packer" and it was. Several thousand people paid 75 cents for uncovered but re-served seats and 50 cents for admission to the grounds, which in-cluded the privilege of sweltering on the benches or destroying their light-colored pantaloons by squatting on the grassy field for the game against the reigning champions from Providence. Both nines were in fighting trim and every inch of ground was hotly contested. There was enough kicking and howling to delight the most exacting crank. The Chicagos edged the Grays 3-2. To his utmost surprise, Kelly made ten plays in right field without error.

Corcoran put on the bracer against the heavy hitters of Rhode Island the next day. According to *The Tribune*, "they went down be-fore Corcoran as though they were some local amateurs who knew nothing about out and in-curves. The champions of 1879 hardly furnished more than a mild recreation for the indisputable champi-

ons of the current season who, with a record of 34-3 are 12½ games ahead of the Grays." With their 7-1 win over Providence on July 6 the Chicagos' winning streak was twenty games. Two days later their twenty-first consecutive victory broke the one set by the 1869 Cincinnati Red Stockings. The White Stockings headed to the train station in a jolly mood. *The Daily Telegraph* said it was beginning to become a wonder if the team would ever lose.

When the White Stockings arrived in Cleveland on July 10 they headed to the Weddell. They picked up their keys at the front desk, went upstairs to drop their bags in their rooms, and returned to the lobby to get their pay envelopes. There wasn't one for Joe Quest.

"What the hell?" Joe yelled at the club secretary.

"Your pay has been garnished by order of the Superior Court of Warren County, Indiana, Quest."

"That goddamed varmit! I only owe the man eighty dollars."

"Well the court awarded him two hundred and twenty."

When Quest went up to his room he found his door open. Inside was a policeman overseeing two men removing his luggage and his suits from the closet. Kelly walked in to see what was going on.

"What am I going to do, Mike?"

"You are gointa take this," said Kel, handing Joe a hundred-dollar bill. "That'll see you through 'til your next pay."

"Thanks, Kel. You're a life saver."

George Core came out of his room and saw Mike and Joe. "Come on then, fellas, there's a few beers waiting for us at Mat Wolford's Tavern. Let's go tickle our innards."

"Sounds like a plan, George, we need to help Joe tie one on so he can forget about the blackguard that's robbin' him."

"Speaking of tying one on, did you hear what happened to Gid Gardner?"

"Did he get into another bar fight?" asked Mike.

"Not this time," said Gore.

"Did he step in front of another trolley bus?"

"No. On the way up the stairs to his hotel room at the Empire after knocking back a few with Pebbly Jack and the Orator he made a wrong turn in the dim light, tumbled over a railing and fell down the atrium through the skylight of the hotel lobby."

"Through the skylight!" exclaimed Kelly. "That's somethin' . . . even for Gid."

"Amazing thing is he lived to tell about it."

Quest shook his head. "Now I know why the two of you always ask for a room on a low floor."

During the first three innings of the first game Flint was the only man to reach the first base and the score-board featured nothing but goose eggs through the first eight frames. The excitement was intense. In the ninth Glasscock made first on a hit. Dunlap brought Pebbly Jack all the way around the bases when he sent the ball down into the left field corner of the grounds for a home run. The Chicagos' winning streak was over.

They got right back to their winning ways the next day when Corcoran, who batted fifth, shut the Blues out 3-0. But lucky willow swinging in the fourth and fifth innings by the home nine the next day, with Corcoran between the points again for Chicago due to Goldsmith's illness, gave Cleveland a 4-1 victory.

The Chicagos pegged more holes in the championship run in their first two games in Troy. By order of his doctor, Goldsmith was granted a vacation by Anson and went home quite sick. Poorman would take his place on the ten-man roster. After the game Kelly went to Martin "Flip" Flaherty's sports equipment shop to buy a new pair of spikes for his base ball shoes.

Frank Bancroft, the secretary of the Worcester Ruby Legs, presented the White Stockings with scarf-pins before the game on July 21. The club had swept his nine twice in two weeks. The pins featured a miniature broom plus a ball and the word "Chicago" on a scroll. President Hubert presented the players gild broom badges emblem-

atic of their ability to sweep everything before them.

Bancroft pulled Kelly aside after the presentation. "I am afraid I have some bad news."

"What's that, Mr. Bancroft?"

"You're a friend of Chub Sullivan, are you not?"

"Aye. I might not be in the league if not for him singin' me praises to the Cincinnatis."

"You may have noticed that Chub's not warming up with the other players."

"I did. He's the best first baseman in the league, I'm sure he'd be playin' if he could. What's the matter?"

"He's got typhoid fever, Mike."

The White Stockings managed to win the first two games in Worcester with little help from Kelly. The crowds could hardly have been referred to as such but it was felt that the home side's prospects, like the weather, were gloomy. Rain fell both days and the ball was as elastic as a pumpkin. In the series finale on Saturday Corcoran twisted the ball in his usual form but when the Ruby Legs did manage a hit it told. After eight straight losses to the Chicagos they finally overcame them by a score of 4-3 and the delight of the spectators was unbounded. Depressed about Chub Sullivan, Kelly was 2-for-12 in the series.

The Chicago players packed their valises and took the noon train to Providence for three games at the Grays' Messer Street Grounds, twenty minutes by horsecar from downtown along a route that ran down the center of the city's glitzy Westminster street past ornate office buildings, pricy shops, and handsome mansions.

During their stay in Providence, they won "flattering encomiums from the best class of citizens by their quiet and gentlemanly demeanor." The local paper said, "the games have not drawn out the professional excellence and comparative strength of the two leading nines in the League for the reason that poor fielding and scattered batting have been insurmountable obstacles. The boys from Rhody

succeeded, however, in giving the coming champions a pair of set-backs which served to revive an interest in the game which had lain dormant previous to the Chicagos' visit."

Anson made the opening run on Kelly's single drive to center field - which reporters unfamiliar with base ball lore sometimes called the "mid-field"—in the first inning on July 31. Start made a one-base hit in the bottom of the inning but was caught at the plate on sharp fielding by Kelly and Quest to Flint. After an extraordinary three straight losses the Chicagos won it 4-1.

On August 5th the Red Stockings were Chicagoed by the White Stockings 3-0 in Boston. The term had been coined in 1870. In front of a huge throng of 5,000 spectators at Dexter Park on July 23 Rynie Wolters had twirled the first shutout in base ball history, beating the invincible White Stockings 9-0.

Mike had breakfast with Dalrymple the next morning. Mike ordered a parsley omelet with bacon. Abner had the mutton chops fried potatoes. Dal sipped on his coffee while Mike read him the Classifieds.

"Widower of means wishes a good wife or housekeeper.

H.H.H.: Tuesday, 10:55 train, Lakeshore. Please don't fail.

Emma: Go home at once, John is very sick.

Left my cane and ring with barkeeper; have forgotten where; wish to redeem same.

A gentleman would like the acquaintance of a lady: church-go-er preferred."

He set the newspaper down and took a sip of his own coffee. It was cold.

"No young ladies lookin' fer romance today, Abner.

Wait, listen to this, Ab. Mr. Garfield is so conscientious that he not only refuses to make political speeches on his journey, he has denied himself the pleasure of kissing babies. He looks forward, however, with considerable fortitude to the time when lovely young women will insist on kissing the next President. Well *I* look forward with

considerable fortitude to the time when lovely young women will insist on kissing the next base ball champions."

The Chicagos trailed the Providence team 4-1 after eighth innings in the August 15 game. Dalrymple led off the ninth with a single to left field and was enabled to reach second on Farrell's neglect to properly cover the base when Houck threw the ball in.

Burns was sitting on the bench beside Kelly. "Dorgan needs to school his men better," he told Mike. "Anson would have my head if I failed to cover a bag like that."

"I disagree, Tom. He'd have ya drawn and quartered."

The Inter-Ocean man was scribbling furiously. "Now came Gore with his first hit of the game and a beauty it was, entitling the striker to two bases and bringing Dalrymple home amid thunderous cheering. Williamson's slow hit and out at first helped Gore to third and Anson tied the game with a safe hit that brought another cheer. Kelly, who had hitherto done nothing with the stick, here drove a tremendous low liner between left and center bringing Anson chugging all the way around to home and himself to third. Burns was forthcoming with an elegant drive just over the head of Peters whereon Kelly tallied to the immense satisfaction of the spectators."

On the 19th Flint received his first serious injury of the season, having his right thumb put out of joint in the ninth inning. In trying to pull it back into place the flesh lacerated so badly that he was expected to be disabled for at least a fortnight. Kelly and Williamson would share his duties and Poorman would tend the right garden wearing goggles with blue lenses to block out the sun.

The new League ball proved a very elastic one for Gore on August 21. He made his eighth consecutive hit in his eighth consecutive time at bat. His runs in the fourth and ninth inning were entirely the product of his own swift legs and Kelly's timely hits.

Batting fifth behind Anson on August 24 Kelly took a spurt with four hits and played flawlessly at third in the Chicagos' exciting twelve inning 2-1 win over the Ruby Legs and their only pitcher Lee Richmond. That made it six in a row for the White Stockings and gave them a 13½ game lead. The White Stockings could pound an opponent hard and rack up runs but they excelled in close games too, having won nine of their dozen one-run games.

Kelly was laid off by a temporary disability. With him and Flint out of the lineup Williamson was sent behind the bat and he struggled there, allowing five passed balls in a 7-4 loss to Worcester on the 28th, just the twelfth loss of the season. On the last day of August only three of the Chicagos hit safe against Tim Keefe, the ex-carpenter from Cambridge who'd joined the Trojans after the Albany club disbanded, leaving the National Association a three-team league. Keefe had an uncanny knack for changing speeds and threw a baffling array of curve pitches, one his own invention that didn't spin but rather dropped at a batsman's feet.

The spectators enthusiastically welcomed Kelly back after a week's retirement through ill-health, and with good reason, his third base play was strictly first-class. He proved rusty with the willow, succumbing to Keefe each time at the bat, but he displayed further proof that he could help them win games even when his bat was stale.

With two hands out and 20-year-old Buck Ewing on third in the second inning Roger Connor hit a hot liner to Kelly. He caught it just before it was about to take his head off then nonchalantly walked over and handed the ball to Corcoran. He sauntered back to third as Ewing took his lead then touched him with the ball he'd *pretended* to hand to Corcoran. It took a while for the umpire and the crowd to realize what had transpired, then a rousing cheer rolled through the delighted spectators.

The rain of Wednesday and the inability of Troy to remain over another day on account of home engagements necessitated the playing of two games on September 2. The Trojans had a runner or more on base each inning in the 11 a.m. game but due to Corcoran's strong pitching and his fielders throwing out runners none reached the home plate. At the end the Trojans sat in sackcloth and ashes contemplating a row of nine goose eggs.

Though he'd thrown 180 pitches in the morning game Larry was

back between the points again at 2 and he proved a teaser once again, allowing just one solitary hit in the first five innings. But the sixth was a Waterloo for Chicago. With one out, Gillespie hit a dribbler to Corcoran, who threw a little wide to Anson but well enough to put the man out as everyone believed but with characteristic cussedness Umpire Chapman decided him safe. A minute later Corcoran caught Gillespie napping and Anson unmistakenly touched him out.

The Tribune man thought the sixth inning offered the home side a perfect opportunity to get the lead. "Dalrymple and Gore hit safe. Dalrymple went to third on a passed ball and scored on Holbert's muff when Caskins threw to the plate after Williamson's hit. Gore got to second and Williamson to first. Anson, after having one strike and seven balls called, lost his head entirely and hit a low ball which, had he let it pass, would have been the eighth ball. As it was, he hit an easy bounder to the pitcher and Gore was forced at third.

Anson now caught the infection of folly and allowed Keefe and Ferguson to entrap him off second. Here there were two men out and only one man on base where the bases should have been loaded and no hands out. Kelly now hit a corking two-baser to right which would have brought in two runs, but Anson was still possessed of the devil. He tried to make it home from first though he was feverishly urged to stop at third and was easily put out at the plate thus frittering away by his egregious foolishness a chance to win the game. After this there were hits by Poorman and Burns but nobody to bat them around." The Troys, who had made but three safe hits, won by a 5-1 count. Corcoran had thrown 308 pitches.

"I've got good news, Larry," Mike told him on their way to the train station. A telegram arrived just before we hopped on the tally-ho. It was from Goldy. Fred'll be waiting for us when we get to Buffalo. Unless you were hoping ta pitch again tomorrow."

Corcoran went to punch Kelly in the arm but couldn't *lift* his.

In the first game of their final road trip of the season in Buffalo on Saturday, September 5 Dame Fortune continued to frown upon the Bisons and the white stockinged nine made a narrow escape.

The Morning Express reported that, "The base-running of Corcoran and Kelly instituted a splendid example for the Buffalo men to emulate." Dalrymple failed to dodge a wild pitched ball in the fourth inning and was almost rendered unconscious by the blow.

Mike had been 'preoccupied' with a lovely female acquaintance before the team left Chicago and hadn't gotten a chance to get his laundry done so he dropped it off at Mrs. Curry's Queen City Laundry then bought cigarettes at Beardsley's. Gerhardt went for some German lager at Baumgartner's saloon on Genesee street, the others went to get their hair cut at Bergin's which had a saloon in the back. They had dinner back at the hotel then headed off to Edward O'Grady's place. He had good whiskey and he always gave Irish ball players the best table in the place.

The playing during the last week left Chicago 12 games in the van. As the case stood, beyond some peradventure, the club had but to win 8 of its last 17 games to secure the League pennant.

On September 7 in Buffalo Kelly, whose gnarled fingers were all thumbs, made two muffs, a wild throw, and a fumble of a bunt, but he threw out three men with lightning line throws. His job was aided by the fact that the Blue-legs had no one coaching on the bases so runners kept stopping when they should have kept going and going when they should have held up. Mike dropped a third strike in the 7th then touched the plate and threw to Anson for a double play preventing a run to score in Hulbert's hard-hitters' 7-4 win.

Kelly had been planning a trip to the dentist to have an infected tooth that was paining him pulled but he reconsidered when he read that a student in a dental office had the flesh on his left hand torn off by the explosion of his dentist's vulcanizer.

The fielding of Clapp, Carpenter, and Kelly in the September 14 game had "marks of greatness." Dalrymple and Gore opened the Chicago first with safe hits and advanced to third and second on a passed ball. When Kelly came to the plate his position was a peculiar one. His feet were well together, the left one a little in advance of the right. He clutched his bat several inches from the handle with

his hands six inches apart to give him quicker command of it and fondled it above his right arm until the ball was a few feet from him.

Mike got a high one and batted both runners home by a clever hit to left. He got second on a fumble but Burns and Anson struck out. It was the club's 73rd game of the season and this was just the third time Anson had struck out. The Cincinnatis scored five runs the rest of the way, the Chicagos none.

Flint couldn't join Mike, George, and Abner that night. His wife, the former Miss de la Motta, was in town. She'd watched the game from behind the netting and had attracted a lot of attention and whispers.

"Tell her you have to go to The Office, Frank, cuz that's where we're headin," said Mike as he put on his hat and opened the door.

"I didn't marry the girl for her brains, but she's bound to find out The Office is a saloon. She'd have my hide."

Mike called back over his shoulder. "Suit yourself, more whiskey fer the rest of us. As fer me, "May I die in bed at 95, the victim of a jealous spouse."

The Cincinnati Enquirer reporter thought there was a distinguished look to the crowd at the September 15 game, the men looking dapper in their plug hats and frock coats, the ladies in their spring-loaded Langtry bustles over tight corsets. Many of them had travelled miles to see the Irish player with the wavy black hair, luxuriant mustache, and matinee-idol good looks their friends had been going on and on about.

The fielding of Kelly, Flint, and Quest had marks of greatness to it. Dalrymple and Gore opened with safe hits and went to third and second on a passed ball by Clapp. Kelly asked him about the hollow on his left cheek.

"It's the result of a hot ball," said Clapp. "My left eye's been closed once, my right one three times, and my nose has been broken . . . I can't think *how* many times."

"You might as well be a prize-fighter, John," said Kel. "You and I

should probably think about wearin' one uv those wire bird cages."

Mike batted both runners home by a hit to left field and got to second on clever running when Sommers fumbled the ball.

"The Chicagos' field work was the finest exhibited by any team that has visited Cincinnati this season," claimed *The Enquirer*. "Every man knows exactly what he will do when he gets his hands on the ball. They don't stand rooted to the ground twenty feet apart as though placed there on penalty of death as other nines do. When Jim White comes to bat Williamson and Burns concentrate over toward third while Gore moves over to left center. When Clapp goes up Williamson takes Burns' usual position, Burns moves down near second, and Quest moves over toward Anson. When Anson got a foul fly Kelly was stooping under him ready to catch the ball should the captain let it drop. When there are plays to first base and Kelly is behind the bat he races to back up Anson in case the throw gets by him."

There was a loud cheer in the eighth inning when Blondie Purcell, seeing that neither Quest nor Burns were at all close to him, took a big lead off second base. Flint took Corcoran's delivery and whipped it into the outfield.

Purcell was stunned. "Who the hell do you think you're throwing to, Flint?" he yelled.

Kelly, who'd signaled to Flint and then raced in from right field like a bat out of hell, finely caught the ball and tagged Purcell out.

"Got ya, Blondie," said Mike.

"Always pulling the wool over *somebody's* eyes, aren't ya, you tricky bugger?"

Reporting from Cincinnati, *The Tribune* reporter told his readers the next day that "the heaviest batting of the season was seen, the two teams making a total of fifty-two bases on clean hits. White was knocked out of the points in three innings. Anson had five safe hits and Kelly three and he scored three times in the White Stockings' 17-9 triumph that put them 13½ games ahead of second-place Prov-

idence. They could have made more but hurried through their last at bats so they could catch their train for home.

Some of the players started drinking as soon as they arrived in Chicago on Thursday night and they went right back to it on Friday night. Their Saturday, September 19 game was the opener of their last home stand of the season. For a time, the Reds' Purcell proved pie for the Chicagos, who opened with a three-bagger and four singles in the first. Kelly, who'd enjoyed the two nights of revelry as much as anyone, went in to catch in the 3rd and his two passed balls, a wild pitch, and an errant throw in by Dalrymple led to two runs. In the 5th two more passed balls let in a third unearned run and in the 8th Anson's failure to trap a ball coming on the bound from Kelly, together with another poor throw from Dalrymple let in two more runs to tie the score. The White Stockings were greatly relieved when darkness enveloped the field and the game was mercifully declared a 5-5 tie.

The Chicagos beat the Reds 5-2 on September 22 and Mike Kelly played a starring role. He was behind the bat and Goldsmith was between the points. It would be a long afternoon. As one scribe put it, "Goldsmith has a style of delivery peculiarly adapted to absorbing a large amount of the valuable time of the habitual members of the audience."

In the second, after Smith was dealt with, Carpenter and Reilly made hits and Sommer got first on Gore's error. With the bases full Will White succumbed to Goldsmith's wiles and struck out, but the crowd groaned when Kelly dropped the third strike.

"Don't worry, Jimmy," a man in a dark grey trilby hat said to his son. "Watch. He did that on purpose."

Sure enough, Kelly picked up the ball and stepped on the plate to force out Carpenter. Then he fired the ball to Anson to put out White. He smiled, turned and headed to the bench. On the way he tipped his cap to the man in the straw hat and winked at his son.

On September 24, Kelly caught the whole game without an error or passed ball and did as perfect work as ever was seen behind the

bat. Anson appreciated Mike running down the line to first whenever there'd be a throw there from third base or shortstop even if it was ninety degrees in the shade. In the first Kelly drove in Gore with a one-baser, stole second, and with great cleverness came in by coaxing McCormick to throw to third instead of home.

"I of all people should've known better than to trust you on a ball diamond," he called out to Kelly.

"Got you again, Jimsy."

In the fifth "Pebbly Jack" Glasscock hit for three bases but was left there by Kelly's quick capture of Phillips' foul bound. Kelly knocked Dalrymple home in the sixth on a speedy hit to "Sureshot" Dunlap, who couldn't handle the ball in time.

The nights were getting cold so Mike stopped at Mabley the Clothier's and bought an ulsterette made of Irish frieze.

When the season closed the White Stockings' record showed that they had decimated all opposition.

> vs. Boston 9-3
>
> vs. Buffalo 11- 1
>
> vs. Cincinnati 10-2
>
> vs. Cleveland 8-4
>
> vs. Providence 9-3
>
> vs. Troy 12-2
>
> vs. Worcester 10-2

"Quite luvly. Yer locket. I especially enjoy the setting."

The Tribune reported that "President Hubert, who is not much in favor of selling season's tickets at less than $21, proposes to shorten the time during which they can be had at low rates. After Wednesday of this week the price will be raised from $15 to $17.50 and after next Saturday to $20."

With the demise of the National Association, the National League would have no competition for the first time in 1881, it would be the only professional base ball league. On December 8 the League reject-ed the Washington Nationals' bid for membership and accepted the Detroit Club as its newest member. They re-elected William Hulbert as president and adopted several new rules.

A.G. Spalding visited one of the club's pre-season workouts to ex-plain the new decrees to the players.

"Good morning, men. Are you ready to go after another championship?"

There was a chorus of "We are."

Spalding took a sheet of paper out of his coat and unfolded it. "There are some significant changes to the rules this year, men. League umpires will now be paid $5 a game. The home team will no longer have to bat in the bottom of the ninth inning if they have more runs than their opponents. A runner will no longer be called out if he's slow returning to a base after a foul ball . . . the way your captain has been on more than one occasion."

Everybody looked at Anson and grinned, but no one dared to laugh.

"The batter will still have the privilege of calling for a high or low pitch, but seven balls will now yield a free pass to first base instead of eight. The pitching box will be moved back five feet to the new distance of fifty feet, so you will have an extra fraction of a second to determine whether a pitch is a shoot or a slow one, and if it is a curve pitch or a straight one. Neither Sunday games, pool gambling, or the sale of intoxicating beverages on the grounds will be tolerated. Teams are to be made up of men with brains and character, not a class of soused loafers who on account of their skill in the field have been tolerated in the professional arena."

Spalding folded up the paper, put it back in his coat, and left. Anson followed him out.

"All right, men," said Kelly. "The sale of intoxicating beverages will not to be tolerated on the grounds this year. Did yas hear me? Not tolerated. I think you all know what that means . . . we're gointa have to bring our own."

Everyone laughed.

Mike continued. "And League teams are to be made up uv men with brains and character, not a class of soused loafers."

He looked around at his smirking teammates.

"So I want yas to get inta three lines, one if you've got brains, another if you've any character, and a third if you're a soused loafer. And I don't want an argument over who'll be at the head of the soused loafers line. Lord knows, we've plenty uv good candidates in this club."

"I hear the Chicago Police have introduced a Patrol and Signal System," said Dalrymple. "They've installed booths equipped with telegraph units that officers and prominent citizens can use to contact the closest police station, maybe Spalding will have one put one in his box so he can report that an umpire stole a game from his club."

Kelly chuckled. "And your man the mayor has bought some new police wagons. Spalding'll probably ask them to have one follow us

around at night."

Gore piped in. "The city's got a new by-law, it's called the Unsightly Beggar Ordinance."

"What in the name uv heaven is that?" asked Mike.

George explained. "Any person who's diseased, maimed, mutilated, or deformed in any way so as to be an unsightly, disgusting, or improper person won't to be allowed on the streets or in any public place under penalty of a fine of $1 for each offense."

"If anybody catches sight uv Flint's mangled fingers he's *sure* ta get fined," said Mike.

The Cincinnati Enquirer posited that the extra five feet the ball would have to travel to the plate seemed certain to increase the chances for successfully stealing bases and that if it did base-runners like Kelly, Gore, and Dalrymple would show to greater advantage than ever and it would require the most perfect work behind the bat to hold men on first base.

In spite of the nasty weather there was a sizable turnout for the season opener on April 30. It was a cold day for fingers - hence the errors. The Chicago players wore their new navy-blue jerseys. They fit them like a second skin and made them look like swimmers or boating men.

Because of Anson the League had instituted a rule that captains were required to submit their lineups by 9:00 o'clock on the morning of a game so Kelly knew when he'd be batting. At 3:00 his royal nob Herr Doescher appeared and the band struck up "All on Account of Eliza."

Dalrymple got his base on balls from McCormick in the fifth inning and went to second on a passed ball of Clapp's. Kelly hit a corker to right and Abner attempted to score. Orator Shafer's throw was in plenty of time to get him but when Clapp went to touch him out Abner veered to his right and ran around him. Umpire Doescher ruled him safe.

The Clevelands' captain McGeary ran in from his third base and

told Doescher that he had a wider concept of what a base line looked like than any one he knew had ever seen and when Doescher refused to reverse himself McGeary protested the game. Anson knocked in Kelly who'd been given seven balls and the White Stockings took the game 8-5.

On May 3 Corcoran held the Cleveland batsmen to three clean hits and was splendidly supported in the field by Burns, Quest, Kelly, and Anson. Kelly and Anson's hits netted two runs in the first. The Blues' captain and change third baseman Mike McGeary resorted to the stale and disreputable trick of trying to trip up Kelly with his foot between third and home. It was reminiscent of the long-gone days when professional base ball was in the hands of loafers and lunk-heads. Umpire Doescher waved Kelly home and promptly fined Mc-Geary $10.

The Troy Budget said, "The position of referee of a dog-fight is preferable to that of umpire of a ball-game." *The Providence Transcript* claimed that "Doescher, the beer-jerking Dutchman, was foolishly within two miles of the city during the past week. It would be best that he make himself scarce."

Still, five dollars was pretty good pay for two or three hours of work. A laborer earned between $1.15 and $1.50 a day, a teamster from $1.20 to $1.65, and a skilled laborer such as a machinist or a cooper anywhere from $1.90 to $2.75.

Kel sent up a difficult fly that "Sure Shot" Dunlap muffed on the run. It was quite uncharacteristic for Dunlap. Kelly had given Fred his nickname after he'd thrown Mike out at first a number of times when Kel was sure he'd made a base hit. Endless practice had made Dunlap as adept as a monkey at grabbing sizzling ground balls in either hand and firing them off from the very spot he'd captured them. His whistling throws, which seemed to clear the grass by no more than half a foot, never seemed to lose more than an inch or two on their rapid flight to first.

Orator Shafer incurred the ill-will of the spectators by his mean refusal to go after foul balls batted over the right field fence. Four

times he stood with his arms folded and delayed the game. Anson and Kelly had to leave the bench to hunt down the ball. As a result the game took two hours and fifteen minutes to play.

When oily-tongued Shafer went up to bat in the fourth inning he asked the umpire to watch Kelly as he was in the habit of snapping his fingers in a manner that would lead the umpire to believe that the striker had fouled the ball into his glove. The first pitch by Goldsmith was about six feet over Shafer's head and Kelly snapped his fingers and demanded a put-out. Of course it was all done for fun but the look that came over Shafer's face put everyone who understood what had taken place into fits of laughter.

Shafer was on first base in the fifth when Dunlap sent a ground-er to Williamson at third. He threw the ball to Burns but it sailed over his hands into right field. Burns spun around to look as Shafer chuckled and headed for third.

Kelly had anticipated that there was a chance the throw might get past Burns and he'd raced in from right just in case. He caught the errant ball on one bounce and fired it to Williamson, who put the easy tag on the no longer smiling Orator.

Gore got in a three-baser the next inning and scored on Kelly's single. Mike neatly stole second, went to third on a passed ball, and tallied on Anson's long fly to center.

After the game the players went for dinner then headed to the Central Hall for the Grand May Party that was being held under the auspices of the Stag Pleasure Club. On their way inside they were told that, "What happens at of the Stag Pleasure Club *stays* at of the Stag Pleasure Club." When they saw nubile young women heading into a dressing room they knew why.

"'Tis a good thing we've no game tomorrow lads, "Kel told the others. "This could be quite an affair."

The Buffalo Morning Express published an analysis of the National Game in its April 5 issue. "The advancement in the art of ball-twist-ing was even greater last year than previously and the curve system

quite reached perfection."

The League blacklisted ten players for "lushnesss and disorderly conduct." Boston owner Arthur Soden wanted to add Kelly to the blacklist but Hubert blocked it, he suspected Soden only wanted to better his odds of beating his club.

The Clevelands hosted the Chicagos in their home opener at National League Park on May 6. *The Cleveland Leader* described the Blues' rowdiest group of boosters. "Among the members of the Blackberriwyne Row gang are prominent streetcar owners Al and Tom Johnson, Charles LeMarche, proprietor of the Weddell House Hotel, cigar magnate George Wilson, and tavern-keeper Mat Wolford. The club was christened such due to their penchant for consuming vast amounts of blackberry wine during Cleveland Blues games and cheering for their home club while heckling the opposition. The necks were knocked off of several bottles of wine during yesterday's game and many bumpers were swallowed."

Burns and Kelly combined for five hits off Jim McCormick, the rest of the team combined for two. Anson won the toss and sent the Blues to handle the bat first. Dalrymple died at first when the visitors' turn came. Gore sent a liner to left and Kelly took a couple of pitches so he could go down to second. Then he rapped a long one over the first base line that landed just foul. Gore had been sure it would be fair and couldn't get back before the ball was fielded to the pitcher and then to second base. Kelly didn't take a chance of hitting another foul and drove one to deep center field, where an epidemic of indecision on the part of the outfielders did the business and Mike raced around to second base. Anson took first on balls but after yelling at Gore for being caught off base the captain was caught off first on Williamson's foul to the right corner.

"Fucking Anson," muttered Gore when it happened. "I'm in the soup for getting thrown out and he does the same damned thing."

Kelly made another hit in the 7th and quickly stole second. Anson retired on a fly that found a resting place in Moynahan's paws then Williamson drove a scorching grounder to McCormick. He deliv-

ered the ball to McGeary to cut his boyhood chum off but it fell out of McGeary's hands. Kelly scored a moment later on a passed ball but the Clevelands had put five runs on the score-board in their half of the inning and the Chicago bats had no answer.

Flint had injured his leg when he fell through an empty coal scuttle at the hotel so Kelly was behind the bat on May 11 and it was dollars to peanuts that Kelly's right arm would keep all base purloiners anchored at first. He garnered two hits and threw out five base-runners in an 11-3 win over Troy. He and Anson collided with each other when they both went after the same foul fly in the seventh. They were too groggy to play the next day and the Trojans overcame the White Stockings 6-5.

The Chicagos eked out a 4-3 win over the Ruby Legs on the 13th. Kelly was behind the bat again the next day and the spirits were still in him. He dropped a foul-bound, muffed a bunt when he fell trying to reach it, and made two bad throws to second as the Worcesters breezed to a 7-1 victory. No one was talking to Anson, he was spitting bullets. The champions' record stood at six wins and five losses.

On the 18th Richmond was batted out of the box for the first time, the White Stockings amassing 16 hits. Kelly had three of them in a 10-3 triumph over the Ruby Legs. In the sixth he lined a ball into the row of chairs in front of the grand-stand. It met the forehead of an old codger who was in the midst of rolling a cigarette. Mike dropped his bat and hurried over to see if he was all right. The man seemed dazed and confused but unhurt.

"You may have knocked some sense into the old fool," said his wife.

The dangerous Bostons and their phenomenal pitcher Whitney were taken into camp on May 20. *The Tribune* thought it great sport to see the wily bean-eaters outplayed at every point, even to the extent of falling into traps customarily successful only against amateur teams.

Burdock noticed that the door of the club-house was open and, knowing that it was home to a big, black dog that had made its way onto the field before, he demanded the door be closed.

"There's no rule covering dogs and doors, Burdock," President Hulbert told the ornery second baseman, "but if it will make you happier the dog shall be bounced and the door closed."

Burdock further delayed the proceedings by making the crowd wait while he dallied lazily in taking his place at the bat.

Hubert's boys cut loose in rattling fashion in the seventh inning with singles by Flint and Kelly, a two-bagger by Dalrymple, a base on seven widely pitched balls to Gore, a muffed throw by Ezra Sutton, a fumbled grounder by Crowley, and some dare-devil base-running by Kelly, the end result being that four runs crossed the plate.

Anson hit a weak grounder with Kelly on second in the eighth.

The Tribune man said, "It was strongly suspected that in his eagerness to reach home from second base Kelly somehow forgot to go by way of third, slighting that bag by fifteen feet and thereby shaving much valuable time and distance.

The umpire of necessity was fixing his attention upon the close play at first and hence the official could not possibly know whether Kelly made contact with the third bag or not. The Red Stockings stormed and kicked but since Barker did not *see* Kelly forego third he could not under the rules give him out."

"What the devil are you doing?" Corcoran asked Kelly when he went to the pitching box the next day.

Kelly was whistling merrily. He had a spade and a wheelbarrow filled with dirt.

"Given' you a wee bit uv a lift," he told the 5-foot-3 hurler as he flung dirt onto the ground.

Fred Goldsmith arrived, towering over his pitching partner.

When Kelly had finished there was a six-inch hill of dirt at the front of the pitching box.

"Give that a try," he told Corcoran.

Larry shrugged and signaled to Silver Flint that he wanted to try a few throws. Corcoran smiled when his shoots flew in even swifter than usual.

First year twirler Charles Radbourn was between the points for Providence on May 26. The 26-year-old had cropped hair over a prominent forehead, leathery skin, a squat neck, powerful shoulders, whip-like arms, and thick legs. He threw a smorgasbord of pitches, a fastball, a drop curve, a reverse curve, and a slow ball. Anson had batted against Radbourn in an exhibition game in Dubuque in '77. "I never faced a pitcher who baffled me more completely with his curves than Radbourn did that day," Cap told Kelly.

He'd do the bulk of the work for Providence in '81 now that 22-year-old John Montgomery Ward, who'd won 47 games in '79, was spending more time tending the right garden. He was a far less daunting twirler now with the new pitching distance.

Though he was a notorious drinker Charlie did so discreetly and always showed up at the park determined to win. Kelly noticed that Radbourn, unlike most pitchers who liked to warm up in front of the stands so women could admire them, preferred to prepare for a game off to the side out of sight and without distraction. Then he plodded to the pitching box sullenly, doggedly and with apparent indifference. He worked so tirelessly his teammates called him "Old Hoss" after the big, plodding horses that could be seen lugging their burdens through the streets.

In the first two innings Radbourn exhibited as many tricks in his delivery as a pig has twists in its tail but after the White Stockings discovered the secret of his crooks Radbourn furnished lively business for Hulbert's aggregation. They avoided his slow balls and waited for swift ones and slaughtered him without mercy.

Kelly reached base on an error by McClellan in the first and was given first on balls in the fourth. Two innings later his furious drive to right was not clearly handled by Ward. Mike made another hit in the final inning. Kelly scored on each occasion. His fly-catching and base-running were features of the game.

The extra dirt on the box didn't help Corcoran much, he went to pieces and gave up six runs. There was a belief that the fifty-foot

range was too much for Corcoran, he was giving men their base more frequently and depending almost wholly on his speed for effectiveness and he was banging up his catchers.

On June 6th Kelly blasted a furious fly to right that was cleanly handled by Ward. The last three of the Chicagos' dozen runs were scored on hits of Kelly, Anson, and Goldsmith, a clever steal of third by Kelly, and a muffed throw by Jerry Denny, whom *The Sporting News* had just labelled "the king of third basemen." The Chicagos won 12-5 to move another game ahead of Worcester and Buffalo. They got $163 as their half of the gate. Kelly's smooth fly-catching was a feature of the game.

In their June 13, 15, and 16 games in Providence the Chicago men had no trouble shooting out the Grays by a combined score of 33-10 and hold on to their one game lead over the Bisons. In the Monday game Mike had three hits.

When Kelly stepped to the plate in Boston in the first inning the next day he was greeted with a perfect storm of hisses, cat-calls, and the like which he received quite pleasantly. Outraged that Kelly had scored the winning run a month ago after bypassing third base, *The Boston Herald* had accused him of all manner of monstrosities in the way of conduct and deportment. He was called a scoundrel and a rogue and was accused of yelling at opposing outfielders, calling for the wrong man to take a ball in order to confuse the fielder who was planning on making the play, and a great many other varieties of infamy.

John Fox, in his first and only big league season, mystified the Chicagos, who'd laid aside the natty white uniforms they wore in their previous contest and appeared in gray suits with white belts and stockings. They made but six hits while the Red Stockings had no difficulty batting Goldsmith for a dozen safe ones. The home nine scored one run in the sixth and a pair in the seventh for a 6-3 win.

Upwards of 1,800 spectators greeted the return of the champions to their home grounds on June 24 after their first Eastern trip. They appeared in lavender uniforms that were thought to be no improvement over the time-honored white ones to which the eyes of Chicago spectators were accustomed. The visiting nine hailed from Providence but as far as furnishing anything like a contest they might as well have hailed from Kankakee. Kelly didn't make much of a contribution to his club's work but little was needed as the White Stockings sandbagged the Grays 8-0.

The visitors presented Bobby Mathews as their pitcher the next day while Goldsmith served for Chicago. The batting of both teams eclipsed anything in sight. The White Stockings seemed to have learned the secret of Mathews' confounding change of pace. The Grays scored four runs in the first and struck another streak in the ninth pounding out another four runs but they were too far behind and only succeeded in helping their batting records a little. Williamson and Kelly did some tall running but Gore was the biggest run-getter with five of them.

Kelly hit a single, a double, and a triple-bagger scoring each time and made a remarkable catch in the 7th inning on the 24th. In the last game of the series he substituted for Flint in the fourth and caught uncommonly well considering the faulty pitching of Corcoran. Mike struck out twice but got in a single in the sixth and hit two-baggers in the first and third innings. After his fourth hit of the game in the ninth he asked for time. Anson had gone to the bat and he looked puzzled.

Mike signaled for him to come toward first. "I've got an idea, Ans," he told Cap in a low voice.

"What is it, another of your tricks?"

"Not a trick, just a thing we could do."

"What's that?"

He nodded toward the pitching box. "We're getting' lots uv hits but we're havin' trouble stealing today, Radbourn's holdin' us all close ta the bags."

"And?"

"What if I were to take off and instead uv you lettin' the pitch go

by in hopes I make it safe ta second, you swing away."

"I swing away?" Anson thought for a moment. "And if I make contact you'll be half way to second and could reach third easily on a single . . . "

"And home as easy as pie if you were ta hit a two-baser."

"Were you thinking of coming back to the bat at some point?" called the umpire.

"I am," said Anson. He nodded and Mike jogged back to first.

The ploy worked. Anson stroked the ball into shallow right field and Kelly, who would never have had a chance to make third, went into the bag standing up.

"You're one jammy bastard you are Kelly," said Denny, the Grays' third baseman.

"Luck's got nuthin' to do with it." He tapped a finger to his right temple. "'Tis *all* up upstairs here, Jerry."

Kelly hurt his hand sliding into second base in the opening game against Troy and didn't play in the other two. The Chicagos won all three anyway to boost their record to 26-10 and stay four and a half games ahead of the Buffalos.

At the end of June Chicago led the League in the matter of runs scored and base-hits made. The team's average was .281 and they were scoring close to seven runs per game but they stood sixth in fielding which showed their games were being won by heavy batting and desperate base-running rather than by faultless work with their hands.

On Friday, July 15 the champions went to Buffalo flushed with confidence. They checked into the Tifft House wearing boutonnières in their lapels that were said to be the gift of admiring lady friends.

"You have to hand it to Hulbert and Spalding, nuthin' but the best for *their* club," said Mike as he looked around the hotel's ornately decorated lobby. "Maybe it's ta make the uther teams think were somethin' special before we even play 'em."

It was hot as blazes. After he unpacked his case he headed to L. Garson & Co. on Main street to buy shirts and collars, a pair of sard sleeve-links, a Canton vest, and a lightweight sack suit and then to Haffa the tailor on Washington street to have it taken in so ladies could admire his physique.

The Buffalo Commercial reported on the action the next day. "The Chicagos scattered over the Riverside Grounds and began to limber up. There was big, brawny Anson and pretty little Corcoran, the mighty batsman Dalrymple, the bold and fleet-footed Gore and Kelly, Williamson, the burly third basemen, bald-headed, sawed-off Joe Quest, and festive, silver-haired Flint. They looked remarkably attractive in their white uniforms and caps of many colors. There were many admiring members of the weaker sex in attendance, ladies being admitted for just ten cents. The excitement of the crowd beggared description; the Buffalonians rose en masse on a number of occasions and applauded vociferously."

During the game the visiting nine "took big chances on the base paths and covered double the territory of an ordinary player" according to *The Commercial*, which berated Kelly for shouting at Bison fielders as they tried to focus on catching fly balls. Mike stole second and third with characteristic ease and scored on Anson's grounder in the first. He knocked in Gore with a single in the fifth and ripped a two-bagger in Chicagos' six-run seventh inning but Buffalo tallied three times in the eighth and triumphed 10-9.

After the game Kelly, Gore, and Dalrymple hoisted a few - actually several more than a few - at Bramer's Tavern. It had one of Edgar Jewett's locally manufactured Bevador coolers that kept beer bottles chilled.

Corcoran pitched the third game of the series. He tried his best to send in difficult curves but acted as though he was playing a game of one-old-cat and was batted out of his position in the fifth inning. Kelly, who stood fifth in the League batting list and was tied for first in runs scored with leadoff man Dalrymple, made two errors, one in the outfield and one behind the bat in an ugly 11-7 loss to Buffa-

lo. The Chicagos, who'd been sure they would crush the Bisons, had been swept by them. The gamblers were stunned. A large sum of money changed hands.

In the Saturday, July 23 game, which *The Detroit Free Press* reporter called "the most brilliant game played at Recreation Park this year" Kelly belted a tremendous drive to the left field fence for a clean home run but that was all the White Stockings could muster against 6-foot novice southpaw George Derby in a 3-2 loss to the Wolverines.

Kelly played a shrewd trick on Derby in the third inning. Dalrymple was on third with two outs and weak-hitting Flint at the plate. Mean-spirited boosters said he couldn't hit a flock of balloons with a bass-fiddle. Derby had two strikes on him when Kelly, who was coaching Dalrymple, stood outside the coacher's lines.

"Wait!" Kelly called out to Derby.

Derby looked over, confused.

"Let me see that ball. I think it's torn."

Derby looked at the ball.

The words . . . **TRADE MARK / SPALDING / LEAGUE BALL** could be read as plain as day. There was hardly a mark on the ball and it certainly wasn't torn.

"No it's not."

"'Tis," said Kelly. "Let me see it."

Derby shrugged and lobbed the ball to Kelly.

As the ball made its way to Kelly he jumped out of its way.

"Go!" he yelled. Dalrymple raced across the plate as the ball innocently dropped to the ground and bounded away.

Kelly did the strong batting and threw out three base-runners in a 6-3 loss to the Blues on July 29. During the last five innings the Clevelands batted Goldsmith as hard as they had Corcoran on Thursday. *The Inter-Ocean's* base ball expert thought the Chicago pitchers had either lost their grip upon the batsmen of other clubs or the change

of five feet being added to the distance had revolutionized the game so completely that even the most effective pitchers had become soft marks for the hitters. "It is very certain that speed alone as the great means of effectiveness in the pitcher's box has become a thing of the past. Perfect control of the ball combined with good judgment and constant hard work will shape earned runs averages in the future."

In an "absolutely perfect" game on August 11 Chicago gave the Wolverines a crushing defeat to the tune of 17-0. Goldsmith's pitching laid over the Detroits' change-pitcher Frank Mountain several layers deep. Mountain, a member of the Freshmen class of Union College, pitched a fearful game, losing his head whenever there were men on bases. Goldy was a marvel of accuracy and effectiveness and received wonderful support. Canadian George "Dandy" Wood was the only Detroit player who struck at the ball with any confidence. The rest hit foolishly, feebly, and hopelessly. Inning after inning the Detroit strikers went out in the order in which they came up. Flint with five hits - normally two weeks' work for him - and Kelly with three were especially strong with the stick.

The Bisons came to town on August 16. They were in second place but trailed the White Stockings by seven games and knew they had better sweep the series. Captain O'Rourke made an egregious error in sending Peters, a shortstop from New Orleans, to right field. He'd never played there before and he never would again. The Chicagos sent nine balls the German's way and he managed to get his hands on only four of them.

"Schei spiel!" he yelled as he watched the ball roll to the outfield fence after his fifth misplay.

Kelly usually hit to all fields to keep the other nine on their toes, but not this time. He aimed strictly for right and wound up with three hits, two for two bases. He scored each time in his club's 13-9 win. On August 18 Kelly played splendidly. He brought down the house when he threw out O'Rourke from deep right field after catching a difficult fly one-handed.

The fielding of the Chicagos was exceptional on Saturday, August

20. Kelly made a terrific throw to Flint to nail Wood at the plate in the eighth inning but Silver muffed it.

"Sorry, Kel," Flint told Mike after the game.

"Don't give it anuther thought, Lord knows I've dropped plenty uv *your* throws. Did Spalding lend ya the money you needed?"

"He did."

A smile spread over Mike's face. "At the usual interest?"

"That's right. Eight per cent."

Of the August 30 game *The Free Press* reporter wrote, "the Detroit spectators were impartial in their applause of all good plays no matter by whom they were made but when Flint let one slip through his hands in the first allowing Wood to score the shouting was, to put it mildly, most ungentlemanly.

Kelly, who played errorless ball at third, spent a lot of the game staring at the Wolverines' catcher Charlie Bennett.

Finally, he yelled over to Tom Burns, "Did Bennett have a big gut when we played these fellows in July, Tom?"

"A big gut?"

"Aye, a big stomach. Look at him, he looks like he's put on twenty pounds. And he's havin' a helluva time bending over."

"You're right, Kel. It's like he's got something stuffed under his shirt."

It turned out Bennett and his wife had conceived the idea of a chest protector. She'd become alarmed by all the ugly purple bruises on his chest and stomach from foul tips. Together, they'd fashioned a shield by sewing strips of cork in between bed-ticking material. Charlie wore the protector under his uniform to avoid detection and ridicule.

The scribe claimed, "As a Boston girl would say, the game didn't look so 'very awfully awful' for the home side until the eighth when Kelly's two-baser, Anson's single, Bennett's drop of Burns' third strike, and Williamson's sacrifice fly to Hanlon added two to the Chicagos' total and Detroit trailed by six." The slugging match ended in a 12-8 victory for the visitors.

Bennett was assessed a stiff fine of $50 by the management of the Detroit club for drinking so much that night that he could not play effectively in the game the next day, a 10-3 win for the Chicagos. *The Post* said, "Bennett played an exceedingly poor game and wore an air of indifference about the result which did not do him credit. He was lazy and inaccurate and the other side stole bases on him audaciously, Kelly touching the plate twice while he was dawdling about."

The Detroits succumbed to their guests again the next day, by a score of 10-3 but Anson was fortunate they weren't awarded the game. He'd done a silly thing in changing the batting order from the list he'd made out the night before, placing Burns ahead of Dalrymple. Bancroft appealed the result to Secretary Young but was denied.

The Chicagos were seven games ahead of the second-place Bisons when they arrived all cocked and ready to give them a sound drubbing in Buffalo on September 8 but they were dished up in fine style instead. The next day *The Buffalo Commercial* gloated over their club's 10-1 win. "The Whitestockings were outplayed at every point. This seems to prove the rumor that the so-called champions are all broken up and don't care a continental whether they win any more games or not. Several members of the team have heard whisperings that they must seek work in other fields in 1882 and it makes little difference to them where Hubert's pride ranks in the list at the end of the season so long as they play well enough to retain their positions. The team cannot in all good conscience deny that they came to Buffalo confident that they would win all three games.

The Chicagos need a grown person for captain. Baby Anson is large but he lacks brains. Williamson, who failed to get Foley's finger burner in the first inning and made a crazy throw after fetching it, is reported to be one of the players who will walk the plank. Burns, the weakest man in the club, made his usual fumble. His decapitation and banishment are certain. The only credible things done by the Chicagos were catches by Kelly and Gore yet they too must go.

In the field the Chicago ball players are louts, at the bat old women. The champions had better jump into the Hamburgh and take a bath. The duffers will appear in a different uniform today - green with frills. Their wardrobe is said to be the most elegant and extensive in the league. One suspects the reason is A.G. Spalding's desire to promote his line of sports clothing."

The White Stockings got into Boston late in the afternoon on September 12. It had been a long trip and most of the players made an early night of it. Not Kelly, Gore, and Dalrymple, they went to Doyle's, the new pub that had just opened on Jamaica street. Gore and Dalrymple drank the new beer the bar was getting patrons to try. It was called Samuel Adams Boston lager. Kelly bought a bottle of Jameson and stuck to that. Each of the revelers went 0-for-3 the next day.

Kelly made three hits in four at bats in his team's 4-3 win on September 14 though. The Red Stockings got five bases on errors in the first inning, the Chicagos six. Mike gathered in four flies in right field but muffed a groundball. The game was played in an hour and twenty-three minutes. Kelly was remembered by Boston friends who presented him with a bouquet and some jewelry. The audience wasn't aware they had. Hulbert wouldn't allow the presentation to be made on the field.

On Thursday Kelly decided to check out The Jordan Marsh & Co. store at the corner of Washington and Avon streets in Winthrop Square. It had developed the concept of "department shopping." The first floor was devoted to the sale of flannels and cottons. On the second floor were dress goods, summer whites, corsets, silks, and muslins. The third floor had gloves, linens, Persian cashmeres, and accessories for gentlemen, and the fourth floor displayed notions—Balmorals, hoop skirts, soaps, perfumery, hosiery, and countless other articles called fancy goods.

Mike decided to check out the fourth floor—he figured there'd be several well-dressed and well-kept women there and he was right, almost all of them were in twos, admiring the fabulous wares.

"Beatrice, look at this shawl! It's absolutely divine, it looks even better than it did in the catalogue," he heard an excited woman in a mauve dress with a hundred flounces say to her friend.

"Look at these cerise and Metternich green poplins . . . and these embroidered sultans," gushed her friend. "And this moon-on-the-lake silk, why it's only nine dollars, Myrtle. And look here, this Bismark Chamelion. It's only *eight* dollars."

"You shouldn't spend *too* much more money, dear, didn't that point-lace handkerchief set you back $29?"

"No, silly, it set my *husband* back $29."

The two women laughed. They were so enraptured with the gorgeous fabrics, beautiful chamelions, and poplin plaids they didn't even notice Mike. He headed down to the third floor in search of a money clip. Its walls were beautifully frescoed, its floors richly carpeted, and its mile-long walnut counters shone in the bright illumination. He looked around at the assortment of expensive suits, Scotch tweeds, English diagonal twills, and pricey French meltens, suede and kid leather gloves, and Balbriggan, silk, and opera hose.

Mike was taken by a splendid collection of cravats, scarfs, and neck-ties. He was even more taken with the fetching, smartly-dressed cash-girl with almond-shaped eyes, impossibly long eyelashes, expertly tinted cheeks, and flowing, sandy hair behind the counter. She was folding a Cardigan jacket and carefully placing it into a Field, Leiter & Co. box. When she finished she looked up and saw Mike staring at her.

"Hello, sir," she said with a hint of an Irish accent. Her eyes sparkled as she asked, "Can I show you anything?"

Mike managed to take his eyes off her and looked down at the counter self-consciously. "I ... I was thinking of purchasing this," he said, pointing to a Norwood watch guard.

"It's one of our most popular novelties."

Mike allowed himself the luxury of admiring the girl's physique. Though her blouse was modestly laced, her generous cleavage was

still spectacular. "Quite luvly."

Non-plussed, the girl looked down at her chest. "What do you ..."

"Yer locket. It's grand. I especially fancy the setting."

Relieved, but somewhat dubious that this handsome man was actually referring to her locket, she said, "Thank you, it was me muther's."

"Do they let you take lunch, Miss?"

"I beg your pardon."

"Do they let you take lunch?"

"Yes, we get an hour, why do you ask?"

"Do you have a beau if I might so bold as to inquire?"

"You may and I've not."

"It's goin' fer noon, would ya join me at a place around the corner fer a bite?"

She looked around to see if her manager was watching. "I'd like that, but I couldn't be seen leaving with you. We aren't allowed to fraternize with the clientele."

"We'll meet downstairs, in the foyer then."

"I should know your name if we're to dine together."

"Mike Kelly. And yours?"

"I'm Siobhan. Give me ten minutes."

Kel couldn't remember enjoying a meal more. Siobhan was a delight. She laughed at all his jokes, including the one about the boy that cried "Out at first!" when the minister called Judgement, and she couldn't get enough of his outlandish stories. They compared their parents' flights from the old country and she talked about her dream of becoming an actress. Then they made plans to see one another whenever the Chicagos were in Boston.

Kelly's batting was on the money in a 4-0 whitewash of Boston on September 16. He slammed two singles and a pair of two-baggers,

scored two runs, and drove in both of the other Chicago runs in the hour and twenty-three minute affair.

The Boston Post was livid with the way Kelly scored in the ninth. It said the victory the Chicagos achieved over the Bostons was "not one to be proud of. But for the contemptible conduct of their player Kelly and the umpiring of a person of the same name they would not have had a run at the end of the ninth inning.

Kelly, the player, came home from second on a ball hit only to the second base line and as it was being fielded to first he went across the lot without going within thirty feet of third base. Many of the spectators laughed at the ploy but those same people roared their disapproval when Kelly, the umpire, refused to declare him out.

This is a trick for which Mike Kelly is famous. It is a disgrace to base ball that a player guilty of such an act should be allowed to continue in the league and some way ought to be found to get rid of him."

One of Mike's friends wouldn't be playing in the league anymore. The next morning Kelly was among the mourners at the funeral of Chub Sullivan, dead at the age of 25. Mike felt fortunate the team happened to be playing in Boston when Chub passed away, he likely wouldn't have been given time off to attend Chub's funeral if the team had been in Chicago.

In the 7th inning of the second game of three in Troy, Buck Ewing muffed Gore's fly. His mind might have been elsewhere. He'd just married Annie Lawson, the daughter of a Confederate soldier. Kelly, who wore crepe on his sleeve in memory of Chub Sullivan, made a three-base hit and scored the winning run on Anson's fly to center after the side should have been out. Fred Goldsmith was given a seven-barrel fine of $150 for abusive language to Anson. When the captain told Goldsmith to pitch carefully to Roger Connor with the game on the line Goldsmith told him to mind his fucking business and get back to first base.

On the 27th of September an audience of a dozen people witnessed a game played under trying conditions. It rained incessantly

and water found its way through openings in the grand-stand so that everyone got a very good ducking.

"Rain or no rain, this club ain't gointa last," Mike told Abner. "They can't draw flies in the sunshine either."

"There are more players on the field than cranks in the stands," chuckled Dalrymple.

The Chicagos batted Keefe soundly but fielded miserably on the muddy grounds. Kelly played right field perched on a small piece of wood. He had a pair of singles and scored two runs in the White Stockings' 10-8 win.

On September 11 the batting records as compiled by F. W. Woodside were released. Anson, with a little help from the Chicago score-keeper, led the White Stockings and the entire league with a .389 average. Dalrymple was second among the Chicagos with a .321 average. Kelly was third at .315 but he was not happy to have struck out twenty-five times. He was second in the League to Gore in times touching home plate and tied for second in hits with Dunlap.

On September 30 the League discussed the need to "weed out dissipated and rebellious members." Kelly wasn't surprised that the list included Lip Pike, Buttercup Dickerson, and Ed Nolan. Providence signed Lip Pike in October. When he made three errors in the ninth inning of a close game he was accused of throwing the game and suspended.

The Bostons were disbanded on October 2. The players had been notified to that effect and they were considerably dissatisfied. They claimed their contracts were for seven months including April and October and they were being deprived of their October salary. In New Orleans in November Kelly received $100, the last of his 1881 salary. He was glad Hulbert hadn't pulled the same shenanigans the Boston club had.

"That fellow could charm a vulture off a carcass."

After he returned from New Orleans, Kelly read in the papers about Wyatt Earp and his brothers and about the soon-to-be-born American Association that was going to charge 25 cents admission, have games on Sunday, and sell beer in the stands. Almost as fascinating was the news about both leagues' uniforms.

"Listen to this, Ab," Mike said to Abner over a drink. "The League uniforms are all gointa feature white pants and belts but each player is gointa wear different colors to signify his position."

"Each man'll wear different colors?"

"Aye, the catchers'll wear scarlet caps and shirts, the pitchers light blue caps and shirts, the first basemen scarlet and white-striped ones, the second basemen'll wear orange and black caps and shirts . . . "

"They'll look like orioles," chuckled Abner.

"The third basemen will be clad in gray caps and shirts, the short-stops maroon ones, the left fielders will don white caps and shirts, the center fielders red and back shirts, the right fielders gray caps and shirts, and substitutes will be required to wear green caps and brown tunics. The *only* team identifier will be the color of our stockings."

"The spectators are going to be taken aback by such a dizzying array," said Dalrymple.

"They're gointa think they've gone to the bluddy circus."

"Who's idea was *that?*"

"Who do we know that sells uniforms?"

139

"Spalding," Abner harrumphed.

Mike, who would split his time between shortstop, catcher, and right field, wasn't happy to have to purchase three new uniforms, though the cost would be $20 not the usual $30.

In March the players spent a lot of time at the gym throwing Indian clubs, racing one another on rowing machines, punching heavy bags, and sparring to "improve the pins." In between they talked about the Earps. Virgil Earp had just arrived in Colton with the remains of his brother Morgan. A body of fifteen men had apparently accompanied him.

On April 4 the players rode the Chicago Street Railway to a studio on State street to have their picture taken. On the way they talked about Jesse James, who'd just been killed in his home in St. Louis. Kelly had his hair cut shorter than usual and, like ten of the other fourteen men, had his mustached trimmed for the photo-mechanical print. Only Anson, Dalrymple, Corcoran, and Flint were clean-shaven. Mike sat in the middle row beside Fred Goldsmith, wearing a sober expression. The players wore the different colored jerseys that signified the positions they played, though it was hard to tell in the black, white, and gray image. The picture had to be taken six times since one or more of the men twitched slightly in the first five attempts.

The National League would have to fight the American Association, their new rival, without the guidance of William Hulbert. He died suddenly on April 10. Kelly had never been close with Hulbert but he'd respected him. Mike wasn't sure how things were going to be with Spalding alone at the helm now.

Though he hadn't confessed to any wrong-doing, Higham - the first umpire to wear a mask - was fired and banned from base ball. He'd been assigned to officiate the Detroits' home games and had done such fine work that a testimonial dinner had been held in his honor. But William G. Thompson, the owner of the Wolverines and mayor of Detroit, had been suspicious of calls Higham had made. He hired a private detective who uncovered a number of telegrams

between the umpire and a well-known gambler. "Buy all the lumber you can" meant bet on the Wolverines. No telegram on a game day meant bet on their opponents.

On Mike's way down to breakfast the next morning the young elevator operator accidentally stopped on the Ladies' floor. Kel assumed they were at the lobby and when he strode out into a sea of women he stopped dead in his tracks. He looked back to the elevator, puzzled.

"I'm terribly sorry, Mr. Kelly, this is the Ladies' floor."

Kelly looked around, smiled his expansive smile, tipped his hat, and got back on the elevator. He handed the embarrassed operator a quarter. "Thanks lad, that was my entertainment for the day. You should uv seen the looks on those women's faces."

The Chicagos batted George Derby liberally in Detroit on May 22 but in most cases after the side should have been snuffed out. The Wolverines put on a ghastly exhibition of fielding. Bennett led the way for the Detroits with four errors. Each time Kelly batted all he could smell was the whiskey emanating from Bennett's pores.

On June 6 in a game in Providence Blondie Purcell, who was in the Buffalos now, took especial pains to get the umpire to put a new ball into play to replace the sodden one they were using. The ball was so wet Galvin couldn't curve it. The umpire refused so Blondie used a pocket-knife to cut off the cover. The umpire slugged Purcell with a $10 fine and Blondie had a second nickname, "Cut Off" Purcell. Blondie was stunned when the Bisons' management fined him an outrageous $100 for his stunt.

After winning the last two games of their road trip by the commanding scores of 9-2 and 12-0 the White Stockings jumped on the unfortunate Ruby Legs, trampled them on the ground, picked them up and mopped the field with their bruised and mangled bodies on June 20 and 21 winning each game 13-3. In the first game the beauty of Kelly's play at shortstop was marred by two bad errors. Anson and Williamson made a number of clock-work putouts. The Chicagos batted with the power of catapults and showed no trace

of timidity on the bases, running them as recklessly as drunkards walk the streets.

In a see-saw 11-innning win over the Bostons on June 15 Kelly garnered just one baby base hit. He shocked Dalrymple when left-handed hitting Sam Wise came to the bat by abandoning his position at shortstop and heading into shallow right field.

"Have you taken leave of your senses, Kel?" asked Abner. "You've left your spot empty."

"Have you not noticed the way Wise bats?"

"What do you mean?" asked Goldsmith.

"With that stance uv his he couldn't hit a ball to the left side to save his life."

"Kel's right," said Abner. "He does nothing but hit to the right side."

A minute later Wise ripped a hard grounder that neither Burns nor Anson would have reached. Mike got it and easily fielded Wise out.

"You're either a genius or one lucky bastard," said Abner as they jogged to the bench.

On June 22nd in the final game of the series 1,200 rooters saw what looked like a certain defeat turn into a victory by pluck and determination. In the fifth inning the Chicagos, who trailed the visitors 7 to 1, showed "what they can do when they expectorate on their flippers and take up another notch on their belts". Kelly changed the program by sending the ball down the left field line. It took off the third baseman's cap and bounded toward the bleacher-boards. Mike capered all the way round to third as the crowd went crazy with delight. When Anson scored the winning run in the ninth the cranks "made a yell that could be heard on the West Side."

The Red Stockings, who'd taken two of three from the White Stockings earlier in the month, came to town at the end of June. Whitney had rejoined the club. He'd been away testifying in a murder trial in Omaha. The Chicago men paid them back in double eagles with 9-2 and 9-0 wins on the 29th and 30th.

Just before the July 1 game Burdock and Rowen ran into each other while they were shagging fly balls. The former fractured his shoulder, the latter suffered a deep gash to his cheek which was sewn up on the grass by a surgeon. Corcoran was Larryupped by the Bostons. Kelly kept busy muffing ground balls and did it with great zeal and effect. His five misplays, two missed flies by Flint, and fumbles by Dalrymple and Nicol and a base on balls by Corcoran when the bases were already filled gave the Bostons their five runs.

The Red Stockings took a one run lead into the ninth but Buffington's wild throw and Sutton's muff gave the home nine the two runs they needed. Kelly counted his lucky stars after his dreadful play at shortstop.

He and Dalrymple went for a drink or two after dinner. On their way into one of their favorite watering holes Abner grabbed Mike by the arm. He pointed to the wall behind the bar and said, "There you are again."

"Poor Custer," chuckled Kelly, "taken down again."

Most of the Chicago saloons that had a painting of Custer's Last Stand hanging on the wall behind the bar had replaced them with one of Kelly sliding into home plate.

For the first time in 1882 on July 9 "the Troy team was compelled to sit down on a nest of goose-eggs." Four thousand people were present, the largest crowd other than on the Fourth of July. Cranks shot off fireworks and guns and shouted wildly with the least provocation. On the hill above the center field fence people were bunched together closer than checks in a dude's wallet.

Rare judgment of the particularities of batsmen was shown by the visitors. Mike got Williamson to plant himself near the foul line for Gillespie and the result was a straight liner right into his hands.

Kelly waved Gore back when Ewing went to the bat and Gore captured a terrific drive off the center field fence and threw him out at second base. The White Stockings scored single runs in the second, third, and sixth and Goldsmith blanked the Trojans 3-0. After the game Chief Roseman said the next time he played against the League champions he wanted a horse to help him chase down the Chicagos' long hits to right field.

In a boiling hot July 14 game at Lake Front Park Stump Weidman and the Detroits were unmercifully walloped 23-4. Kelly reached base on Morrisey's misplay in the fourth, hit a three-bagger in the fifth, and wielded the ash for a bag then scored on Morrisey's fourth gaff of the game in the eighth. He stole three bases, twice while Wolverines' catcher Bennett was dawdling, and scored three times. After the game Bennett was fined $50 for having had too much to drink the night before.

Kelly bought a blue chevriot diagonal suit for $15, some shirts and collars, and a pair of Cordovan leather shoes at Commonwealth Clothing store the next day. He dined alone at the Palmer House that night. A waiter held a chair for a woman sitting down at the table next to him. Already seated there was a young girl in a Pinafore hat, her daughter no doubt, thought Kelly. The girl was pretty, her mother was an absolute corker. She wore a light ecru princess line dress without a horizontal waist seam that molded snuggly to her body by means of vertical seams and tucks that created a body-hugging silhouette.

It was fringed with strings of gold beads and she had diamonds in her bangs, on her neck, on her billowy bosom, about her wrists, and on her fingers. Her luminous hair was piled up in intricate knots and braids and cascades of curls fell down her back. On her head was a precariously tipped bonnet trimmed with flowers and ribbons.

As she was delicately sipping her soup her daughter noticed someone across the room. She smiled and said, "Mother, there's my friend, Edna. I heard she and her mother might be stopping here on their way back to Philadelphia. Would you mind terribly if I went over and talked with her?"

"Not at all, dear. I am perfectly fine, go on ahead."

As the girl got up to leave, the bustle of her dress knocked her mother's clutch purse onto the floor. Mike looked around for a waiter

who might pick it up and seeing none wiped his mouth, got up and got it.

When he handed the woman her bag a look of recognition swept across her face. "You're Kelly, the baseballist, are you not?"

"That I am," said Kelly, a little taken aback. "Have we met? I don't think I'd forget a woman as striking as yourself."

She smiled. "When we checked into the Palmer House the other day the manager told us that a White Stockings base ball game was a must see in Chicago. He added, rather proudly, that their best player, Mike Kelly, stays at the hotel."

"Which game did you see?"

"The one on Friday against the Detroit team."

"The Friday game. That was a barrel uv laughs. We did up Stump Weidman pretty badly didn't we?"

"Yes, you in particular. I thought the poor man was going to cry when you hit for three bases and sent three of your mates across the plate. But I felt a little sorry for *you*."

"Sorry for *me*?"

"Yes, all that running of the bases you did."

"I think I lost three or four pounds. I needed a lot uv refreshment after that one."

"Speaking of refreshment, are you finished your supper, Mr. Kelly?"

"I am so. Why do you ask?"

"I thought you might join me in some refreshment. My husband left me quite well off, but it means I have to drink alone and that is quite an unseemly thing for a lady to do in a hotel."

"Did you want me to call for a waiter and the wine list?"

"I want you to do no such thing."

Mike was puzzled. "I thought . . . ."

"What I would like you to do is come up to my suite. I have plenty to drink there."

"Well I'm afraid I can't do that."

"Oh. Why not?"

"Because you've not told me your name."

"Land sakes, I'm sorry, it's Hazel. Hazel Sykes."

Fitzgerald and Jeffreys, two investment bankers, sat at a table nearby. They watched as Kelly headed for the elevator with yet another attractive woman on his arm.

"Look at Kelly," said Fitzgerald.

"That fellow could charm a vulture off a carcass."

Kelly's apartment was large and handsomely furnished but it was no comparison to Hazel's suite. The "common room" was anything but common. It was huge and richly carpeted, with high, frescoed ceilings, enormous plate glass windows with a spectacular view of the lake and city, velvet upholstered chairs, oriental divans and foot stools, a polished mahogany escritoire, and a marble mantlepiece with a mirror over it in which Hazel quickly checked her hair and makeup.

"How long are you staying at the Palmer, Hazel?"

"Actually, I'm in no hurry to leave. As I said, my husband left a considerable sum, but a suite such as this in one of the best hotels costs only a fraction of the price of maintaining a mansion or a large private home with comparable amenities.

Hazel's daughter came in. She looked at Kelly, then her mother, then Kelly again. "Is that the man who sat at the next table in the dining room, mother?"

"Yes it is. Does he look familiar?"

"He does. I was going to say something during supper but I feared you would chastise me for looking at strange men. Aren't you Mike Kelly from the White Stockings?"

"Guilty as charged."

"I'm Effie. We attended one of your games. We often go in Boston

on Ladies Days, but we'd never seen *your* team before. I think your club would make mincemeat of the Bostons. You certainly had your way with the Detroits."

"Yer muther told me you'd gone to our game on Friday. We knocked the Detroits around pretty smartly."

"Well, I must get to bed, mother had me in about a hundred stores this afternoon. A pleasure meeting you Mr. Kelly, I imagine mother and I shall be attending more of your games." She went to the bedroom on the far end of the suite, turned and smiled back at Mike, and went in.

When Mike woke up in Hazel's enormous bed he had to think for a moment where he was. Then he smiled. Oddly, he was alone. He'd hoped that Hazel, whom he'd been glad to discover was 'no lady' between the sheets, would want to carry on some more. He looked across the room and saw a tray with a glass of orange juice, a carafe of coffee, and a plate with toast and jam sitting on a mahogany chiffonier. A note was attached to the mirror above the dressing table. He got up and read it.

"I would love to have enjoyed your company again this morning. I should have said so last night, but I am meeting with my financial advisors. I had breakfast sent up for you. Look forward to seeing you again, have a good game, Hazel."

Mike picked up the tray and took it back to bed. He was about to pour himself a second cup of coffee when he heard the door handle being turned. He presumed Hazel's meeting had been cancelled. It wasn't Hazel. It was her daughter.

She was faintly redolent of hyacinth or lavender, Mike couldn't tell which. She was in high heels and wore a silk French Coutel corset that struggled to contain her breasts. The corset was the same color as her eyes.

"Mother left a note on my door that said she would be out all morning on business." She waited a beat. She'd had her hair up. She pulled a ribbon and it fell to her shoulders. "I thought you might like some company." She looked at Kelly.

Mike looked down and realized there was a swelling beneath the sheets.

The Chicagos played fifteen games between June 17 and July 11 and lost only one. The League had abandoned the different colored uniforms. The result had been sheer chaos, collisions when base runners arrived at a base whose defender wore the same color they did and other equally confusing and embarrassing incidents on the field.

In the first inning on July 18, after Dalrymple had swung at air three times and Gore had grounded weakly out to Galvin, Kelly drove a hot one at Force's feet. He muffed but picked it up in time to catch his man with a good throw. In his hurry to make up for lost time he threw short and wide of Brouthers and Mike was safe. Kelly winked at his captain that he was about to take off for second. Anson nodded and hit a liner that bounced off the right field fence. Had Kelly been standing near first he wouldn't have been able to score. With his head-start toward second he made it around easily. Kelly's run was the difference in the Chicagos' 3-2 win.

Spalding had invited Carter Harrison, the mayor of Chicago, to join him in his private box.

"You've got yourself a gem in Kelly," said Harrison as they got up to leave.

"We were lucky to get him from the Cincinnatis, your honor."

"The man is an absolute genius on a ball diamond. The last time I was here he decided to forego third base when the umpire had his eyes on first base."

"Oh, the man has pulled a lot more fast ones since then. He was coaching third base in Detroit and he got their rookie pitcher to toss him the ball because he claimed it was damaged."

"Did he throw it to him?"

"He *did* and Kelly stepped out of the way. The ball fell on the ground and the runner trotted home."

The mayor laughed. "Could I borrow Kelly and turn him loose on the city counsellors."

The White Stockings, with the exception of Flint, had their mustaches taken off on July 19. Samson-like, they attributed their one-run losses to Detroit and Boston games to the loss of their whiskers. The attendance at the three Chicago vs. Troy games aggregated fully 13,000 - by far the largest for any three games in League history. The Troy team took away as its share a sum not far short of $2,800, which was as much as Chicago had taken away from Troy in the last three years.

The players got a tip on a horse called Charley. It was a sure thing. They headed to the Trotting & Jockey Club and everybody but Quest placed sizable wagers on him. The horse took an early lead then pulled up lame.

"Look at your Charley horse," chided Quest, a big smile on his face.

The others sneered at him.

The Chicagos lost the next day. A correspondent of *The Tribune* said that a great many people wondered why Captain Anson didn't coach his men during games but contented himself with sitting on the bench chewing his cud with the regularity of a Passamaquoddy school-girl bruising her gum and then swearing at them when they came in to the bench. All clubs were now required to provide a bench so players wouldn't have to sprawl on the ground or sit with the spectators.

The Clevelands took their soup with the same old ladle at the hands of the Chicagos on the 24th. The audience of 2,000 delighted to see their club appear in another new uniform, a sensible and tasteful hot weather outfit and the neatest one yet - a flannel shirt trimmed in red with elbow sleeves trimmed with scarlet at the neck and on the breast a large C.

"Look at Mike Kelly," a woman in a soft straw outing-hat in the front row whispered to the friend next to her. "Do you see how close-fitting his shirt is?"

"I haven't looked at anything else, Maude."

Mike sensed they were admiring him and tipped his cap to them.

"Oh!" gasped the admirers loud enough that their escorts frowned at them in admonishment.

The Clevelands, who wore white shirts with the familiar blue hose and their potato-bug caps, had a change pitcher they'd kept in the background and the local paragraphers had been pitching into manager Doescher because he still hadn't trotted out his dark horse. Now he released him from his stall and he proved a phenomenon. He accomplished what no other league pitcher before him ever did in the most remarkable game ever played. His name was Rowe and he hadn't set foot on a big league diamond in five years. The White Stockings were indebted to Doescher for the privilege of his acquaintance. In all their lives the Chicago batsmen never enjoyed a game so thoroughly. Why Doescher should have kept him in the dark so long was a mystery. Equally so, why had Rowe been kept at all? The 27-year-old threw seven wild pitches and was death on his catcher.

The game was of a teeter-board variety. Wild pitches, wildly thrown balls by "Alderman" Briody, a fumble by Dunlap, a fine base-hit by Kelly that scored Dalrymple, a single by Anson, and a double by Burns gave the White Stockings five unearned runs in the first inning. The home side scored four more runs indebted to errors in the third.

Gore pulled up with a leg strain in the midst of running down a long fly ball in the third inning.

"Hey, laddies," Mike yelled to the others, "now *George* is the Charley horse."

During the Clevelands' at bats Maude was hit in the mouth with a swift foul ball. Mike rushed over to see if she was all right. She was thrilled, as was her friend. Their perturbed escorts were not.

"Such a pretty mouth to suffer so," consoled Mike, "Keep this as a souvenir," he added, pressing the ball into Maude's white-gloved hand. He smiled and turned to Anson. "I'm good for that one, get us a new one."

Anson requested the umpire to call play until a new League ball could be procured and told Dalrymple to go to the clubhouse for one. In the confusion Dunlap and Briody stole bases but given the beating their team was laying on the Blues neither Kelly nor Anson kicked.

Flint got a jammed finger in the fourth so Nicol went to short and Kelly behind the bat. Nine runs were made that inning on a single by Gore, a triple by Kelly, doubles by Burns, Williamson, and Nicol, a one-baser by Dalrymple, a base on balls, a home run by Flint of all people, a fumble by Glasscock, and three wild pitches from understandably rattled Rowe. Anson was the last batter and the crowd yelled "Give 'em a chance," so he hit an easy one to Dunlap and mercifully closed the inning. The Blues' white uniforms were drenched.

In the eighth a base on balls and Kelly's two-baser brought in another run. In the ninth Burns singled, Flint and Nicol each hit for two bases, and Dalrymple singled. Gore, like all men from Saccarappa disliked derby dicers, and he landed a screamer into the first base bleachers that skimmed a Trilby from an unsuspecting head as neatly as old Sitting Bull ever essayed to raise a scalp. Kelly and Williamson's doubles and a muffed fly by Willigrod produced another three runs. The crowd roared with laughter and applauded frantically.

The White Stockings added yet another three tallies in the ninth for a 35-4 win. They had set League records for clean hits, total bases, and runs and Maude would always treasure the League ball given to her by Mike Kelly.

On Saturday, July 29 in Detroit the Chicagos had a regular melon-cutting picnic, taking their revenge on Wiedman for a previous loss by pounding him without remorse. Kelly "wielded a vigorous wagon tongue." He garnered four hits in his five times at the bat and scored four times in the White Stockings' rattling 17-1 rout of the Wolverines.

The talk in the tally-ho on the way back to the hotel was about how managers of the League clubs had started to fine their players

for fielding errors and misplays.

"It's bad enough they dock us for stayin' out late and partakin' in a bit uv innocent revelry," groaned Kelly, "now we have to pay for *muffs*."

Mike and George had breakfast together the next morning. Gore had bought a newspaper in the lobby. He finished eating and flipped to page 4, the Sports page.

"Anson's second to Brouthers in batting. Of course you need to take that with a grain of salt. I'm at .323, you're hitting .315."

Kelly gave him a vacant look.

"I know. You don't give a rat's ass what your numbers are, so long as we win."

Gore looked back at his newspaper. "F. B. Brainwood thinks Ned wants to go over to the Detroits on account of Anson fining him for getting to the grounds late last week."

Kelly winked at a pretty girl at a nearby table who'd been eyeing him. She blushed but didn't look away.

"Brainwood thinks you and I are the best base runners in the game. He says I'm swifter than you, but you make up for my speed with your keener judgment as to chances and openings."

"Who the hell is F. B. Brainwood?"

"Haven't the foggiest." Gore went to take a drink of coffee and nearly spit it out.

"What?"

"The Buffalo Courier says the Bisons are being paid to play ball, not to get drunk."

"Well if there is a club that's payin' their players ta get drunk they need to let me know cuz I'm all in."

On August 8 all of the scheduled games were cancelled due to the funeral of General Ulysses S. Grant. Kelly was glad the team was on the road, snow was falling in Chicago.

On September 5 the Trojans arrived in town for a three-game series. President Spalding sat in his private box with the President of the Union Pacific closing arrangements to have a special car take the team on an extended trip to the prominent towns of Iowa, Nebraska, Colorado, and Kansas in October.

In the first game "the White Stockings ran rampant on the bases in true Chicago style and played with all their old-time dash and confidence. Their change of caps may have had something to do with their change of luck as they appeared in their old harlequin parti-colored headgear. If such a change helps them win games they may want to change all their clothes when the Providence club comes here right down to their socks," wrote the *Tribune* man. Kelly made three hits and scored once in Corcoran's 10-0 whitewash. Mike admired his concentration, Larry had just gotten married.

Three of the Troy infielders talked after being retired again in the eighth inning. "You know how Kelly signals Corcoran what manner of pitch to throw when he's behind the bat," Buck Ewing said to Tom Burns.

"He uses his fingers. He started doing it last year," said Burns. "He studies every batter and figures out his weaknesses."

"What about it?" asked Roger Connor.

"There's more to it than that, have you noticed that he makes other signals?"

"*Other* signals?" asked Connor.

"Haven't you ever noticed that when *he* catches the fielders always seem to be in the right place?"

Connor thought for a moment. "Come to think on it, I've hit three balls on the nose today and every time I did a fielder was right there waiting for it."

"Kelly lets them know what he's signaled Corcoran to throw," explained Ewing. "If it's a shoot he knows the batsman won't be able to pull it down the line so Kelly nods for the fielder to shade more toward center field and if he's called for a puzzler he signals to the

fielder to move over close to the line. And we haven't had many men on base, but did you notice that when we *have* Corcoran hasn't had to watch them very closely?"

"Come to think of it, you're right," said Ewing. "Why's that?"

"Kelly sees if a runner's talking a big lead and if a throw is needed to first he taps his right knee and if Corcoran needs to throw to third he touches his left knee. If he has to throw to *second*, Kelly grabs the bill of his cap."

"So Corcoran never needs to take his focus off the man at bat. No wonder they beat us all the time," sighed Connor.

The Trojans presented a woebegone, hopeless style and seemed beaten from the start. They lost the second game 7-1 and looked for a better result in the final game of the series but things didn't go their way again. "There was no limit to the batting possibilities of the home team or the muffing possibilities of the visitors. Welch was fearfully punished in the second, third, fourth, and fifth innings. Corcoran was hit clean but three times. Chicago's batting prolonged play so that it was necessary to call the game at the end of the eighth inning on account of darkness."

Gore, Kelly, Anson, and Flint, who no one ever accused of being a batter, each made four hits in a 24-1 lark on September 9, knocking Troy's ace twirler Welch out of the box. The White Stockings had gone into the series three games behind the league-leading Grays and had expected to gain ground on them but they'd counted their chickens before they hatched. Radbourn and Ward had held the Blues to three runs in their three-games series in Cleveland and Providence had swept the Blues to stay three games up.

Before the game there was a long-distance throwing contest between Williamson and Troy's Fred Pfeffer. Kelly wagered $5 on Ned. Umpire Bradley measured the ground with a surveyor's tape he carried to check if the bases were positioned correctly. Pfeffer's best throw was 396 feet and 5 inches long. Williamson's was 397 feet.

"The drinks are on me tonight, boys," said Mike as Troy players handed him his winnings. "We're goin' to Paddy Ryan's new place."

154

After the game Kelly headed to Nicoll "the Great American Tailor" in the Lakeside Building on Clark street opposite the new Post-Office. It featured gentleman's furnishing goods that included fine all-wool suits for $20, gabardine ones for $12, skeleton flannel sack coats, neckwear, suspenders, handkerchiefs, and hosiery as well as fine linen and muslin shirts for a dollar.

The White Stockings and Grays began a crucial three-game series at the Lakefront Grounds on September 12.

"We can't lose today," Anson sententiously told his players as they warmed up later in their new uniforms with red trim.

"And why is that?" asked Mike.

"Because I've just got a telegram. It's a boy, ten pounds."

The others looked at one another. Finally Kelly raised his right arm. "We can't lose!"

Every play of the all-important match was watched with breathless intensity. Kelly made fine catches of difficult flies and drove in runs in the 3rd and the 8th. With one out in the 9th and Dalrymple on third and Kelly on first after a third safe hit Anson grabbed his big bat.

Kelly took a lead, hoping to coax a throw from Radbourn. Anson batted a swift ball that landed in George Wright's hands on the first bounce. Wright, who was fond of posing for effect, made a show of deliberately stepping on second. At the crack of the bat, Kelly had set sail for second. Wright had plenty of time to get lead-footed Anson at first.

Kelly ran at Wright like an express train and, just as he raised his arm to throw, Mike ran into him pell mell. Wright's throw sailed fifteen feet over Joe Start's head and into the seats. Dalrymple scored easily. Anson lumbered around the bases and scored the winning run. Harry Wright, the Troy manager, kicked and kicked about the interference on his brother but the umpire ruled that Kelly had the right to the basepath and allowed both runs to stand. The Chicago papers claimed Wright's bad throw was simply the result of his haste

in trying to complete the double play.

The next day's game was even closer. The Grays were certain they'd win. What they didn't know was that Kelly had stolen their signs. He made two hits in a 6-5 win that edged the Chicagos to within a game of Providence.

On the 14th Kelly served as captain and he ran the team excellently. Anson was in Philadelphia. Tragically, one of his children had died two days after his wife had given birth. Milt Scott, a local amateur, took Anson's place at first base. When he threw to Burns at second the ball got by Tom and rolled into left field. The runner went all the way to third. Kelly called time and waved Dalrymple and Hugh Nicol, who was playing right field, in for a chat.

"Tom should uv made the catch, but the runner shouldn't have made it to third. Have you not seen that when Silver throws to Anson I run in from right to back him up in case it gets by him? Abner, when you see a throw comin' from first to second you need ta get on your horse and be ready to back up the base. And Hugh, if there's a throw from third to second I want you to back up the bag. Do yas get me drift?" They nodded and returned to their positions.

Corcoran took care of the Grays, granting them just a half dozen hits. Kelly drove in two of his club's three runs in the sixth and the Chicagos won 6-2 to tie Providence for first in the race for the championship.

The Chicagos had trailed the Grays by three games on September 9. As they took the field against the Ruby Legs on Saturday the 16th after sweeping the three games from Providence and then three from the Troys they were a game ahead.

Richmond was in fine fettle and the White Stockings' trailed 1-0 when their turn to bat came in the sixth. Dalrymple went over to Spalding's box. Mike was puzzled. As captain he felt he should know what Abner was up to so he followed him over.

"Could you move down a couple of chairs, Mr. Spalding?" asked Abner.

"Move down a couple of chairs? Why would I do that?"

"That was the seat Harry Wright occupied during the games we had with his club. I made a lot of hits when he sat there."

Spalding shrugged and moved down.

Flint led off with a single but in trying for second was put out Stovey to Corey. Dalrymple went to the plate and nodded to Spalding. Then he smashed the ball to deep right for two bases and nodded to Spalding again.

Gore died on a foul bound to Richmond then Williamson hit a slow bounder down toward first base and by fast running and Richmond's fumble he made it safely to first. Dalrymple flew around third and scored. Williamson made second on Bushong's muff of Smith's throw. The side should have been a blank but Goldsmith's drive for three bases and Kelly's liner for two added another pair of runs and the Chicagos captured a convincing 5-1 victory. When the bulletin-board showed a defeat for Providence in Detroit the crowd uncorked their lungs and roared.

The Chicagos lost the first game of their series in Cleveland on Friday, September 22 by a score of 15-6. Mike, Abner, George, Silver, and newlywed Corcoran started that night at Mat Wolford's Tavern. A saloon called the Arch was a short stagger away on Prospect avenue. Orator Shafer, Jim McCormick, and Jack Glasscock were there celebrating their unexpected win. James waved his old friend and his drinking comrades over to their table.

"Larry's a newly-wed, he can only revel on road trips now," Mike explained.

"Well let's see that he does," said Shafer. He called over to the barkeep, "Another round, my good man."

"And keep 'em coming," added James.

Flint, Gore, and Dalrymple staggered back to the Weddell House around 1 a.m. Luckily, it was just around the corner. Mike and Larry stayed a lot longer.

The next morning two touts talked in hushed tones in the lobby of the Weddell House.

One of them, a tall man with a black beard, said to the other, a sleazy-looking character with a scar over his right eye, "Drunk as a lord, Kelly was."

"Was he alone?"

"No."

"Who was he with?"

"Corcoran."

"Corcoran?"

"Are you sure?"

"I am."

"Isn't it his turn to pitch?

"It is."

"We need to put together a big pool on the Blues to beat the Chicagos this afternoon."

The two touts met up after the game.

"Was Corcoran able to pitch?"

"He was."

"And?"

"He must have learned from Kelly how to drink all night and still play the next day."

"How's that, what did Corcoran do?"

"He cost us a bloody fortune is what he did. Son of a bitch threw a three-hit shutout."

The White Stockings played in Buffalo on Tuesday, the 26th. The day was a chilly one and winter wraps were in demand for all except the players.

"I'll bet the Bisons wish they had Buffalo robes," chuckled Kelly.

They eked by the Bisons 9-7 then the two teams took the just finished Nickel Plate Road, an extension of the New York, Chicago and St. Louis Railroad, to Chicago for the last three games of the season. The train was fully booked so the teams had to share a sleeping-car. Kelly and his teammates didn't mind, they knew that if they won just a single game and the Grays lost one they'd have their third consecutive pennant. An 11-5 win over the Bisons, their fifteenth in their last sixteen games, did the business.

The Greys matched the Chicagos over the last three weeks of the season. Providence won 15 of their last 16 games but they never made up the three games they'd lost in the Windy City in early September. They finished in second place, three games behind the White Stockings.

The White Stockings and the Cincinnati Red Stockings, champions of the American Association, agreed to face each other in a pair of exhibition games, the first time in major-league baseball that two pennant winners would meet.

The first of the historic games took place on October 6 at Cincinnati's Bank Street Grounds. Kelly didn't play. His usual spot in right field was taken by Corcoran. Mike was in Paterson marrying Agnus. He was happy that four of the men he'd played with would be attending the ceremony.

Blondie Purcell's Bisons had finished their season in Chicago and he and Mike had gone out on a toot while he was in town. The two headed for Paterson as soon as the Saturday, September 30 game ended. Ed Nolan and Buttercup Dickerson, who'd sat out the '82 season after stints in Troy and Worcester, were already there. They were three sheets to the wind when Mike and Blondie arrived. James McCormick was Mike's best man. His club had finished their season at home after placing sixth. James had won 36 games but they weren't enough to carry his Blues higher than fifth place. He envied Mike and his three straight championships.

"I hate to rain on your parade, but are you sure you want to do this?" James asked Mike when they got together with Blondie, Ed,

and Buttercup the night before the wedding. I mean Agnus is a fine lass and all, her folks and mine often get together and talk about the old country, but the two of yas aren't exactly what you'd call *lovey-dovey*."

"Agnus doesn't make me heart flutter and she's no ravin' beauty, but beauty doesn't boil the kettle. I'm not marryin' her on account uv romance, call it a marriage uv convenience. She's a fine and proper, church-goin' woman who doesn't want to be a spinster the rest uv her life and she'd like a man to take her to the opera. I'm a fun lovin' sod that needs a woman to cook a meal and darn me socks and organize the check book so I don't end up as poor as a bluddy church mouse."

Mike didn't stay with his new wife long. He headed out West for the nine-game exhibition series against the Providence club Spalding and the Grays' director had organized. Being under contract until the end of October he hadn't much choice and, as usual, he needed the money.

The Grays and White Stockings split the first eight games, which made for an exciting finale in delightful weather in Fort Wayne on October 24. Unfortunately for the enthusiastic audience of 600 the players, who just wanted the lengthy exhibition to be over, played in a "don't-care-a-cent" fashion.

After the game Mike and his teammates boarded the Nickel Plate Special and headed back to Chicago. When they arrived, Kelly headed for the homes of three handsome lady friends whose charms he'd badly missed these past few weeks.

10

"Depends how long the thing goes."

On November 14 a "combination team" put together by "Cut Off" Purcell boarded the City of Grenville for New Orleans. A number of games had been organized there and in other nearby towns. Newlywed Kelly and the other players would spend the winter in the South. Corcoran would pitch, Flint would catch, Purcell, Gore, and Foley of the Buffalos would play the outfield, and the infield would feature Brouthers at first base, Farrell at second, Williamson at third, and Kelly at shortstop. They wore a variety of colors, the battery dressed in white like priests of old at a sacrifice ceremony. The basemen wore gold and black striped shirts and caps. Kelly's clothes were made tight to show the exact molding of his fine figure and the Southern belles in attendance were suitably impressed, twirling their parasols and giggling to one another.

In December the White Stockings sold Joe Quest to the Wolverines. After leading the League in errors with Indianapolis in 1878 he'd done a complete turnabout and led the league's second basemen in fielding percentage in both 1880 and '81. Anson liked that Joe was not a drinker or a carouser but he'd always been a hole in the batting order. That's why he'd had to share second base with Burns in '82.

Quest's replacement was Fred Pfeffer. In 1879 he joined the semi-professional Louisville Eclipses, for whom he played the next three years, gaining a reputation for his fielding ability. During a 19-inning tie game with Akron on June 26, 1881 Pfeffer put out six runners and assisted 12 times, cutting off three men at home and a like number at third with his swift, accurate throws. He played for the Troys in '82 but when they disbanded in October Anson had

161

recruited him to play shortstop for the nine-game exhibition series. Anson liked what he saw and Fred was given a contract.

During his time with the White Stockings he'd be given the nickname "Dandelion" because he was death to dandelion burners and he'd become the most important component of Chicago's "stonewall infield." Chicago had a massive German population so Pfeffer's popularity was assured once he demonstrated his ability. He became affectionately known as "Unser Fritz." Years later Kelly would nostalgically say, "Pfeffer was the greatest second baseman of them all. All you had to do was throw the ball anywhere near the bag and he'd get it—high, wide, or on the ground. And what a man Fred was to make a return throw; why he could lay on his *stomach* and throw a hundred yards."

The White Stockings moved into their new home, Lake Front Park II. Its grand-stand was no rude succession of benches but was laid off into 2,000 numbered and separated spaces so a spectator could buy a reserved seat instead of just the right to sit on a bench. The seats had been painted, the cost a whopping $1,800 for the paint alone. Reporters were treated to procession velvet-carpeted boxes with cushioned chairs.

Overlooking the main entrance was an elaborately ornamented pagoda in which the First Cavalry Band would play the anthem and popular airs. Above the band-stand was a row of eighteen private boxes cozily draped to keep out the sun and wind and furnished with comfortable armchairs big enough for affluent and oversized derrieres. Spalding had his own roomy private box. It was equipped with a telephone so he could send orders to his team without leaving his seat. The players were not to utter profanity or spit tobacco juice on the infield grass and they were to have their shirts tucked in at all times - not just to appear neat and tidy - to show off their manager's uniforms to best effect. Spalding knew there was no better advertisement for the tight-fitting outfits than Michael J. Kelly, though he certainly wasn't paying him to wear them.

The services of 41 people were required for each home game: seven ushers, six "moonlighting" policemen, four gate-keepers, three

field men, three cushion renters, six refreshment boys, eight musicians, and four ticket takers. At other parks, players who weren't in the lineup were still acting in that capacity. Over the center field fence was a huge sign that read.

CHICAGO BASE BALL PARK
Home to the League Champions

———

1876 • 1880 • 1881 • 1882

The total expenses for the coming season were projected to be $60,000 so the club would need to average $625 at the gate for the 96 League games. Competition from the newly formed American Association had put pressure on the National League to find bigger markets. This spelled doom for Troy and created a spot for the New York Gothams. In 1882 the Trojans had finished in seventh place with continually dismal attendance, this in spite of a lineup that included Connor, Ewing, Welch, and another future 300 game winner, Tim Keefe. The entire Troy roster became free agents. Ewing, Connor, and Welch were pursued by every team in both the American Association and National League, but millionaire owner John B. Day was able to sign the big three. Day also signed Tim Keefe, but placed him on the American Association New York Mets which he also owned. Al Reach, a sporting goods magnate who'd been a star player in the National Association from 1871 to 1875, and John Rogers, a pompous attorney, were granted a National League franchise after the Worcester club quit the league in December.

The White Stockings travelled to Detroit at the end of April and checked into the Russell House. On his way though the enormous, high-ceilinged lobby he picked up a brochure from the front desk to learn more about the place and overheard the desk clerk tell a registering guest that Thomas Edison had worked at the hotel as a newsboy and candy butcher when he was young.

Kelly knew he'd be sharing a room with George Gore. Mike carried his bags for him, George was too sick to. Soon after they settled

in a physician visited their room and told George he was dangerous-ly ill with inflammation of the lungs and wouldn't be able to play for several days.

To take George's mind off his miserable condition Mike read the brochure out loud. George coughed, sneezed, and tried his best to sip the hot broth the doctor had ordered sent up to him.

"The offices, lobby, and reading rooms, which are fitted up in handsome style, are on the marble-tiled ground floor. The 225 guest chambers open into commodious halls and corridors and are reached by wide marble stairways and swift elevators. Electric lights, electrical enunciations, call bells, prompt and efficient service, and superior tonsorial and bathing establishments assist in rendering the Russell House one of the most comfortable, convenient, and desir-able stopping places for tourists seeking immunity from monotony and its incident cares."

He paused. "Listen to this, George, you aren't gonna smell like a mule anymore. Thirty additional bath rooms have recently been added as well as gentlemen's public and private toilet rooms exqui-sitely furnished in Italian marble."

Kelly was still reading the brochure at breakfast the next morning. "The breakfast room has been remodeled and wainscoted in Spanish mahogany ornamented with elegant chiseled stone and tile," he told Williamson.

"That's grand, Kel," chuckled Ned. "I can hardly get down my sau-sage and eggs unless I'm surrounded by Spanish mahogany orna-mented with elegant chiseled stone and tile."

"Wait, there's more. The appointments and fixtures are of the most modern description and conform to the essentials of cultivated tastes … as are found among the likes of us refined base ballists," he added. "Say what you will about Spalding, he does put us up in might fancy places."

"And here's something for Anson. A splendidly appointed billiard parlor affords a pleasing recreation to the lovers of the captivating sport."

"Good. Maybe he'll be too busy to notice what time we come in."

The Chicagos started the defense of their third consecutive championship at Recreation Park on May Day. *The Free Press* described the festivities. "The capricious weather of the past month smiled upon the ball tossers. By 2 o'clock there was quite a crowd around the ticket office and when the gates opened an hour later there was a squeeze and the turnstile clicked merrily. At 3 p.m. the gates were thrown open and the champions came onto the grounds. They were greeted with a hearty round of applause and began practicing immediately.

It was evident that the rumor that had been circulated to the effect that the Chicagos had done little during the spring to prepare for the season and were not in condition was without foundation. They looked as fit as fiddles and ran and threw the ball around spritely as if they'd played their last championship game the day before and hadn't missed a beat. Fifteen minutes later the Detroiters came through the gate attired in their neat white uniforms and were received as cordially as the visitors had been.

Joe Quest, the new Detroit captain, came out for the spin of the coin.

"No hard feelings," said Anson.

"Fuck off and spin the damn coin," said Quest. "I call heads."

Anson spun the half-dollar and it landed head up.

"You and your friends can go to the bat first. Wait, they all hate your guts."

Anson clenched his fist and the umpire stepped between the two. "That'll do, Quest. Get your men on the field."

Dalrymple was made out at first and Gore, still coughing but somewhat recovered, went up to bat. Stump Weldman gave him his base on balls. It was an act of generosity he should not often repeat as this season they'd be considered errors. Kelly got his bat from the Chicagos' new mascot, a pleasant dark-skinned lad named Clarence Duval whom Anson called a "little coon" and a "no account nigger."

"Thanks, Clarence," said Mike, "yer a good lad."

Kel hit the first pitch down the third base line. When he got to first he looked across the diamond at Gore. He looked as though he might die. Williamson pounded the air three times. Anson grounded to second. Quest scooped up the ball, smirked at Anson and threw him out.

Gore somehow managed to make it through one more inning. Thankfully, he hadn't needed to bat again. The game was delayed fully fifteen minutes while Corcoran arrayed himself in 19-year-old Dick Burns' Detroit uniform. It was the only one that wasn't too big.

The Detroits led 3-2 after six and the spectators began to imagine they saw a victory in the offing, but the seventh inning put an end to any such hopes. Goldsmith and Pfeffer hit past second for singles and Dalrymple hit the smudged ball down the left field line to fill the bases. Corcoran hit down the left foul line bringing in Goldsmith and leaving the bases still full.

"Bring us in, Kel," yelled Fred from third.

Kelly winked at some girls in the front row of the grand-stand he'd noticed ogling him. They blushed and hid behind prim-rose-yellow fans.

"That I shall, Goldie," yelled Kelly. "Hop on yer horse and get ready ta go."

Kelly spanked the ball over Hanlon's head and capered around to third. He could see the girls clapping madly away.

"That damned Kelly. He kills us every damn time," groaned a man in a fashionable plug hat. He looked at the ladies around him and apologized for the profanity.

Williamson popped a little one to right field and as soon as it landed in Mansell's hands Kelly was off. The Chicagos won 7-4 but Gore's illness left them with not a man to spare.

Kelly liked Detroit. There was plenty to do of an evening and scores of places to drink. He supposed it helped that the mayor was in the wholesale liquor trade. If the gang wanted to go somewhere that was upscale they went to Churchill's on State street or drank imported beer and ate frog legs and soft-shelled crabs from the East Coast at Thomas Swain's Saloon. William Buesser's saloon on Miami Avenue had fine liquor and cigars and ball pool tables as well. Sharpe's Chop House on Jefferson was a favorite of sports enthusiasts, gamblers, and newspapermen. George Gris' beer hall sold 5-cent cigars from Soper's and 1- cent ones from the Royal Banner and featured "entertainment for men", comely and partially clad young women.

The Penobscot welcomed ladies and was where Mike and his gang headed on nights when the temperature refused to fall below eighty degrees. It had washed air blown over a ton of ice by huge fans. Gate's Oyster House had the best seafood in town. William Dolph served the best beer, but not on Sundays. His place was in the theatre district. Pfeffer liked going there because the sign on the window read Pfeffer's *Famous* BEER.

Dolph's lovely "restaurant girls" delighted in seductively blowing the foam off the top of overflowing beer steins, but Dolph insisted that his customers behave like gentlemen, which was fine with Kelly and he didn't mind if some beer foam landed in his mustache, especially if some also landed in the cleavage of the restaurant girl doing the blowing.

After escorting the daughter of a Wolverines' shareholder to one of the theatres on Woodward Avenue Mike took her to Ardussi Garibaldi's for a late-night supper of stuffed peppers, Chianti, and spaghetti. He liked to get Ardussi to mix his specialty, a Tom & Jerrys, a rum-based eggnog. The girl had one too many and forgot herself.

When Gore and Kelly breakfasted the next morning a well-dressed middle-aged couple and their attractive daughter sat at the next table. Kelly happened to be looking up in hopes of getting the waiter's attention when he heard a smash and was stunned to see a baseball zooming straight toward the three. He leapt up, dove in front of them, and snatched the ball out of the air.

"Good God!" gasped the osseous gentleman. "One of us might have been killed."

A waiter scurried over. "Thank heavens you were here, Mr. Kelly.

I'm afraid this is not the first time that has happened. An amateur team that calls themselves the Early Risers practices in a field beside the hotel. Several errant balls have smashed through our windows."

"How can we repay you for your gallantry?" asked the still startled gentleman.

Kelly looked at the man's daughter, who wore a yellow summer dress. Curls of light brown hair cascaded along the sides of her beautiful face. "You could introduce me ta your lovely daughter."

The girl didn't wait for her father. She set down her napkin and said, "I'm Penelope. Could I know your name, sir?"

"Michael Kelly," said Kel, taking the girl's hand and bowing slightly. "I play base ball … in the Chicago club."

"Perhaps we should go to see Mr. Kelly play," suggested Penelope's mother, who hadn't taken her eyes off Mike. "If he's this skilled in a breakfast room, imagine how he must be on a base ball diamond."

"Three o'clock," said Mike. "That's when we take on the Detroits. I'll make sure they set a box aside for you." He bowed again, gave Penelope a long look, and returned to his table.

"How do you do it?" asked George.

"What?"

"Meet beautiful women everywhere we go."

"I don't know. Just seems ta happen."

"It happens more to you in a week than it does to me in a year."

Mike was glad to see Penelope and her parents in the box he'd asked the Wolverines' manager to arrange. See had a refreshment boy deliver a note to him. When Mike read it he knew that between Penelope and the shareholder's daughter—and they'd be a *fine pair* to be in between—he was going to enjoy coming to Detroit even more from now on.

The White Stockings swept the Wolverines and the two teams travelled to Chicago for the White Stockings' home opener on May 5. Mike and Anson hoisted the *1882 Championship* flag before the

game but their club lost a close one, 3-2. After the game "certain mischievous parties" threw cushions at the umpire and two of the men were arrested. Spalding said other arrests for such atrocities would follow.

"Christ almighty," Mike told Abner, "they was only *pillows*. Lucky they weren't stones. Spalding woulduv asked for the death penalty!"

The new Philadelphia team came to Lake Front Park II for the first time on May 11 and were defeated, though the Chicago victory was hardly one to crow over. Of the nine runs made by the home side only two were earned. Kelly put in a clean hit and scored on Anson's blow in the fifth and Mike's rattling three-baser sent Dalrymple home in the sixth. Anson made four errors that led to three runs by the Quakers as the Philadelphias had been dubbed.

Kelly belted a home run and threw out two runners from right field in the Chicagos' 5-1 win the next day. *The Minneapolis Star Tribune* said, "Gore and Kelly are great throwers and it takes the swiftest of runners to make a base when the ball is in the hands of either one."

On the 15th the New York Gothams came to town. A critically important piece to their success had been added. John Montgomery Ward had won 47 games as a 19-year-old right-hander for the '79 Providence Grays. At the age of 22, the age by which pitchers were often already burned out, Ward was an afterthought. Fearing he would never regain his old form, the Grays sold Ward to the Gothams. Before long he'd be their captain and have his law degree as well.

The White Stockings commenced the three-game series with a close shave, an 8-7 win they nearly lost by poor fielding. Williamson, Flint, and Pfeffer each made two errors. Burns had three. Surprisingly, Dalrymple had none. So far Abner had made more errors than put-outs. Kelly belted two three-baggers and threw out three of the New Yorkers.

In a 15-2 clubbing of the "nickel-plate nine" on Friday, May 17 the Chicagos batted Welch at will and fielded flawlessly while the New Yorks could do nothing with Corcoran and went all to pieces

in the field. Kelly drove in Dalrymple in the first inning and Gore in the third. He changed places with Flint in the seventh and in the ninth one of Corcoran's swift deliveries struck him in the knee cap. The resounding crack could be heard up in the luxury boxes. Several women gasped. Kel "wriggled around about ten square feet of grass" and the ladies were treated to some top-quality cussing.

The May 23 game between the Bostons and Chicagos was "decidedly off color in point of science" according to *The Inter-Ocean*, but "those who admire batting and base-running were doubtless well surfeited." Sullivan filled the vacancy caused by the compulsory retirement of Odlin. William L. "Billy" Harris of *The Boston Globe* opined that Sullivan displayed "lamentable ignorance of the game. He not only gave bad decisions but also abused one of the spectators who happened to express his opinion on the right and wrong of the matter. Umpires are not hired or paid for the purpose of paying attention to remarks made by spectators however uncomplimentary they may be. He knows or ought to know that he is guaranteed protection from bodily harm and should not heed the talk of outsiders."

The Bostons won the toss of the cent. Anson called tails and lost.

Kelly groaned and turned to Ned.

"That's eight in a row, maybe he should let one uv us call it."

John Morrill, the Boston's captain, sent the Chicagos up to bat. Gore made a baser and reached second on Hackett's overthrow. Kelly smacked a ball through the infield and Anson followed with a drive to the outfield that scored both runners.

In the second Goldsmith secured a base hit, Flint got his base on play, and Pfeffer's single brought Goldsmith home. Gore hit for two bags to score Flint and Pfeffer and Kelly drove a hot one north for three bases letting Gore stroll home. Mike made another hit and scored another run in the eighth as the Chicagos clobbered the Bostons 19-8 to maintain their 1½ game lead.

In a 9-5 loss to Providence the next day Burns got a ball in his right eye in the preliminary practice. For reasons known only to him, Anson put Kelly at second base, Pfeffer at shortstop, and called

Fred Goldsmith down from the audience to play right field. *The Tribune* pulled no punches. "Kelly's play at second was about as bad an exhibition as has been seen at that place this season." *The Inter-Ocean* man, who considered the Chicagos' red and black stripe shirts, white pants and caps very neat and tasteful, was a little kinder but not much. "Kelly took the medallion for expensive misplay by making four errors."

In the seventh inning the White Stockings had runners at second and third with none out, but Radbourn struck out Goldsmith and Corcoran and Flint followed suit and the champions were rewarded with a cipher. Then the umpire, Mr. Furlong, who hails from Kansas City, made an incorrect decision at first. Anson put out Hines with time to spare but Furlong, who remained behind the plate, could not have been more mistaken if he had been seventeen Furlongs from Chicago. The crowd hissed the umpire but ex-Umpire Odlin of Lancaster, who sat in the reporters' box, applauded the decision by vigorous hand-clapping. It was not a graceful thing for young Mr. Odlin to do under the circumstances as it indicated that his recent removal had left him with a wire-edge on."

The White Stockings travelled to Philadelphia on the 30th and when they arrived they checked into the Continental Hotel on Chestnut street. It was notable for its technologies: gas lighting, central heating, air ventilation, and interior plumbing as well as bell wires and speaking tubes, a passenger elevator, and laundry service. The players, who were glad Anson and his wife Victoria were staying at her parents' house, delighted in calling one another's rooms on the speaking tubes pretending to be bill collectors or proprietors of establishments where friendly ladies could be visited on an hourly basis.

The hotel's management told the players while they were perfectly welcome to eat in the main dining room they might be 'more comfortable' in the Gentlemen's Café. They said thanks but no thanks and went to the Washington Hotel's kitchen, where they dined on delicious terrapin soup, quail, mutton chops, and oyster pies. After dinner they headed to McGillin's Olde Ale House on Drury street,

then finished the night at Finelli's.

The Chicagos had a rare Wednesday double header the next day. Clad in their smart new blue flannel shirts and high white hats they clobbered Quaker twirler John Coleman 15-8 and 22-4. He'd lead the league in '83 by running up 48 losses and surrendering 772 hits, 291 earned runs, and a whopping seventeen home runs. Kelly took over behind the bat in the first inning of the morning game after Flint hurt his finger. He ran the bases "with alacrity and daring" and scored three runs. His hand was hurt in the third inning of the second game but the injury didn't affect his stick-work, he had three hits and scored four of his team's runs for a total of seven on the day.

During the trip Fred Pfeffer failed to appear at the hotel three nights in a row. Kelly was pretty sure he was spending his time at Bube's German Brewery on North Market street and may have found a frisky fräulein to cavort with. Each day he was told how much he was fined - it was doubled each time - and each morning that amount was found in a sealed envelope at the hotel's front desk.

The Pale Hose moved into first place by beating the Quakers 4-3 on Thursday and swept the series with a more convincing 10-1 win on Friday. When the team left town the hotel manager gave Pfeffer's envelopes to Anson. He was puzzled. "I never *did* see the man," the manager told Anson.

Feeling good about themselves after sweeping the Philadelphias the players made their way to the Broad street station and hopped aboard a Pennsylvania Railway train for New York. Around one in the morning Kelly, Flint, Gore, and Dalrymple played a game of what they called "freight train base ball" on top of the cars, pausing frequently to take pulls from the pair of whiskey bottles they'd appropriated from the bar car. They played until all of the balls they'd brought had disappeared over the sides into the pitch darkness. Then they shrugged and headed off to their berths.

The team was booked into the Windsor Hotel in New York. It occupied an entire block along Fifth avenue from 46th to 47th street. Though it featured a bath-room in each of its 139 suites critics said

it was too far uptown to succeed. But the proprietor, Gothams' own-er John Daly, was banking on visitors coming to and from the new Grand Central Terminal stopping in. For now, he was letting the oth-er National League teams stay there - on different floors than the high paying guests - at a discount. He told the lounge's barkeeps to keep them drinking as late into the night as they could. After check-ing in the players headed off to see the latest wonder of the world, the just completed Brooklyn Bridge. Though it was not a wonder of the world, back home Chicago's El had just opened to traffic.

Mike was excited to be in America's biggest, busiest city. He hadn't been in New York since he went there to pick up newspapers and back then he hadn't seen anything but the receiving dock at the train station in the middle of the night.

Grounds waiters in striped shirts went along the grand-stand and bleaching boards calling out, "I gawt score cards, ham sandwiches, 'n cold beer here" in thick Brooklyn accents. After winning their first game in the Big Apple the Chicagos lost the next three by a combined score of 36 to 13 - they'd been indulging exhaustingly in New York's late-night entertainments. On the train ride to Providence Anson was livid. His mood didn't improve when his club lost the first game in Providence 10-2, Kelly being the only Chicago player to muster more than one hit against Radbourn. The loss dropped the White Stockings into second place.

Providence manager Harry Wright put Lee Richmond up against the White Stockings on Saturday, June 9. After losing 33 games in '82, Richmond was mostly an outfielder now. Although seven of the runs he allowed were scored when the side should have been put out, Richmond lost 11-0. The Grays tried Charlie Sweeney between the points on Monday and he proved a treasure, prevailing by a score of 6 to 2 and the Chicagos fell to third place. Radbourn pitched a tidy game on Tuesday, downing the westerners 8-1. The White Stockings managed only four hits - one of those a scratch - and they fielded like clumsy children.

In the June 14, 16, and 17 games in Boston Kelly was as conspic-uous and far-fetched in his conduct as ever, shouting and bawling

at the top of his voice to disconcert the Beaneaters as the Bostons were now being called. Kelly played effortlessly at short with gilt-edge pick-ups and sensational throws, but he went 1-for-5, 1-for-7, and 1-for-5 again. It was his worse series ever with the willow so he set fire to his plunket-driving bat at the end of it.

The Boston Globe expressed the view that every club should have a player ready in uniform to take the place of another in case of an accident. It groused that Boston audiences had twice been kept waiting through a team's failure to have a substitute ready. "The reserve player also should be where the field captain will not be obliged to hunt him up."

Rumors were circulating about the evening activities of the Chicago players while they were in the Hub. They were said to have spent much of their free time in the Crawford House in Scollay Square in the company of female entertainers. Corcoran was mortified that his young wife might get wind of it.

The champions met an ignominious defeat in the first game in Buffalo. After four days off Corcoran should have been well rested, but the Bisons did work with the stick in the third and fourth that made him very tired indeed. *The Tribune* lamented the depths to which the Chicagos had fallen. In its "Fly-Tip" section the lead items read:

"To the Chicago Club: Return and all will be forgotten.

It is a pity the grounds at Buffalo were not too wet for play yesterday.

One hit, with a total of one base! That was the record made by the champions yesterday.

For the choicest selection of goose-eggs contributed this season see the score in the game yesterday.

The severest drubbing ever administered by one League team over another was the beating of the Chicagos by the Buffalo Club yesterday."

The players wore their zebra Spalding shirts the next day but were no match for Galvin, who pitched a game scarcely second to that of the day before. The result: Buffalo 6, Chicago 2. The White Stockings

now sat six games out of first.

They finished the road trip that had started out so promisingly and turned disastrous in Cleveland. Before the series opener on Saturday *The Cleveland Voice* warned that "the bulldozing players of the Chicago nine must be on their best behavior. A Cleveland audience would despise one of their players if he should intentionally run into a member of their club and they will brook no such action. This is official and don't you forget it." Kelly had a good laugh at that idle threat.

Throughout the game a crank from the Blackberriwyne Row gang with a bowler perched precariously on his head called out to Kelly on the bench.

A harsh-tongued shrew wearing a leghorn hat bent into an outlandish shape bellowed something about how well Kelly's uniform fit him.

"That's quite the quail pipe on that one," said Abner.

"Hey, Kelly, do *you* ever drink during a game?" yelled a crank who was a few sheets to the wind.

Mike exhaled a puff of smoke, tossed his cigarette to the ground, stomped out the butt, then answered over his shoulder as he went to get his bat.

"Depends how long the thing goes."

Kelly, Gore, Goldsmith, Pfeffer, Billy Sunday, and James McCormick went to LS&F Burgess Grocers after dinner at the Burgess Grand Café that night. They found the dining room of the Weddell House a tad stuffy on a Saturday night. The Chicago men were puzzled but McCormick knew that the grocery housed a tavern. After several rounds Gore said, "Let's go find some dirty puzzles, boys."

"Your tallywags aching again, George?" chuckled Mike.

All of them missed curfew - by several hours - but there was no game the next day.

The carousers were, however, fined $70 by Anson for taking a trip to Haltnorth's beer-gardens Sunday night and having "a little time".

Kelly and Williamson went to the Glenville Track on Monday. Kelly won big on Maud S., who railroad tycoon William H. Vanderbilt had bought for $20,000.

The Chicagos finally stopped the bleeding on the 26th with a 3-0 win but it was hardly one to savor, all of their runs were unearned. Kelly made two safe hits off James McCormick but he muffed a fly in right and later got thrown out at the plate.

The Buffalo men appeared in their dirty, drab gray uniforms at Lake Front Park on the third of July. The Chicagos, who'd won the first three games of their mid-season homestand and now trailed Providence by four and a half, were in their Spalding zebra-striped outfits again, Mike's cleaner than all the others as usual which greatly pleased Spalding. The White Stockings annihilated the Bisons by a count of 31-7. George Derby, the Buffalo pitcher, was given his release the next day. According to *The Trib* man, "When a Gatling gun can be made out of a stovepipe a pitcher might be made out of George Derby. He was safely hit 32 times for a grand total of fifty bases.

Kelly, Anson, Gore, and Dalrymple ran until they dropped from sheer exhaustion. It was only the torrid temperature that kept the Chicago track team from scoring somewhere in the neighborhood of fifty to a hundred runs. Kelly had eight of the Chicagos' sixty-seven at bats, making three singles, a two-baser, and a three-baser that loosened the cover of the weary ball. Derby was warmly congratulated at the end of the game. The rumor is he is to remain in Chicago and will pitch for the cash-boys, the rumor that he will pitch in a millinery house is denied."

Six thousand persons witnessed the game with the Clevelands on the Fourth of July. Eleven men were put in uniform by the home team. Goldsmith had a fingernail knocked off in the fifth inning by a ball from Dunlap's bat. Corcoran was called in and soon after Flint was disabled. Kelly went behind the bat and as soon as Sunday could put on a uniform he was relieved in right field by Flint. Of course Sunday did nothing at the bat, nor did Kelly, though his work behind it was beyond all praise in the 10-6 loss. Even though his left hand

was in a disabled condition he drove in Gore with a robust baser in the afternoon game played in scorching heat, a 5-1 Chicago win. The umpire was sweating so profusely Mike took pity on him and gave him his fan.

Kelly made the best catch of the day in the ninth. A crank in the stands above right field called to him.

"It looks as though you could use a beer, Kel." He stretched out his hand. It held a tall glass of beer.

"Aye, that I could," said Mike, going to the fence, taking the glass, and nodding thanks.

He walked back to his position and took a big slug of the beer.

Crack!

The ball came whizzing toward him. He reached up with his free hand, made the catch, and threw the ball in to Burns. He held his beer up for the crowd to see. "Didn't spill a drop," he yelled for their amusement.

The July 8 issue of *The Tribune* left no doubt in its readers' minds how its base ball man and sports editor felt about a certain official. "Only upon the theory that league umpire G.W. Burnham is a pool-room shark can his action in the Chicago-Cleveland games of Friday and yesterday be accounted for. When Gore's body was squarely across the home-plate Briody touched him with the ball. Burnham declared Gore out and the run thus stolen from the home club by the pool-room shard gave the visitors the game."

A lovely young girl walked along the sidewalk toward Kelly and Dalrymple as they headed for breakfast the next morning. She had long, ash blonde hair put up in a pompadour style, the waves starting at her forehead and running up and down the back of her neck. She wore a skirt composed of plaited flounces of pink sateen peeping out through other ruffles of oriental lace and a small Tuscan braid bonnet trimmed with two curled ostrich tips. Her shoes were the very latest style of button gaiters.

A woman was meticulously tending her garden nearby.

"Did you ever do any gardening, Kel? asked Abner.

"I sewed a few wild oats when I was young."

The girl looked at Mike and smiled, then she dropped her hand-kerchief. It was no accident. Mike picked it up and handed it to her.

She looked into his eyes and said, "Why thank you, you are very kind," she said. "Aren't you, Michael Kelly, the base ball player?"

"That I am," said Mike. "And this is my teammate and boon companion Abner Dalrymple."

The girl looked at Abner for a beat and returned her gaze to Kelly.

She handed Mike something. It was a piece of stationary. Mike looked at it. A few words were carefully printed on it. Mike read them. "One forty-five North Rush Street."

"My father has built a rather grand new home there. There are several rooms where you and I could share a cup of tea ... or a mint julep if that would be more to your liking."

"I believe that would be fine, or a glass of your father's oldest whiskey perhaps," said Mike.

"Irish or Scotch?" she asked.

"Either would serve, Miss. Can I know your name then?"

"It's Abigail. A pleasure to meet you Mr. Dalrymple. I look forward to seeing you soon, Michael."

"We have a day off next week. Monday."

"Some time around three then?" suggested Abigail, a sparkle in her eyes.

"Three it is," said Mike, stuffing the piece of paper into his watch fob pocket.

"Until Monday then," said Abigail as she strode away.

Abner stared at the beauty as she left them, then turned to Mike. "What is it about you that mashes all the girls? The rest of us have to search high and low for women and they stop you in the street."

"It's me wavy hair and winnin' ways," Mike answered breezily. "Now let's track down some breakfast, I'm starved."

He took out his watch, dropping Abigail's address on the sidewalk. He picked it up and grinned. "I wouldn't be wantin' ta lose *that*," he said, putting the paper in his vest pocket.

On Monday afternoon he was definitely glad that he hadn't lost the paper. Abigail offered him more than fine whiskey.

On July 17 *The Boston Globe* advised that: "The Beaneaters, who were shut out today by the Chicagos, would do well to think twice before trying to take an extra base on Kelly's arm. He threw out four of them from the right field today."

Anson made a mistake when he made out the lineup for the July 26 game. He put light-hitting Flint in the third slot and Kelly ninth. It worked, Silver surprised with four runs and five hits that would help boost his season average to .265. He'd bat just .204, .209, and .202 the next three years. He would have felt a lot prouder if he'd pounded so many hits off a hurler other than 20-year-old Art Hagan who'd finish his rookie season with a sparkling 1-14 record. The Chicagos banged out two dozen hits on their way to a 17-5 trouncing of the Quakers. Kelly had two of them, one a three-baser in the ninth, and he made two fine running catches in right field, a one-handed one near the fence, the other a two-hander on the foul line.

After the game *The Inter-Ocean* scribe stopped Anson on his way to the dressing-room. He said, "That was quite a game your man Kelly played in right field today, Cap."

"It was. You know, Kelly makes more errors than a lot of men that play the outfield but you couldn't ask for a better man to play right field."

"Not even Orator Shafer?"

"Not even Shafer. I know you haven't been going to ball games all that long but right field is different."

"How's that?"

"The easiest and simplest thing for an outfielder to do is judge and

catch a flyball hit straight to him. But a large portion of the hits to right field are sent there by right handed batsmen and they're generally curving toward the foul line. They're harder to judge and even if they're judged correctly they're damn difficult to hold as such balls have a way of gettin' through a fielder's hands. Since the right fielder's the only one who has a chance to throw a runner out at first he needs to play closer to the infield and must run back for more fly balls than the other two men. Kelly makes a specialty of retiring batsmen out at first base. He is one great thrower. It takes a mighty swift runner to make a base when the ball's in *his* hands."

On August 4th *The Tribune* predicted that the Chicago Club could still bring the pennant again to Chicago. "The team has outplayed the crack nines of the country in every respect. Daily may tell funny stories in the Clevelands and Whitney in the Bostons may pound the hands off a brace of catchers but Flint, Corcoran, Goldsmith, and Kelly turn up every time as able-bodied men."

Summer beer gardens were popular on the largely German North Side of Chicago. They included Belmont Grove, Rainbow Gardens, Brands Park, and Scheiner's Grove among others. They were festive places that offered respite from the summer heat. On an off day between wins over the Gothams, Kelly and the other White Stockings rabble-rousers headed to Brands Garden. Fred Pfeffer spoke German, which helped. Brands was a cheery place, it had lively polka music, good food, a merry-go-round, and an endless supply of locally brewed lagers.

"Ein Bier für einfach von uns bitte hübsche Mädchen," Pfeffer said to the buxom fräulein who came over as he and Mike and Abner sat down at a table with a red-white check tablecloth.

The girl smiled at Fred and then turned to take in Kelly. "I vill be right back vith them," she said.

"You'd better hope a foul ball in the face doesn't ruin those good looks of yours or knock out one of those straight white teeth," chuckled Abner.

Fred saw Mike watching the fräulein fill three steins from a beer

tap. She was looking straight at him and the suds were spilling over the rims.

"Lookin' to munch on those dumplings, Kel?" asked Fred.

"Something like that, Fred. A fellow's got to keep up his strength."

"Keep in practice, don't you mean, Kel?" asked Dalrymple.

"That too."

When the fräulein brought the beers she leaned over in front of Mike so he could take in the scenery. "I live around za corner, number vun hundred and six. I'm done at twelve." She touched his shoulder. "Vy don't you join me for a midnight snack?"

Kelly went to answer but he was distracted. Dalrymple had fallen off the merry-go-round after a few too many steins.

Heavyweight champ John L. Sullivan, the "Boston Strong Boy", umpired the August 9 game in Boston. He attended many of the Beaneaters' games. Many a time he shook his head after an umpire made a bad call and mumbled, "I could do better than *that* duffer."

Three weeks ago he'd pummeled Charlie Mitchell and knocked him repeatedly out of the ring at Madison Square Garden. The police had put a stop to the fight after four rounds. Not surprisingly, not a single one of Sullivan's calls occasioned as much as a murmur. When a poor ball was called a strike, a circumstance that would usually have been the cause of lively kicking, the victim looked at the champ timidly and appealingly like a lamb led out for the slaughter.

The Chicagos played an exhibition game in Toledo the next day. *The Daily Blade* called Moses Fleetwood Walker, the mulatto catcher of the Toledo club and a law student at Ann Arbor University, "a gentleman on and off the ball field entirely lacking in bummer instincts. Walker, who by the way is a gentleman and a scholar in the literal sense, was the source of contention between the home club and the Chicagos, whose arrival caused a sensation at the Union depot yesterday. They wore white ties and dark blue uniforms and were under the command of the swelled baby from Marshalltown. Shortly after his arrival he informed the managing director of the local club that

he objected to the Toledo nine playing Walker.

The director grumbled, "The New Yorks, the Metropolitans, the Buckeyes, and the St. Louis club have had no problem playing against Walker and nothing untoward transpired when they did."

The Toledos hadn't intended to play Walker on account of his having a sore hand but they decided to put him in the lineup in right field after Anson's gesticulations. When the Chicagos arrived at the grounds and the beefy captain saw Walker warming up he exclaimed, "We ain't playin ball with no damned nigger!"

Anson was informed that he could play his team against Walker or go home. After considering the cost of the train tickets to transport his club to Toledo and the loss of his share of the gate Anson reluctantly conceded to play the game under protest but stormed, "We'll play this here game, but we won't play never no more with the nigger in!"

Mike approached O'Day, the Toledos' first baseman. "Just so you know, I got no problem playin' with Fleetwood in your nine. "I hear he's a grand player. Anse is still stuck in the Fifties."

The White Stockings boarded a steamboat and crossed Lake Erie for a series in Buffalo. As they headed to the ball grounds they saw that horse-drawn carriages were being replaced by cars powered by storage batteries. Mike liked Buffalo, the city's saloon owners openly flouted the law by selling alcoholic beverages on Sunday. The Chicagos downed the Bisons 4-2 on Saturday, spent Sunday in McBride's Pub on Chicago street, and whipped the Buffalos 14-8 on Monday.

The Bisons, who'd been delayed 40 minutes by an accident on the road, won the toss and elected to go first to the bat. They faced the Sphinx-like Corcoran. O'Rourke and his men had on their batting clothes, they swung their ash sticks for keeps, retiring with four runs in their favor. Larry got his knickers in a twist and started kicking at the umpire like a buck-eyed Texan steer but got no satisfaction. He took his revenge on Flint, causing him to hop around like a man with St. Vitas dance. Silver let one ball go by and two more Buffalos stampeded across the plate.

Cushman, a 31-year-old Ohioan with a hair-brush for a mustache, was in the pitching box for Buffalo. Dalrymple was back at the top of the batting list. With Derby pitching the day before, Abner had been dropped to the bottom because of his utter inability to judge left-handed twirlers. Cushman sent three white-stockings to first on balls and they got around on five Buffalo errors. The Bisons closed their half of the fourth with five runs for a total of fifteen to the visitors' ten. O'Rourke decided there were enough bees in the butter and it was time to relieve the wild ex-railway conductor and try his own arm in the box. He surrendered another seven tallies but he and his mates tacked on another nine of their own.

The Buffalo Commercial reported that on Tuesday "the Chicagos faced Cushman, who swung his arms like a wind-mill in a gale. He was as wild as a March hare, sending three visitors to base on called balls and they got around on five errors. Three runs without a hit were rich pickings.

Umpire Lane called the game on account of it being too dark for fielding at 7:10. Everybody pronounced it the most exciting game ever played in Buffalo."

"Praise the Lord," the weary scorekeeper said to the reporter beside him. The final register was 19 runs, 27 hits, and 22 errors for the Bisons. The Chicagos managed a mere 17 runs.

The White Stockings lost their last three games in Buffalo, partly as a result of frequent consumption of the city's Bowker's birch beer, then lost four of five in Cleveland. By the 21st they'd fallen back to six games out of first. Anson ordered each and every one of the players to be in their rooms by 8 p.m. and to stay there. He'd told them to avoid spirits or else, but he knew they were working behind his back. Just after ten o'clock Anson was playing billiards in the hotel's games room, which provided a clear view of the elevator and stairs and he kept checking to make sure no players made use of either. He happened to look out the window and see something white shoot by. He set down his cue stick, stuck his head out the window and looked up. He saw Dalrymple pulling as hard he could on a rope. On the other end of it was a large water pitcher.

"You rotten fly flushers!" he yelled.

His players had bribed a bell-boy to fill the jug with beer every half hour and they were going to keep it up until their arms were too tired to pull anymore.

Kelly was embarrassed on August 29. He was the only one of the Chicagos that didn't make a hit in their 7-0 shutout of Cleveland. William Harris, *The Boston Globe* man, wrote that "the number of players who go in for playing for their side is very small, most are record-hunters or sluggers who try to slam the ball as if they want to send it over the fence every time. This is miscalled batting. There are few instances of men who make sacrifice-hitting a study. It is more difficult to advance men on bases than to strike safely, the latter generally a matter of luck in landing the ball where there is no one to catch it. With the skilled pitchers in play today 'duffer batting' as the slashing style can aptly be termed is almost wholly useless and it is strange that veteran players persist in it."

At the end of their last home stand of the season the Chicagos swept Buffalo by scores of 3-1, 4-1, and 18-14, beat Cleveland 7-0, 9-1, and 21-7, then swept Detroit by scores of 13-1, 14-1, 26-6, and 12-8 to pull one and half games ahead of Boston.

The White Stockings rode roughshod over the Clevelands and Detroits from August 20 to September 8 by scores of 9-1, 21-7, 13-1, 14-1, 26-6, and 12-8. The 26-6 win included a streak of hitting unparalleled in a League game, 28 at bats, eighteen clean hits, 29 total bases, and eighteen runs in one inning! Kelly made three safe hits and scored three times. After the closer on Saturday the Chicagos went out to celebrate their eleventh straight win, their train didn't leave until noon and they were in first place.

When they arrived in Boston on September 10 they learned that the Triumvir, the Red Stockings three principal stock-holders, had promised each of the Beaneaters $200 and a new suit of clothes if they won the pennant. One of Kelly's legs was torn open when he slid into second in the fifth inning of the Monday game. "Black Jack" Burdock, the Boston second baseman, kept sharp stones in his pock-

ets and when he suspected an opponent was going to be sliding into his base he sprinkled them on the base path.

"Ya rotten cheat!" Kelly yelled at Burdock as he watched the blood ooze from his fresh wound.

"No idea what you're talking about, Kelly," said Burdock.

"Those damn stones, you liar," retorted Mike.

"Stones? Couldn't tell ya how those might uv got there. But I'll be sure to tell the groundskeeper. Lucky you didn't slide headfirst and cut up that pretty face uv yours."

Umpire McLean was overcome by the heat for a second time and had to be replaced by retired AA umpire Blakiston. Kelly made two hits and scored three runs in a 4-2 defeat. The Bostons won again the next day, and then the next - by a humiliating 13-2.

The band from the *Globe* played several selections with great flourish before the September 13 game, the last one of the disappointing series. The grand-stand was well filled, the fair sex turning out in number. Whitney was unfathomable to the Chicagos. They had little opportunity to do base running, their batting being of the light-weight order. Gore and Kelly were badly bowled up from the night before. Mike made one scratch hit in seven tries and Gore made three muffs in the outfield in a 3-1 loss that dropped them into unfamiliar territory - fourth place. No one celebrated on the steamboat ride to Providence.

On September 15 in Providence Umpire Bradley fined Corcoran $20 for insulting language. Little Larry addressed an opprobrious epithet to him and threatened to hit him over the head with a bat if he was fined.

The Boston Globe had fun at the expense of the Windy City's newspapers the next day. "We knew the Chicago papers would dance a war can-can over the defeats of Anson's excursion party here. When their agony was at its height the headline read 'An afternoon devoted by the Boston club to larruping the Chicago Crew'. The game was characterized by a bucolic exhibition of fielding by the white-hosed men.'

The Times added editorially that, 'The Chicago club cannot play base ball away from home.' The reason is probably that Mr. Anson and his young men are bashful and don't like to play before strangers. The Times has undoubtedly hit upon the right idea. Modesty has always been the failing of Anson and the silent Kelly."

Kelly had three hits in the season finale in Philadelphia on September 29 but he finished the season with the worst numbers he'd ever post, a .255 batting average and a paltry .282 on-base percentage. One of his hits soared over the center field fence. The ball was absent about five minutes and was brought back by a small boy who rode back to the grounds on a Ridge avenue car. The Chicagos had won their last five games but their hopes of winning another championship were crushed, the Bostons were invincible, winning 14 of their last 15 games.

Mike headed to Paterson to spend some time with Agnus. She told him about all the things her church society was planning and about the sewing she was doing. Just now she was making dresses for dolls for parents in the neighborhood to give their daughters for Christmas. As usual she didn't ask about Mike's doings during the season - the less she knew the better. She heard women whisper about her handsome husband as they passed her on the street. Most of the murmurs in the press were about Mike's tendency to imbibe too much too often and she was well aware of his fondness for whiskey, Lord knows he'd been no teetotaler when they'd been married. As for anything else - any women - he was discreet about it. She'd read about other players frequenting houses of ill repute or being in the company of 'painted ladies' but Mike's name was never mentioned. She could read her scriptures and pretend. She wasn't sure if praying for her husband would do any good.

"Let's Go Spend that $50."

In November Kelly was back in New Orleans to play an exhibition game. A local took him and Sam Wise of the Bostons on a Saturday hunt. Mike had spent a lot of the off-season in the Catskills shooting all sorts of game. They returned with a fine bunch of fish, eight snipes, and thirty ducks. Kel shot only at birds in flight, Sam elected to fire at sitting ducks in the water.

Most of the other White Stockings headed to New Orleans after Christmas. They enjoyed themselves - a lot - they were smitten by the southern belles that attended their games. George Gore ran out of money and wired Spalding for an advance.

"It is unaccountable to me that players who go to New Orleans require so much more money than players who stay home and do nothing," Spalding chided Gore. "You must make this last $100 do you until the season opens."

Kelly, Flint, and Williamson hit up the boss for fat advances as well. "Have already advanced you seven hundred dollars with the distinct understanding that no more would be requested, I cannot comply with your request," Spalding snapped at Williamson on January 16. He added tartly that "Attempting to keep Williamson in funds is a good deal like pouring water into a rat hole, you don't know the depth and consequently can form no sentiment as to the amount required to fill it."

The League expanded its schedule to 112 games and there were a number of rule changes for the 1884 season. "Six balls will constitute a walk. The Pitcher's Lines must be 6 feet long and 4 feet wide. Each

corner, i.e., point, of the box must be marked by a flat iron plate. The Captain's Lines must be drawn 15 feet parallel with the foul lines. The Players' Bench must be 12 feet long and located on the left side of the Home Base. At each end must be a bat-rack with fixtures for holding 20 bats.

No Club shall allow open betting or pool selling upon its grounds. No Club shall sell liquor upon its grounds. Every Club shall furnish a sufficient police force to preserve order. No Umpire, Manager, Captain or Player shall address the audience during the progress of a game except in necessary explanation. A Substitute shall not be allowed to take the place of any Player unless such Player be disabled by reason of illness or injury. The Batsman on taking his position must call for a "High Ball", a "Low Ball", or a "High-Low Ball" and the Umpire shall notify the Pitcher to deliver the ball as required. A staff of four League Umpires shall be selected by the Secretary before the 1st day of May. The Umpire shall not reverse his decision on any point upon the testimony of any player or bystander."

Kelly had inspired one of the new rules. It said that a Base Runner must touch all four bases to score a run. The attention of the Umpire is particularly directed to violations of the purpose and spirit of the Rules including:

Laziness or loafing of players in taking their places,

Failure to keep the bats in the rack provided for them,

Calling out to an opposing fielder to disconcert him,

Indecent or improper language addressed to the audience, the Umpire, or another player.

In any of these cases the Umpire should promptly fine the offending player."

In February Kelly went to Chicago to see Spalding. He gave Kelly a loan of $100 on top of the $600 he'd already extended him. Before handing it over he required Kelly to sign a contract agreeing to surrender $100 per month from the 1st of May until the following April.

Travel, especially between the East and the West was a lot less con-

fusing now. Standard time had been instituted by the railroads the previous November. The time of day had always been a local matter maintained by a clock on a church steeple or in a jeweler's window.

Kelly and Burns played handball together on a day when it was too cold to practice out of doors. Goldsmith and Williamson had made the papers for numerous incidents in beer gardens and street corner grogeries. Gore and Dalrymple were reportedly acting wildly too. After Mike and Tom had finished playing they went for a Turkish bath. Amid the clouds of steam Burns asked Mike, "Why do you and Fred and Abner and George get more attention for breaking the rules than Sunday and I do for *obeying* them?"

Kelly wiped the sweat from his eyes and chuckled, "Why don't you dubs break a window and get *yourselves* talked about?"

Agnus had finally moved to Chicago. The Flints and the Kellys went to see *My American Cousin* at the Grand Opera House. Tickets for the popular new show were hard to come by, the theater was jam-packed.

"There are Mike Kelly and the estimable *Mrs.* Kelly," a base ball enthusiast told his wife.

"Such a dowdy looking-woman," she declared.

"You'd have thought he'd have landed some beauty, an actress perhaps."

"I hear she's from his hometown."

"There must be slim pickings wherever it is."

The Chicagos opened the season with games on the Southeast Diamond of the Polo Grounds. The Northwest diamond was home to the AA's New York Metropolitans. Sometimes a ball batted from one diamond onto the other would interfere with play.

After their strong finish to the '83 season they hoped to get a good start out of the gate. Three thousand New Yorkers were in the grandstand by 2:30 on May Day and elevated trains loaded full of more enthusiasts were arriving every other minute. Almost every important man in New York occupied a seat in the boxes. The ladies' gallery was especially full. Many bright faces beamed out of fur capes or broad-shouldered ulsters. Welch handed the visitors their hats, Kelly was 0-for-4.

That night he and George and Abner sat in the lobby, where they spotted one of the New York base ball writers.

"Where might we go for a bit uv fun while we're in town?" Mike asked him.

"Let me think, a colleague of mine works the crime beat. A large red lamp marks the establishment of Harry Hill at 25 East Houston where an hour cannot be spent more pleasantly and the bewitching smiles of fairy-like creatures who devote themselves to the service of Cupid at 84 West Houston are unrivalled by any of the fine ladies who walk Broadway in silks and satins. But beware of smartly-dressed, comely young ladies of extinguished modesty unattended by male companions who can be seen along the boulevard. They're Nymphes de Pave, cruisers who've robbed many an unsuspecting stranger of his all.

The worst dives are between 24th and 40th streets and 5th and 6th avenues. That's a region of such depravity the reformers call it Satan's Circus. Half of the buildings are devoted to some form of sin or another. Sixth Avenue is lined with dives, saloons and all-night dance halls. The Tenderloin's between Gramercy Park and Murray Hill on the east and Hell's Kitchen on the west. It stretches north from 23rd street between Fifth and Eighth avenues. No neighborhood in New York has more saloons, music halls, gambling dens, and brothels than the Tenderloin, it's a sink of iniquity. Amid all the sex that's openly for sale one street stands out, 39th street west of Seventh avenue. It's called Soubrette Row."

Mike and the others looked puzzled.

"A soubrette is a saucy, flirtatious girl," the reporter explained.

"It's around the corner from the new Metropolitan Opera House. It's run by French madams. The rich swells can enjoy an evening at the opera and then turn the corner and have all of their fantasies fulfilled. The girls specialize in some rather scandalous practices. The

French girls resort to such unnatural practices the other girls won't associate or eat with them."

Mike looked at the others. "I'm not sure we're in the mood for anything *that* racy. We're lookin' for flirtatious chorus girls, not prostitutes or salacious - what did ya call them - soubrettes."

"We're not for looking for disorderly houses of assignment," added George.

"Well, the Broadway Garden runs from Broadway to Mercer street, it's conducted on the pretty-waiter girl system. On the other side there are three concert saloons that are quiet and orderly - the Dew Drop Inn, the Eureka, and the Palace Garden. A little further, on West Houston, you'll encounter the Judge and Jury, a great resort for sportsmen where everything's conducted in a respectable manner and there are blondes and brunettes who are always ready to receive gentlemen into their tender arms. Their sallies are calculated to dispel the clouds of melancholy."

"And if we're just thirsty?" asked Mike.

"If you're just thirsty, there's a thirty-two block section on the Lower East Side that has two hundred and fifty lager-beer saloons and about sixty liquor saloons. Again, there are places you will certainly not want to frequent. Some sell liquor mixed with liquid camphor and those that sell a punch composed of whiskey, hot rum, camphor, benzene, and cocaine sweepings for six cents a glass. Kit Burn's Sportsmen's Hall on Water street has an amphitheater on the first floor. Contests to the death are held pitting terriers against giant rats. Their champion terrier slew a hundred rats in eleven minutes. There are some Bowery dives that have no glasses, only barrels of booze connected to rubber tubes. For three cents you can drink till you run out of breath."

"We're not *that* thirsty," said Abner.

"McGlory's Armory Hall on Hester Street is a haven of beastliness and depravity. It's frequented by thieves, pickpockets, and procurers. If you fancy thugs wearing pistols, knives, brass knuckles, and bludgeons, bar-room brawls and gang violence you'll love the place.

Drunken customers are robbed by the female regulars who flirt with them. Then they're dragged from the table by a bouncer and thrown into the street. Once outside, the victim is searched for anything of value and stripped of his clothes. You won't see McGlory there, he's still in the Tombs for running a disorderly house."

"Sounds divine," chuckled Mike.

"There are plenty of other places you'll want to steer clear of. Milligan's Hell, the Tub of Blood, and the Chain and Locker to name a few. At the Slide on Bleecker Street young men solicit other men. And some of the upstanding citizens of the Big Apple you'll not want to encounter are Piggy Noles, Boiled Oysters Malloy, Slops Connolly, Goo Goo Knox, Eddie the Plague, and Baboon Dooley. Oh, and Happy Jack Mulraney. He killed a saloon-keeper for making fun of his facial twitch."

"I think I'll just stay in my room while we're here," said George.

"There must be *somewhere* we can go without gettin' ourselves mugged," said Mike.

"If you're looking for a Men's Only Irish pub there's McSorley's Old Ale House on East 7th street," said the reporter. "Their motto is be good or be gone. Neir's Tavern is a bit of a hike from here, it's out by the Union Course Race Track. The White Horse Tavern opened a couple of years ago at Hudson and 11th street, you'll find mostly dock workers there."

"I could've been a dock worker meself," said Mike. "I say we head ta the White Horse, gents."

"Let's," said Abner.

"Yes, indeed," agreed George.

The White Stockings lost the first three games in New York and allowed 37 runs in doing so. They beat the Quakers 12-7 on May 5th at Recreation Park in Philadelphia for their first win. It was underserved in the mind of *The Philadelphia Times* reporter. "A rank decision by the umpire and two accidents to players gave the Chicagos all the runs they needed in the third inning. "

Anson opened the inning with a base hit and Williamson was sent to first on six balls. Burns hit to Coleman who threw out Anson at third. A double play should have been made but in catching the ball Mulvey broke the third finger of his left hand. Then Coleman sprained his neck and had to do slow pitching. Pfeffer filled the bases on a short hit to left field. Corcoran hit to McLellan who threw to Cowley cutting Williamson off at the home plate.

"Not out!" declared Mr. Van Court and the crowd yelled in derision. Sunday, Dalrymple, and Anson followed with singles. Kelly rapped a two-baser and when the dust cleared eight men had crossed the plate. After the game the umpire admitted he had been wrong. He thought there were only two men on the bases.

Mike did even more the next day. In the first, Gore hit for two bases and singles by Kelly, Anson, Sunday, and Pfeffer yielded four earned runs. Manning's muff of Corcoran's fly, coupled with Kelly's single and two wild pitches gave the Chicagos two more runs in the third. In the sixth bad errors by McClellan and Andrews and singles by Gore and Kelly gave the visitors another two runs. Mike ended up with four hits and three runs in his side's 13-0 rout.

On Saturday, May 10 in Providence the Grays did the Chicagos to a nice brown and turned them over in a loss that bordered on the burlesque. Irwin reached base on Kelly's bad throw in the second and scored when Denny's easy flyball went over sleepy George Gore's head. Farrell scored on Dalrymple's terrible throw to the plate in the third. Denny got a life at first on Kelly's errant throw in the fifth and scored on yet another wild throw to the plate by Abner.

Kelly gave Umpire McLean a bad time. When a call didn't go his way he went up to him and said in a loud voice, "'Twas a bum call, Billy. Our man Gore was safe by five feet."

"Mike, I am gointa have to fine you another $5 for that, the people in the stands heard you, but I have ta say, you're the only man in the League who calls me by me first name and asks after me family. You may be one uv the biggest kickers in the game but you are one uv the few that never cusses me out."

Radford went to first on called balls in the seventh and in stealing second caused Flint to throw so poorly that Carroll was allowed to slip in with yet another unearned run. The calamity ended in the ninth when a fumble of Dalrymple's allowed Irwin and Denny to cross the plate.

After the game Spalding fined Gore and Silver Flint $50 for "allowing dissipation to diminish their skills." He threatened to double the fine if they showed up drunk again.

Anson's men seemed in better shape to do battle on Monday. Radbourn, who was itching to beat the Chicagos, got the start but couldn't muster the strength or control to keep Providence in the game. Kelly, playing shortstop, stirred things up when Radford tried to sprint to third base. Mike, whom *The Providence Journal* had labeled "the conspicuous sneak of the white-legged ex-champions", jumped into his path and blocked him, earning the crowd's fervent maledictions. This time, Umpire McLean had seen the whole thing. He waved the runner to third base and sternly reprimanded Kelly. All the same, Goldsmith cruised to a 5-0, four-hit shutout.

On May 14 The *St. Paul Globe* proclaimed that it was evident from the first 28 games of the National League schedule that "the western clubs are having a very bad start this year. The New Yorks, clad in handsome shirts and caps chocolate in color with white-striped flannel, seem to have found out how to play ball, Boston is playing a grand game, Providence is powerful and dangerous, and Philadelphia has braced up wonderfully under Harry Wright. The Chicagos are 0-2 against the New Yorks, 0-4 against the Bostons, and 1-3 in their games with Providence. The once mighty champions are mired in seventh place with an overall record of 4-12. They had the misfortune of losing the services of Flint and Burns and neither Corcoran nor Goldsmith have thus far showed the pitching form to keep their club anywhere near the front."

The Chicagos suffered an eighth consecutive loss on the 22nd. *The Tribune* moaned, "there is nothing to encourage the expectation that the Chicago club will be better than fourth in the race." They dropped five of their next six to fall to second last place, better

than only Detroit's 2-17 record, and Anson instituted a regime of no late hours, no bumming, no indifferent play, and double the fines for each succeeding offence. It worked. The White Stockings took ten of their next twelve.

The Buffalo Commercial's man reflected that: "it stirs the blood of an old patron of the game to see men play ball like Gore, Williamson, and Pfeffer but Kelly is the captain of the base-runners."

On Saturday, June 6 the east end of the field at Lake Front Park was filled with barouches, demi-landaus, phaetons, and clarences and the neighboring roof-tops were packed with on-lookers. When the tally-ho coach arrived with the players the horde of boys outside cheered the men to the echo. When the band struck up "The League March" and Captain Anson brought his team out in single rank there was sent up a cheer that must have warmed the cockles of the hearts of the nine athletes. The home side batted Harkins at will. Kelly made a single, a drive good for two bags, and a home run in the Chicagos' 11-2 win.

After the team got to Detroit on June 11 and beat the Wolverines 8-4 Mike felt bad for Billy Sunday so he invited him to come along with the gang to one of their favorite haunts, a place on Ellicott Street.

"The place used to be half grocery store but they shut that part down," Mike told Sunday as they went in.

Billy looked up as he followed Mike in.

"The upstairs is a hotel now," Kelly explained. "If it weren't for our damned curfew, it'd be tempting ta lay yer head up there after a couple too many."

After a few drinks they walked to a nearby saloon. They were accustomed to swinging doors that led to a bare, simple room with plain furniture and rusty spittoons. This one was large and richly decorated.

"Must be one of the ones the breweries are sponsoring," said Gore. "They pay for everything from the furniture and the bar-rail to the food."

The players were shocked to see that many of the customers were young women chatting and merrily drinking. Had they been prostitutes, the men would have flirted with them or called them over but it was awkward to acknowledge a woman who was on her own. When two of the girls turned to talk to the players they laughed when Sunday ran straight out the door.

The second game of the series was a Ladies Day. According to *The Detroit Free Press*, girls and women could "walk right in at the big gate without being interviewed by the ticket-takers." Of course some of the ticket-takers were players not in the lineup and they were known to take a little too close a look at the ladies.

Kelly's two-bagger to left scored Dalrymple in the first. With the bases loaded in the fourth Fritz Pfeffer sent a grounder to Geiss and in his eagerness to make a double play Geiss failed to make *either* out. Kelly hit a wicked baser to score the two and Williamson drove in the other runners. Corcoran's thumb was sore so he could curve the ball only slightly and there was no speed to speak of so Kelly went in to pitch in the fifth. *The Free Press* said, "the Detroit batters went up to the plate with the intention of paying their compliments to Kelly but Hanlon and Scott were thrown out by Pfeffer and when Guiss and Bennett struck out Kelly was cheered to the skies." Whispered words were exchanged behind parasols by admiring females.

The Wolverines loaded the bases in the sixth but Kelly got Hanlon to hit a weak grounder to second to end the inning. Mike allowed one run in the seventh on a fine three-bagger by Meinke and Detroit notched another in the eighth when Corcoran, who was in Mike's usual spot, let a soft liner get by him. With the game on the line Billy Sunday missed two balls in center. Anson could see Kelly was getting frustrated and had him change places with Williamson. Wood hit a puke pop fly over third that Kelly muffed. Williamson threw one over Flint's head and the Chicagos, who hadn't scored in five innings, lost 9-7.

The Chicago Herald published an anonymous accusatory letter. "When the Chicago base ballists, who were again beaten in Detroit today, get demoralized by drink, why don't you reporters say so? The

public should be warned. Fifteen thousand people have extended their cash within the past week only to witness games played by men too full of Detroit liquor to play ball."

After the game Spalding told reporters, "Kelly is a born leader and his teammates are more than willing to follow him on his nightly bar-hopping escapades. I'm fining him five dollars for loafing on the basepaths today."

When the reporters asked Anson for a comment he told them, "Mike is a white-souled, genial fellow with a legion of friends and but one enemy in the world, that one enemy being Mike himself."

When Spalding took Kelly to task for his behavior Mike asked him, "What are you runnin' here, A.G., a base ball club or a Sunday school?"

After a 6-5 loss in the Friday game Kelly had three hits and scored twice in a much-needed win in the Saturday matinee and the White Stockings ended up splitting the four-game series in Detroit. During their stay *The Detroit Free Press* announced that "M.J. Kelly, the light-ning player of the Chicagos, would take part Saturday night in Frank Lane's farce "He Would Have a Benefit" at White's Theater. The the-atre manager had organized a benefit performance for an attendant. While clinging to the outside of a crowded street-car he'd attempted to get money from his pocket to pay his fare and when he lost his hold he'd fallen under the wheels and been severely injured. He was his widowed mother's sole support.

Penelope, looking radiant, was in the audience with her parents. Kelly didn't exactly receive rave reviews. *The Free Press* theatre critic wrote that "the handsome ball tosser acquitted himself creditably." But the performance had been a challenge as the entire Chicago team sat in a private box above the stage heckling Mike throughout the show.

"Kelly, you must do Hamlet, no wait, Macbeth," bellowed Dalrymple.

"Absolutely divine, the handsomest soul ever to grace a stage," yelled Flint.

In a squeaky female voice Gore called out, "Oh, Michael, you simply must attend one of my garden parties this summer."

The farce closed with Frank Lane slapping Kelly on the back with a clapboard.

Anson leaned out over the front of the box. "Give it to him, Frank, give it to him."

The White Stockings took a steamboat across Lake Erie for a series in Buffalo. Kelly and company spent Saturday night and most of Sunday at McBride's Pub and it showed when they got hammered in another manner in a 20-9 loss to the Bisons on Monday. Anson could see Kelly had got in a good jag and was in no condition to play and punished him by having him play shortstop. When Mike botched O'Rourke's easy grounder in the first inning Anson was furious. He threatened that if Kelly and his cronies ever showed up in that condition for a game again they'd have the devil to pay. Mike made sure he was clear-headed for the Tuesday game and played well. The Chicagos made it close but still lost 8-7. They traveled to Cleveland and lost both games there. Sobriety didn't help.

When the team's train stopped at the little station in Fremont on the way home a group of women boarded. The White Stockings sat across from them at supper in the dining car. Three young women sat with a well-dressed woman in her fifties at one table. Another three young women occupied a second table headed by a scrawny woman in her thirties with a weather-beaten face. Off in the corner were young ladies by themselves. They were easily the most attractive of the bunch and the liveliest as well. The rest sipped their lemonades, ladled their soup, and rarely spoke. The pretty girls were having a great time and they spent a lot of it looking over at George, Abner, and Mike's table.

Eventually the other girls and the two women left. George, Abner, and Mike went over to the lively girls' table. "Would you mind if we joined you girls?" asked Gore.

"Not in the least," said the oldest girl, a redhead who looked to be nineteen or twenty. "I'm Beatrix, that's Edith," she said, pointing to

the girl across the table from her, "and this is Adeline," she said indicating the prettiest of the three, a striking, blue-eyed blonde.

"You girls are more tanned and ... athletic looking than most of the young ladies we see, might I inquire how you come to be travelling together?" asked Abner.

"We're all members of the same group," said Beatrix.

"I hope it's not the Young Women's Christian Association," said Dalrymple.

"Or the Young Women's *Temperance* Society," chuckled Kelly.

The girls giggled again.

"We're members of the Kalamazoo Young Women's Cyclists Club," explained Adeline. "We're on our way to Chicago to compete against a team from the West Side."

"We apologize for eying you throughout your supper, but you look familiar, should we know you?" asked Beatrix.

"Would yous like to get to know us?" muttered Abner under his breath.

"Our pictures are in the paper sometimes," said Gore. "Especially Kelly's. Cameras are kind to him."

Adeline smiled at Mike. "Who are the *older* women with the group?" he asked.

"The highfalutin one is our sponsor, Mrs. Wainwright. The sourpuss is our coach, the Spinster Humphreys, I mean *Miss* Humphreys."

The other girls laughed.

"She doesn't let anyone have the least bit of fun," said Edith. "It's all about training and winning every match."

"Well if you would like some fun," said Gore, looking around to see if any of the servers were watching," I happen to have a bottle of bourbon in my room."

The girls' eyes lit up.

"Grab us some glasses," George told Abner.

Abner waited a beat until the last of the servers headed into the galley and then stuck three fingers of each hand in three empty glasses on a tray.

"He has a great pair of hands," explained George.

The girls giggled again.

"Edith certainly takes her training seriously," said Gore as he and Mike and Abner had breakfast. "She rode me for a half an hour last night." He looked at Gore. "What about Beatrix?"

Gore wiped his mouth and set down his napkin. "She's even more rigorous, rode me for *forty-five* minutes. What about Adeline, Kel?"

"Couldn't say, George … we weren't watchin' the clock all that much."

The June 30 game was well nigh given away in the fourth on singles by Denny, Gilligan, and Paul Radford, a passed ball, and a genuine South American muff of a gentle fly by Kelly on which the visitors secured three runs. Radbourn got in a four-bagger over the right field fence in the fourth and that was the last time a Providence player crossed the plate.

In the home side's half of the ninth with the score four runs each Dalrymple gave Gilligan a foul fly and Gore hit to Farrell and was fielded out at first. The Chicago rooters were on pins and needles as Kelly went to the bat. He squared himself to do business to right field then indicated that he wanted a high pitch. The umpire nodded and when Radbourn complied Mike sent the ball far over second base and under a handsome four-wheeled trap that was being driven out of the gate. Kelly hurried around the bases as fast as he could, given that he'd packed on twenty pounds, and scored the run that won the game. The crowd erupted in delight.

Roger Connor hit a long one to right field in the fifth inning of the July 5 game in Chicago. Kelly, playing third base, took the relay throw from Pfeffer as Connor slid into the bag just under Mike's tag. As Connor beat the dirt off his uniform Kelly pretended to throw the ball to Corcoran and winked as he did it. Larry went into his windup and when Connor took his leadoff Kelly pulled the ball from under

his arm and tagged him out. Connor's manager fined him $10 for being caught by such an old trick.

Kelly spent Sunday afternoon at Guttenberg Race Track. He had exactly $100 in his pocket and placed the crisp note on the nose of a horse called Play or Pay. Mike had chosen the horse because he'd negotiated 30-to-1 odds with Chicago bookie Ike Thompson. Play or Pay won at the wire, allowing Kelly to pocket $3,100 but he dropped $2,000 betting on nags.

Before Kelly returned home he gave more than $500 to friends and admirers. He stopped in at his favorite saloon and bought drinks and cigars for everyone. Later, when he headed for home, Kelly saw a little girl sitting in the gutter crying. He scooped her up into his arms and asked what was the matter. She told him her daddy had died the previous week in a railroad accident. Her mother was ill, but the family had no money for a doctor. Kelly handed over what he had left in his pocket to the girl, a little more than $100. He proceeded home, stopping on the way to negotiate a loan from a friend so he could buy dinner.

Chicago won an easy victory in Cleveland on the 22nd by all-round superior work. The White Stockings' fielding was grand, their base-running energetic, their batting hard and Haskins suffered steadily. Kelly had three hits and scored after each one as the visitors blasted the Blues 12-3. Haskins wasn't fooling many batsmen, he'd lead the League in losses with 32.

After spending a few hours at Mat Wolford's tavern that night with Kelly, Gore, and Flint, Fred Goldsmith was between the points the next day. The White Stockings lit James McCormick up for 22 hits, but hung-over Goldsmith gave up six runs in the second and was exhausted by the ninth when he gave up another four and lost 16-13.

John Gaffney umpired the game. He'd begun playing baseball as a third baseman but his promising career was ended when he injured his arm throwing a snowball just before being promoted to the National League so he became a printer and started um-piring Ivy League games. Gaffney pioneered the practice of mov-

ing from behind the catcher to behind the twirler when a batter reached base. He made other innovations as well including calling balls fair or foul depending on where they cleared the fence rather than where they landed and making a shirt with pockets in which to store extra baseballs.

He and Kelly provided the cranks with great amusement throughout the afternoon - though it was not the umpire's intention to. After grounding to third in the second inning Kelly raced to first. It was close, but he just beat the throw.

"Out!" yelled Gaffney.

"Are you kidding me, John?" asked Kelly.

"I'm not, Mike," said Gaffney.

"Well you're dead wrong," said Kelly. Gaffney looked up into the stands. Everyone was smiling. "I'm going to have to fine you $5, Kel."

A crank in a brand new boater turned to his friend, "The air of injured innocence Kelly puts on is worth the price of admission alone."

Two innings later Mike was catching. The runner on first headed for second. Kelly nailed him with a great throw.

"Safe!" cried Gaffney.

"What! I got him. Didn't we get him, Fred?" Mike called to Pfeffer.

Even the base runner seemed to think he was out.

"Did you bet on the Blues, John?" Kelly asked Gaffney. "The man was out by a Mississippi mile."

"I am going to have to fine you another $5 for that, Mike, the people in the stands heard you."

Mike said, "Well it's a free country and there's no law against exercising your vocal organs."

The spectators howled.

Later, Kelly was at the bat. A pitch was clearly outside.

"Strike four. Batter out!" announced Gaffney.

Kelly turned to address the grand-stand again.

The man in the new boater elbowed his friend. "Here he goes again."

Mike addressed the rooters sincerely. "Won't one of yas please lend this poor man your glasses?"

He paused a beat. "And a white cane."

The spectators roared. "That'll be fifteen," said Gaffney.

Kelly ran for a pop up the next inning and just caught it before it hit the grass.

"Not out," declared Gaffney.

"Really, Gaff!"

"The ball hit the ground."

"Is it true you fined the proprietor of the Gibson House $10 for talking back to you when he asked Is it hot enough for you?"

"And that's another twenty."

Gaffney was in the Café of the Weddell House that night talking with some local men he knew. The swing doors flew open and half of the players of the Chicago team - Kelly in the lead - marched in. A look of concern spread across Gaffney's face, he'd heard that Kelly had vowed he 'would attend to Gaffney' and the umpire expected trouble.

"Hello, Gaf," Mike shouted jovially when he saw Gaffney. "Have a drink on me ... your friends too."

"Much obliged Kel," said Gaffney nervously, "but I'm not drinking tonight."

"Say Gaf," Kelly went on, "how much did you soak me for this afternoon?"

"An even $50," replied Gaffney.

"Reported it to the boss yet?"

"Not yet."

"Tell you what I'll do," said Kelly, grabbing the dice box. "I'll shake

you to see whether it's a hundred or nothing."

Gaffney started to walk away.

"Come on, Gaf, be game," the other players called.

He came back.

"Horses?" asked Gaffney.

"Nope," said Kelly. "One throw."

Gaffney spilled out two pairs, aces and fours.

The players looked at Gaffney's dice.

"That was a mighty fine roll, wasn't it, Kel?" chuckled the bar-tender.

Mike said nothing. He turned the box bottom side up and, lifting it again, turned up three fives.

The players roared at Kelly's luck and turned to see Gaffney's reaction.

Gaffney paused a beat then shrugged. "All right, Mike, the fine don't go."

Kelly patted Gaffney on the back, turned to his mates, and smiled. "Come on, fellers," he shouted as he started for the door, "let's go spend that $50."

One of the men Gaffney had been talking with at the Weddell House Café was a reporter. He sought out Kelly the next day and queried him about the conduct that had led to his fines.

"People go to see games for excitement," said Kelly. "They love to be worked up. That's one reason why I believe in chin music now and then on the diamond. The people want good play with just enough kicking to keep things interesting. Audiences won't keep goin' to ball-grounds unless they can see something in the nature of entertainment and excitement. You won't find the ordinary man going to a game on a day when it's eighty degrees in the shade to see two nines play each other for a couple of hours without a word being said. Our team draws more people than any club in baseball and a lot of that's on account uv us bein' known as chronic kickers."

Sweeney stunned the Grays by defecting to the St. Louis Maroons of the Union Association. The move came after an exhibition game in Woonsocket, Rhode Island. Sweeney, who'd been drinking throughout the game, refused to return with the team to Providence and chose to stay in Woonsocket with a woman he'd escorted to the park. When he woke up the next morning he realized he'd missed the morning practice. He raced to make it back to Providence for his start that afternoon. When he arrived just in time Frank Bancroft, who'd let Radbourn take a few days off to rest his sore arm, was left with little choice but to start his still drunk ace.

Sweeney continued drinking but somehow held a 6-2 lead through five innings. Fearing his luck wouldn't hold, Bancroft attempted to make a pitching change, but Sweeney verbally attacked him, refused to leave the game, and continued to pitch another two innings. Before the start of the eighth, Bancroft ordered Charley to vacate the mound and move to right field. When Bancroft threatened him with a $50 fine if he didn't, Sweeney told him to take his fine and the rest of his salary and shove it up his ass. He quit the team and spent the rest of the game in the stands with a pair of prostitutes. The now eight-player Grays lost the game.

At that point, Radbourn made a deal with the Grays. He offered to start every game for the rest of the year in exchange for a raise in pay and having the reserve clause stripped from his contract. Ownership relented and Radbourn began the most incredible performance in baseball history. He started, and completed, 40 of the Grays next 43 games, including 20 in a row at one point. His hair was a mess, he wasn't able to lift his arm high enough to comb it.

Mike hit a single, a double, and a home run and scored two of the Chicagos' runs on Saturday. It took the worst kind of double-dyed muffing to give the Buffalo men the game but the White Stockings were equal to the emergency. It was all too typical of the '84 team's struggles. They scored nine runs but the Buffalo club scored eleven on seven hits. Gore made three muffs.

"If you like makin' muffs so much you might just as well go inta the fur business, George," Kelly chided him.

"You're a fine one to talk," sneered Gore.

The Detroit Free Press had taken to calling them "a chump team." A frustrated booster telegrammed Anson inquiring whether the contest had been on the level. Anson tartly replied, "I would not disgrace my players by showing them your telegram, nor degrade myself by answering your ridiculous question."

To change their luck the club got a new mascot, Little Willie Hahn, a flaxen hair, blue-eyed boy who doted on Williamson. Ned told reporters that every man in the nine firmly believed the club can't lose if Willie is present and just as confidently believed that they can't win if he fails to appear. Anson was happy to be rid of Duval, "the no account nigger." He didn't believe in mascots but thought Willie was a good advertisement for the club.

On August 19 John L. Sullivan was an interested spectator at the Boston vs. Chicago game. The bases were loaded in the ninth when Kelly hit the ball on the nose and sent it clear to Randolph street for four runs. The crowd rose en masse, giddily threw their hats into the puffily clouded sky and cheered themselves purple but the Beaneaters scored two of their own in their half of the inning and beat the White Stockings for the fifth consecutive time.

On August 24 the White Stockings purchased John Clarkson from Saginaw of the Northwestern League. Clarkson was born into a family of means. His father owned a prospering jewelry and watchmaking business in Boston.

Clarkson played amateur ball for the Beacons of Boston for two years. He was one of their star hitters and eventually developed into the club's leading pitcher. The team played all comers, including major-league clubs and John gained a reputation as one of the area's leading hurlers.

After the 1882 season Clarkson signed on with Saginaw club of the Northwestern League and played every position but catcher. The club directors were unimpressed and soon discussed releasing the young player. The manager put him between the points and those thoughts dissipated. The manager spent hours working on John's

motion behind the team's hotel and converted Clarkson into an overhand pitcher - the overhand style was about to become legal in the National League.

Clarkson returned to Saginaw in '84. In 45 games he accrued a 34-9 record with nine shutouts and a stunning 388 strikeouts as well as an ERA of 0.64. He hit .306 as well. That caught the eye of major-league managers. On August 14, the Northwestern League ousted the Saginaw club for nonpayment of dues and the club disbanded.

Now a free agent, Clarkson fielded offers from Boston, Cincinnati, and Chicago. Anson thought John was "in possession of a remarkable drop curve and fast, overhand lifting speed, and a most deceiving change of pace." To add to hitters' difficulty Clarkson wore a big, shiny belt-buckle that flashed sunlight into their eyes. Kelly thought that was very clever.

The Chicagos were in Providence on August 27. Kelly noticed that there was now a "bull pen" outside the center field fence and wondered why, since Radbourn pitched virtually every inning of every game. The White Stockings presented their new pitcher and he proved a valuable acquisition. He pitched a swift, curving ball which the Greys did not succeed in finding. He had "a Hot Spring arm" and his speed was such that Kelly's hands were black and blue and after the 5th. He moved to third base.

On September 1st two of the Chicagos - the newspapers declined to say which ones - were fined $50 each for drunkenness. Two days later Kelly hit a home run in the seventh inning that was one of the longest made at the new Polo Grounds. In the 8th the team made it to the .500 mark with a 15-10 win at home over the Quakers, part of a ten-game winning streak.

The Boston Globe's base-ball column's headline on September 9 reflected Kelly's status in the Chicagos.

"KELLY & ANSON'S NINE BEAT THE METROPOLITAN NEW YORKERS

The visitors hit Begley with perfect ease. A triple by Gore, a dou-

ble by Kelly, and a single by Anson gave them two earned runs in the first inning. Three errors allowed them to score in the sixth. Kelly opened the seventh by spanking the sphere over the left field fence for a home run. He went to the bench, got the box containing a new ball and smashed it with his bat. After freeing it from its coverings he laid the ball gently on the bench with a look that said, "You'll be needed directly." Sure enough, none of the spectators returned the ball so Kel tossed the new one out to Begley with a flourish. Three singles led to another tally. Fair-skinned Umpire Billy McLean was overcome by the heat again.

Kelly wore his batting clothes on September 16, he had four hits and scored three times in a 17-0 win over Boston. Morrill's men couldn't fathom Corcoran's sneaky pet curves and only two of them saw third base. Ferguson's decisive umpiring left no chance for kicking on either side. The Chicagos were on a tear, but Providence - or rather Radbourn - was unstoppable.

On September 25, while Radbourne was beating the Chicagos again Kelly sat beside Dalrymple on the bench waiting for the inevitable.

"Do you realize Old Hoss could win sixty games, Kel?'" said Abner.

"Aye, I wouldn't bet against it."

"How does he do it?"

"Radbourn has made a wonderful record because he hasn't tried for what most of us consider a pitching record."

"What do you mean?"

"He doesn't care a lick about shutouts and the like. Haven't you noticed? When he's in a game and it looks like his team is going to win he throws the balls right down the middle and lets his fielders do the work. That way he saves his arm and he can go right back to the box the next day."

On the verge of the ripe old age of thirty, Radbourn would finish the season with a record of 60 wins, a 1.38 ERA, and 441 strikeouts in 678 innings.

Kelly led the way with three hits in the once mighty Chicagos' last game of the season played in bitter cold. The win ran their September record to 21-4 but they'd dug far too big a hole for themselves with their shoddy play in May and weren't within a whiff of first place. Providence had won ten in a row in June and then 28 of 29 later in the season. The White Stockings finished in fifth place, 12 ½ games behind the Grays. *The Providence Transcript* boasted that the emblem of the championship would be kissed by the breezes from Narragansett Bay.

Kelly led the league in batting with a .354 average and 120 runs scored. Though few paid attention to the statistic, he placed third in runs batted home as well with 95.

Tribune and *Sporting Life* reporter Harry Palmer talked to Mike over dinner at Williams & Newman. He wiped his mouth after finishing his steak and turned to Kelly. "You batted .255 last season and .354 this year, Mike. That's a hundred-point improvement. What changed?"

Mike took a swig of his drink and said, "Last year I was too fat to play good ball, Harry. The idea of a man carrying 185 pounds around the bases! I know what ailed me battin', too much trying to hit to right field. There's nuthin in it. Wait till you get a good ball over the plate and then crack away. That's good battin'." He looked at his glass. "And that's good whiskey."

THE
$10,000
BEAUTY

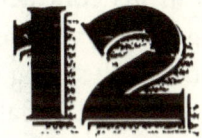

"Not Going Away Anytime Soon."

Kelly wintered in Hyde Park, N.Y. with Agnus. Next door was a family named Roosevelt that had a baby named Franklin. Agnus knitted him a blanket and some booties.

In early March Kelly returned from the South, having spent several weeks there for the benefit of his health. He'd intended to pass the winter months at the home of his brother but a throat trouble forced him to seek out a milder climate.

He badly wanted to win another championship. Surely the Grays would have a hard time repeating their success of '84, Radbourn couldn't possibly win sixty games again. The Bostons would certainly be contenders, the Buffalos would be heavy batsmen as usual, the Detroits could hardly do worse. The Gothams could well be the biggest threat.

John B. Day was determined to make his team champions and to that end the Metropolitans, his AA team, were sacrificed. The Mets' manager, Jim "Smilin' Jeems" Mutrie, indulged in some rule-bending chicanery to bring Mets stars Keefe and Esterbrook over to the Gothams whom he would now take over. Shortly before the start of the 1885 season, Mutrie took the two on a voyage to Day's onion farm in Bermuda. Once Keefe and Esterbrook were safely out to sea, Day released them from the Mets roster. While the two were out of the country and incommunicado the ten-day period other teams had to sign them elapsed. Once that happened, Mutrie inked the two to Gothams pacts.

Buffalo's Jim O'Rourke, an implacable foe of the reserve clause, had operated without one in his contract. He and the club owner proceeded under a yearly gentlemen's agreement that he'd maintain allegiance to the Bisons. But in the spring of 1884 Jim served notice that this would be his last season in Buffalo. Despite his impending departure, he continued to serve the club diligently and led the team on the field by example, batting .347 and pacing the League with 162 base hits.

O'Rourke's daughter Anna had died in '83 and he was determined to find a club close enough to his home in Bridgeport to allow him to spend Sundays with his remaining children. Using a bidding war among interested teams, Jim extracted a $4,000 contract from Day. O'Rourke joined Buck Ewing, John Montgomery Ward, Tim Keefe, Mickey Welch, and Roger Connor, a fellow Connecticut Irishman as taciturn as O'Rourke was loquacious. The Gothamites would be a force to be reckoned with.

The Chicagos wouldn't repeat the folly of last Spring and practice on the home grounds in April when the weather was "reliably bad." The men headed South on the April 1 evening train to play exhibitions in Cincinnati, then Nashville, Chattanooga, and Atlanta. They cancelled their other exhibitions with Atlanta after beating their local Picked Nine by a score of 24-3 on the 15th and spent the rest of the month in Nashville, the town, the park, and the people having made a very favorable impression on them. Mike was especially impressed by two local gals, Ella-Mae, tall and 28, and Clementine, petite and 22. Anson imposed a total abstinence condition on the players, anyone violating it would see his salary reduced.

The team arrived in St. Louis on April 30 and rode to the Union Base Ball Park for the season opener in barouches. On the streets they saw a dozen shiny cabs the St. Louis Hansom Cab Company had imported from England. They were the most stylish vehicles Kelly had ever seen. The cabs were pulled by big, strong-boned horses at a much quicker gait than an ordinary hack team. People with no particular place to go were hiring them for one-mile rides at a cost of 25 cents purely for the fun of the thing.

Hack drivers were jealous of the sporty rigs. One of them had purposely rammed one that happened to be carrying Mr. D. B. Gould, the president of the St. Louis Hansom Cab Company, and a lady friend. The cab stood the collision without damage, the hack lost two of its spokes.

In spite of unfavorable weather that had left the grounds heavy and slippery, ten thousand base-ball cranks crowded Union Park to witness the opening game of the series. They were delighted to have a League team to root on now. The Maroons had debuted the year before as members of the Union Association, which was derided as "the Onion League" by the NL and the AA. Henry Lucas, founder and president of the Association, owned the Maroons and stocked his team with the league's best players. They started the season with twenty straight wins, sweeping the Altoona Mountain Cities, the Washington Nationals, and the Baltimore Monumentals and finished the season with a 94 and 19 domination of the league, which led to its untimely demise. The Maroons wouldn't fare so well against major league competition.

The home side scored twice in the top of the first. Lewis knocked the ball over the fence in the sixth. He'd had only reached third base but was given home on a new rule that granted a home run on a hit over a fence at least 210 feet from the home plate.

That gave the Maroons a 3-1 lead which they held until the ninth inning when an error of local boy Billy Alvord gave Gore first base and a fumble by Fred Lewis of Kelly's single let George to third and Mike to second. Anson flew out to Fred Dunlap, the Maroons' captain, and Pfeffer went out on a foul tip. George Baker, another native of St. Louis, threw to second base to double up Kelly but Dunlap wasn't there for some reason known only to himself and the ball sailed into center field. Boyle scooped it up and threw it to third. Hapless Alvord missed it. Gore ran to the plate and Kelly raced for home behind him. Glasscock retrieved the ball and fired it to the catcher Fatty Briody just in time to head Kelly off and the game was the property of the Maroons. Great excitement prevailed and the crowd yelled itself hoarse.

Henry Boyle pitched a swift ball the next day but walked six Chicago men and hit three as well in a 9-5 loss. The White Stockings whomped the Maroons 16-1 and 7-2 in the other two games of the series then trounced the Bisons 13-4 in Buffalo on May 8. The fifth inning was a rattler for the visitors as the Chicago men put nine runs on the score-board. Kelly had three hits in five visits to the plate. The big news in the evening papers was from the lumber-yard district of Chicago, where $1.5 million worth of boards had gone up in flames.

The White Stockings suffered their second loss in New York on May 11. The next day, the home team's rooters came away disgusted after the Chicagos walloped the Giants 10-2. Keefe was "all at sea, having no command over the sphere and surrendering a dozen hits." None were by Kelly, though he was praised for his work in the right garden. Mike had one hit in his club's 9-3 win in Philadelphia on the 13th and just one again in a 3-0 win in front of an enthusiastic crowd of 5,000 at Recreation Park the next day.

The Tribune base ball man opined that, "A club's reputation depends in a great measure on their gentlemanly deportment. With our club the social relations are of the pleasantest. Clarkson and Kelly, who are becoming fast friends, possess splendid voices and greatly enliven our tours away from home."

Among the society notes of May 12 was an announcement that Abner Dalrymple, left fielder of the Chicagos, was married last week to Miss Winnifred S. Green, niece of Capt. John Prindiville, a wealthy vessel owner of Chicago. James McCormick and his wife Jennie were witnesses.

In New York on the 16th the Chicago nine made silly errors at an alarming rate in the fifth inning. Young Richardson pitched for the Gothams, whom *The New York World* had started to call Giants due to the size of their men, and did excellent work, winning 13-4.

The White Stockings scored a run in the 8th and another in the 9th to beat the Quakers for the fourth consecutive time on May 19. Getzien was charged with fifteen errors but almost all of them were actually bases on balls.

The Giants downed the Wolverines 12-4 in New York but that wasn't the talk of the town. When the Brooklyn Bridge opened in May of 1883 it gained fame for its beauty and convenience. Soon it became known for its jumpers. The first person to leap from the bridge was Robert Odlum, a 34-year-old swimming instructor who tried it that day.

After going to church he assembled an audience: a tugboat full of spectators in the East River and a rescue swimmer who waited below to help him onto the boat after he hit the water. Around 5:30, just as the ball game was ending, with the bridge packed with pedestrians strolling the walkway, Odlum climbed over the rail and took his plunge. To lower the impact when he hit the water he held one arm above his head and the other pressed to his side.

As on-lookers held their breath Odlum rose to the water's surface motionless. A man on the tugboat swam out to get him and brought him on board. His insides were thoroughly lacerated, he died that night.

Of the Chicagos' May 25 game in Boston, William Harris wrote, "Both clubs are imbued with a determination to present themselves in the most favorable light. The two organizations are old rivals and know each other's strong and weak points to perfection. Boston spectators delight to witness Anson the chronic kicker and his able assistant kicker and lieutenant Kelly. Clarkson delivered the ball seemingly without the slightest exertion. To say that Kelly supported him admirably only faintly expresses it. The Chicago ace allowed just three hits, oddly two of them by Jim Manning who was suspended last week because of his weakness at the bat. It may have been that Clarkson was laying off on him and saving his energies for Boston's stronger batsmen.

The crowd grew excited in the sixth when Joe Hornung strode to the plate with men on first and second.

"Now, Joe," shouted an enthusiastic rooter.

The spectator got his wish when Hornung smashed the first pitch into right field for what seemed a sure base hit but Kelly scooped up

the ball and whipped it to Anson just quick enough to cause Joe to resume his seat.

Kelly proved himself a jewel in Providence on May 30. He was left nursing his earned bag each time he made his three safe hits, but he drove in all of the Chicagos' runs in a 3-2 win. The game took an agonizing two hours and forty-five minutes, partly because two balls were lost and new ones finally had to be put into play.

The White Stockings finished their 24-game season opening road trip in grand style with a four-game sweep of the Wolverines that put them in second place, a game behind the Giants and two ahead of Providence. As they were leaving Detroit Buffalo Bill was arriving with the members of his Wild West Show for their performance at the Driving Park.

On June 5 the 10,327 patrons, including all of Chicago's Who's Who, were loud in their praises of the barely-completed West Side Park. It was located on a small block bounded by Congress, Loomis, Harrison and Throop streets, with the diamond toward its western end. The elongated block lent a bathtub-like shape to the park, with foul lines as short as 216 feet. A bicycle track encircled the playing field to accommodate the cycling craze that was sweeping the nation.

The stadium held roughly 10,000 fans. It had brick outfield fences, grand-stands supported by sturdy oak trusses, and a series of private boxes for the wealthiest citizens, visiting club boosters, and the owners and administrators of the White Stockings. The press had their own private box to cover the action on the field. The entire outlay of money on the grounds would aggregate to nearly $30,000, the sum of $10,0000 alone for the brick wall surrounding the park.

The Tribune reported that, "At 2 o'clock a tally-ho coach and four-in-hand landed the teams at the east end of the grounds and the Lucas team in their gay maroon and white uniforms took the field for practice. After throwing the ball around for an hour they gave way to the White Stockings. As Anson and his men crossed the outfield the immense audience rose to its feet and gave them a welcome of which the club may well feel proud.

In the third inning Gore sent the leather into extreme left field and scored amidst wild and long-continued applause. Kelly then got a base on balls and cleverly stole second and third before being brought home by Anson's long hit to Lewis. Triple baggers by Flint and Kelly and a single by Gore together with a sacrifice by Anson yielded Chicago three runs."

Briody scored on an error by Kelly in the ninth but Mike was hampered by a rush of spectators who were anxious to beat the crowd and ran across the field to the gates.

After a satisfying 9-2 win Kelly took Agnus to see "The Drum Major's Daughter," which had opened at the Chicago Theater while the team was on the road. Fred Pfeffer and his wife Ida and George Gore and his wife joined them. Abner and his new bride Winnifred had other plans.

On June 12 John L. Sullivan arrived in Chicago for his fight with Jack Burke at the Driving Grounds the next day. The previous Wednesday night in Philadelphia Sullivan had gotten very drunk, eaten six dozen clams at one sitting, and put the inmates of several saloons to flight. A dozen of his friends overpowered him and by main force put him to bed.

A 17-9 win over Detroit on the 13th moved the Chicagos into a tie for the lead with a 24-6 record. Kelly played first base and racked up three hits and three errors. In a 17-5 win on Monday Kelly scored five runs in the White Stockings' 8-6 win over Providence. He was knackered from running the bases and his uniform was filthy from all the sliding he'd done.

The Detroits had a decided advantage for the first six innings on June 16 and it looked very much like a defeat for the hosts. Left-handed Elmer Sutcliffe, who had gotten into just four games in '84, was behind the bat the first four innings but played so loosely that Kelly was put in his place. Mike hit for a base in the first, stole second, and scored on Quest's error. Kelly hit safe again and scored another run in the third.

He got a square hit to the outskirts of left field in the fifth. He stood

at first base a picture of studied nonchalance, not a muscle twitching as he stared blandly in the general direction of the pitching box with the most enigmatic of looks on his handsome and much-admired face. Ten thousand throats created a wall of sound, half exhorting the pitcher to throw the ball, half beseeching Kelly to "Go!"

After what seemed an eternity the pitcher sent the ball plate-ward. There was a deafening roar as Kelly took off. Bennett hurled the ball to second. His throw was perfect. Shortstop Marr Phillips cupped the ball in his hands and turned grimly as Kelly thundered toward him. The boosters were on their feet now, screaming "Slide, Kelly, SLIDE!" at the top of their lungs.

Suddenly Mike's body dropped to the ground and a cloud of dust rolled toward the base. Phillips lunged to where Kelly should be, where any *other* base stealer would be.

Kelly wasn't there. He was off to one side. He and Phillips looked down at the bag at the same time, Phillips puzzled, Mike grinning. The toe of his base ball shoe was hooked around the bag.

"Safe!" yelled the umpire.

"Yaahhh!" roared the crowd.

After Mike took third base a stockbroker in a private box said to his wife, "Do you notice the way Kelly slows down while he's running the bases to coax a throw. When they do, the other runner has time to score."

Kelly reached base and scored on Anson's two-baser in the seventh and got his fifth hit and scored his fifth run of the game in the ninth. His runs were needed, the Chicagos squeaked out an 8-6 win. To top things off Kelly threw out three Detroit base-runners.

"What would they do without that scalawag Kelly?" a man with a pepper gray goatee said to his friend as they left the grounds.

"Let's hope they never have to find out," replied his friend.

The Chicagos put in their best display of fielding of the season on June 24 against Philadelphia, making just one error. After Mulvey put in his home run they drove every ball that looked the least bit

favorable and the result was seven long fly hits. After a 12-2 win, the White Stockings' 18th straight, Anson felt that the boys had made up their minds to equal or surpass their 1880 record of 22 straight wins.

"We beat the Quakers four straight on their grounds and I reckon we can do the same thing here," Kelly told the others.

The Chicagos dropped the next two games. Kelly going 0-for-7 didn't helped.

The sports editor of *The Louisville Courier-Journal* wrote that, "Kicking may make umpires sad but it adds spice to the game and it tickles the crowd. It draws too. People turn out to see the Chicagos for the pleasure afforded by the lively way in which they play ball and you can always expect to hear Anson and Kelly chin the umpire. If they don't, the crowd is disappointed. A game between Anson & Co. and Comiskey's Browns would fill every available spot on any ball grounds."

John A. Brown, the General Secretary of the Chicago Base Ball club, was interviewed at the Sturtevant Hotel. He attributed the success of the White Stockings to "Blue Lick Water." Asked to explain, Brown said that the decision was taken to spend the month of April in Nashville but it was in Kentucky on the team's way home where they had good food and plenty of practice in the delightful climate and healthful Blue Lick water that caused them to sweat away every ounce of useless flesh and they couldn't help but become as supple as cats.

The question of healthy, substantial, well-cooked food is so important the Chicago management chooses stopping places a good deal on the merits of the table, which requires them to stay at the most expensive hotels in all the cities excepting Boston and New York."

Asked about the character of the club's players Brown confessed that he knew nothing about the players apart from their salaries, which he kept secret to avoid jealousies.

Just then Dalrymple happened by and was asked to describe his teammates. He started with the club's only college man. "Clarkson is 24, unmarried, and a jewelry-man in the intervals between the seasons. Fred Pfeffer is from Louisville. Gore is 29, married, and the game's only player from Saccarappa, Maine. Anson is the oldest player at 32. He has a delightful home in Chicago for which he paid $8,000 and he's worth probably $15,000, all earned on the diamond field. My own home in the off-season is a cattle ranch outside of Franklin, Nebraska. Among the accomplishments of individual members, Anson is noted as a billiardist, Sunday is the fastest runner in the league, Kelly is the greatest base runner. A successful base runner must combine coolness, quick perception, instantaneous decision-making, but above all nerve and those Kel possesses in spades."

What Dalrymple failed to mention was that at the ripe old age of 25 the club's former star twirler Larry Corcoran was done racking up wins. He was ordered to go home and put his arm in a sling for two months. He'd pitch only six more big league games.

Kelly rapped three hits off Daisy Davis and made two sparkling catches of long flyballs in a 12-8 win over Boston on the 27th. *American Sports* magazine noted that the Chicagos had the same number of runs as hits while the other League clubs had made three hits to each of their runs, they attributed it to the White Stockings' fine base-running.

The crowd at the Cincinnati grounds that day was the most disorderly ever seen there. Umpire McLean gave dissatisfaction to the crowd of 4,000 spectators by his decisions, especially on base play. Incensed by a crank's taunts Billy grabbed a bat and flung it viciously into the grandstand, braining an innocent bystander named T.J. Watson and nearly inciting a riot. The assemblage of staid businessmen, demure maidens, and blushing damsels going frantic over a game of ball was a sight to behold. It was with great difficulty that McLean was protected from the mob.

The game was finished at the highest pitch of excitement and the umpire was smuggled from the grounds in handcuffs and hauled off for summary justice in a police wagon. McLean escaped a prison sentence by paying a $500 fine, a sizeable chunk of his annual income. In a public letter, he apologized and pleaded for understanding but

didn't sound terribly contrite. "Goaded by uncalled-for, as well as unexpected taunts, I, for a moment, and but for a moment, forgot my position as an umpire and did what any man's nature would prompt if placed in a similar situation."

As June turned to July Kelly had more runs than hits. He was drinking heavily but when Spalding was asked to comment on it he shrugged and told the reporter, "Nobody likes having so many micks in the club and Kelly is the worst of the lot. He loves to spread his enthusiasm for drinking and carousing no matter what hour of the night. Anson tells me that on road trips Kelly will have everybody rip-roaring drunk by midnight and after they howl like wolves for a while they all pass out, all except him that is. But we need to sell tickets and no one does that like Michael J. Kelly."

There was now a good deal more snap and vigor in the Chicagos' play than there had been in either of the previous two seasons. The last game of the series resulted in another victory for the home nine and it came by a powerful aggregation of hard ball striking. Kelly had three of his club's twenty-three hits in a 24-10 win that moved them two games ahead of the second-place Giants.

Mike read *The Inter-Ocean* during breakfast the next morning and saw that someone had written in to inquire as to whether Cal McVey was still alive. Kelly chuckled when he read the response. "Answer. - Calvin McVey is now living on his ranch in California. As a side speculation he has gone into individual sports. He has come off the winner in several wrestling matches and has captured gold medals for all-round athletics."

Kelly's bat was full of holes in a 6-4 loss to New York on July 3. He couldn't contribute with his arm as not a single ball was batted his way. The Giants downed the White Stockings 6-3 the next day and Kelly was stymied with the willow again. Pfeffer pitched and was batted freely, the crowd calling out loudly for Clarkson, who was playing right field as Kelly was employed in Pfeffer's place at second. The Gothamites completed the sweep on Monday the home team making a dozen errors none by Kelly. He knew that if it hadn't been for their dismal record against New York the White Stockings would

hold a commanding lead.

On July 9 Kelly got in a triple in the first and a single in the fifth. Behind the bat he made two errors and had one passed ball but threw out three runners in his club's 8-5 defeat of the crippled Providence nine.

W.I. Harris opined that, "If the Chicagos lose out on the pennant this year it will be due to the niggardly cheeseparing by the management of the club. Messrs. Spalding and Anson have outlived their usefulness. When Captain Anson indulges himself in his favorite pastime of billiards after a game his players quickly hie themselves to the nearest gin-mill, well knowing that if Anson once gets interested in a billiards game his otherwise watchful eye is off them."

The Chicagos headed out on the road on Sunday, July 12 for a five-game series in Buffalo with a half-game lead over New York. Mike wanted to win every game.

"These fellas should be easy-pickin', lads. They're bringing up the rear. They've played fifty games and won but fifteen uv them."

The Tribune reported on a new addition to the Chicago team on July 29. "This afternoon's game with the Providence team will be the last played in Chicago until August 17. Kelly and Kennedy, who has surrendered five home runs in the seven games he has pitched thus far, will form the battery for the home team. The question that has so long proven a source of anxiety to the ball-going public of Chicago – viz.: That of securing a quality pitcher to alternate with Clarkson has at last been satisfactorily arranged. President Spalding has arranged the release from the Providence team of James McCormick.

When The Tribune man asked Spalding about the acquisition of McCormick A.G. said, "Given that Kennedy has surrendered five home runs in the seven games he has been assigned to pitch I'd say it was high time we got someone else to alternate with Clarkson. McCormick is very popular with our boys, a good fellow and a thoroughly good ball-player. If he continues his record as a pitcher and will follow the example of the other boys in abstaining from anything stronger than milk and water until the close of the season he

must prove a welcome acquisition to the ranks of the Chicago Club.'"

When Kelly read that he was in a bar. He waved the waiter over and pointed to his glass of whiskey. "Could ya pour a drop uv water into that for me?"

James umpired the first game in his Chicago uniform owing to the non-appearance of a League umpire. The Buffalo cranks felt McCormick handed the game to his new team in the 8th inning when the visitors scored three times to pull ahead 6-4. Kelly appeared to have clearly run outside the base line in his attempt to reach second but after hesitating McCormick did not give Kelly out. Mike scored on Anson's baser and that was followed by two base hits that gave the Chicagos the lead and the game as it turned out since a summer shower washed out the ninth inning. According to *The Buffalo Express* the next morning "the feeling manifested by the crowd need not be described."

The paper ran a pithy account of Tuesday's game. "The bulldozers from Chicago won another game at the Park yesterday. Clarkson pitched and Flint caught until the seventh when Williamson stepped into the box and Kelly caught. It all seemed mere child's play for the visitors. They laughed and joked each other all through the game. Umpire Gaffney fined Gore $50 for wagging his chin too freely."

The state of things in Buffalo was so bad that there was talk the club would be disbanded at the end of the week. The fact that they'd sold Pud Galvin who'd won 46 games each of the past two seasons to the AA's Pittsburgh club didn't bode well for their future. Their departure would make it difficult for the League, one team would be idle whenever it had a series scheduled with the Bisons.

A large crowd turned up the next day to see Galvin's replacement Pete Wood, a 19-year-old Canadian. It was hoped that he would have an auspicious send-off but no one expected that he would give such a splendid exhibition of pitching as he did. He seemed conscious that every eye was upon him but displayed little uneasiness. The Chicagos were fortunate to bunch enough hits together in the third inning to win the game, but Wood limited them to just seven in total and he

struck out every man in the list with the exception of Pfeffer. Anson was as pugilistic as ever, disputing Gaffney's calls, especially on third strikes, and he received a generous and well-deserved hissing from the spectators.

The teams played twice on Thursday. The Chicagos had all the fun they wanted with the Bisons during a 9-3 victory in the morning. The home nine was rattled from the start. Serad sent Gore to first on balls, to second on a wild pitch, then allowed him to steal third from whence he scored on Kelly's hit to left. Anson hit safe sending Kelly to second and both advanced on Pfeffer's grounder to Serad who vainly endeavored to throw Kelly out at third. With the bases full, a balk was called on the hapless Serad and Kelly was waved home. The Chicagos ran up five runs in the 8th for a 9-3 win.

The Bisons sent Wood to the box for the afternoon game, the re-scheduled postponed game of May 10. Wood told Captain Richard-son he had sore arm and a lame back but Richardson was unmoved. The White Stockings were a lot more familiar with the young Ca-nadian's delivery now and it was quite a different story this time. To the chagrin of the audience he was bombarded from the get-go. The greedy Chicagos scored twice in the first, three times in the second, and six times in the third, then coasted to a 13-9 win and a sweep that moved them three games ahead of New York. But the Giants wouldn't be going away any time soon.

"Can They Slay the Giants?"

The White Stockings took the long train ride from Buffalo to Boston and checked into the United States Hotel late Friday afternoon. After dinner most of the players smoked a cigar in the lobby and then headed up to their second-floor rooms. Not Kelly, he headed to Doyle's. After a few hours of throwing back whiskeys and reveling with Beaneater boosters of Irish descent he headed to the Bell in Hand.

The place sold mostly beer but Mike was able to talk the white-haired bar-tender into finding him a bottle of Irish whiskey.

"The first owner, Jimmy Wilson, was Boston's town crier for fifty years," the bar-tender told Mike. "He announced news of everything from the Boston Tea Party to the war for independence. When he retired, he opened this place."

He pointed to the name of the tavern above the bar. "He named it for the bell he carried on the job. Jimmy didn't go for the hard stuff, he refused to sell whiskey, rum, or even gin. You needed two glasses for his ale. It was so thick it was served in two mugs, one for the ale, the other for the froth."

Kelly was glad all the other patrons were drinking ale - he didn't have to share his bottle.

On Saturday there was enough heavy batting, clever base-running, and phenomenally bad fielding to satisfy even the wildest enthusiasts. The fielders were kept on the hop-skip-and-jump and covered more ground in two hours than they generally would in two weeks.

One of the most exciting incidents of the afternoon was a foot race by Kelly and Sunday to the lower fence for the ball when old Deacon White made his home run. Anson, Pfeffer, and Kelly were ridiculed for their noisy attempt to bull-doze the umpire on more than one occasion, especially when the agile Mike was caught napping at first by Brouthers, which created a jubilant storm in the stands. After the game Spalding fined Kelly $250 for incessantly missing curfew.

Brouthers was interviewed by a man from *The Sporting Life.*

"Who is your favorite man to play against, Dan?"

"Mike Kelly. He has a bluff, genial manner that disarms suspicion and makes you like him from the first. He's like a fox. Every time the umpires are asleep or looking the other way he pulls one over on them. Of course there are some people who believe in playing base ball on the level but a good many other birds realize that it's played on a diamond so take advantage of all the corners. Kelly could sell earmuffs in the Philippines or palm-leaf fans in Alaska. He's a wonder as a baseball player but as a trickster he's a marvel. Whenever he's on the field the umpires spend half their time combing the wool away from their eyes."

The reporter chuckled.

Brouthers carried on. "In a game in Detroit I came to bat in the ninth inning, there were two out and three on base. Moments like that are big ones in a batter's life. I got a toe hold and made my mind to tear the cover off the first good one that came across. I believe we needed three runs. Kel was playing in the field that day. I picked out one that I liked and hit it hard enough to drive it out of the lot. I was sure the ball was going over the fence because Kelly was running like a mountain goat in that direction. Just as he got near the fence he made a wonderful jump and got the ball. That made three out; the game was over, and Mike kept running into the clubhouse, taking the ball with him. We lost the game, of course. Some time later Kel confessed to me that he'd never even touched the ball he'd apparently caught. It had cleared the fence by ten feet, the one he held up for everyone to see had been in his pocket."

On July 24 the Boston fielders were kept busy leather hunting the whole afternoon. They surrendered fourteen runs to the visitors from the Windy City.

A stout man in the stands above the Chicagos' bench with a thick Boston accent shouted, "We could sure use ya on awer club, Mike," when Kelly got back to the bench after hitting a ball over the left field fence." It was his third hit of the afternoon.

The Boston Globe mourned, "When Capt. Anson repaired to the ticket office after yesterday's game and drew his club's share of the gate he saw how local attendance has decreased. One hundred and twelve dollars was the grand total. Boston people have grown tired of paying fifty cents to see their nine go on the field in a don't-care manner and act as if they are beaten before the game commences. How different is the Chicago club. If only Boston had a Kelly or an Anson in its nine."

Mike had ridden to the grounds with Nat Goodwin in a barouche. Goodwin spent most of the ride talking about the new novel he was reading called "Huck Finn."

A huge crowd passed through the Polo Grounds' turn-stiles on August 6 for the first game of an all-important series between the League's frontrunners. The Giants had won 12 of their last 13 games and the Chicagos could feel them breathing down their necks. The excited spectators were on tenterhooks throughout as Welch and Clarkson each allowed four hits and no runs in nine innings.

When Ewing opened the tenth by driving the ball out of the reach of the agile Kelly it was a signal for an outburst of applause. On the fourth pitch to Ward, Ewing started for second. Ward hit the sphere on a line to right. Kelly smiled, other teams were copying his run-and-hit play. He handled the ball magnificently and threw New York's crack base-runner out at first. As he did, Ewing headed to third at his utmost speed. Anson fired the ball to Williamson. Ball and runner seemed to arrive simultaneously but by a headlong dive Ewing gained the base.

Gillespie tipped the third ball pitched to him, a slow curve, slowly

toward second base. Pfeffer stooped to handle it but it took a sudden bound over his shoulder. He retrieved the sphere and at once it was off like a rifle-shot toward Flint. As Ewing slid into the plate a thick cloud of dust concealed all.

"Is he out?" asked Ward.

"Does the run count?" queried Esterbrook.

The dust finally cleared and Ewing's hand was seen to be on the plate. Flint sat staring at the ball, which lay in the dirt in between his legs.

With two hands down in the bottom of the tenth Pfeffer was put out at second while trying to steal that point and there was a perfect storm of applause. Governor Hill fired his hat high into the air, chair cushions were thrown about promiscuously, and every person present was happy save the Chicago players who presented a pitiful spectacle as they dragged their bats behind them like so many mourners returning from a funeral. Anson was the saddest man in the party, visions of the championship fading from his gaze.

"Tough luck," Abner Dalrymple ventured to remark.

"Yes," said Gore.

"Those fellows played good ball," interpolated Kelly.

"But they had the umpire with them," said corpulent Williamson.

"Let's blame it on the umpire," was Anson's rejoinder.

"Yes, let's," agreed Fred Pfeffer.

Kelly contributed three hits to the Chicagos' much needed win the next day. He handled McCormick's baffling curves splendidly behind the bat and James kept the Giants to five one-basers. A loss would have given the Giants a tie for first place.

In the last game of the series the New York men appeared far and away the League's superior nine, scoring four runs in the 4th, two in the 7th, another four in the 8th and running roughshod over the visitors 12-0. The Giants played errorless ball and went to town on Clarkson's twists. He'd never looked worse, allowing a whopping sev-

enteen hits - as many as he usually surrendered in *three* games.

After the game a red-faced Anson, who'd been criticized in the press along with Gore, Pfeffer, and Williamson for making inexcusable errors, told reporters the White Stockings would get square with the New Yorks when they came to Chicago in September. Anson was in a little better mood after his men won a make-up game in Buffalo on their way to a four-game series in Detroit.

After the 1884 season Frederick K. Stearns, argumentative, aggressive, and not to be ignored when his interests were involved, had joined the Wolverines' ownership group. He spearheaded the purchase of the Indianapolis franchise and the transfer of its players to Detroit on June 15. Stearns then rounded up Sam Thompson and most of the other former Hoosier players and put them on a train bound for Detroit with the intention of using them in the next Wolverine game. But before the train arrived he received a wire from National League Secretary Nick Young informing him that, according to the directives of the National Agreement, ten days had to expire before released players could be signed by another team.

Stearns hired a yacht and sent the players on a cruise around Lake Michigan. Out of sight of land, they had no idea where they were. Farm boys who'd never been on the water, they were sea-sick most of the time. A couple of the players demanded to be put ashore but the captain refused.

Rookie slugger Sam Thompson, the Hoosier player most coveted by other League clubs, said the men spent their time in fishing and playing poker - chips having thoughtfully been provided - and were entertained royally with food and drink, anything in the line of creature comforts you could find packed away on ice, until the time limit expired. Then they were brought back to Detroit where they all immediately signed Wolverine contracts. After signing, the players went to their hotel to check for messages. They found scores of letters and telegraphed offers for their services from other clubs that had piled up during their captivity. With the addition of the new men the Detroits turned things around. They'd soon be a force to be reckoned

with, but not yet, they'd need another influx of quality players.

The Chicagos took all four games in Detroit. None was especially close but the last one was nearly not played. Tommy Bond, now an umpire, was working the series and his decisions in the third game had been questionable to say the least. When he arrived for the final game of the series he was handed a telegram by Bill Watkins, the Detroit captain. It read:

> **Mr. T. Bond, your services are no longer required by the National League, effective immediately.**
>
> **Nick Young, Secretary, National League**

Young had arranged for Harry Chipman, a Detroit attorney who'd umpired while he had studied law, to work the game. Anson insisted that since Bond was there anyway it made a hell of a lot more sense for him to do the game.

"The League said effective immediately," said Watkins.

Anson pointed at Bond. "We ain't playing unless he umpires."

"Well he can't," said Watkins.

"He can and he fucking well will!" stormed Anson.

The crowd was getting restless. Three police officers arrived on the scene.

"You'll play with Chipman as umpire or you'll forfeit the game!" the spectators heard Watkins exclaim.

Anson's face was bright red, as it often was. "We … we …" He looked at the stands and saw outrage on the spectators' faces.

"We'll play. Under protest."

The Chicagos played the first game of their 11-game homestand on August 18 in front of two thousand cheerful boosters. The sea of brown and gray suits was enlivened by splashes of red and yellow. Having indulged in liberal doses of whiskey and gotten absolutely foozled the night before, Kelly was in a stupor. He let a lazy fly off the bat of Glasscock go over his head in the third inning and two run-

ners scored on the play. He left the game at the end of the fifth. Kelly was lucky his team held on for a 9-4 win. *The Inter-Ocean* reporter wrote, "Victory once more perched upon the banner of the Whites and another game on the winning side makes the title to the pennant more certain, though it may have been somewhat presumptuous on President Spalding's part to put the year 1885 on the flag that flies over the grounds at the beginning of the season." As penance Anson put Kelly at the bottom of the batting list the next day. He was 'under the weather' when he showed up for the third game of the series. Anson didn't even put his name on the list. Kelly didn't play the last game of the series either.

Kelly was back and in fine form for the September 2nd game, a 12-9 win over Buffalo. *The Inter-Ocean* reporter thought the Chicagos' fielding "was perfect, with the exception of the regulation errors by Anson and Burns. Not a single error was charged to pitcher McCormick or catcher Kelly, a remarkable thing in the present method of scoring passed balls and bases on balls in the error column. The nine played a game that would have beaten any club in the League and if they can only do as well when they stand up before the New Yorks the championship is certainly theirs. Kelly did as much if not more than any individual toward winning the game. He by his splendid batting, base running, and coaching enthused the team into turning a defeat into a victory. *The Tribune* noted that "Kelly's coaching of the home team, his schemes and his ability to rattle his opponents wrought his friends up to a high pitch of enthusiasm."

The White Stockings' bats were tied quiet in a 7-2 loss in St. Louis on September 9. Kelly's run-scoring baser in the ninth was one of just three hits. But when the Boston-New York game was bulletined the Chicago players gave a shout of joy. They trounced the Maroons, whom the St. Louis writers had dubbed the Black Diamonds, 8-1 the next day but 19-year-old Egyptian Healy, fresh from the Southern League, proved a tougher challenge on Friday. The only runs scored came in the seventh inning. Kelly was sent to first on balls. Anson swore Kelly had rubber knees that he could adjust at will to fool the umpires on low balls. Mike stole second and third then Pfeffer hit past Dunlap and Kelly scored. Pfeffer stole second and came home

on Burns' clean drive to left.

After the game Mike went over to Alex McKinnon, the Maroons' first baseman. "Why are you lads callin' your new pitcher *Egyptian*? He looks American ta me. And I didn't see him ride into the grounds on a camel."

McKinnon chuckled. "He's from Cairo."

Kelly gave him a blank look.

McKinnon chuckled again. "Cairo, Illinois."

On their way out of the park Mike heard the sound of hooves and saw a team of six massive Clydesdale steeds pulling a scarlet red wagon with the word BUDWEISER along the sides.

"They like their suds here in St. Louis," said Mike.

"Why don't we do some tot-hunting while we're in town," said Abner.

"Let's get some neck oil first," said Gore. "This burg's got more breweries than bordellos."

Healy proved a mystery to the White Stockings again the next day to the delight of the St. Louis cranks. He shut them out on five hits, none by Kelly. The Giants clobbered Providence 9-1.

"That Egyptian fella's gointa cost us the damn pennant," groaned Kelly.

The team boarded an Atlantic & Great Western Railroad train for the trip back to Chicago that night. The railroad was known for its excellent safety record and comfortable, elegant, luxurious cars. The Atlantic & Great Western also boasted that its passengers, traveling in its beautifully appointed Pullman cars, would not have to leave the train between Chicago, Cincinnati, and St. Louis. The players didn't have to get off the train, but they weren't travelling in Pullman cars. Kelly drank a whole bottle of the railroad's whiskey on the way.

He was behind the bat for the first game, catching, or *trying* to catch his friend James. The boosters were happy to have their favor-

ite entertainer back but Mike was in no mood to entertain them.

When a crank yelled "Razzle Dazzle, Kel" he uncharacteristically ignored him.

He tried to leave the game after six innings due to illness but Boston captain Morrill wouldn't allow Flint to substitute for him so he was forced to carry on. The newspapers put it bluntly. "Kelly was unable to hold the pitching of McCormick, six pitches got past him." Mike's *illness* was a terrific hangover. He could hardly wait for the game to end.

The Chicagos beat the Bostons the next two days. Kelly read that Detroit owner Stearns had telegraphed his bank to request that it take care of his draft for $7,000 and the bank had done so. Mike's eyes widened when he read that the money was for the purchase of each and every one of Buffalos' players. The Bisons would have to finish out the season with local amateurs. With Hardy Richardson, Jack Rowe, Dan Brouthers, and Deacon White in the first four places in their batting list the Bisons had just swept a four-game series from the Wolverines. Now "the Big Four" would be playing for the Detroits. Or would they?

The papers announced that Richardson, Rowe, Brouthers, and White would be in the Detroit lineup on Saturday, September 19 against the Giants. They were not. Secretary Young had ruled that the transfer of the Buffalo players to Detroit could not take place until the end of the season. "The Big Four will play in the Buffalo club or not at all," he decreed. Without them in the lineup the Giants beat the Wolverines on Saturday to stay within two games of the White Stockings. As for the Big Four, they didn't play for Detroit or Buffalo the rest of the season - they just disappeared but they'd certainly make the Wolverines a powerhouse in '86 and '87.

The Chicagos beat the Grays on September 22 and 23 then lost to them the next day. The two teams would journey to Providence for a make-up game and then back to Chicago for another single game. Spalding had protested that it was ridiculous to go back and forth like that but the Giants wouldn't stand for the White Stockings having an extra home game. Playing in Providence hardly bothered the Chicagos, they hammered the Grays 21-3. Kelly had three hits and scored four runs. When the two clubs got back to Chicago the White Stockings whitewashed the Providences 6-0. The Giants had downed the Bisons 15-1 and 5-1.

The National League's juggernauts would meet with just two weeks left in the season. Both had astounding winning percentages, Chicago's .798 and New York's .779. The Giants had won 10 of their last 11 games and the Chicagos had won 10 of their last 12.

All four games of the eagerly anticipated series were sold out in advance, an unprecedented occurrence. The Giants were confident that they could win three of the games and tie the race. They would be two ahead if they swept the series. They'd won 9 of the 12 previous head-to-head matchups even though Clarkson had pitched almost every game. Mickey Welch was a perfect 7-0 against the White Stockings.

The New Yorks were staying at the Clifton House and were accompanied by a large number of admirers. Several cars had been added to the Chicago Express to transport them. Many of the leading eastern newspapers had sent representatives.

The people of Chicago had seldom been so wildly enthusiastic over the result of an opening game of a series. The betting odds were even in Chicago betting emporiums but in New York the Giants were favorites at 100 to 75. Ten thousand people, including a great many that rooted loudly for the visitors, witnessed the Tuesday, September 29 game which was "played for blood on both sides."

Anson chose McCormick to pitch. To the surprise of no one, New York went with Welch. With fans sitting in foul territory and standees strung out down the outfield fences, Giants captain Ward insisted on ground rules giving three bases on hits into the overflow.

He quickly regretted it. The crowd was hysterical when their darlings put up four runs in their first at bats on hits by Pfeffer, Williamson, Burns, and a ground-rule triple by Kelly. Welch was walloped all over the field and Kelly was the chief pounder. Chicago added two

runs in the fifth on Kelly's three-baser. He hit another in the ninth for his club's final run. He'd gone five times to the bat and knocked out two doubles and three triples and he scored three times.

Kelly hopped from side to side all afternoon to capture his old friend's twisters. He snapped them up like the grip of fate, threw with wonderful quickness and precision, and captured bamboozles - foul balls caught before the first bounce - like a frisky kitten would its favorite toy mouse. W.I. Harris wrote, "What would the Chicago nine be without Kelly? If only the Bostons had a player like him."

The down-town pool rooms were crowded all afternoon the next day in the Big Apple. New Yorkers were slightly cast down but still came to the front with their money. Returns were received as each club retired from the bat and were posted on the board to cheers and groans. At the close of the fifth somebody offered $10 to $9 but found no takers. Thousands of dollars changed hands on the result of the game.

Streets were blocked by the crowds who watched the huge bulletin boards for the two hours the game was played. In front of The *New York Sun* office three policemen had all they could handle to keep the sidewalk clear.

People flocked to West Side Park in droves. Every street-car was crowded to its utmost capacity and vehicles of every description were hailed for passage to the game. Hundreds stood or sat in chairs in front of the center field fence that was 560 feet from home plate. Many were compelled to become squatters on the outfield grass while small boys pre-empted telephone poles and store windows commanding a view of the field. The roofs of the colony of boarding houses swarmed with long distance baseball enthusiasts who aimed scores of opera glasses and telescopes at the diamond. Men roosted upon the last tier of bricks of the grimy chimneys while others clung to lightning rods like shipwrecked sailors to a spar. It was nearly impossible to hear the umpire when he yelled safe or out or the name of a player that was being substituted.

The game abounded in great plays by both sides. Kelly, who was

still recovering from his celebration of yesterday's win, succumbed to Keefe's wiles in the three-strike order in the first inning. Shaking hands with Willie Hahn before his at bat hadn't helped this time. Mike tried to find the outside of the left field fence with a long fly ball his next time up but the wind was against him and it fell into Gillespie's hands.

The home team finally broke open a game of goose eggs in the last half of the fourth inning. Dalrymple sent a hot grounder to left and sprinted around to second just ahead of Gillespie's throw. Gore followed with a hot grounder of his own that shot through shortstop John Ward and allowed Dalrymple to score.

After Kelly and Anson were retired on flyballs to open the seventh Pfeffer hit a skyscraper the wind couldn't keep inside the park.

The Gotham City nine were unable to gauge Clarkson's curves and the score remained 2-0 until the ninth. Connor opened with a walk and Ewing struck out. Gillespie reached base when Anson muffed a throw. With two on, Mike Dorgan bounced to Burns who tossed to Pfeffer to force the runner. Fred's desperate attempt to complete a game-ending double play went wild and before the dust cleared Connor had scored and Dorgan was perched on second with the tying run but Clarkson snagged Richardson's come-backer and tossed it to Anson for the final out.

The Giants' 2-1 loss caused gloom in New York. Though there was still a possibility of them winning the pennant it was regarded as a weak straw to catch.

The third game was played on Thursday, October 1. Prolonged cheering greeted the Chicagos as they came into the field at the call of the bell. Anson walked at the head of the line of players and his huge form towered over Willie Hahn who carried a bat as big as himself. The wind blew hard from the northwest and made cats' paws in the soft grass of the outfield. Down in the clubhouse the janitors pranced around like dancing masters, dusting the uniforms of the coming champions and laying wagers on the day's contest.

Welch lost to McCormick again, 8-3 this time. A two-out error

by Ward prolonged the Chicagos' second inning, then second base-man Joe Gerhardt let a grounder go through his hands and two men scored. With White Stockings on second and third and two out in the fourth, Ewing let a passed ball get by for one run then threw wildly over third to give the home team two more gift tallies. New York counted one in the third and two in the sixth and the score stood at 4-3 before Chicago put the game away with four clean hits in a four-run top of the ninth.

Thousands of people rose to their feet as if launched by a spring and from many throats came sound indescribable, a hurricane of hullabaloos. Men jumped up and down like Comanches and hugged one another in delight. Willie Hahn was beaming. He walked off the grounds on his hands. The next morning *The Decatur Herald* said the mortgage the Chicagos held on the League Championship pennant was foreclosed yesterday afternoon.

When Nat Goodwin, who travelled with his own skull for use in the grave-digger scene in Hamlet, heard of the White Stockings win-ning the championship he treated them to a performance of "The Skating Rink" at Hooley's Theatre. After the overture the orchestra struck up "See the Conquering Hero Comes" and Goodwin led the eleven Chicago players to their box.

Leading the race by five games with five to play, the Chicagos aimed to mathematically clinch the championship in the series fi-nale on Saturday with Clarkson pitching against Keefe. Paced by a three-run poke over the left-field fence by Kelly, they roared out to an 8-2 lead after three innings but the Giants showed their mettle by tallying one in the fourth, two in the fifth, and, with the help of a controversial call at second base, five in the sixth to take a 10-8 lead. They added two runs when the gloaming was not far off in the bot-tom of the eighth and the game was called.

The pennant was officially decided on Tuesday, October 6. When the Philadelphias were retired with neatness and dispatch in the ninth the Chicago men threw their caps into the air in jubilation. The score-board showed that the once mighty New Yorks had fallen

to the lowly Maroons by a score of 7-4 and now had no chance of catching the White Stockings.

According to *The Spalding Guide* Buffalo's Jim O'Rourke had finished first in the League with a .351 average. Boston's Ezra Sutton, who looked more like an accountant than a ball tosser, was right on his heels at .350. Kelly wound up third at .341.

Years later, as baseball researchers became increasingly diligent and combed through old box scores to see if there had been any mistakes they discovered that there had been a few in 1885. Correcting them caused a new king to be crowned. O'Rourke and Sutton each dropped three points - to .347 and .346 - but the contemporary tabulations had understated Mike Kelly's average by 13 points, so his revised average became .354 and that topped the list. Kelly was happy to have led the league in runs scored with 124.

The Boston Globe ran a piece on Kelly. "The king of the base ball profession is Mike Kelly, the Chicagos' right fielder and change catcher, who first saw the light of day in Troy, NY in 1857. Everybody who ever saw the Chicagos play knows Kelly by sight simply because they keep their eyes on him from the time he strides onto the field 'til the time he exits it. He is the best base-runner and the hardest and most clever kicker who walks the ball diamonds - the air of injured innocence he puts on is worth the price of admission itself. His batting and fielding figures rarely lead the list but if it is possible to strike a general average for stealing, batting, conscientious fielding, persistent kicking, skillful base-running, knowledge of the game, and all the tricks which help a club to win he would stand alone."

Spalding was so delighted by his team winning the pennant he gave each player a $100 bonus for abstaining from intoxicating beverages and orgies and winning the pennant. He was looking forward to the series he'd arranged with the AA champion St. Louis club.

The Browns scored two runs in the second on Chicago errors in Game One in Chicago. They added four more on two hits and four more White Stocking errors in top of the fourth and Kelly scored the Chicagos' first run in the bottom of the inning. Gore got a base on

balls in the eighth and scored off singles by Kelly and Anson. Pfeffer followed with a home run that tied the game. As it was now too dark to continue play the game was called.

The game the next day broke up in the sixth inning which nearly culminated in a riot. The Chicagos were without the service of Gore who had been suspended by Capt. Anson for indifferent playing and indulging to freely in stimulants. He didn't accompany the team to St. Louis. Comiskey hit hot to Pfeffer who threw home to Kelly to catch Gleason but the ball arrived too late. Kelly sent it to second to catch Comiskey but Pfeffer muffed it and Welch ran home and Comiskey took third. He scored on a passed ball.

The Chicago Tribune reported the near riot that occurred in detail. "The Browns held a 4-2 led when the Chicagos came to bat in the sixth. Umpire David Sullivan had given several close decisions against St. Louis and he was subjected to considerable abuse from the crowd. Sunday hit a tremendous drive over Nichol's head and reached second. He reached third on a wild pitch while Kelly, who was the target of numerous furtive glances, giggles, and whispers from elaborately dressed Southern belles, was sawing wind at the plate. Kelly finally got on to the sphere and landed it in Gleason's hands. As Gleason threw the ball to first, Sunday started for home, attracting Sullivan's attention. He didn't see the play at first. The ball had beaten Kelly to first by ten feet. Sunday scored and Sullivan declared Kelly safe and the crowd erupted in protest.

All of the players gathered around Anson, Sullivan, and Comiskey and outrageous words were exchanged. As they were, Kelly snuck over to second base. Comiskey threatened to take his men off the field and Sullivan told him if he did the game would be given to Chicago. He told both captains to have their men in their places in the next two minutes and they were. Play resumed amid curses and jeers.

Anson hit safe to center field and Kelly came home to tie the score. Pfeffer hit a fly back of first base which Nichol dropped, but he fielded the ball to second to force Anson. With Pfeffer on third,

Williamson danced around the plate for five minutes, during which Kelly trotted to third on a passed ball. The big third baseman at last hit the ball and it struck outside the foul-line but curved in to fair ground. Comiskey gathered it in and fielded the ball quickly to first base which was covered by Barkley. Williamson beat the throw and Pfeffer came in.

Comiskey claimed the ball was foul. Sullivan agreed and told Williamson he would have to come back. Then Anson and Kelly came to the front and in a few minutes convinced the umpire that the ball was fair. Players had congregated around Sullivan again and another scene occurred. Two hundred men jumped onto the field and made for Sullivan. Security officers reached him before he could be manhandled. Now nearly all of the male spectators came onto the field and took sides in the trouble. The Chicago men seized their bats and held their ground while Sullivan was escorted off the field by the security detail. The White Stockings claimed victory because the Browns left the field. From the safety of his hotel room Sullivan decided the game 9 to 0 in favor of Chicago. Comiskey contested his decision.

When the two teams met again the next day, Harry McCaffrey, who'd played for the Browns in 1882, took over the umpiring duties. The game was played with little controversy in front of a disappointingly small crowd. The White Stockings went to pieces in the field flubbing away the game in the first inning when a two-out error led to five unearned St. Louis runs. From there on Caruthers and Clarkson, dominated, with Caruthers eventually prevailing, 7-4.

The rest of the series was almost an afterthought. None of the games was well attended and a few more were called early for darkness. Though the series was supposed to go 12 games, due to the lackluster attendance, both teams agreed to cancel the series after Game Seven. St. Louis had easily won the seventh game, which was also called early on account of darkness - hardly a thrilling end to the final game of a championship series.

Anson and Comiskey, who insisted that Game Two should not have counted, had a fistfight that nearly led to a riot. It started when

Anson told Comiskey that the umpiring in St. Louis had bordered on criminal. Both men landed in jail and had to be sprung by Spalding and Van der Ahe. Eventually the two sides agreed to split the $1,000 prize.

When Kelly returned to Paterson he was given a parade that wound through the city streets. "Kelly the Giants Slayer" people called out as he waved his hat in the air. After the politicians feted him he and James McCormick drank all night in David Treado's saloon. Treado was a local ball player. McCormick liked the place so much he decided to buy in. He knew sales would be brisk whenever Mike was in town.

THE
$10,000
BEAUTY

"Another Pinkerton, is it?"

On March 13 the team headed to Hot Springs which was known for its warm temperatures, the medicinal and curative properties of its natural springs, and its abundant hotel accommodations. They would undergo a regimen of training and bathing.

Billy Sunday came in from Marshalltown, Iowa where Anson had discovered him. John Clarkson and his bride Ella arrived fresh from their wedding ceremony and gala reception in Boston.

Jimmy Ryan came in from Lawrence, Massachusetts. He'd started playing ball at Holy Cross College and had just 29 games of minor league experience when Cap Anson signed him. *The Chicago Tribune* noted that "Ryan, the young Bridgeport player, proved himself a strong batter, a quick fielder and very clever between the bases." Ryan had played in the closing games of the season in Philadelphia. He'd made six hits in 13 at bats and with his speed and his arm would be a much better replacement for Kelly when he was catching McCormick than Billy Sunday. Ryan was Irish but Anson liked him in spite of it.

McCormick and Williamson arrived on the 9:00 train from Philadelphia. Dalrymple had come in ten days earlier, weather-beaten from tending to his ninety head of cattle on his ranch in Nebraska and sporting a full beard. Pfeffer arrived looking hale and handsome. Mike Kelly showed up right after Fred Pfeffer. Kelly had recently given Sam Morton's sliding pads his hearty endorsement, saying that his invention would enable runners to steal bases without injury to their cuticles. From all appearances his stay in New Orleans, where he'd

captained a nine made up of League players, had put him "in splendid condition." Spalding told him he'd never seen him looking better. Kelly told his boss he was the recipient of excellent treatment in the Crescent City and had never passed a pleasanter winter. Then he introduced himself to the team's new battery, Jocko Flynn, who Kelly figured wasn't any bigger than Larry Corcoran, and his 19-year-old catcher George Moolic.

"We don't know a lotta the players but we know who you awer, Mr. Kelly," said Flynn.

"What part uv New England you boys hail from?"

"Lawrence, Massachusetts," said Jocko. "George and I been playin' catch with one other fer years."

"Just like me and James," said Mike. "Now we're gointa have a Jersey battery and a New England one."

Kelly came within an ace of getting left behind when the team departed for Hot Springs. He stepped into a store across from the train station to say good-bye to some friends and set his satchel and the cage containing his parrot on a counter. He lingered longer than he meant to and in his blurry to leave he secured his valise but forgot the cage. Halfway across the street he realized he'd left the parrot behind. He went back and got it but made matters worse when he sprawled over a baggage cart on his flight across the station platform.

"Darn it, Mike. Are you drunk?" asked the parrot when its cage tumbled across the cement.

Kelly grabbed his bag and the cage and leapt at the rear end of the train.

"You may be a crack ball catcher, Mr. Kelly," remarked the conductor as he caught Mike by the back of his coat and pulled him up onto the platform, "but you are a darn poor train catcher."

Harry Palmer, who was covering the doings of the White Stockings in their winter abodes for *The Sporting Life*, stated that, "Several of the men, notably Flint, Williamson, Burns, and especially Dalrymple, who is apparently quite fond of his new wife's cooking or more likely that of her servants, will have to drop a few pounds before they can get around the bases in their old-time form, but the majority are all solid bone and muscle and ready to play the best ball of their lives."

Palmer and some other reporters sat down with Kelly, who was sweating from a workout and had a towel around his neck.

"How's the bird?" asked Palmer, who'd visited the Kellys in Paterson in December and had been told Mike had brought the bird with him to Hot Springs.

"Paul?"

"Yes."

"Mike and Agnes named their pet parrot Paul," Palmer explained to the other reporters. "They hung a chestnut bell on the side of his cage. He rings the damned thing like a maniac whenever anyone does something he doesn't like. Tell them about the preacher's visit, Kel."

Mike chuckled. "On our last trip East last year I popped in at the house and Mrs. K had invited the minister, a red-haired gentleman, for dinner. There was only one breakable thing left in the house that Paul hadn't broken, a green vase. Nobody noticed when the bird perched on top of it. After a few minutes he fell asleep, lost his balance, and slid inside.

The minister was quite interested in base ball and I was explaining the rules to him. He picked up his glass of water and was asking me about sacrifice plays when we heard, 'Hi, there, red-head, drop that.'

"The reverend felt the top of his head and stared around the room. I told him we had a parrot and it must be concealed somewhere in the room. I looked all over and couldn't find him, then we heard, 'Mike, old sod! It's rotten hot in here. I'm dead for a drink. Who's his nobs? Rush the growler there, will you?' Mrs. K and the preacher looked at each other with apprehension and dread."

"I asked Mrs. K who'd taught the bird such profanity as he had not known how to utter an oath when I was last there in the spring. 'He doesn't often do that, in fact he's a very good bird. He says his prayers every night before he goes to bed.' I said, 'Come, wife, that's putting it on too thick.'

"I searched for that parrot like a hound after a rabbit but still couldn't find the rascal. Then we heard a crash as the vase fell to the hearth-stone and Paul looked at his bloodied foot, raised his head, and flashed defiance at us. I made a leap for him but missed.

She pulled Paul out from the broken glass, bound up his bleeding toe, and smoothed his feathers. Then she sat him on the back of a chair and bade him say his night prayer. Paul chanted,

'Now I lay me down to sleep,

I pray the Lord my soul to keep,

If I should die before I wake...'

At that point I'm afraid I broke into laughter. Paul glared at me and shrieked, 'Shut up, Mike, you damned fool. I pray the Lord my soul to take.'"

The players had breast bars for increasing stretching, a wrist machine, air punching bags, a vaulting bar to condition them to catch high balls, and a nautical wheel to widen the chest and give them increased wind while running. Spalding had thought of everything, there was even a doctor on hand.

After breakfast the men walked seven or eight miles, then took hot and cold bathes to reduce the extra winter flesh, went to the gym where they took turns smacking a ball suspended from the ceiling to heighten their hand-eye co-ordination, and practiced sliding on sand spread over the floor. Then they ate lunch and went for another long walk before afternoon practice and scrimmage games.

Ned Williamson thought the curative properties of the Hot Spring waters were wonderful and could knock rheumatism higher than a kite. He wrote to Spalding, who had just told reporters that his team would abstain from all alcoholic beverages until the last pitch of the season has been thrown, that their stay at the Arkansas resort has been a very pleasant and beneficial one. He related that all off the big fellows were rapidly reducing and the lightweights were gaining flesh. The players were leaving the hotel at 5 the next morning on eighteen of the best saddle horses in town for a fifteen-mile ride over the mountains to Sulfur Springs.

Abner Dalrymple fell victim to one of Kelly's practical jokes on St. Patrick's Day. The day before Mike had developed quite a thirst after a run through the woods and went looking for a spring. He found one that had water bubbling through the sand and the pebbles. Its bright green color made it quite inviting. Kel lay flat on the ground and was about to put his mouth to the water when he was startled by a yell. When he turned around the dead cut of Kit the Arkansas Traveler was running toward him.

"What's the matter with you?" asked Mike.

"Don't drink none o' that ar water, young feller. The spring's like as not ta make ya feel sick to yer stomach. If yer mustache had touched it, it would've turned greener than grass."

Kelly asked him if he could buy his flask. He said he could and Mike filled it with the water. When he got back to the resort he snuck into Abner's room and filled his water-pitcher with the spring water.

When Dalrymple came down for breakfast the next morning his beard and hair were rusty green. Within an hour they were as green as any St. Patrick's Day badge in the place. Dal was mad but he had to stand the guying. He swore he'd get back at Kelly even if it had all been for fun.

The Chicago Tribune devoted an entire column to the travelling White Stockings on April 1. "When the train over the Memphis & Little Rock Railroad pulled into the Union Depot yesterday a dozen active-looking young fellows sprang out upon the platform, the last of whom, Mike Kelly, stopped to assist a pretty woman and a cor-pulent man, the club Secretary and Treasurer John Brown, in their descent to terra-firma. The party was the Chicago Base-Ball Club. They left Hot Springs on Tuesday morning over the Iron Mountain Road with some misgivings owing to the strike as to whether they would get through. All but Sunday and McCormick did, though they

arrived several hours late. Mac sprained his ankle severely when exercising last week and was left behind with Billy as his nurse.

The men were assembled in Secretary Brown's temporary office where they were measured to ascertain the development of body and limbs at the present time. Williamson boasted the largest chest at 42 inches, Anson the biggest biceps at 15 inches and the greatest height at 6 foot 2. Kelly measured 5 foot 11 and a half and had the third largest chest - an even 40 inches. Kel was a little above the team average in weight at 177 pounds - he'd been 182 two weeks earlier. He teased McCormick, who turned out to be the club's heaviest player at 213 pounds, having surpassed Williamson and even Anson.

After being measured they donned their white-flannel tourist-jackets and were driven in carriages to the Southern League grounds, which was filled with a large and enthusiastic crowd." The visiting celebrities trailed the amateurs 2-0 after six innings but racked up five in the seventh. Kelly, the visitor who attracted the most attention, disappointed with no hits in five attempts.

The White-Stockings will play the Memphians tomorrow and Saturday then leave Sunday for Atlanta where they are to meet the Pittsburg American Association team. They will then travel to Savannah, Macon, Columbus, and Nashville then go to Kansas City for the opening game of the season."

On April 29 in New York a photographer took a live action picture of play during the Giants' home opener against the Beaneaters using one of the new "detective cameras", so named because they could be disguised as parcels, cases, bowler hats, or pistols. Exposures in bright conditions were done in fractions of a second. No longer did a man need to have his coat sleeve pinned to a tablecloth to ensure he remained absolutely stock-still for a full minute. Outdoor "snapshooting" with the new ready-made gelatin coated plates was becoming all the rage and "magazine" cameras allowed people to take several photos before reloading the film.

The White Stockings travelled to Kansas City on the newly amalgamated Chicago, Kansas & Western Railroad to play the Cowboys

at Association Park. Stump Weidman pitched to Fatty Briody. The Kansas City team had a "burly colored gentleman" as their good luck charm. The "tall raw-boned Ethiopian" was dressed in an old team uniform and paraded to the team bench at 3:15 to the tune of "While I Behold His Manly Form." The game was recreated for boosters back home at the Chicago Music Hall, using a picture of Association Park and transparencies with the players' names on them.

The Kansas City Times reported that, "The spectators were wild to see the kicking and guying of Anson and Kelly. Every play was applauded heartily, the audience rising almost in a body, shouting and waving their hats and umbrellas when a good hit or a brilliant field play came along."

McCormick sat in the west side-box with Jim Cooke, a ticket seller.

"I've never seen your nine play," said Cooke. "Does the audience always have their eyes glued on Kelly?"

"They do," said James. "Especially the ladies."

In the thirteenth inning Dalrymple was given his base on balls, stole second, went to third on Lillie's muff of Gore's long hit to left, and scored on Kelly's hit to center which closed the game.

"I'm coming back tomorrow, Eunice," Cooke and McCormick heard a woman behind them tell someone she was with."

"To see the Cowboys, Abigail?"

"No. Mike Kelly."

Eunice and Abigail were lucky to have Kelly to ogle the next day. The White Stockings scored five runs in the first inning and four in the second and coasted to a 17-8 win.

Kelly went 0-for-5 in a 6-5 loss in St. Louis on May 4, the closest thing to a hit being a puke fly to the shortstop, but *The Globe-Democrat* man was impressed. He said Kelly "caught in fine style and threw to the bases with perfection." He had obviously not been watching when Kelly had a pitch get past him in the second inning or when his throw to third to get Glasscock sailed over Burns' head. It was important that Kelly handle pitches well, nervous Jocko Flynn was

making his debut between the points. Mike wasn't sure why he was catching him instead of Moolic but the kid hadn't batted worth a darn in the South and, having never eaten good restaurant food before, he'd actually *gained* weight instead of losing it. He'd had more than a few pitches skip past him. Of course, he'd never caught big league twirlers with deliveries like Clarkson and McCormick's.

The White Stockings arrived home on May 6 to take on the Wolverines. Talk amongst the cranks on their way into West Side Park for the home opener focused on the widespread labor unrest in Chicago after the Haymarket Riot two days before and the discovery by police of a plot to burn much of the city. The demonstration at the Haymarket had begun as a peaceful rally in support of workers on strike for an 8-hour work-day. Someone had thrown a bomb at the police when they tried to disperse the crowd and the resulting gunfire had left eight policeman and four demonstrators dead.

The sun shone brightly, the air was balmy, and the band discoursed lively Mikado airs as policeman wearing black armbands scanned the crowd. Little Willie Hahn sat on the bench with the players in a club uniform. Presently a bell rang and the players rose and advanced to the flag staff. Anson and Kelly seized ropes and after a few pulls a pennant bearing the legend "Champions of the United States, 1885" wafted in the breeze. The audience let out a cheer. Suddenly a big dark cloud loomed up and before the startled assemblage could draw their linen dusters closer around their shoulders an Arctic blast swopped down upon them and 6,000 sets of teeth chattered. The game went on and the hosts prevailed 5-1. Kelly banged the sheepskin to right for two bases scoring Jimmy Ryan in the third inning. He maneuvered to get first on balls his next time up. Whenever a fair ball was pitched he held up his bat and tipped the ball, making it foul. Baldwin pitched seven or eight more balls right over the plate and Kelly made fouls of them all then Baldwin tired and threw enough pitches outside and high to put Kelly on first.

The Chicagos were handy at the bat on the 10th, their hits well divided up. The runs in the opening frame were made by Kelly and Anson and were gifts from the Bostons. Kelly put in a fine two-bas-

er in the third and Dalrymple and Gore both came home. The 7-1 victory put the White Stockings into first place a game ahead of the Giants and the much improved Wolverines.

May 18th was the first appearance in Chicago of the new Washington club, who were being called the Nationals. In the pitching box was Daily. The team would use fifteen different pitchers in '86, the ace being Dupee Shaw who would win 13 and lose 31. They used everyone from Larry Corcoran, washed up at 25, his arm dead, to Hugh "One Arm" Daily. *The Cleveland Herald* described Daily as "a strong man and a remarkable batter for a one-handed person." He had a bad reputation though; his horrific, cuss-laden outbursts shocked well-heeled spectators and he once punched his catcher for throwing the ball back too hard and making his stump sore."

Kelly did well behind the bat with the exception of a wild throw to third that gave the Washingtons a run. Curry umpired and gave fresh evidence of his incompetency. His permitting of Baker to hold second when the latter was clearly out from Kelly to Pfeffer in the third was so glaring an error of judgement that he got the full benefit of the crowd's contempt. They hissed like snakes in nettle weed and jeered until the welkin rang with their indignation but Curry was as unmoved as a stone.

Kelly was struck in the knee by a pitched ball but after some delay he gamely continued his work and scored twice in the home side's 7-5 victory. When he hit the ball away off to left field in the fifth inning he did some of the greatest base-running ever seen upon the home grounds. Even Sunday would have had hard work to get more than two bases on the hit so promptly was it fielded.

Three thousand people saw the Phillies jump on Clarkson with both feet on the chilly 22nd of May, pounding him for four singles, two three-baggers, and two home runs. But the White Stockings more than returned the compliment by hitting Mr. Ferguson for eight singles, three three-basers, and a home run. The Phillies tied the score in the top of the fifth but the Whites rolled up two runs by Dalrymple and Kelly's tremendous hitting and fine base-running.

On May 27 the White Stockings, winners of eight straight, began a road trip in Washington. They stopped at the Imperial Hotel on Pennsylvania avenue between 13th and 14th streets in the heart of Rum Row, one of Washington's liveliest and most notorious districts. The hostelry featured fashionably rich, dark furnishings. The first floor was tiled in marble with heavy black walnut furniture in the lobby. Dominating the new bar-room was a large walnut bar paneled in Hungarian ash as well as a tall mirrored side-board, a cigar stand, and a raw oyster counter. The room was fitted out with a gong connected to a booth at the National Theatre next door. The theatre had burned to the ground in '85 but had been quickly replaced.

Originally a line of federal town houses, Rum Row had changed character dramatically during the Civil War when soldiers swarmed the streets of Washington looking for cheap entertainment. The row's previously respectable homes and commercial establishments had been gradually replaced with saloons and gambling joints.

Police raids repeatedly swept through Rum Row in the late 1870s, but the gamblers were usually tipped off in advance and didn't get caught. Then one night in February 1881, a coordinated surprise raid was simultaneously launched on five suspected gambling houses, resulting in the arrests of the proprietors and numerous patrons, including many members of Congress. All sorts of fancy mahogany faro tables, various roulette wheels, stacks of poker chips, and other gambling paraphernalia were also confiscated. The luxurious furnishings were all broken up for kindling wood and the police counted the raid as a notable success. A week later the charges against two of the gambling houses were dropped and all of them were soon back to business as usual.

Anson liked the National. A poolroom had just opened in the hotel's former bar-room after the billiard parlor next door was destroyed by fire. While he played pool most of his teammates frequented Ebbitt Grill on 15th street and Beucher's Saloon and drank the mint juleps Henry Clay had introduced to Washington at the Round Robin a short walk away on Pennsylvania. Mark Twain and Walt Whitman had apparently been there in the Spring.

Kelly was otherwise engaged. He'd been delighted to learn that Sarah Cowell was in the cast of *Erminie*, the show the National Theatre was currently staging. She was thrilled when he visited her dressing-room and immediately invited him to her hotel room.

"Let's skip dinner, there's a book I want to read to you, well parts of one."

This was a first for Kelly. Women had invited him to their boudoirs to do a variety of things, but never to *read* to him. He was even more taken aback when she told him this new book was written by an Indian philosopher named Vatsyayana.

"What's it about?"

"It's about everything from urban living to statecraft, from perfumes to gardens."

Now Mike was *really* confused.

"What's it called?"

"The Kama Sutra."

Mike and Sarah had tried - quite successfully, as he'd lost count of how many times she'd climaxed - seven of the suggested positions from the book by the time the sun began peeking through the window and he decided he'd better head back to his room for a couple of hours of shut-eye.

The Nationals, who would suit up an incredible 37 players over the course of the season, were in the rear of the procession with a dismal record of 4-13. Bookmakers wouldn't even take bets on the game. Bob Barr was in the box for the Nationals. He'd racked up 18 wins and 52 losses in the AA and then gone to work for the government. He'd lost his job and signed on to pitch for the Nationals, for whom he would win two and lose eighteen. Shockingly, Barr shut out the badly hung over visitors 7-0. They'd had two days off when they came home and, knowing they'd be facing the sad-sack Nationals, they'd enjoyed themselves, especially at Beucher's Saloon. The bar-maids were quite alluring, especially in the rooms upstairs.

After being raked over the coals by Spalding and Anson the Chicagos turned in early that night and plastered the Washingtons with a 20-0 shutout the next day. They scored four runs in the first, five in the third, and another four in the fourth off Ed Crane. Mercifully, Joe Yingling, a 19-year-old amateur from Baltimore, was finally sent in to take Crane's place. Yingling gave up seven runs in his only major league appearance. It was that kind of year for the Nationals.

The White Stockings bested the Washingtons 4-2 in the series finale then moved on to Philadelphia where they edged the Quakers 4-3. In New York, the Giants put an end to the Wolverines' 15-game winning streak before a crowd of 20,632. No baseball audience had ever approached 20,000. The game was called in the first inning when hundreds of people spilled onto the field. Many of the spectators went home, but mounted police cleared the field and, with a rule that any ball hit into the audience would be a single, the game was played.

Kelly had a problem and he needed to solve it. Anson had taken to sitting in the hotel lobbies and watching the elevators to see if any of his men were slipping out of the hotel after curfew. He knew he couldn't wait until the wee hours to catch them coming in, he wanted to keep them from leaving. The trick was, how to get past him without being spotted.

The "white-hosed giants from the West" had an easy time of it in Boston, winning all three games. Only the second one was close. The headline of the June 8 *Tribune* sports page read:

Kelly Pulls Game Out of the Fire for Chicago
A Big Day for the Best Living Ball Player

New York held a 2-0 lead in the 7th when Kelly met with an accident to his clothing. Time was called to give him a chance to change. He was greeted with laughter when he reappeared in light knickerbockers. Kelly removed his cap and bowed from the waist.

Dalrymple, the first striker in the ninth, sent the ball to the picket fence in right field and succeeded in reaching third base. Gore was

retired at first. Kelly came to the plate and slashed a high one to left which Gillespie allowed to go over his head. Dalrymple scored in a walk and Kelly raced around to third base. Anson batted next and hit a long field fly to Dorgan. As soon as the ball touched Dorgan's hands Mike was off and running and slid into home seconds later with the winning run. The laughter changed to applause.

On June 12 against Kansas City the Chicagos played like a $25,000 nine, it was their best game of the season on the home grounds. *The Tribune* opined that "they worked well together and partook of the inspiration that Kelly and McCormick were full of. This battery is certainly the smoothest pair in the league, they perform in perfect harmony. Their work was a special delight to all lovers of the game."

Mike went shopping right after breakfast the next morning. He'd gone backstage at Haverly's Theatre the last time the team was at home and sought out Louise Hagemann. When he introduced him-self she seemed to have heard his name and thought she'd seen him at the Palmer House but clearly had never been to a ball game. He asked her where she got the costumes for the shows.

"Well as a matter of fact, I've just found a new place. I wasn't over-ly happy with the quality of the costumes I was getting and I heard about a young German immigrant, a producer of operas and oper-ettas whose made several trips back to Europe to purchase costumes from leading opera companies. He's just opened a store here in Chi-cago. It's called Fritz Schoultz and Company Broadway Costumes. Wait, I have one of their cards."

She went to her desk and gave it to Mike. Now he was on his way to Fritz Schoultz and Company Broadway Costumes.

"Can I help you, sir?" said a tall, thin, young clerk when Mike entered the store.

"I don't want to look like this," said Mike.

"I beg your pardon," said the clerk.

"I said I don't want to look like this, I want to look like someone else."

The young man looked Mike up and down. "I don't quite under-

stand, you are one of the most strikingly attractive men I have ever seen. Why would you want to change your appearance?"

"There is someone who watches me and I need to get past him without him knowing it's me."

"I see. And you don't have a particular costume in mind?"

"No. I just need to be unrecognizable."

"Well then, let's see what we can put together for you."

On Saturday, June 19th came news from Detroit that "McCormick and Kelly, the 'great Jersey battery' who have not lost a game this season, are very happy over the 5-4 victory that gave their club a one and a half game lead over the Wolverines." During play in the fourth inning Kelly ran out to the shortstop position to provide a distraction for his runner. Coachers' boxes would be introduced the following year. It was McCormick's fourteenth game of the season and he had yet to lose.

"Have you ever been to the Two Way Inn, me sun?" asked Mike as he patted his old friend on the back when the last Wolverine was dispatched.

"I've stopped there for a bite a couple of times. Why do you ask?"

"They're celebratin' their tenth anniversary and your arm must be some sore. I'll wager they have some medicine in stock. I'd recommend whiskey."

James felt his shoulder. "Now that you mention it, it is a might sore. Certainly sore enough to warrant some medicine. How much should I take?"

"Fourteen wins. Fourteen doses."

"On my own!"

"No. I'd not been any sort uv a battery mate if I didn't help ya take it. Me hands are pretty damn sore, I'll drink seven uv 'em for you. What are friends for after all?"

After taking two games at home from the seventh place Kansas City Cowboys and one from the sixth place St. Louis Maroons, the

Chicagos headed to Detroit on Saturday, June 19th for three against the first place Wolverines. The players liked going there, they lived in style at the Griswold House. Spalding liked it, the rates were $1 per day and up. The dining room sported a Victorian motif in red and gold. Large crystal chandeliers dangled from the ceiling and each table was draped in white damask and had ornate lamps with pink and gold shades. When the clock struck 8 p.m., the dining room was transformed into a cabaret.

As soon as the team reached the hotel Kelly started off up Woodward avenue. Anson dropped his bag and darted out the door after him.

"Come back, Michael," he called.

"I am only going a little way," Kelly called back over his shoulder without turning around.

"Never mind," said Anson in his loftiest manner. "I want you to come back."

"I'm only going to call upon Goldsmith, he's tending bar in a turf exchange."

"You can do that in the morning."

Kelly shrugged, muttered to himself, and turned around.

The Woodward and Bush street-car lines put on extra cars to accommodate the people heading to see the first Detroit-Chicago game at Recreation Park. The papers would call it "the most exciting game of base ball in the history of Detroit."

A large delegation had come from Chicago and excursions arrived on nearly every railroad line into the city. The Chicagos' procession of carriages was noticeable to the throng of Detroit boosters for there were brooms bearing the words "Record breakers" in the whip sockets of each carriage. The Detroit management saw their brooms and went them one better, procuring an immense broom five feet across which was carried across the field amid the wildest yells of the spectators.

The White Stockings were a game and a half behind the Wolverines and looked to sweep them. Rows of chairs were placed in front of the stands ten rows deep and a rope was stretched halfway between the diamond and the back fence to keep the spectators back, necessitating special rules barring all home runs and three base hits. The crowd of 12,000 was Recreation Park's largest ever.

At 3:35 the Chicago team arrived in their carriages, the first containing Captain Anson and Willie Hahn who carried an immense broom on which was printed "our mascot." The Detroits had hustled to find a mascot of their own and the result was the appearance of Charlie Gallaher, a Sixth Ward kid who was said to have been born with a full set of teeth and was guaranteed to possess all the magic charms of a genuine mascot.

Kelly hit to right for a base in the third and scored on Thompson's wild throw. His mistake was forgiven - Big Sam was still suffering from a bout of malaria - but Ned Hanlon was fined $25 for poor play after the game.

Mike hit to left for two bases in the 5th and scored on a hit by Anson. With the score tied 4-4 in the 9th McCormick reached first on a fumble by Richardson, went to second on a passed ball, to third on Gore's hot bounder, and scored the winning run on another passed ball by Jack Rowe who normally played shortstop, Charlie Bennett having traded places with him due to mangled fingers.

On Sunday the White Stockings, some badly hung over from having gone on a tear the night before, hopped on a Michigan Central train and headed to play a game in Kalamazoo. After the Chicagos hammered the hapless amateur nine it was noticed that a half dozen of Spalding's best League balls had mysteriously disappeared and the jackets of Kelly, Williamson, and others were gone. They came to the conclusion that the balls were stowed away in the jackets. The thieves also laid hands on Chicago bats and Anson's mitt and made off with them.

"We've been Kalamazooed," chuckled Kelly as they left for the train station.

The Detroit Free Press man took great delight in writing his piece on the Monday game.

"The White Stockings strut around with a lordly air, talk loftily of their great feats on the diamond, and pityingly descant on the short-comings of benighted ball tossers who are unfortunate to belong to some "inferior" organization. The hilarious ecstasies of a Fourth of July are melancholy compared with the rapturous delight which filled the hearts of all Michiganders when the simple story, Detroit 4, Chicago 1, was borne to them. About 6,000 people had the exceeding pleasure of seeing the Detroits take some of the conceit out of Anson's Babies."

Anson didn't play, Kelly held down first and played it well, as he played any position in which he was put. When asked the cause of his captain's absence, Kelly related that he, Williamson, McCormick, and Anson had taken a tug and gone up to Lake St. Clair for some fishing yesterday. They'd made several hauls when Anson got something on his line that nearly broke his pole in two.

What he reeled in after a 45-minute battle had one eye, red whiskers, and a tusk jutting from its lip. Anson was the glummest duck all the way home. "That was a Jonas, boys," he said. "I swear I won't play ball tomorrow if I have to quit the business. You'll see Kelly at first tomorrow as sure as the game comes off."

The clouds hung low and threatened rain as the champions with Willie Hahn in tow jumped into the two hacks in front of the Russell House. All were in uniform except Anson who wore a long plum-colored Prince Albert coat and a look of distress. Kelly carried a string of frog bones as a sort of fetich, but the fish with the tusk was constantly before his vision. *The Inter-Ocean* had run a picture of the monster based on Kelly's description of it. Willie Hahn turned his stockings inside out to break the spell and Dalrymple refused to ride backwards.

In the bottom of the first inning Thompson, the man who hits base balls as though they had insulted him, cracked a Clarksonian curve into the left field for a base and Richardson scored amid tu-

multuous cheering. Thompson wanted to get home before it rained so he tried to steal second. Flint made a quick throw to Pfeffer who was crouching over the bag like a man suffering from dyspepsia but stood up and tagged the slow-footed slugger.

The Chicagos succumbed to the curves of Getzein, the gritty German, batting only three balls out of the infield. They were nothing but a lot of wooden figures to the pride of Grand Rapids. He had a no-hitter going until the ninth when Flint directed the ball to left for a base and Dalrymple sent it down the right field line for three bases. Kelly pounded the air three times and Getzein settled the business by striking out Ryan. The Wolverines won 4-1 to take a 2½ game lead.

A half hour after curfew Kelly took the stairs down to the lobby and walked slowly past Anson and out the front door of the Russell House. He got into a hack and told the driver he was going to Andrew Sheeler's saloon on Fort street. The hack driver had taken Mike there before, but he didn't recognize him.

When he sat down at the bar he asked for his usual, a bottle of Jameson and a glass.

The bar-tender looked at him, puzzled. "I know that voice, and I know it to ask for a bottle of Jameson, but your face doesn't ring a bell."

"It's Mike, Tom, Mike Kelly."

"Mike Kelly? But …"

"Wait, I'll go and get out uv this get-up and you'll see."

Mike went to the bathroom and took off the red wig, tinted glasses, bushy black beard, Falstaffian prosthetic nose, and theatrical green cloak he'd purchased at Fritz Schoultz and Company Broadway Costumes and went back to the bar.

"It *is* you then. Why the hell were you dressed like that?"

"I needed to sneak past Anson. It worked, he had no idea 'twas me. I walked right by him. Now fetch me that bottle, will ya."

Gore thumped a two-bagger in the fourth the next day. Kelly got in a corker to right and both of them scored. An event that created

more than unusual stir and bustle was an altercation between Captain Anson and Umpire Gaffney. The game had hardly begun when open hostilities were inaugurated by Anson, who frequently left his base to protest Gaffney's decisions.

The Detroit spectators' jeers, catcalls, and shouts didn't dissuade Anson one iota. His biggest kick came in the third inning when Hanlon struck three times and Kelly dropped the ball and attempted to make a double play. Gaffney wouldn't allow it.

Anson advanced from his position and it was plain to anyone without an opera-glass that he was mad. Gaffney waved the big bulldozer back to first bag but he kept right on toward the plate. The Chicago infielders followed him but Kelly told the boys to go back and then told Anson to stop yawping his yawp and making a fool of himself. His advice wasn't heeded.

"I fine you ten dollars for questioning my decision," said Gaffney.

That only made the big captain madder. "Does that go?" he asked in an insulting tone.

He stepped up to Gaffney with his fists clenched and his eyes blazing.

"You are a fucking idiot, Gaffney," declared Anson loud enough for most of the spectators to hear.

"Fifty more for that, Anson," snarled Gaffney.

"You are nothing but a gib-faced meater!" yelled Anson.

Gaffney tore off his mask and faced Anson, who looked as though he was about to strike him. Kelly pushed Anson back and he finally shrugged, waved his hand derisively at Gaffney and stormed back to his position.

The Detroits scored two runs in the first inning and another pair in the fifth and went on to win 5-1 and give themselves a 3 1/2 game cushion over the White Stockings.

As he was leaving the grounds a prominent gentleman from Chicago told his companion, "I am a staunch supporter of the Chicago Club, but after witnessing Anson's villainous conduct today

I'm glad they lost."

The Inter-Ocean ran an account of the 10-6 win over the Nationals' on June 23.

"Today's game was of the jug-handled sort, the two nines combining for sixteen errors. Kelly made three hits and scored two of the victors' runs. Shaw, "the Washington wizard", had a serious lameness in his arm, the five runs he yielded in the fourth inning were his undoing. The basepaths were buzzing and the manner in which the ball was pasted was a reminder of the old days of straight-arm twirling and a ball with a lot of rubber in it."

The newspapers weren't sure if Anson had paid the $110 he owed the League for the fines Gaffney had imposed on him but *The Philadelphia Times* reported that the Detroit Base Ball Club had preferred formal charges against him for his disgraceful conduct at Recreation Park. President Young chuckled when he'd heard about the fine. "I imagine that man has walked about a hundred miles up and down the first base line in depreciation of the League's umpires this season."

The White Stockings beat the Nationals 16-5 on Friday, June 25 in Chicago. Dalrymple hit safe for a base in the first inning. After Gore flew out, Kelly helped Abner to third by a long single. Then he drew a throw to second by a steal and Dal started home. Knowles returned the ball to the plate too late and Kelly took the opportunity to make for third. Gilligan threw to Hines to head him off. "Deafy" Hines muffed the ball and collided with Kelly. Both fell, Hines landing on top of Kelly.

Hines seized Kelly around the thigh, pinning him to the ground while Carroll raced after the ball. It took the crowd ten seconds to realize Mike's predicament and then there was a storm of hisses and cries of "Foul!" and "Fire him."

Pfeffer rushed over and broke Hines' hold. The umpire raced down to third and reprimanded Hines and waved Kelly home amid the cheers and plaudits of the audience. A single by Anson and home runs by Pfeffer and Williamson footed up a total of five runs

in the inning.

"It was a thrill to see Pfeffer and Williamson hit those home runs," a man in a bowler hat told his wife. "But there's never anything more entertaining than watching Mike Kelly run the bases."

There was a reasonable explanation for the Chicagos' 4-2 loss to the Philadelphias on Tuesday, the 29th. When they reached the grounds they saw that the Stars and Stripes near the marker's blackboard hung at half-mast.

"It's a hoodoo," said Fred Pfeffer. "And I walked under a ladder this morning, I hadn't wanted to say anything."

"I passed three white horses on the way out of the park yesterday," said Dalrymple.

"Billy Hahn said he dreamed of rats all night," added Williamson.

"And I spilled the salt at breakfast," moaned Billy Sunday.

As could be seen, the club hadn't stood a chance.

On the last day of June *The Sporting Life* reported that five of the top seven batters in the American Association were pitchers and that Jerry Denny of the St. Louis Base-Ball Team had been fined $150 and indefinitely suspended for drunkenness and ungentlemanly behavior.

On July 1 the Chicago men picked up the game by the right end at the outset and completely batted down the New Yorks. McCormick and Kelly, the great unbeaten Jersey battery, made the visitors heartily sick and the arm of Kelly prevented any thefts on the base-paths. Two days later Kelly and McCormick were finally defeated, a 7-3 loss to the Giants.

The Chicagos jumped on Welch with a vengeance and wiped the grounds with the New Yorks on the 7th. Captain Ward gave up the game in the 8th. McCormick, who was badly out of shape and struggled in hot weather, let down in the 5th and the visitors got in six runs. But the rest of the White Stockings played with a vim seldom equaled. The Giants were all broken up and made stupid errors. The home nine won 21-9 to stay 4½ games behind the Detroits, who

blanked the Quakers 2-0. Their aces were having banner seasons. Lady Baldwin was on his way to 42 wins and Pretzels Getzien would rack up 30.

The cocky first-place Wolverines came in the next day accompanied by 200 enthusiasts from Detroit equipped with fish-horns, whistles, and kazoos. They'd come in on a special train decorated with banners that read "1886 Champions". At 3 o'clock the big gates at Throop and Congress were thrown open and a platoon of police and the teams in barouches pulled by huge white horses entered to the strains of Austin's First Regiment Band.

The Wolverines sent their supporters back to their hotel in a somber mood after a 9-4 loss, then lost again the next day and made it three straight with a 3-1 defeat at the hands of Clarkson on Saturday. The newsmen berated them for such feeble play in a crucial series and said, "The White Stockings are all experts but not players for individual records. The club is the Marshall Field of the base ball business."

On July 13, Chris Von Der Ahe, who'd taken to calling enthusiastic base ball boosters fanatics, was so confident his team would win the American Association pennant again - even though their lead was just 2½ games - that he hosted a celebratory banquet in right field. The tables were "loaded down with good things" and "wine flowed like water." The Chicagos were in town to play the Maroons.

The St. Louis Dispatch remarked, "The Chicagos and Detroits, the two great powers of the League, have drawn large crowds in their respective towns especially when they have come together. Of course it was not to be expected that the White Stockings' power to attract would be as great when the contest was to be with such manifestly weaker talent as the Maroons. Still, the Chicagos ought to be a great attraction in any city, they have some famous ball players and two at least who have been apotheosized by Chicago people and regularly damned by every other city, north, east, west, and south.

Kelly and Anson, both stock-holders in the club, have probably done more to make Chicago famous and keep its name before

the public than anyone. Kelly and Anson on the ball field are one thing. Kelly and Anson in private life are another. Judging from the way they play the national game they are two gruff, unpleasant and decidedly fresh fellows with a marked inclination to bulldoze. But when in citizens' clothes and with friends they are very different indeed. Anson has a good heart and kind, pleasant manners and Kelly is a boon companion of the first water.

The only objection to his character perhaps is the extreme prodigality of his nature and the loose way he gets rid of his money. It is said of him that at the end of last season he had drawn his pay up to the notch and had spent it all in regular order. He found himself high and dry without a copper and the only thing clearly present to his mind was that he had to have more money. To facilitate the accomplishment of this very much to be desired end Kelly beat his steps to that part of Chicago wherein he knew Mr. Spalding hung his shingle.

He met him very opportunely and said, 'How do?'

'How do?'

'I'd like to have some money, Al.'

The abbreviation of the president's name is one of Kelly's old gags used to intimidate.

'Money! You've just been paid off.'

'I know. But that's all gone and I must have more.'

'Well, I'll endorse your paper for ... how much?'

'Oh, $200."

'For $200. If the bank thinks it good, you can go down and draw it.'

The bank thought it good, the note was endorsed and Kelly got the money - with a subtraction of eight per cent interest.

When he got back he met Anson and, drawing forth the roll, he showed him the amount. 'Where did you get it?'

'From Al.' He returned the bills to his vest pocket and remarked, 'This is what I call tough, Ans. Us fellows invest our money in an enterprise like the Chicago club and get six per cent for it and then I

have to pay *eight* for it when I want a smell.'

When Kelly was young he worked briefly as a bell boy in a hotel and he acquired considerable cheek in the occupation. An example of the latter trait is given in an incident that occurred while the White Stockings were stopping at the Southern Hotel.

He collared a young clerk in the lobby and, tongue-in-cheek, told the lad, 'Say, you go up to Spalding's room and tell him I signed on to play right field and I don't catch any more. Tell him I'm here if he wants to see me and tell him I'm not going' away.'

Taking Kelly seriously, the bell boy nodded vehemently and headed for the elevator.

By the time he reached it, Kelly was gone. He'd gone to join a friend who'd invited him for a drink."

In a jolly mood that night, Mike and George and Abner went to a place at Wells and Jackson streets. Kelly looked around as they entered. Tumblers clinked merrily amidst the smoky haze. Men in various stages of intoxication smoked, drank, and laughed at their own witticisms in stalls along the sides of the room. With them were brazen painted ladies who made no effort to hide their calling. Heavy curtains partially screened the couples from view but they were parted in the middle. The woman had taken special pains in arranging their toilettes with the most outrageous immodesty in order to display their charms to best advantage. Their dresses displayed their lower limbs and were so low in the neck as to be absolutely indecent.

"Put your eyes back in yer heads, lads," said Mike.

He led them to an unoccupied table in the middle of the room and signaled to the bar-keep for a round of drinks. As the insane revelry carried on around them they felt a breeze as the door opened and a stunning vixen in dashing attire came in, a hint of petticoats swooshing about her laced boots. Her entrance caused a profound sensation and there was a moment of hushed silence followed by a boisterous huzza. As she passed Mike she tossed her red gold hair back, looked at him, smiled a smile with luscious pouty glossed lips that showed she was more than a little impressed, and strode to the

bar where the bar-keep grinned and filled a glass for her.

"I'm no masher, but did you see that?" Abner asked the others.

"She's a sight for sore eyes," said Gore.

"The girl's a vision, an absolute stunner."

"A creature of rare beauty ta be sure," said Mike.

Abner looked at the expression on Mike's face and chuckled, "Methinks there may be trouble afoot."

A pock-marked man in fine toggery who'd been sitting alone sopping soup from a bowl, wiped his mustache, got up and approached the girl. She looked him up and down and when she waved him away he shrugged and slouched back to his broth like a beaten puppy.

Mike lit a cigarette and to the shock of him and his teammates the girl picked up her glass, went over to their table and sat down on Mike's knee.

"Have you one for me?" she asked suggestively.

"I … I do," answered Mike. He pulled another cigarette out of his pack, gently put it in her offered mouth and lit it. He was about to ask the beauty for her name but she'd read his mind.

"Rachael. I'm Rachael." Her China blue eyes sparkled in the light from the kerosene lamp on the table. They were streaked and circled with a darker shade of blue. Her mouth was parted slightly to reveal perfect white teeth. "And you are?"

"Kelly, Mike Kelly." He indicated the others. "These sots call me Kel."

Rachel exhaled a puff of smoke luridly. "Kelly, the base ballist?"

Mike nodded. "One and the same."

"That explains the tan on your handsome face. I've heard men speak of you. You must be rather good at it." She looked at her empty glass, stroked Kel's arm, and purred, "Would it be wicked of me to ask you to buy me another?"

"A little, but I will anyway," said Mike. He waved to the bartender,

who hurried over.

"Leave it," said Mike, meaning the bottle. After the bartender had done as bidden and left Mike poured three inches into Rachael's glass. She smiled and drank down half of it.

Two women in thick make-up came in and sat at a nearby table. They looked over and smiled.

"Those gals look mighty thirsty," said Gore jocosely.

"And lonely," said Abner.

They picked up their glasses and went over to their table.

Rachael put her arms around Mike's shoulders and said, "So you play ball. Do you relish any other pleasures?"

"Perhaps. What is it you have in mind?"

He nearly spilled his drink when Rachael said with a mischievous grin, "I rather enjoy being tied up, how about you?"

In Kansas City on the 17th Anson's pair of doubles and Kelly's pair of triples came at opportune moments when teammates populated the bases. The crowd enjoyed the sprinting around the bases and applauded the long hits.

The Chicagos played a clumsy game on the 19th. Kelly's error in the eighth inning permitted four runs but the White Stockings scored three of their own that inning and added another two in the ninth to best the Maroons 9-4.

Back at home to take on the Maroons on July 20 the Chicagos won in a landslide, 20-4. Kelly was pitched out just once. He registered four hits and scored four times. Three days later the White Stockings roughed up Kansas City by a count of 11-0. Kelly gunned down three Cowboys from behind the plate. The White Stockings were on a roll but they were playing the weakest clubs in the League. Things might change when they faced better nines.

On the 22nd McCormick, Flint, Gore, Williamson, Ryan, and Kelly were fined $25 by President Spalding for breaking their temperance pledges. Actual drunkenness was not charged, but they had all

been drinking more or less for the past three weeks, especially on the road, and the fines were imposed merely as a warning. Their indifferent playing was laid to drink though Gore, Kelly, and Williamson were known to be suffering badly from "Charley-horse" and could hardly walk. Kelly's arm had been bothering him since the start of the season. On the field, the Chicagos batted Conway "with great freedom" and stampeded the Cowboys 14-1. Kelly stole two bases and scored a run to add to his league-leading total.

Somewhere in the neighborhood of 5,000 people, some of whom surrendered half a dollar, the balance filling the observation stands outside the grounds at ten and fifteen cents a head, attended the July 29 game in Boston. They came in carriages with footmen in livery, spindly-wheeled Goddards, horse cars, and on foot. Hundreds of stiff, white felt dicers loomed in the grand-stand, contrasting sharply with the evergreen headgear of the ladies.

Billy Harris wrote, "Gore opened the second with a three-bagger to left field and scored on Kelly's beautiful clip to right. Foxy and never sit still for a second Kelly proceeded to steal second base. When Ryan hit a fly to Hornung, Kelly looked longingly at third base but reckoned it wasn't worth a try but he danced off the bag far enough to tempt Joe to throw to Burdock. Hornung took the bait and threw to second. His throw was wild but Kelly's hopes were dashed to earth when 'Burdie' made a nifty one-hand stop and he had to scramble back to second. Ryan struck out but a passed ball gave Kelly third base. Another pitch got by Gunning but rolled to a stop near the plate. When he picked it up Kelly was flying toward home. Gunning reached out to touch him with the ball but Kelly slid safe just under his hand. It was close work and the crowd thought Kelly was out but their judgment didn't count. Umpire Eagan's did.

Kelly made a beautiful running catch in the bottom of the inning and had another close shave minutes later when he ran home in the sixth on Anson's short single to center field and again just beat the throw.

When the Chicagos went into the field in the 3rd Kelly rolled up his sleeves, sauntered out to his position by second base, struck

an attitude with his hand on his hips, and awaited further develop-ments. When Hornung drove the ball toward Williamson Kelly re-membered that as good a thrower as Ed was, Anson had been known to drop some of his best ones. Kelly took off like a deer and was behind Anson as the sphere settled in his hands. He had nothing to work off his superfluous nervous energy until Poorman made a dash for second. Kelly was on the bag in an instant. His quick eye told him that Flint's throw was high and with a bound he went into the air. His left hand shot up like a jack-in-the-box and it intercepted the ball as it was tearing toward center field. Poorman was contemplating going to third but he changed his mind and then contemplated whether Kelly was an India rubber ball.

He stationed himself in the third base coaching box when the Chicagos went to bat but when Anson drew a base on six bad ones Kelly rushed around to coach him at first. Anson took his lead and Stemmyer made a feint to throw over.

"How's that for a balk?" shouted Kelly.

In the fourth inning Kelly actually spent his time on the players' bench, but when he went back to the field he had nothing to do but hitch up his breeches and chin a little more vigorously. When Gore reached third on a long hit over Hornung's head it was just the sort of position the great Kelly likes to be put in. A base hit was wanted and this is the way he went to work to make it. He tried his pet bat on the ground as if he feared some one may have cracked it, rapped the plate affectionately, planted his feet heel to heel, cut off half a dozen slices of the air, glared at Stemmyer with evil intent, and was set to do the deed. He struck a mighty blow at the ball but missed it. Then he twisted the bat to see if he couldn't find a flat side.

This time the ball ran up against his bat and Kelly was off to first in a jiffy. Then came some base running such as is seldom seen. He gave his breeches a true sailor hitch, informed Umpire Eagan that Anson wanted a high ball and the next one pitched fixed itself between Pop Tate's stomach and his air cushion. 'Lucky Kelly' dashed for second. When within a few feet of the bag he went down and ploughed into Burdock, who held the ball and claimed out.

270

'Oh,' was Kelly's ejaculation as he jumped to his feet and tried to show Burdoch how far he had missed the touch by spreading his arms apart as far as they would spread. Councilman Eagan called 'Safe'.

'You were lucky *that* time, Kel,' yelled someone from the stands.

'The luck of the Irish as we say here in Boston,' added another spectator.

'The man's never still for an instant,' said a third.

He was not. Two pitches later he stole third. Then he began a war dance up and down the third base line far enough to tempt Tate to throw to third. The bait took and Pop fired a ball well over Billy Nash, who leapt high into the air and hauled it down with his right hand. Kelly dove back to the bag.

'That was some catch,' he told Nash. 'Time to play ball,' he yelled, as Williamson went to the bat.

Two strikes were called on the big shortstop and then he aerialized a flyball into Hornung's clutches. Kelly gazed longingly at the plate but concluded it would not be a safe trip there just now.

On the next pitch the ball bounded away from Tate's hands and rolled a few feet away. It stopped so close to him that there was not more than one chance in a hundred Kelly could score but he'd take that chance in a heartbeat. He gave one glance at the ball and then off came Kelly's hat as he flew down to third and rushed at the plate as though shot from a cannon.

Tate recovered himself and also dashed at the plate. He saw a dark blue streak, heard a fall and Kelly was at his feet in a heap. He didn't stop to say a word but picked himself up and walked away, rubbing a strained wrist.

In the front row, Arthur Soden, the owner of the Boston club, turned to his nervous treasurer James B. Billings, who was certain he would be killed by a foul ball and usually sat in the top row of the right wing of the grand stand. 'Now *that* is how the game should be played, J.B., we need a man like Kelly to wake our nine up and keep the other side on their heels.'

After regulating the fielders to places that suited him in the seventh Kelly leapt high in the air to save an errant throw from Flint. When the Chicagos came in Kelly was in a hurry. He called out 'Striker up' then recognized a pretty lady friend in the grand stand and raised his cap gracefully, showing his manly face and got his 42-inch stick. Six balls sent him to first and again he went from pillar to post by daring base running, sliding home just like he had before except that now his clothes were black instead of blue. He went over to the water pail for a drink but kept his eye on the game. 'Get on your base!' he yelled to Anson as a foul fly went into the air.

'That settles it,' Soden said to Billings when the game ended 6-2 Chicago. 'If there ever comes a time when we can get Michael Kelly for our club we must do it, come hell or high water.'"

Tim Murnane had joined William Harris on *The Boston Globe*'s base ball reporting staff. He was more qualified for his job than most newspaper men, which was why his wages were $15 a week, not $10. He'd played four seasons at first base in the National As- sociation. He had also played three seasons in the National League for Boston and Providence. After his playing days ended he was a scout for League clubs.

His many connections throughout major-league base ball and lo- cally in the New England League served him well in his capacity as a full-time baseball writer. He could inform *Globe* readers not only about game details but also give them the inside "dope" he gathered, some of which came as return favors for his scouting of local talent.

Murnane wrote. "There is not another man in the base ball profes- sion who plays the game just as Mike Kelly of the Chicagos does. He is never satisfied with working like a beaver in the field or between the bases but must be on the move from the time the umpire shouts "High ball, play" until he calls "Batter out" and the players leave the field. When the other members of the Chicago nine are occupying the bench awaiting their turns at bat Kelly is invariably along the coaching line. And if he does once sit down for a minute's rest he never forgets that it is a free country with no law against exercising your vocal organs and he always backs up his big captain Anson in

his many kicks. You can't keep Mike Kelly either quiet or still when he is on the ball field. It would be easier to induce the three directors of the Boston club to divide up their salaries in a dividend for the other stockholders.

This king pin of the diamond is an interesting study. Today I followed his every move as closely as I could - as did many in the audience—particularly the ladies who fanned their lovely faces. Kelly was the life of the game. When Dalrymple led off Kelly stood as close to the right of the plate as Eagan would permit, leaning on his bat and watching every pitch intently. He managed to stay quiet while Dalrymple struck out but when a strike was called on Gore he yelled 'What's that?' at Eagan. The umpire frowned, then grinned, knowing it was just Kelly's way."

The Chicagos lost the last game in Boston July 30 then boarded a New York, Providence and Boston Railroad train to New York for three games. Kelly's muff of a foul fly in the eighth cost his club the first game, though he and Anson were the only Chicagos to make hits off Welch. Two wild throws by Kelly in the third inning the next day gave the New Yorks a lead they never relinquished. With a two-run lead in the ninth inning of the series finale the next day the White Stockings thought they'd salvaged at least one game from the Giants—until the New Yorks tallied three runs in their half of the inning.

The White Stockings redeemed themselves somewhat by sweeping their series in Washington but it was hardly a feat of which to be all that proud as the Nationals had won 11 games and lost 58. Kelly saw in *The Tribune* that the players' nighttime activities had become a topic of interest among base ball cranks. "Within the past month the champions have frequently played a careless, indifferent game that would have disgraced a barefooted nine of urchins who play in Millcreek Bottoms. They shuffled around the grounds today like a parcel of old women. It is currently rumored that several of the boys are cracking their temperance pledges. They have been a little gay this year, believing perhaps that corned or not they can beat any club in the world, but they will find that, unless they settle down to work,

they will forfeit all claim to the respect and confidence of admirers of the game, as well as the championship pennant."

The White Stockings arrived in Philadelphia on August 8. Kelly and the gang had the lay of the land by now. They ate dinner at Campiglia's on Eighth street below Walnut. It was famous for its spaghetti, Chianti, and Neapolitan cookery. While they were eating they talked about which places they should hit. Tom Green's place at Green's Hotel had a showy bar-room. It was popular in the blistering heat of mid-summer because it had a ceiling suggestive of the Arctic, with tapering icicles and vistas of shimmering snow and frost.

"Andy" Moore, a millionaire distiller, had remodeled the bar-room of the old Girard House at Ninth and Chestnut on a scale of garish magnificence that threw every rival establishment into the shade. It featured heavily carved, massive mahogany fixtures, velvet fittings and paneled paintings of scantily arrayed nymphs. It was far too high brow for play tossers. De Waels's was out of the question too, it was managed along very strict lines and was frequented only by the very best class of drinkers.

The group decided on "Billy" McGonegal's saloon on Chestnut street under the Opera House. It was a favorite tippling-place for the journalistic and sporting crowd. They spent a while there, a while at "Squire" McMullen's Randall House on Bainbridge street, then finished their night at "Billy" McLean's. Sunday, Clarkson, and of course Kelly, were the last ones to head back to the Weddell House.

The Chicagos were badly trounced the next day. *The Philadelphia Times* said, "The game was too one-sided to be really exciting but the bludgeoning of the champions kept the crowd in a continual yell. The enthusiasm was greatest in the second inning when the home nine made five runs. There was a new umpire and his name is Skinner, from Washington. He is a right pleasant little fellow with a blonde mustache. He wears a continual smile and is disposed to be accommodating. Mr. Skinner twice changed his decisions to please Captain Anson.

Clarkson started in to pitch but appeared to be out of sorts and

was knocked out of the box in the fifth. The Chicagos played without spirit but only Anson with two muffed foul fly balls and two fumbled grounders and Ryan with two wild throws played badly. Kelly saved the visitors from a dose of whitewash in the ninth when he made two bases on a long drive to left center, went to third on Anson's fly hit to Ferguson, and scored on Pfeffer's grounder to Irwin."

The Philadelphia Times noted that: "The members of the Chicago team who were fined $25 each for loose habits tried to have them remitted but President Spalding refused to do it. This may account for the champions' poor play here and in Boston. It is more likely, however, that they are playing in bad luck, with several crippled players."

Spalding sent a telegram to the management of the Weddell House asking at what hour his players had been returning to the hotel at night during their stay. He didn't like the answer he got back. Not at all.

When the team got back to Chicago Spalding called Anson in and told him, "You must be more strict in your discipline, Adrian, and you can start by enforcing our eleven o'clock curfew."

"Well, I can't be expected to play ball and manage the team if I'm out 'til all hours following the men."

"If you need detectives to keep the players in their rooms, I'll get them."

The next day Spalding paid a visit to his friend William Pinkerton, who had just become head of the agency after the death of his father Allan.

"I need some of my players followed, William. These ones."

He handed Pinkerton a list.

William's eyes widened as he read the list of men Spalding wanted tailed. "Gore, Flint, Ryan, Clarkson, McCormick, Pfeffer, Dalrymple, and Kelly? Isn't that your whole team?"

"All but Anson and Burns. Be on the alert, they're tricky devils," said Spalding, "Mike Kelly's even been known to put on a disguise to sneak out of a hotel after hours."

William's eyes widened again.

On August 12 it was reported that, "Kelly of the Chicagos is a phenomenal run-getter and leads the League in this respect. Though he has played in seven less games than Brouthers of Detroit the upshot of the matter is that he has made four more runs. Kelly has made one-sixth of the runs scored by the Chicagos and nearly one-half as many as the whole Kansas City Club."

"My players don't touch a drop!" said Henry Lucas, the owner of the Maroons, as he sat in Spalding's private box while his club played at the West End Grounds on August 13.

"Read the reports from the Pinkertons, Henry. Even men you're convinced are temperate and men who've sworn not to imbibe were seen throwing whisky in their faces in the same dives my players were seen in."

Lucas thought about it. He recalled Jerry Denny looking more than a little unsteady in the game the day before. He decided to confront him.

"I only took a glass of beer yesterday," was Denny's response.

It turned out the detectives had watched Denny toss back thirteen glasses of beer and more than one slug of whiskey in the early morning before the game. Denny was hardly the only player found out. The report outlined "a pretty state of things" among players. It stated that there was not a single League club which didn't have players in their ranks who indulged in spirits freely, even copiously while they were in Chicago.

Spalding called the seven offenders into his office. They marched in like penitent school-boys, all except Kelly who breezed in like he hadn't a care in the world. When Spalding finished reading the Pinkerton detective's report there was a profound silence.

Kelly finally broke it. "I have but one amendment to that report, A.G. In that place where your man has me drinking lemonade at three a.m. he's off. I've never touched lemonade at that hour in me life, 'twas whiskey."

On his way out of the office Kelly let the others go on ahead and lingered by the desk of a comely stenographer. A lavender ribbon held her beautiful ash-blonde hair in place. She'd made eyes at Mike before and he recognized her as one of those women who beckon slyly - by implication if not by actual open suggestion.

She wrote something on her legal pad, tore off the page, looked around the office to see if anyone was watching, and slid the paper to the side of the desk where Mike stood. She'd written 311 Franklin street, Apt. 12 and the words, "Tonight, if you are interested. 8 o'clock."

Mike was very much interested. He had a most enjoyable evening in Apartment 12. The girl was not new to the practices she encouraged. They both knew he'd be back.

Kelly played a remarkable game on Saturday, August 14. He scored three runs and garnered three hits off Egyptian Healy including a brace of two-baggers in the Chicagos' 5-2 win over the Maroons.

On Sunday afternoon, Billy Sunday and several of his teammates were out on the town on their day off. At a street corner, they stopped to listen to a gospel preaching group from the Pacific Garden Mission that was near both the ballpark and Sunday's rooming house.

"Those are the same hymns me muther used ta sing," said Billy.

Sunday began attending services at the mission. After talking with a former society matron who worked there, Billy - after some struggle on his part - decided to become a devout Christian. He began attending services and youth group meetings and swore off the drink. Kelly was surprised but told Billy he respected his decision.

In the 7th inning of a 15-1 romp over the Kansas City club on August 17 Anson got hurt so Kelly went to first base.

The Cowboys' Pete Conway hit a single, then headed toward second base on a passed ball. Kelly cried out, "Foul!"

Conway was confused. He stopped and asked Mike if the hit was a foul ball.

"'Twas indeed," Kelly told him.

Conway shrugged his shoulders and started walking back to first base.

McCormick threw the ball to Pfeffer, who tagged Conway out.

Conway looked at Kelly. "You said it was a foul!"

"Oh, I thought you asked if it was a passed ball," said Mike.

The Kansas City players were livid.

Captain Dave Rowe raced in from his place in left field and charged at Umpire Grayson Pierce.

"You have no right to call our man out on such a play!" he stormed.

"What are you going to do about it?" demanded Pierce. "It wasn't me that told him it was foul."

The Sporting Life said that "the ploy was typical of the great Sir Michael Kelly."

As the team's train was about to pull out of the station for their trip to Detroit, Kelly spotted a tall man in a green suit staring at him. He jumped off the train and charged at the man full tilt.

"Another Pinkerton, is it? Here put *this* in your report."

With that he punched the startled gawker in the nose.

He turned and ran to the accelerating train and hopped aboard to the applause of his teammates.

It turned out the man was a drayman, not a detective.

"Whenever Kel's in Town."

The Chicagos had closed to within a half game of the slugging Wolverines and got ready to face them in a crucial three-game series in Detroit that began on August 20.

The Free Press was positively giddy over the result of the first game. "Were 100 calliopes, 500 Wagnerian orchestras and ten tribes of Comanches to unite in one grand vocal and instrumental effort the result would give one a mild idea of the concerted screech of delight emitted by 10,000 throats at Recreation Park yesterday evening when the runs by which Detroit won came in. The Wolverines toyed with Clarkson's curves and Baldwin was altogether too deep for Spalding's batsmen."

Kelly's second hit of the game made things look chilly but Baldwin snuffed the rally out and triumphed 6-4. *The Free Press* man thought the Detroit management should sit down on the cushion-throwing nuisance as several ladies were struck by the missiles.

McCormick was knocked out of the box the next day and Sunday was sent out to pitch. The first man he faced hit the ball out of the park. Anson got so flustered by the Wolverines' run scoring he took Kelly's place behind the bat. It didn't help, the Detroits won 12-5. *The Chicago Herald* moaned, "Chicago is still struggling in second place. *The Tribune* was gloomier. Its headline read, "Farewell to the Pennant."

It was *The Free Press* man's turn to be glum after witnessing the final game of the series.

"There was a stillness in Detroit on Monday as a result of a beating of the League leaders by the men from the city on the lake. The defeat was the worst the home nine has sustained this season and the first time the sluggers have produced nothing but blanks. It was whispered about on Saturday night that the reason for Chicago's terrible playing in their drubbings in the first two games of the set was that certain of Anson's men had regarded the club's present visit here as an excursion for personal pleasure and had made the most of it.

"Swish! Spat! These were the sounds that fell with monotonous frequency on the ears of the 5,000 people at Recreation Park. The swish was caused by the mighty swinging of the Wolverine bats cleaving the murky atmosphere and the spat was the result of the ball striking Mike Kelly's hands.

In Brouthers' last at bat he was completely fooled by an upshoot and swung so hard he nearly fell down.

'That swing near sucked the air right out of the place,' chuckled Kelly.

Kelly led off the first inning with a single to left. He went to second on a passed ball and scored on Anson's cracking two baser to right. With two men out in the ninth Mike hit to White who threw wild to Brouthers. Kelly scurried to second. Anson hit down the left foul line for two bases and Kelly raced home.

It is certain that the Chicagos observed the Sabbath, for a fresher looking set of ball players never appeared on any grounds than those that thrashed the Michiganders today. The air was close and sultry but it proved cold enough for the host side. The Detroits were all out of tune and failed to make a base hit. Ten times the sluggers sawed wind. There were lots of complaints about the umpire's strike zone. 'Give us a wooden man or a cigar store Indian, but not *this* nincompoop again,' yelled one crank."

The White Stockings began a 16-game homestand on August 24 against the Beaneaters. A sizable crowd arrived at the West Side Grounds to greet the White Stockings, heartened by the shutout of Detroit on Monday that had pulled them to within a game and a half

of the Wolverines. The Chicagos got off to a terrific start, knocking Radbourn out of the box. Kelly was bristling all over with base hits and scored five times in an 18-6 win over the Beaneaters.

The Tribune man was impressed with Kelly's contribution to his team's 8-1 win the next day.

"Kelly's work behind the bat fully sustained his reputation as the 'greatest ball-player in the world.' He caught McCormick who was a trifle wild without letting a ball pass him and he kept the Boston runners hugging the bag."

The home nine kept hammering away at Radbourn until they had him so discouraged he didn't try to pitch but just tossed the ball over the plate. Kelly singled and scored in the first, second, fourth, and fifth innings, and scored yet again after a base on balls in the eighth. As the 18-6 rout ended the telegraph wires that led to Spalding's box brought the unexpected but welcome news that the Quakers had battered the Wolverines 10-2.

After thumping the Beaneaters 8-1 the next day the Chicagos took over first place with a 10-4 win over them on the 26th. As Kelly strode to the plate there was a bubbling of cheers and delighted comment as spectators pointed him out to their neighbors, shouted his name, begged him to hit, and laughed in ecstatic anticipation. Gore scored on Kelly's ringing double in the fifth but the game was tied 1-1 until the seventh inning and it was a crusher. The White Stockings struck for seven runs beginning with a drive by Kelly that shot over Billy Nash before he could react.

Anson and Kelly gave their averages a boost. In six times at bat Anson made six runs, two home runs, a double, and two singles. Kelly made two singles and a double off Buffinton in four times at bat. Both had been hitting the ball vociferously the past fortnight. If they kept it up there would be a tight race for the batting record. Anson was leading the League with a .372 batting percentage. Kelly was close behind at .365. Almost as much interest was being taken in the result as in the neck-and-neck contest for the coveted championship.

When Mike caught Burdock's pop up to end the game he

tossed the ball to Anson, the winning captain, and pointed over his shoulder.

Anson smiled when he saw that Mike was pointing to the scoreboard, which displayed.

PHILADELPHIA 11

DETROIT 10

After three months of lurking in their shadows a game or two back, the Chicagos had finally overtaken the Wolverines.

The Philadelphias came in for three games and left town licking their wounds after losing by scores of 13-1, 13-8, and 13-10. Crane could hardly be blamed for giving up eleven hits to the mighty Chicagos on September 1, but sending fourteen men to base on balls certainly contributed to the Nationals' 15-2 defeat. Washington had Shaw in the box the next day and "his gymnastics apparently queered the boys, for they could not hit him." They managed to scratch together three runs but trailed by a run in the ninth when Anson pasted a pretty three baser to center field sending Gore and Ryan across the plate.

Kelly was hot under the collar when he read the *Inter-Ocean* man's account of the last game of the series. He chastised the team for allowing six runs to be scored on them in the last three innings.

"That pompous little pop-in-jay!" said Kelly the next morning loud enough that Agnus nearly dropped her tea-cup.

"What ever is the matter?" she asked.

"*The Inter-Ocean* man, who wouldn't know an inshoot if it struck him on the nose, says there is no reason why we should have let down in our play. Games should be played from first to last and it is just as well that the Chicago batsmen and fielders arrive at a knowledge of this fact at once."

"But didn't you have a sizable lead yesterday?"

"Fer the love uv ... he was about to say God and changed it to Pete . . . we had the buggers beat thirteen ta nuthin."

Eugene Field, who wrote a humorous piece called "Sharps and Flats" for *The Chicago Daily News*, stated that "To secure their end there is nothing the Chicagos will not do and Kelly is chief among the originators of their schemes. He has more brains than all the members of the club combined. There is more pleasure to be had from seeing him run the bases than there is in the entire nine innings of the average game. The ordinary ball-player goes about his business as a day laborer would go about sawing wood, but Mr. Kelly wearies his opponents with all kinds of devices and in the invention of these harassing tactics we are free to say that he is exceedingly felicitous and fertile."

The second-place Wolverines fined their captain Ned Hanlon, who had batted over .300 in '85 and now stood last among the Detroit nine with an average hovering around .230, a whopping $300 for insubordination. Kelly wondered how much grumbling was going on behind closed doors among the Detroits when they should be focused on the pennant race.

Mike paid a visit to 311 Franklin street, Apt. 12 that night. The stenographer was more amorous than ever. It was lucky Agnus was accustomed to Mike getting home after midnight.

Kelly was almost too tired to play the next day but he had a smile on his face and a hitch in his step. Anson hit a triple in the bottom of the 9th. He rounded the bases at the approximate speed of a street sweeper and as he chugged into third gasping and wheezing Kelly broke into hysterical fits of laughter until a look that could kill silenced him and he walked away smirking. The Chicagos won their 9th straight and now had a 2½ game lead. A rumor was making the rounds that Dalrymple's days with the Chicagos were numbered and that he would retire and go back to his farm.

After a 7-4 win in the opening game of the New York series, Kelly had three hits, one an exciting inside-the-park home run, off Keefe and scored twice in the Chicagos' 13-11 win over the Giants on September 7, their twelfth straight. After Mike sent a vicious grounder up the middle and stole second in the fourth inning a wildly pitched ball went under the chairs to the left of the backstop and was lost so long that Kelly went home from second.

There were fewer than 1,000 persons at the postponed meeting of the Chicago and New York clubs on the morning of September 8. Gore opened for the home side with a safe hit and Kelly followed with a hard smash to left and planted himself on second base. Williamson got his base on a muff by Gerhardt that let in two runs. The Chicagos scored eight in the sixth and went on to maul the Giants 12-3. They took the afternoon game 9-4 by hard hitting at an opportune moment, Kelly's home run over the Harrison street wall broke the visitors' hearts. The batting of the New Yorkers in the afternoon game was anything but gigantic. Flynn unwillingly set a record that would never be broken by winning 23 games in his only season in the major leagues.

There was a great deal of excitement and anticipation when the Wolverines came to Chicago for a pivotal series. Shortly after 1 o'clock on September 9 the Clifton House was over-run with enthusiasts. When the blue-uniformed Chicagos arrived an hour later in two fine carriages headed by Austen's Military Band the street outside was jammed. The Detroits climbed into two other carriages and headed to the grounds. On the seat of one carriage was a white bull dog gaily decked with ribbons, a gift to the Wolverines by a Chicago gentleman.

Thoughts of the one-hitter Clarkson had hurled in Detroit were on the minds of the Wolverines as they went to bat in the first. Hardy Richardson surprised everyone when he drilled one of his initial deliveries into the gap between Kelly and Gore. By the time agile Mike retrieved it Richardson was at third base having a conversation with Burns. Spectators turned their heads to see when delighted screeches came from a box occupied by a group of Detroit cranks. They went into ecstasy when Hardy scored on Brouthers' hit past second a moment later. The game was close until the seventh when three Wolverines crossed the plate for an 8-3 win. The visiting cranks reveled at the Clinton House that night, their heroes trailed the Chicagos by just a pair.

The heavy hitting of Brouthers was the feature of the second game. He batted for fifteen bases with three home runs, a double, and a single. Kelly yelled at him when he arrived at first after the one baser. "Are ya takin' it easy on us us now, Dan, or are ya just worn out from all that runnin'?"

Mike doubled in the fourth and the seventh. Ryan led off the eighth with a two baser and scored on Kelly's third hit of the afternoon. Mike started for second and Conway threw to Dunlap. He never saw the ball because of the sun. Kelly ran home while Hanlon was chasing it.

"You couldn't have done much more than you *did*," Mike told Brouters when the game ended 14-8 Chicago.

"I suppose that will put me ahead of you on the batting list, Kel," said Dan.

"Oh, I don't pay much attention to that."

"I'll bet you'd like to beat out Anson though."

"That I would, Daniel. That I would."

Thousands of White Stockings rooters filled the streets outside West Side Grounds on Saturday in hopes of getting a ticket for the last game of the series. Kelly hit a ground rule double into the crowd in the first inning and scored on Pfeffer's hit to Ganzel. Mike sent a vicious grounder past Richardson in the fifth and came home when Anson's long hit to center went through Hanlon's hands. The game was stopped after eight innings with the Chicagos in the van by a score of 12-3.

Spalding had dinner with *The Inter-Ocean*'s base ball man that night. The reporter ordered twice as much food as he normally did, Spalding was paying.

"You've had great luck ... I mean success in keeping your Club together, Mr. Spalding," he said after a mouth-watering bite of roast quail. "And quite an aggregation of star ball tossers they are, another pennant in the works I should imagine. How much longer can you hold them all?"

Spalding set down his snifter of cognac, "Being a member of the Chicago nine a player has reached the acme of his profession, he can never hope to win a better place or get more money with any other club. When they stop playing with the Chicagos my men will have ceased to play ball or will be useless as players. By a strict adherence to the club and its rules they will achieve a comfortable competence for their declining years."

"I see," said the taken aback reporter returning to his quail.

The Chicago aggregation began their extended final road trek with two wins in their three games in St. Louis, both by close scores. Then they journeyed to Kansas City and won all four games. *The Globe-Democrat* in its report of the second game said: "There is a crowd or roughs that make it their principal business to hoot and jowl the umpire. The gang of hoodlums that generally infest the upper portion of the grand stand had some remarks to make on every decision Quest made. This so rattled him that his calls in the remaining innings were not as good as they might have been. When he favored the Chicagos the crowd would open up on him and when the Windy City people thought they were getting the worst of it Anson, Kelly, Williamson, Pfeffer, and the other pets would set up a howl."

Time was running out for the Wolverines as the Chicago sluggers rolled into Detroit on September 22. They stood four and a half games behind the White Stockings and would have to win either two or all three games to stay in the hunt.

The Tribune gloated a little after the first game of the series.

"The Detroit Base-Ball Club was buried this afternoon. The grave-diggers from Chicago slaughtered them first then interred them with no funeral worth speaking of. Their Dakota dog mascot will be shot or given away to-night."

Kelly's crew had a delicious dinner at Sharpe's Chop House & Saloon on Griswold Street. Then they went to Tommy's Bar & Grill and finished their revelries at the Firebird Tavern, where they nearly got into a fight with some drunken cranks that threw insults at them.

With two hands out in the first inning of the second game of the series Jocko Flynn hit a grounder that Dunlap got and put to first well in time. Phil Powers called him safe. After the side was fairly out the Chicagos made four runs. At the end of the fourth, after Powers had made another debatable call, the Wolverines' supporters voiced their sentiments with his decisions in a series of hisses and catcalls. In the sixth, Gore and Kelly got bases on balls owing to Powers' poor judgment then Anson and Burns made singles. Burns ran down to steal second and was so palpably put out that when Powers called him safe he sat down on the bag and laughed heartily.

It was 4:40 when Powers announced that he would call the game back to the sixth inning. He gave no reason why. It had been overcast but the clouds had begun to break and it was getting bright.

A wild scene followed. Enraged spectators chased Powers into the dressing-room then waited for him to come out. Friends of the en-caged umpired shouted that a row was taking place in the street and when the crowd ran to see what it was Powers was smuggled into a hack which drove off quickly with the mob in chase. The carriage was soon so closely surrounded that it was impossible for the driver to proceed faster than a walk. Imprecations were heaped upon the umpire, who sat in the back deathly pale and cowering with fear.

When they passed an excavation on the street the mob procured gravel and small stones, which they showered upon Powers. Further on, eggs were procured from a grocery store and hurled at the car-riage, which soon resembled a yellow circus chariot. About that time a carriage containing some of the Chicago players drove up and a large stone was thrown at it, striking Burns and hurting him badly. Mike leapt out and tackled the man who'd thrown the stone, but the fellow's friends rallied and Kelly received several stunning blows to the back of his neck and his face. Burns sprang out to help his friend and the two players made a desperate fight against the crowd, finally getting the stone-thrower in a position where he was terribly pun-ished. The fellow proved to be an excursionist from Toledo.

When Willie Hahn heard about the attack on Kelly and Burns he packed a cap pistol and a blow-gun into his little suitcase and begged his father to buy him a ticket for Detroit.

The Detroit Free Press was blunt, almost threatening.

"Never was a Detroit base ball audience so aroused. That Phil Powers escaped without injury is due to the strategy of friends. If he knows when he is well off he will never again show his face at Recreation Park. The management has sent a formal protest to Nick Young and it is hoped here that Powers' days as a League umpire are numbered."

After the long train ride to Philadelphia Kelly's crew split their Friday night between the two Billys -McGonegal's and McLean's - and as a consequence played "listlessly" the next day. Mike had but one hit in a twin bill loss.

According to *The Enquirer*, the visitors endeavored to escape defeat on Monday by "resorting to all the obstruction tactics for which they are famous." After the home side scored three runs in the eighth Kelly pretended to be hurt and Anson called for Lew Hardie to replace him. The sky darkened while Hardie got himself into uniform and Umpire Fullman decided it would not be possible to see a thrown ball much less a batted one. He announced that the game was called due to darkness and the three runs the Phillies had just scored would stand under the provision of Section 4 of Rule 43, giving them a 6-5 win. While Anton kicked about it a dozen enthusiastic rooters carried Fullman to the club house on their shoulders.

Anson put his best possible nine on the field for the series finale on Wednesday and they played the rankest kind of game he'd seen, some of their errors being simply ridiculous. Flint was miserable behind the bat. In what *The Philadelphia Times* called "the most brilliant series ever played at Recreation Park" Kelly'd had a grand total of two hits in the five games, four of them Chicago losses and one a draw. The Phillies had "outperformed the champions at all points."

The Wolverines started October four games back of Chicago and it looked as though the White Stockings would prevail, but the Detroits won six games in six days. At the Polo Grounds on the 5th, Kelly was on second base when Anson drove the ball into right field for a hit. As Kelly rounded third Giants right fielder Mike Dorgan

uncorked a wild throw to the plate. The ball sailed up the third base line and through a gate that led under the grandstand that happened to be open. As Giants' catcher Tom Deasley and pitcher Tim Keefe ran under the stands to retrieve the ball, Kelly raced over and shut the gate, standing in front of it to prevent the ball from coming back onto the field. Anson circled the bases and scored a run for the White Stockings. The New Yorks prevailed by a score of 7-4 anyway. Worse, the Wolverines had beaten the Nationals in the morning and again in the afternoon. They won in Washington again the next day, though it took them eleven innings. That brought them to within a game and a half of the Chicagos, who knew that they were on the ragged edge.

The White Stockings watched the score-board nervously on Friday while they played in Boston. The score from Philadelphia was posted as PHILA 1 DETR 1 after two innings and it was the same up until the same score was posted after nine. Everyone waited for the score-board boy to hang numbers under the tenth inning but he didn't stir. Kelly had two hits, drove in a run, and scored twice as the Chicagos went on to win 8-4. When they got back to their hotel the White Stockings were glad to learn from the desk-clerk that the game in Philadelphia had ended in a tie after being called due to darkness.

On Saturday, October 9th Chicago beat 12-3 Boston. There was tremendous excitement from the start and when it was over hundreds of boosters who'd travelled to Boston escorted the team from the grounds and repeatedly cheered them as they took their seats in the coach. The Tribune man happily reported, "Nothing here is too good for them, they are heroes of the hour. Mike Kelly, who has distinguished himself by fine base-running and good batting and delighted the crowd when he stole third base while Stemmyer was getting ready to pitch, was clearly their favorite and was hailed as the greatest ball-player in America."

The Quakers' Charlie "Jack-in-the-box" Ferguson pitched both ends of a double header against Detroit and had anything but a pleasing effect on the Wolverines, beating them 5-1 and 6-1. In Chi-

cago, crowds of men hung about the tickers waiting with absorbed interest for the news to come over the wire. When the news came in of Chicago's victory and the Detroits' pair of losses in Philadelphia the cheering and applause were deafening.

Spalding fired off a telegram. When Anson got it the White Stockings crowded around as he read it. "Chicago, Oct. 9 A.C. Anson, CAPTAIN, CHICAGO BALL CLUB, BOSTON: You have clinched the pennant in grand style. Knew we could depend upon the old war horses in a pinch. You have captured the League championship, now come home and win the world's championship. As a token of my appreciation of your work I herewith tender each man of the team a suit of clothes, awaiting their order and the team collectively one-half the receipts in the coming series with St. Louis. Accept congratulations, A.G. Spalding."

"A set uv clothes and half the gate from the series. Will wonders never cease?" said Kelly.

"Never thought the skinflint had it in him," said Gore.

Williamson, Dalrymple, Pfeffer, and Kelly sat in the easiest chairs the Boston Press Club parlor afforded and told stories that evening. The scribes that sat around them lapped up what Kelly had to say.

"We play in Adams Tuesday and after that we go to St. Louis to tackle the Browns and you can wear bradiggan clothes all the winter by bettin' we'll win it easy," said Kelly as a pretty serving girl set a glass of whisky on the table in front of him and whispered, "This is the good stuff from the back," winked, turned and left.

Kelly smiled and picked up the glass. "I think we'd uv batted hard today if there had been a cannon throwing the balls in. Rad did himself up the day before. I was walking out to the field after striking out and I said to him, I wish you would throw that arm of yours off of you. He never said a word. He's a terror. He fooled me on a couple uv 'em. I thought they were up across my neck where I like 'em but I couldn't uv hit 'em with a ladder."

He took a drink and went on. "I never strike at a low one ... I can't

see the damned things. You can take my dying oath if I didn't think I was up to the top of the batting list after all ... by the official averages." He looked around. "You cranks here don't know how to score ball. I ain't afraid of Brouthers, he may be ahead uv me. I ain't been watching what he's been doing these three or four days."

Then he sat back in his seat and puffed violently at an Old Judge cigarette.

"Hanlon says he's afraid to try to steal bases on you, Mike," suggested *The Tribune* scribe.

"I'm always watching for a man like Hanlon. I'm right there close up behind the bat and they give me balls a little high so I can throw him out."

"Who's the worst kicker in the league?" asked *The Inter-Ocean* man.

"John Morrill. There's none uther," declared Kelly.

Pfeffer exhaled a puff of cigar smoke and interrupted. "Unless, we tell him to. Then he'll make a bold bluff." He turned to Dalrymple. "Ain't that right, Old Whiskers?"

"When Kel does, the crowd eats it right up," said Abner. "A lot of the other kickers just make them weary, dragging games on past two hours often as not."

"There are different kinds of chin," said Pfeffer. "The cranks don't mind so much if they can hear what you're jawing at the umpire about. When Morrill kicks they can't hear a damn word he says."

A waiter went by. "Ginger ale, please," said Pfeffer. "I'm not that keen on playing in Adams. We get beat by those cheap clubs. It doesn't pay to take chances where nothing's on the line. I sprained an ankle in Rochester and had to lay off League games for six days."

"You ought to pitch in one of these exhibition games, Kel," said Dalrymple. "The cranks'd *love* to see you in the box."

"I pitched a game last year against the Buffalos. Old Brouth made a home run the very first inning and then Jack Rowe got in a three bagger so I retired. His Whiskers here went in the next inning but

they knocked him around just as bad. Then Pfeff went in and they couldn't knock him out."

"Why's that?" asked *The Tribune* man.

"There was no one else to put in."

Everyone laughed.

Kelly turned to *The Inter-Ocean* fellow. "You know that piece you wrote about me the last of July? Well I sent a paper to a cousin of mine. I never saw the girl but I had a mash from that time out. I'll send her a telegram tonight. I've got a lot more to send too … one to my wife, one to Nat Goodwin and one to my sister in California." He pulled some papers out of the pocket of his Prince Albert coat. "I got it here, just what I'm going to say. No, I ain't either, they're all in my ball clothes."

"How about that row you and Burns had in Detroit?" asked *The Tribune* man. "Did we get that straight?"

Mike set down his glass. "No. Yous got it all wrong, yas did. We had beat 'em two straight, see, and they were all dead sore. Williamson and Burns and His Whiskers there got me into trouble. We were coming out uv the grounds and about two hundred kids follied us up to the cab. When one of the gang threw a brick through the window and hit Tom in the neck it made me mad, you know. I put after the kid but a big fellow with whiskers tackled me. Well I sized him up and saw he was as big as I was. I chased him around the crowd for a minute and finally let go at him with my left duke. Burns had follied me out and he gave him another one in the neck and he staggered. Tom's wrist is lame from it now, he couldn't play for a cent yesterday and he didn't go in today. Then a fellow in the crowd yelled lynch them and Tom and me piled into the cab and escaped."

The only Mike drained the rest of his glass, stepped to the piano, deposited his 186 pounds of shape and sinew on the plush-covered stool and sang a ditty to the most familiar tune in "The Tin Soldier", playing his own accompaniment with his big, bruised hands.

"Chicago has a ball club,

The finest in the land,

A detective brought news,

That seven drank booze,

And Burns with a smoke in his hand."

Pfeffer sat down beside Kelly and joined in.

"Twenty-five it was the damage,

The club house suffered the pain,

The director had gall,

But when we played ball,

We got there just the same."

The whole room cheered and applauded.

"Me friend Jimmy McCormick wrote that himself," said Mike. "Good, ain't it? Oh, that was rank, fining us $25 apiece. Spalding pulled us all up before him and read off all we had been doing … according to the detective, the son of a gun. He had Burns down smoking cigarettes and McCormick drinking three soda lemonades. Mac spoke up and said it wasn't true, one would kill him, and me having three bottles of beer in my room and I says, 'What, only three? Take my dying oath I never drank anything in me life."

'Yes," broke in Pfeffer. "It was dead wrong. Here we'd won sixteen out of our last seventeen games and then we got fined and told off and we went East and lost six out of ten and that liked to have done us in."

"Young Ryan owned up to drinking beer three times," added Dalrymple. "Said the water didn't agree with him."

All this time Williamson didn't say much but only talked quietly at one side, smiling and admiring Kelly and acting like the fat, good-natured, homely, earnest fellow that he was.

"After all," said Kelly, "the cranks abuse us wherever we go, but they like to see us play just the same."

The players got up, stretched, and walked out of the club as the

October sun peeked out above their heads.

The first three games of the championship series were played at West Side Park. In the first game, on Monday, October 18, Chicago quickly jumped out to a two-run lead powered by Anson's RBI triple to the gap in right center. Pfeffer drove Anson home with a single and the blue-uniformed home team took a 2-0 lead. That was all the scoring the White Stockings needed for the win, Clarkson pitched a 5-hit shutout.

Bob Carruthers' curves proved a mystery to Anson's men the next day. They managed just two hits while the Browns got to rheumatic-footed McCormick for eleven hits and a dozen runs.

The Detroit Free Press base ball writer was in the press box. He told his readers he'd witnessed "one of the worst games ever played" by the Chicagos, who not only failed to hit Carruthers but "fielded like a bindle of schoolboys out on a lark and missed nearly every opportunity given them to do effective work." The National League champions committed a dozen errors. Tom Burns, one of the only players not hung over from the celebration of the easy win in Game One, was responsible for four of them.

After being tied in knots by Carruthers the day before, the Chicagos batted him around the park in Game Three on Wednesday. He threw six wild pitches and walked six men in the first. The Browns stared daggers at Charley Comiskey. They'd warned him not to send Carruthers to the pitching box two days in a row. Clarkson was on top of his game again, the right-hander struck out eight Browns in an 11-4 win.

In the second inning Kelly dropped the third strike to Hudson and threw to third, picking off Curt Welch. Hudson stayed at the plate and after a lengthy dispute was granted first base even though he hadn't run. Yank Robinson reached on Dalrymple's muff of his fly ball. Doc Bushong conked up a fly to Gore who captured it and threw a strike to home. Kelly stood on the plate waiting for it.

When he tagged Robinson, Yank drove his shoulder into Kelly's face. The only Mike tumbled over, his face badly cut open. The crowd cheered Gore's throw and hissed at Robinson's hoodlum act.

In the third inning Clarkson flew out and Gore was retired on a little groundball. Kelly came to the plate, blood caked beneath his eye. When the second pitch came his way Kel lifted it clear over the left field fence. He made a tour of the bases amid a storm of cheers and the spectators seemed to feel that Mike had gained some revenge.

When the series shifted to St. Louis the Browns turned it around. Clarkson was between the points for Game Four, pitching for the third time in four days. McCormick didn't make the trip due to a recurrence of the rheumatism in his feet. Jocko Flynn was already lost to the team for the year - and his career - with arm trouble. In an effort to overcome the pitching deficit the team hurriedly signed a young 39-game winner from a minor league club in Duluth, Ward Baldwin, but the new addition to the team didn't see action in the series. Browns' owner Chris von der Ahe objected to the Chicagos' use of Baldwin declaring that there was an understanding that the series was a competition between the two teams that had won the championships of their leagues and no additional players were to be used by either side and Spalding hadn't let the Browns use Ramsey, the catcher in the Louisvilles.

A.G. remonstrated for the new addition to his stable and the two owners stormed off for speedy decision of the dispute by the board of umpires appointed for the series, a process specified by an earlier agreement between the teams. Three of the four umpires two from each league were located and it was determined that the matter should be left to the toss of a coin. Anson lost the flip and Baldwin was barred from the series.

After the starting bell rang at 3:15 p.m., the Chicagos managed to rack up a 3-0 lead in the top of the first inning. The Browns narrowed the margin with a run in the second inning and another run in the third. The tide turned decisively in the fifth inning. Clarkson tired and gave up a two-run single by Gleason, followed by an RBI single by Charlie Comiskey.

The White Stockings managed to get two runs back in the top of the sixth but the Browns put the game away for good with three more runs in the bottom half of the frame. The game was called after seven innings due to darkness, the series knotted at two games each. Anson was angered by the decision to call the game after 7 innings, claiming that sufficient light remained to see the ball when the game was ended, but his plea went unheeded as the crowd of about 8,000 scurried for the exits.

Anson trotted out Williamson to start Game Four, only to see the hapless conscript knocked out of the box after giving up three hits and two runs in the first inning. Jimmy Ryan went in and showed himself a better pitcher than Ned but he still took the loss as his teammates blundered the game away defensively, Burns, Gore, Pfeffer, and Williamson, "fumbling, juggling, and fooling with balls at critical junctures."

The final game of the 1886 Series was a legendary affair. Bob Caruthers made his third pitching start for St. Louis, with John Clarkson pitching for a fourth time for Chicago. Under threatening skies the White Stockings took a 2-0 lead into the fourth inning when a rain shower prompted fans to leave the grand-stand and run onto the field demanding that the umpire call the game because of inclement weather. Order was restored only with the assistance of the police.

A 3-0 Chicago lead held until a dramatic comeback by the Browns in the eighth. Charlie Comiskey began the St. Louis half of the inning with a single to right field and was sent to third on Welch's bunt. He managed to beat out the throw to first base, putting runners on the corners. Burns threw wildly to first in an effort to pick off Welch only to see the ball skip away and Comiskey score. The home crowd erupted. Clarkson managed to collect two outs, but he kept the inning alive with a walk of Doc Bushong, the hitter in the 9-spot that brought the potential go-ahead run to the plate, leadoff hitting Arlie Latham.

Anson had been riding Latham throughout the game from the

third base coaching area, taunting him as a soft spot in the Browns' defense. Latham delivered his answer with his bat, hammering a long fly ball that Dalrymple misjudged. Running on contact, Welch and Bushong both scored on the play, knotting the game at 3's.

Neither team scored in the 9th, sending the game to extra innings. Chicago failed to score in their half of the 10th, but in the bottom half of the frame the Browns started a rally with Curt Welch advancing to third base. Clarkson wound up and threw a pitch that got past Kelly and Welch came home to win the game and the series for St. Louis.

There was disagreement as to whether the final play of the game was made possible by a passed ball or a wild pitch. Kelly told the press he was willing to take the blame. "I signaled Clarkson for a low ball on one side and when it came it was high up on the other. It struck my hand as I tried to get it and I would say it was a passed ball. You can give it to me if you want to. Clarkson told me it slipped from his hands.

The Tribune reporter differed with the official scoring decision, asserting that the passed ball was really a wild pitch by Clarkson. Unfortunately, he'd be remembered best for throwing the famous wild pitch. Compounding the seriousness of the loss were allegations that he'd failed to make his planned start in Game Five because he'd been out drinking the night before.

Some disgruntled teammates said publicly that they held no ill will, but they were suspected of giving less than their best efforts for Clarkson when he was on the mound. Others treated Clarkson with hostility for the remainder of his career.

Total receipts for the series were $13,920.10, from which was first deducted the $100 salaries of the umpires. The remaining funds were split in half between team owner Chris Von der Ahe and the St. Louis players with each one pocketing slightly over $500. Spalding was so livid that his club had lost he told the players they could pay their own train fare back to Chicago. Kelly was one of the men who'd bet on his team to win and spent a tidy sum living it up in St. Louis. They

had to borrow money from the Browns.

The White Stockings were invited to meet President Grover Cleveland at the White House. As the president went down the line of players shaking hands, Kelly, ever the jokester, on a dare from Dalrymple, decided to see if he could squeeze the president's soft pudgy hand hard enough to make him wince. He succeeded.

When Mike and James returned to Paterson they were given a parade that wound through the streets. After the politicians had feted them before an adoring crowd, the two friends drank all night in David Treado's saloon. He'd played ball with Jim and Mike in his teens and now he was looking for a partner in the establishment. He got one in McCormick.

"I know we'll do well whenever Kel's in town," chuckled James.

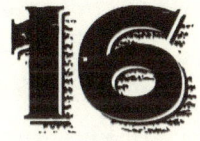

"The $10,000 Beauty."

On November 1 *The New York Sun* stated that Mike Kelly, the most famous of the champion Chicago White Stockings, would not play ball next season because he had made over $100,000 speculating in wheat.

"More like a thousand," Mike told a reporter who asked him about it.

In hopes of generating more offence, a Joint AA/NL Rules Committee voted to have four strikes and five balls. The strike zone would be from the knees to the shoulders. Pitchers were restricted to one step and would have to start with one foot on the back line of the box, which was reduced from 4 x 7 feet to 4 x 5 ½. The pitching distance would now be 55 ½ feet. Batters would be awarded first base if hit by a pitch but a batter's right to call for a 'high ball' or a 'low ball' was abolished. Thanks to players like Kelly, coaches would be required to stay inside their boxes. There would be no more coin tossing. The home team would choose which side would bat first.

Spalding returned from a hunting retreat in the wilds of Dakota in November and one of his first acts was to release Abner Dalrymple, Kelly's best friend next to James McCormick. Mike had been afraid it would happen. Now far removed from the slugging of his early years in the League, Ab had batted .233 in '86.

Then Spalding sold George Gore to the New York Giants for $3,500. *The Tribune* said, "The Chicago Base-Ball Club has released Dalrymple, its famous left fielder, and he has signed with the Pittsburg club. The release of Gore and Dalrymple thoroughly breaks up the best outfield that was ever seen on these grounds. For five years they and Kelly were an unapproachable trio."

Now Williamson badly wanted to get away from the Chicagos and play in the Browns.

At the beginning of December one of Kelly's admirers ran into a *Tribune* reporter and accosted him with: "I see the Tribune thinks Mike Kelly will play here next season. Does anybody want to bet anything on that?"

"Is it a good bet he will not?" asked the reporter.

"Yes it is. If Spalding don't pay him that money he won't be back."

"Do you mean the fines that were imposed for drinking?"

"No, I don't mean the fines for drinking. Spalding promised some of the players bonus money and I'll tell you all about it if ya promise not to use my name."

The man was assured that his name would not be mentioned. He took a note book out of his pocket then a paper from inside of it. Then he told the reporter that in spite of the $2,000 salary limit, Gore was supposed to get $2,275, Williamson $2,275, McCormick $2,375, Kelly the same, and Flint $2,800. When the season was over the boys came around for the extra money but Spalding held onto it. Gore stuck it out 'til he got his release. Kelly made a big kick but it was no use and he took an oath that if Spalding didn't pay him that money he would never play another game as a member of the Chicago club."

In January Spalding was still fuming about McCormick's performance in the postseason. Of McCormick's claim of rheumatism, he said, "Rheumatism! Bah! It was drink and nothing but drink. He drank about as much as the rest of them put together."

President Day of the New Yorks was heard to say that he was very interested in acquiring Mike Kelly but knew he couldn't be bought for any price. "Kelly is a wonderful player and Spalding wouldn't part with him any sooner than I would with Ewing, Connor, or O'Rourke. Kelly's loud talk about leaving Chicago was all bluff, he told reporters. President Hewitt of the Washingtons said his club was as willing as ever to get Kelly but knew the prospect of securing him did

not look particularly bright.

According to *The Philadelphia Times* no new developments were reported in the Kelly negotiations. "At present a sort of armed neutrality exists, neither side knowing what the other is preparing to spring. It is certain that if Kelly will come in on terms not too exorbitant and sign a temperance contract that all Chicago players are required to agree to he will be back with them. Spalding has no hesitation in praising Michael's ability to play ball. He believes him to be one of the best ball players in the world."

On February 6 Spalding went to Hot Springs to meet with the players who remained and extracted from each a pledge of total abstinence. Two days later he met privately with Kelly, who demanded the $375 bonus he'd been promised for good behavior. Spalding refused and wouldn't rescind the additional $225 that had been withheld from his salary in fines for drinking. The pair did not part on speaking terms.

The news the next day was that the Kansas City Cowboys had folded up their tent. Pittsburg had already been granted permission to take their place. The Maroons had sold their franchise to the Indianapolis Hoosiers. There would be much bigger news the next week.

On February 15 a shocking report came in from the Nelson House in Poughkeepsie, N.Y. As a result of a month of negotiations between the Boston Triumvir of Soden, Conant, and Billings and A.G. Spalding the next time the "only Mike" Kelly stepped to the plate at the South End Grounds it would be in a Boston uniform. The final disposition of Kelly had been almost the sole topic of discussion in sporting circles ever since he declared that he wouldn't play if it had to be in Chicago.

Arthur H. Soden, who'd made his fortune in the roofing business, was the President of the Boston club. J.B. Billings, the club's Treasurer, was a shoe and leather maker. Secretary William Conant was a man of less means than his partners but liked to smoke big cigars and drive around town behind a frisky span of horses. The Triumvir ran a tight ship. They encouraged the players to go into the stands to retrieve foul balls and firemen who jumped down from their lo-comotive cabs to pick up balls on Walpole street were as good as criminals to them.

W.I. Harris had gotten wind of what was going on and he'd hur-ried to Poughkeepsie. He relished in the pleasure of witnessing Kelly sign his name to his new contract. He said, "The beaming smile on Treasurer Billings' face would melt away the chilly sensations Cap-tain Anson will experience when he learns that he will have to pilot the Chicagos without the assistance of the able lieutenant he has had for so long. After Kelly, clad in a tight-setting Prince Albert coat, had signed, Billings folded the contract and put it into his innermost pocket and tuned to Harris, "Good things come high, but we must have them."

The contract was for the League maximum $2,000 but to get around the salary cap the Boston club would pay Kelly an additional $3,000 for the use of his image in the team's advertisements. Billings told Harris how the deal had been consummated.

'Well, it's a long story, Bill, but now that the chase is over and I've got Mike's signature I'll tell you the whole thing. As soon as the sea-son finished we began to hear all manner of reports of hard feelings between Kelly and Al Spalding. At first I paid very little attention to them thinking that Mike was mad because some fine had been de-ducted from his salary and supposing that he would get over it very soon and sign. When he said he would never play with the Chicagos again unless what he lost in fines was made up to him I took no stock in the threat. But one day it occurred to me that Spalding would like to sell him and that's where I started. I suppose if anyone had told me before that time that the Chicagos would let Mike Kelly go I would have laughed at him, but somehow I was impressed with the feeling that here was a chance for us to show that we meant business.

I went to Soden and Conant and told them about it and they laughed at me. They didn't believe anybody could get Kelly away from Chicago. I didn't know as I could but I was in for trying as I have long considered him to be the greatest player in the business. I told them if I had my pick of one player in all the League I would

take Mike Kelly. Mr. Soden said the same thing. We talked the whole thing over and decided to make an offer of $5,000 for Kelly's release and I wrote Spalding to that effect.

After a while I got a letter from him stating that he could not think of disposing of the best man he had for $5,000. He said he was not anxious to release him but perhaps for double that amount he might consider it. Ten thousand dollars is quite a sum for one player we thought, but we were bound to have him. We offered $9,000 and Spalding replied that he would take the matter to the other stockholders and let us know by the middle of March. We were not prepared to lose our chance for him over a thousand dollars so we told Spalding we would pay the full $10,0000 if Kelly agreed to sign with us but that we needed an answer immediately.

We received a reply that we could have Kelly for $10,000 and we were at liberty to sign him as soon as we could. The only condition was that if at any point we thought of releasing Kelly the Chicago club would have the right to buy him back. The letter gave us Kelly's address and on Friday evening Soden, Conant, and myself met and decided that I should start on Sunday night for this place where I telegraphed Kelly to meet me. The rest of the story you know. Kelly's contract is on the way to Washington accompanied by a check for $10,000. Nick Young has been instructed by Spalding to consider Kelly released by Chicago and the contract approved upon receipt of the check."

President Young told *The Philadelphia Times* correspondent that he was surprised by Spalding's decision to sell Kelly but knew he could never play his old game with the White Stockings and that Boston sorely needed just the strengthening that the acquisition of the great player would add. "I am very glad to record the deal," he said.

Kelly was asked how much he thought Boston had paid Chicago for his release.

He thought for a moment. "I'd wager three thousand, five hundred dollars, the same as the New Yorks paid for George Gore."

"Guess again," said the reporter.

"Five thousand."

"Higher."

"Seven thousand?"

"No, Kel. The Boston directors handed over ten thousand to get you."

Kelly was flabbergasted. He shook his head. "Ten thousand dollars? Well I'd better play like the devil himself to warrant *that* amount."

As soon as Kelly signed the contract he went down to the telegraph office and sent a message to Nat Goodwin: "I am now a beaneater and shall be in your town all next summer."

Mike told Harris, "You can take me dyin' oath, Billy, I'll play hard enough to be worth every cent of it. I'm not one of your fancy players who can catch today but has to lay off tomorrow to get back in condition again. I can play every game and when I ain't catching I'm always ready to fill some other place. I was taught to be any every-day man in the Chicago club and last year I played in all but two or three games, I've forgotten which. That man Anson is a holy terror. Why, he's made me go in and catch when my hands were in a frightful state. I could hardly hold the ball but that was nothing to him. I had to play anyway."

Harris asked Kelly if he would have gone back to play for Spalding if he hadn't signed to play in the Bostons and Mike said he would have played in New York but that he would not play in the Chicagos again. I tell you one thing, if we can't clean out Anson's crowd this season I'll quit the business. Just think of it, all the old outfielders have left and the three of us scored and thumped in a good many runs. Perhaps they'll wish we were back when they run up against our boys from the Hub."

Billings told Harris that it was virtually decided by the directors that if they succeeded in making Kelly a Beaneater they would anoint him captain. Kelly seemed reluctant to say anything about such a possibility. When Billings asked him about the captaincy and

pressed him on it all Mike would say is, "There isn't a nicer fellow in the game than John Morrill."

Of Kelly's influence on a team Harris said, "When on the ball field Mike is fairly boiling over with enthusiasm and he always goes into a game with such a whole-heartedness that his spirit becomes infectious and spreads over the whole team."

"Is Kelly worth the price paid for him?" asked *The Philadelphia Times*. "As a star attraction, yes. Kelly is arousing an enthusiasm in Boston which will tell in the way of greatly enlarged gate receipts and consequent profits. Much will be expected of him and everybody will go to see him and hurrah for him and the team. For anything else than a drawing card he is not worth anything like the sum paid, nor is any player who ever batted a ball in the national game. Kelly is a great player. Of that there cannot be the slightest doubt. But one man cannot win the championship."

Spalding told *The Herald* that Kelly "has been with us seven years and a more genial, willing player does not live. He has my best wishes for success. Boston can say it has the *king* of ball players." The name would stick.

Ned Williamson was asked to comment on Kelly's departure. "Mike was a huge attraction. He's unquestionably the most popular player on the diamond. He brought thousands of dollars to the Chicago treasury and Spalding will never again have a man in his team who will be to it what Mike Kelly has been. More than that, he was the life and soul of the Chicagos."

When Ned was asked about Chicago's chances for a pennant without Kelly a hang-dog expression came over his face. "No, we surely will not be able to do that. His loss is going to be rough on us holdover players." Asking first that his next remark would be off the record he said, "I regret my decision to sign with a team that was determined to clear out my friends and battle-tested teammates. When I signed I supposed we'd have the old nine; if I had thought that Kelly and Gore were going to be released my signature would never have gone on that contract."

In March a list of the top run scorers in the League since the 1879 season was printed in *The Tennessean*. Kelly led with an average of 100 runs per season. Gore was close behind at 96, O'Rourke next at 88, then Brouthers at 87, Dalrymple 83, and Anson 77.

Kelly's 155 tallies in '86 were five more than second-place Gore and 16 better than third-place Brouthers. Behind Mike's league-leading .388 batting average were Anson at .371 and Brouthers at .370. Kelly was way ahead of the pack in on-base percentage. His was .483. Brouthers and Gore were well back at .445 and .434.

A Detroit barber offered a ticket good for 100 free shaves to the first player to hit a home run in Detroit. There was a pretty good chance Dan Brouthers would be the most clean-shaven man in the game in '87. After all, he'd led the League with 11 home runs in '86.

The Chicago batting list *had* started with Dalrymple, Gore, and Kelly. Now it would be Billy Sunday, Jimmy Ryan, Dalrymple's replacement in left field, and 24-year-old rookie Marty Sullivan. They wouldn't be striking fear in the hearts of many enemy pitchers.

After leading the League in RBIs five of the last six years, the big captain would have a lot fewer base runners to hit home. His total would plummet from 147 to 102, sixty-four fewer than Detroit's Sam Thompson. In '87 the White Stockings would score almost a hundred fewer runs. They could have used Mike Kelly. His total of 120 would be among his best.

The March 15 evening headline read "Kelly, the Ten Thousand Dollar Beauty Welcomed by the Boys". Though people recognized the honorific, many had forgotten its origin. In 1881, circus owner Adam Forepaugh had held a contest for the most beautiful woman in America. The winner was promised $10,000 and the lead in his spectacle entertainment entitled Lalla Rookh's Departure from Dehli. When actress Louise Montague, a demi-blonde who had blue eyes and a mass of wavy dark chestnut hair combed well down over her narrow Grecian forehead, was declared the winner she'd been promoted as the "$10,000 beauty."

There wasn't anyone at the Winslow rink on skates or playing polo.

Twelve players under contract to the Boston club awaited the arrival of their new matinee idol teammate. Half of them were stationed across one end of the rink, the rest lined the other. Balls flew back and forth between them. Several base ball enthusiasts watched from the perimeter and an equal number of youngsters tried to nudge their way forward to catch a glimpse of their hero.

"Kelly's nawt here," said a boy with a thick Boston accent.

"Where can he be?" asked another kid.

A man overheard them. He chuckled and said, "Knowing Mike Kelly, he could be almost anywhere, boys."

Suddenly the door burst open and a tall, finely formed fellow stepped through it. His clear eye and ruddy complexion reflected his fine condition. His splendid physique filled out a handsome Prince of Wales suit and there was a rosebud in its lapel.

"It's him! It's King Kelly!" yelled one of the kids.

A murmur went through the spectators and the players as well.

Joe Hornung stepped forward and grasped Kel by the hand. "Mike, old man, we're glad to have you."

Hoss Radbourn gave him an equally hearty greeting and as each of the other players welcomed him Kelly was ready with a bright and witty remark.

"Not much of a stache you have there, Kid," he said to 19-year-old, peach fuzz-faced Madden.

"How's the missus, Jack?" he asked dapper Burdock, "still waiting up nights for you?"

"Are the bartenders back in Richmond missing you yet, Pop?" he asked Tate.

"Still picking nags at the track, John?" he wanted to know from Morrill.

Kelly hadn't come to the rink to take part in the practice and didn't have his baseball toggery with him but he couldn't stand by when he saw the rest of his new teammates going at it. He pulled off his coat,

grabbed Pop Tate's catcher's glove and stood in the center of the rink while Kid Madden pitched to him.

"How are you feeling?" Hornung asked when Mike took the glove off and handed it back to Tate.

"Never better, Joe," said the king of the diamond as he put his suit-jacket back on. "I struck the town yesterday and my address just now is the United States Hotel. If anybody is going to call on me he had better do it pretty soon or he'll find me in a boarding house. I'm no bondholder."

Outside of the gym later a boy approached Kel and asked him something.

Joe asked, "What does he want?"

"He wants me to sign something for him," answered Mike.

Joe chuckled, "Sign what? A check?"

"No, a score-card."

"I've never heard tell of such a thing. Are you going to sign it?"

"I suppose."

Mike took the boy's score-card and signed it.

A small group of boys huddled nearby. They saw Kelly sign the card and hurried over.

"Can you sign your name on something for me too, Mr. Kelly?"

"I can, sun, but what?"

The boy hadn't realized that he had nothing for his hero to sign. He looked around desperately and spotted a discarded peanut bag. He grabbed it and gave it to Mike. As he signed it the other boys scrambled for things that could be written on.

"This had better not catch on or I'll be late for the bar every afternoon."

"Don't worry, Kel." said Joe, "I'll save a seat for ya."

"I'm hanging this on my bedroom wall," the boy with the signed score-card told the others.

"This'll look kinda strange on *my* wall," said the boy with the signed peanut bag.

The March 28 *Globe* related that, "Kelly, whose particular pet at present is a Skye terrier named Bess, said Saturday that he was going to work with a will this week. He proposes to do some tall running. He has just returned from Hyde Park, New York where he went to see his wife who is ill with a severe attack of rheumatism. Kelly has been obliged to indefinitely postpone his intention of bringing her to Boston."

Mike was making himself solid with the Boston reporters, telling them how he had always liked Boston and the people and that he had a great many friends in the city. He explained how he was going to win the championship for the Bostons.

"Kel is always a great kidder," wrote Billy Harris. "He's never said more than that he would try and help the team to win. His head fits his hat snugly."

Within a month of the purchase, the Boston club publicized a $10,000 life insurance policy they'd taken out on Kelly to protect their investment. It was well worth it, average game attendance for Boston would be nearly double that of the previous season.

At the beginning of April Kelly officiated as a referee at a Benefit for an amateur club. "He was the cynosure of all eyes and his personal appearance and base ball abilities were the main conversation. His image had already found its way onto the walls of Irish pubs throughout Boston. Reproductions of a painting of Kelly sliding head-first into second base in front of a cheering crowd had replaced paintings of Custer's Last Stand just as they had in Chicago. Mike was already enhancing his income by endorsing products such as a "Slide, Kelly, Slide" model sled and a Kelly-branded shoe polish.

At a team meeting Kelly appointed himself ticket agent for his theatrical friend Floyd, who was staging a Benefit that night at the park and he succeeded in disposing of quite a collection of pasteboards. Then he assisted Wise, Buffington, and Nash in settling the merits of certain bats and showed them one that was "full uv liners."

Then Kelly got out a sheet of paper and asked for everyone's attention. "We got a bunch uv new rules this year, boys, listen up. Pitchers,
your box is bein' reduced in size to four by five and a half feet. I think
you all knew that was coming, but there's ta be no more callin' for
high or low pitches. Five called balls'll get ya first base, four called
strikes'll get ya called out. Whatever you batted last season you'll
likely add forty or fifty points ta your mark. The League's decided
bases on balls are gointa be scored as hits."

Sam Wise interrupted. "Did you say bases on balls are going be
scored as *hits*?"

"I did."

"Whose cockamamie idea was *that*?"

"I've no idea, it's about as ridiculous as countin' bases on balls as
errors against the pitcher. There's good news for us sliders … the
home base is ta be made uv rubber and nuthin' but rubber, and it's
gointa be a twelve inch square. And the best news uv all… if ya get
hit by a pitch you're ta be awarded your base."

"About time," said Sam Wise.

"Aye, it bluddy well is," said Mike.

Then Soden came in and laid down *his* rules for the coming season. He wore a dark grey frock coat that seemed ridiculously formal
for the occasion and his chest was swollen out like a bantam roost-
er's. "Faithful observation of the following club rules is expected
from each and every one of you," he said. He cleared his throat and
read from a sheet of paper. "One, there is to be no intemperance, dissipation, or excess of any kind. Two, there is to be no loitering about
or frequenting of liquor saloons, gambling houses, or establishments
of ill-repute. Three, you are to have no truck with known gamblers
or disreputable characters. Four, you are to report twice a day, at ten
o'clock and two o'clock. Five, you will not engage in disorderly conduct of any sort. And six, there is to be no keeping of unreasonable
hours. You will be in your rooms by 11:30." He paused and looked
straight at Kelly. "Captain and all."

During the delivery of this unusual and unprecedented screed the men listened intently. Kelly tilted his stool back against his locker. He only once lost his balance and that was during the reading of Rule number one. Then he pointed at good-natured Tate and said, "That means you, Pop." Morrill kept his head down and stared at the floor.

Soden wiped his brow and stowed away his manuscript. Silence reigned for close to two minutes, then Morrill stood up and said, "As manager I have charge of the selection and placing of the men to play, but if Captain Kelly desires to play anybody differently I should not hesitate to play the men in that order. I think we can all get on harmoniously."

The Boston owners knew that pitching would be the main issue for the Beaneaters in '87. Old Hoss Radbourn's glory years in Providence were well behind him. Twenty-two-year-old Bill "Cannon Ball" Stemmyer from Cleveland stood 6-foot-2 and weighed 190 pounds. Billy Nash said he was the fastest pitcher he ever saw. No catcher could handle him if he was even slightly off target though. Stemmyer had won 22 games for the Bostons in '86. He'd win just six in '87, batters laid off his shoots and belted his changeups and curves.

Michael "Kid" Madden was frail and almost childlike in appearance, 124 pounds spread thinly over a 5-foot-7 frame. "An assortment of breaking pitches second to none and the most puzzling of drops" was how a sportswriter who covered the Portland Atlantics of the New England League summed up the Kid's stuff. John Morrill was so impressed when the Beaneaters played the Atlantics in an exhibition that he signed Madden as well as the Kid's batterymate Tom O'Rourke to Boston contracts.

William Harris was the envy of *The Boston Globe* staff when he was given the plum assignment of covering the Beaneaters' match with the Baltimores on April 8. He sent a detailed account of the game back to Boston that night.

"There was fun and excitement without end at Oriole Park today. The 5,687 people got a big return for their money. The bats on both

311

teams were knocking the cover off the ball. It was thought that the Bostons and 'the only Mike' would prove a good attraction but no one dreamed of the extent.

The boys from the Hub rode out to the grounds on a coach of 1850 vintage. On the way, it ran into a procession. Out of the window went Kelly's shoulders and in his stentorian voice he shouted, 'Here, you mogul, don't cross that funeral. I never crossed a funeral and won a game in me life.'

It happened that the procession was not a funeral, however, only the Sons of Ebenezer on parade. 'Kel' made conquests of several Baltimore's fair damsels en route.

Of course Bostonians will want to know how the boys deported themselves, particularly what Kelly, who has been extensively advertised here as the '$10,000 beauty', did for the honor of his new found constituents. Well, he made things lively and interesting and I am glad to say he covered himself with glory. He had only one fielding chance and he handled that with ease though there was no moss on it. Where Mike got in his work was with a 42 by 2½ inch club. Three successive times did Kelly hit the ball and after that in seventeen balls 'Allentown' Smith put only four over the plate and gave 'Kel' his base twice.

When Oyster Burns made a two-base hit in the third the crowd yelled. Then Blondie Purcell lifted the sphere away into right field and a regular storm of applause went up but Kelly pulled it off the clouds after a hard backward run and the yells subsided. After the game Joe Hornung said that if 'Kel' had made that catch in Boston he would have owned the grand-stand.

Kelly hit a daisy cutter too hot for Greenwood to handle his next time at the plate. His subsequent chance came with two out and three men on base and Mike was in his element. He faced Phenomenal Smith with an attitude of defiance. He pounded the plate then spit on his hands, rubbed them in the dirt, and pounded the plate again. His bat bounced, which it had never done until this year. The League has adopted the white rubber plates Robert Keating patented after playing a single game with the Orioles and deciding he needed a different vocation. Kel was glad, he has ruined many a leg and uniform on the stone ones. Then he gripped his club like the man looking for the fellow who stole his wife.

There was a wicked gleam in his eyes and a force in his arms that sent the first ball pitched whizzing between Burns and Jumbo Davis and four men made the dirt fly on the base lines. Burdock came home on play and Tate trying to do the same was clearly out at the plate. But Umpire Skinner had run down to second to watch Kelly and having his back to the plate didn't see the put out and wouldn't allow it. Thomas Burns, Esq. raised his voice in high disgust, but Skinner would not listen to his dulcet tones and made everyone play ball. That set the crowd going and between the hard knocks of Burns, who wanted to know if Skinner was going to 'give them duffers everything', and the assertion of the wrathy Mike, who with great naivete informed him that he had never seen a better umpire in his life, they were fit to be tied.

Not long did the Bostons kick dirt in the eyes of the Baltimores, who scored four runs in the fifth to make a game of it. Sammy Wise lifted the ball into left center in the sixth for three bases and Smith refused to give Kelly a chance to drive him home and gave him his bases on calls instead. Kelly stole second, skillfully evading Greenwood's touch then called to Nash at the bat 'Now then Billy, every good one lay into it' and Billy did for a rattling two-baser that brought in Wise and the Beauty.

The game was still in doubt in the ninth and the crowd pushed in on the diamond to the discomfort of the players. Greenwood led off with a base hit then Tate and Burdock disposed of him at second on a clever force. But Skinner said 'not out' in spite of the hard kicking of Burdie and Kelly. Greenwood scored on Tate's bad throw and Tucker managed to get himself hit with the ball. Burdie caught him at second but Skinner was blind as usual. A hit would tie the game but Grimm was not equal to the emergency and hit an up-fly to Morrill and the match was decided.

The Bostons piled into their 'bus' amid the jeering of the crowd that poured from the grounds. A number of small stones and lumps of dry clay were thrown into the coach as it moved away. Kelly shouted to the driver of the coach to stop but Morrill said 'go on' and on we went, the boys singing 'Rock-a-bye baby.'"

On April 12 Harris wrote, "Mike Kelly is a tower of strength in the team. He knows the points by heart and works them for all they are worth. The youngsters have the most sublime faith in him and try to emulate him in everything."

Most of the members of the Boston team bought new derby hats and every one pasted a postage stamp photograph of Mike Kelly in the crown of his hat.

"I hear Spalding signed Willie Hahn to a contract. He's eleven now isn't he, Kel?" Burdock asked Kelly while they rode to the practice grounds the next morning.

"That's right."

"Apparently he and his dad were a bit stunned when Spalding read them the sobriety clause."

The Haverhill team visited the Hub on April 25. They chased the ball until they were weary and the Bostons were just as tired from running the bases. The pros made no pretension of trying hard after racking up a 14-0 lead in the first two innings. Kelly was on base five times and laughed when he dropped two flyballs and even when he was hit by a pitch from the soft-throwing Haverhill twirler. In the third inning he knocked a foul over the left field fence. A policeman was enjoying the game from a ladder propped up against a telegraph pole from which Operator Tobin sent the Western Union bulletins of the game. The ball fell near Tobin's roost and the cop earned a round of applause by making a fine catch. After the game Kelly announced tongue-in-cheek his intention to wear roller skates and goggles when he tended the right garden.

The thirteen Boston men left from the Boston & Albany depot on the 9 a.m. train the next morning to play the Yale team at New Haven. Then they'd travel to New York - where they would end up

cooling their heels for an hour at the train station - Newark, and then to Washington, where they'd booked rooms at Willard's, to open the season. Of course General Dixwell, the Boston team's most devoted crank, went with them as well as several other noted base ball enthusiasts. Dixwell was 5-foot-4, with a high forehead, a round chin, victorious blue eyes, and a flood of wavy golden whiskers. He wore bright-colored vests and looked like a Merovingian prince. Dixwell had never been near a battle field. The title was bestowed on him for the General Petition, a request for season tickets that he sent to the Boston owners.

Dixwell had given Kelly, Radbourn, Daily, Burdock, Madden, and Wheelock handsome leather bags to carry their bats in.

The general sat beside Kelly on the train ride.

"We're all grateful for the gift uv new bags," said Mike. "You're always giving us things."

"And I take great pleasure in doing so," said Dixwell.

"How can you afford it all, General? I see you at every one of our home games, you travel with us during spring training, and I know you go with the club on the road as far away as Chicago, so I'm thinkin' that you don't work."

"My father died when I was a lad, Mike. He was a banker and he left me with a comfortable trust fund … $10,000 annually, and an additional $10,000 if I maintained any sort of useful employment. I honored my father's wish by opening Dixwell's Art Furniture Parlor on Park street in '76, but the enterprise went bust in '84. I reopened it at 175 Tremont street as the agent for Marks' Adjustable Recliner Chair."

"An adjustable recliner chair? That sounds mighty darn comfortable."

The general looked around the car to see if anyone was listening. "Don't tell any of the other players, but if you win the pennant I'm giving every man one of my chairs."

"That'd be grand uv ya, I'll keep it under me hat, Arthur."

"Did you ever play the game, General, you seem to know a

lot about it?"

"I always keep score and I never get so distracted that I fail to record a play. In fact, Billy Harris and Tim Murnane often ask me to look over their accounts of the game to see if they've made any mistakes."

"And they ask you to do this over a couple uv drinks at a nearby watering hole and you end up with the tab."

"Why, yes, as a matter of fact. How did you know?"

"Lucky guess."

"I also keep impeccable records of every professional player, including their height, age, average ability, and previous condition of baseball servitude. That's how I knew Murnane had played the game and umpired a little."

Kelly took a puff of his cigarette and blew a perfect ring of smoke into the air. "But did you ever *play* the game?"

The general chuckled. "Once they put me out in right field on the Common. No offence to you, Mike, but in *those* days if you couldn't play ball worth a lick they put you in right field. I know they *play* you there because you can throw runners out at first and third base better than anyone in the game. At any rate, there was one ball knocked out my way in the first part of the game and I disgraced myself by running away from it. That settled my career as a ball player but I've been a crank of the game for many years. Last season I missed but one championship contest played by the Bostons."

"Well we all luv to hear your 'Hi, Hi' every time somethin' good happens."

"It's my way of expressing appreciation of a good play. I do not consider it too noisy, and it's not half as bad as the way *some* of the cranks give expression to their feelings."

On April 28 the team met at the N.Y & N.E. depot to board the train for their season opener in Washington. Kelly talked to a reporter during the trip. "Just because a player fumbles a ball there's no reason why he can't make the play anyway. It's often the case that you

can put your man out by a good throw after a bad fumble. When I juggle one I'm all the more anxious to make the put-out and I always throw to the base. That's the way we're going to play this season. If we make some errors we won't care a snap about them but will play harder than ever."

'Featherweight' called the Beaneaters a happy lot of ball tossers after their 9-4 defeat of the Nationals in their first game. He said professional players were thought not to care whether they won or not but the croakers who sang that song were way off key.

Mike had dinner with Billy Harris at the Horseshoe Café in Billington that night. "Tell 'em up in Boston we've got a lot uv ginger in us," Kelly told Harris. "And we play with a lot uv life and snap," he added as he tucked a piece of roast beef into his mouth then smiled at a woman who was trying hard not to stare at him.

From a Washington standpoint the game wasn't up to the handle or the heart. Each of their players dropped to the vicinity of his boots when the Bostons tallied four runs in the fifth inning and came from behind to win.

The game the next day was a hard one for the Nationals to lose as well. Four Beaneaters crossed the plate in the first inning but they barely held on as the Washingtons scored a run in each of the last three innings only to fall 4-3 to the visitors. It was the President's reception day and five of the Bostons Beaneaters had visited the White House in the morning.

"I'm very glad to see you, gentleman," said President Cleveland when the players entered the reception room. "I heard you were in town to play our nine. It has been a long time since I played ball but I still follow our national game. I was hoping to see $10,000 Kelly to tell him that hereafter he shall see that the Thirteenth Amendment to the Constitution which prohibits slavery and involuntary servitude is enforced."

The headline of *The Globe* sports page on May 3 read, "Captain Kelly Steps into the Breach and Makes Big Stemmyer Steady as a Rock." When Mike missed two flies in succession in the fourth in-

ning of the previous day's game and his team trailed the Quakers 6-1 the Philadelphia crowd yelled themselves hoarse and wondered why the Big Three in Boston had paid $10,000 for that man. But they didn't think it so strange when the sixth inning had been played.

Umpire Powers had been hammering Stemmyer about his position in the box. "I must be able to see light between your feet, Mr. Stemmyer," he kept reminding him.

The Ohioan was so afraid he'd commit a balk he could hardly throw the ball.

Kelly took over for Tate behind the bat and settled Stemmyer down.

"Don't worry about balks, Bill," Mike told him. "I'll watch your damn feet."

The Philadelphias didn't score another run. The Beaneaters scored six in the fifth, two in the sixth, and another three in the seventh for their third straight win.

Captain Kelly and his men were at the mercy of auburn-haired Casey on May 4. Outside of four square hits the Beaneaters were entirely at the mercy of the occupant of the central position. Two of the Big Three watched from the Directors' box and saw their players get painted with a thick coat of whitewash by Harry Wright's slender southpaw. With the score 8-0 Philadelphia Kelly stooped to catch a ball in the dirt and suddenly doubled up in pain holding onto a finger he'd hurt in Newark. Time was called and after consulting with both managers Kel took off his catching paraphernalia and went to the bench.

The 12-0 defeat didn't seem to depress the Bostons, who began a concert when they left the ground and kept it up until they reached their hotel. Wise was the only man wearing a hangdog face and Kelly tried to console him. "We'd won every game we'd played, Sam. There are some days when you couldn't win a game with twenty men."

Billings told the Chicago press, who were still taken aback by the sum he'd paid for Mike's services, "Rest assured Kelly will pay back our outlay for him. Since we made that deal the whole of Boston has

gone mad on base ball and from all indications our attendance at the opening games will be greater than has ever been seen in Boston."

'Uncle Bill', who'd started out as a hoop skirt maker, often met Kelly for drinks. Conant, who often travelled with the team, found that wherever Kelly was there were bound to be at least a couple of beautiful women.

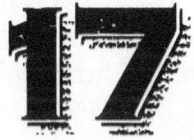

17

"The Hub has got our dandy."

In New York on May 5 darkness saved both sides from defeat. That it was a tie instead of a Boston win rested squarely on the shoulders of Captain Mike. He still had a sore finger and muffed two fly balls in the 9th that had given the Giants the lead.

Harris, who'd now been assigned to travel with the Beaneaters all summer, wrote "Manager Mutrie's nickname is Truthful James but he is loyal to his men so he says that Buck Ewing is the best general ball player in the land and Mike Kelly is second. Jim fielded his best possible lineup, even having Gore, who was used up with malaria, suit up. He put Smiling Mickey Welch who has always been a stumbling block in the Bostons' path in the pitcher's box. Leadoff batter Sam Wise, who'd told the team that all the talk of him getting married was silly chaff, waved at Welch's curves and struck out. The Boston rooters groaned but the sight of Kelly stepping to the plate was cause for rejoicing. He rapped the plate with the end of his bat, faced squarely to the pitcher's box, sized up the first pitch and sent the ball a ways over second base.

Wise struck out again his next time up and it was the $10,000 beauty's turn again. Kelly stood at the home plate with every nerve strung up to the highest tension, his bat nervously describing eccentric areas over his right shoulder. The New York twirler gave him a high one and the next second it was making straight for Gore. It sailed over the big center fielder's head and Kel tore around the bases like a dancing master doing a Virginia reel and crossed the plate before the ball got back to the diamond.

Mike faced towards right his next time up, hoping to put one into the deep expanses of right field. He put a ball up into the warm bosom of the air but it was foul. Then he lined another one just outside the foul line and on his third try he belted the battered ball to smithereens just inside of it. Hornung scored and Wise went around to third.

The Beaneaters held a 6-1 lead when the fifth inning ended. Roger Connor lifted a ball high into right field. Mike who had his mind on who was likely to win the Suburban and the Brooklyn Handicap, misjudged it and ran too far. He had to take it over his head and missed. The crowd exploded. A run scored and it seemed to turn the tide. The New Yorkers scored three in the seventh and the visitors' lead was down to one. The excitement was intense and the specta-tors watched every motion of the players with a critical eye. Director Conant pulled on his cigar like his life depended on it and Treasurer Billings was squirming in his seat as if there were ants on it.

Ewing doubled to left field to open the inning but Sam Wise threw Ward out at first and Connor fouled out to Daily. O'Rourke was next up. "Rad" was as cool as if Boston held a ten-run lead. Two strikes were called, then Lord James nearly flattened the ball with a terrific clip that sent it to deep right field. Kelly couldn't reach it before it struck the ground and bounced off the fence. The three-bagger easily scored Ewing and the game was tied.

In the tenth Kelly lined a pitch toward left field. Richardson in-stinctively put up his hand without the remotest hope of catching the ball, but it smacked into his hand and he grasped it for the out.

"Three inches higher and it would have gone for a home run," groaned Mike as he kicked the dirt in frustration.

The teams began the eleventh, but it was too dark now. Umpire Powers, dressed in the regulation gray flannel suit Nick Young has ordered umpires to wear, waved his arm in the air and called out, 'That's game.'

We were standing talking in the hall of the Grand Central Hotel just after coming from the game when a gentleman came over and

said to Mike: 'I understand the finger you injured during the game caused you to miss a fly which prevented your team from winning.'

Kel unrolled the bandage around the forefinger on his left hand that Ewing had stepped on while Mike was sliding into second base. The iron spike in the New Yorker's shoe had cut right through the nail and into Kelly's finger causing a painful wound.

'The finger had nothing to do with it,' responded Kelly. 'I ought to have caught that ball. It was an easy fly and I made a bad mess of it.'"

The headline the next day was,

"KELLY SPOILS A GAME BY A BAD MUFF."

That Kelly still had a host of friends in the Windy City was shown during the game in Chicago that day. When the scorer embellished the blackboard with the Bostons' 10-4 triumph over New York the crowd burst into a wild, exultant cheer. Cries of 'Hooray for Kelly' were heard above the storm of applause. The outburst reddened the roots of Spalding. He knew why the crowd had erupted in glee.

"There were 10,000 spectators at the game, a huge number for a Monday. All the regulars were in attendance and many hundreds of others who want to be in fashion as it's now the fashion to be a base ball crank. Hardly had the game commenced when a large number of ladies, fair admirers of the Bostons, arrived and found that they could not get up the long flight of stairs in the grand stand. Gallant Michael Kelly decided that their pluck was deserving of something better than 'Standing room only' so with the assistance of a chair for a step-ladder they climbed into the grand stand. But it wasn't like a horse-car where there is always room for one more so Kelly escorted the ladies for whom there was no room to the Bostons' bench. When his confused teammates looked at Kelly and wondered where they were to sit he pointed to the grass in front of the bench.

Irwin made a nifty stop of Kelly's bounder that had speed and was full of coiled springs in the third and got the ball to first just in time to make his out. Wise took care of Wood's fly in the fourth then Sammy settled Buffinton at first. Irwin sent a line hit down to right

field that seemed safe enough for two bases but Kelly made a quick dash then a pretty catch of it.

No runs were made in the sixth, sharp fielding being the rule. Ferguson made a beautiful stop of a hot ball from Kelly's bat. Michael J. made a splendid catch of his own in the seventh when he pulled down a hard one near the fence. In the end the cause of the Bostons' defeat was simple. They could not manage to put a rally together against the Phillies' erstwhile second baseman now twirler Charlie Ferguson.

A large delegation from the Elks Lodge who had driven to the grounds in a tally-ho cheered Kelly's every move. The man who could make the most noise was the best fellow." Harris advised Kelly's boosters that they could give their hero cigars or they could give him peanuts - but outside the grounds.

In the second home game, a convincing 17-4 win, Kelly did splendid work in right field. None of the Quakers dared take an extra base on his still lively arm. He batted hard and did wonderful base running while urging his new teammates do follow his lead. "I don't care how many errors we make if only you win," he called out to them. "Take all the chances, it's runs that count." The spectators, who were still getting used to seeing Kelly in red and white, enjoyed his constant refrains. That night the Boston Lodge of Elks presented Kelly with a $500 diamond-studded watch.

The Washingtons made their first appearance of the season in Boston on the 12th. With their ace Whitney needing a rest they put their left-handed twirler Dupee Shaw in the box. He really was a twirler. Shaw, who some called the "Wizard", had an unusual windmill delivery and his gyrations provided amusement to the spectators. He was careful not to do his windmill act with men on base, however.

Alfred Henry Spink described Shaw's wind-up in *The Sporting News*. "After considerable swinging and scratching around with his feet, during which he delivers a lengthy speech to the batter to the effect that he is the best pitcher on earth and the batter a dub, he stretches both arms at full length over his head. Then after gazing

fixedly at the first baseman for a moment, he wheels half around and both arms fly apart like magic. He winds his left arm around again and lets the ball fly, running at the same time all the way from the box to the home plate."

"What crazy shite Shaw does before he pitches is enough to give a timid man the delirium tremors," Kelly told Sam Wise as he was getting ready to lead off. "The man's right off his trolley."

"Then when the man finally does throw the ball it comes in like a blue streak," said Sam.

"Be careful if you get on, the man watches first so close you don't dare take any kind uv a lead."

Sam reached on a base on balls when a pitch flew past his head, then got picked off first in spite of Kelly's warning.

The Nationals didn't expect much from Shaw, who'd racked up 31 losses in '86. Dupee received a warm reception but was batted until his fielders wore their spikes out chasing the ball all over the South End grounds. Kelly, Nash, Wise, and Radbourn smashed the ball about as they pleased. Kelly had four safe hits and a base on balls in his five trips to the bat. The Bostons chalked up 19 runs and the crowd yelled and laughed themselves silly. Wise, Johnston, and Kelly did beautiful work in the field. "The only" caught a liner in the eighth inning and made a lightning fast throw to second base. It was so quick that for a moment the crowd was stilled with wonder.

In its account of the next day's game in *The Boston Post* included comments about the change in the Beaneaters' attitude, which was now one of confidence. "The tower of strength upon which this confidence is founded is Mike Kelly. Great are his individual attainments as a player; his knowledge of the capacity of his men and his ability to command at will the power of the team is remarkable."

The Beaneaters took control of the May 14 game in the very first inning. O'Day commenced business by sending Hornung to first on balls. Joe surprised Connie Mack, the Washington catcher, by a clean steal of second. Kelly now had *all* the men taking chances on the base-paths. Then the real fun began. Kelly hit an easy ball to Kreig which he allowed to roll past him and Hornung ran all the way home. Mike rattled O'Day by starting for second then stopping and O'Day threw a wild pitch. Mack fumbled the next pitch and Mike took off for third. Connie's throw was so far offline that all Donnelly could do was slap it down and watch it roll toward second. Before anyone could get it Kelly had stolen home.

The crowd let out a roar that could be heard a mile away.

"He pulls out all the stops every time," a man in a gray fedora said to his son.

The man in front of him was puffing on a cigar. He yelled down to Kelly. "I like these, Mike." indicating his cigar. The label read "The Only Kel."

Mike chuckled. "I'm glad uv it. They turned out better than I'd expected."

"Are they selling well?" the man asked.

When Kelly called back, "All the profits are goin' up in smoke," the grand-stand roared.

Four more runs crossed the plate before the side was retired. The Nationals braced up after that and played with greater earnestness but to little avail. The final was Boston 10, Washington 2.

The Beaneaters took eight of their nine games in the middle of May but couldn't gain an inch of ground on the front-running Detroits who won eight in a row.

Morrill, Nash, and Kelly made Pud Galvin weary before they got through with him on May 17. They didn't make many long hits, but they hit the ball hard every time and piled up eighteen safe ones. Kelly got in two terrific drives and according to *The Post* "the commanding presence of 'the only' maintained among the Bostons that steadiness of play and mutual confidence which ultimately enabled the home team to pull the game out of the fire in the last inning."

The Beaneaters trailed the Pittsburgs 5-1 when they took their turns at the bat in the fourth. Little Madden, who had shown no remarkable aptitude with the bat to-date, put the first pitched ball just

over Smith's head. A yell went up when Hornung made a safe hit to center. An ardent crank yelled, "Now, Kelly, hit her in the neck," and Mike did as requested. He sent a ball at Barkley, who made a heroic attempt to stop it but it bounded off the man like a rubber ball from a stone wall and Madden and Johnston ran home. Wise drove one at Galvin but he muffed it. Pud tried to catch Kelly off second but forgot to pause and Umpire Hengle called "Balk" and pointed for Mike to take third base. Morrill cracked a ball that danced in flames as it tore along the turf and Kelly dashed in with his team's third run.

After Hornung fouled out to Miller in the seventh Kelly made a line hit to left field that netted two bags. Wise was given a life on Barkley's muff then Nash belted one through Whitney's hands and the bases were full. When Morrill walked to the plate Mike yelled at the stands, "I'll bet a quarter he'll make a home run!" Morrill knocked a couple over the fence foul then hit a sledgehammer blow fair over the left field fence. Kelly was pelted with quarters from delighted cranks as he crossed the plate.

The Beaneaters swept three games from Washington and their May 18th 9-2 defeat of the Alleghenys made it three straight over Pittsburg. Before the game Kelly, who was cracking low balls with a vengeance, told William Harris to keep an eye on him because he felt finer than silk. Harris did as usual and Mike made three hits off his old friend James McCormick. Said Kelly, "When I get a high ball it scares me so they call a strike before I know it. You see I don't except anybody to give me one. I'm laying for low balls now and you want to watch me."

In the sixth, Kelly's towering fly knocked "Cowboy" Jim Whitney off his horse and onto the seat of his pants. He must have thought he'd run into a Western cyclone. By true Chicago-style running Kelly reached second before the hit could be fielded. In the eighth Kelly took first on a smoking hit which no one cared to handle and then stole second. He was still wearing Sam Morton's sliding pads, which weren't fastened to his trousers but played loosely over his hips. Morrill had copied the design. Sam Wise and Billy Nash, who had badly bruised knees and thighs, stuffed their pants full of cotton batting.

Con Daily had invented a sliding suit made up of towels. Mike told him his knees looked like balloons.

In the ninth Hornung struck to right center for a base and trotted home when Kelly sent the ball over the left field fence. Mike had a chuckle that night when he found out his old team was mired in seventh place. His replacement Marty Sullivan had made five errors in the Chicagos' fifth straight loss.

At home to Indianapolis on the 23rd the Bostons lost a heart breaker. Kelly made three hits including a ninth inning drive over the left field fence but the Beaneaters fell to the saffron-hued buttercups 10-9.

Kelly took Siobhan to dinner at a place that specialized in seafood and French cuisine that night. He told her how good it was to see her again.

"I can't believe how people around town are obsessed with you," she said. "It seems they've nothing else to talk about."

Siobhan wore a handsome silk suit of a dark mushroom color with a front of chenille fringe and a crystal beaded passementerie and beaded lace with knots of blue ribbon.

"You're even luvlier than the last time I laid eyes on you," Mike told her.

They had wine with their meal. Neither had more than a glass. Siobhan's father had been an alcoholic and she had eschewed liquor. Kelly had no need for whiskey when he was with her, her company was enough. He asked about her dream of becoming an actress and she told him that she was taking acting lessons. Siobhan was thrilled when Mike told her he'd be happy to introduce her to Nat Goodwin and some of his other friends in the theater.

When they went for a walk after dinner they got a lot of stares.

"I don't think that's Mike Kelly's wife," a woman with raised eyebrows told her husband, an investment banker.

"I'm no gambling man but I'd wager a considerable sum of money she's not."

Siobhan pointed at a passing street-car and laughed. "There you are again."

Kelly smiled when he read what *The Fall River News* had to say. "Without Kelly, Gore, and Dalrymple the Chicagos are about as effective as the Mayflower would be without a centerboard." The journal had joked that "water never did agree with Kelly's complexion."

Billy Harris wrote, "With the loss of Mike Kelly the granite outfield of the Chicago team is shattered. Dalrymple, Gore, and Kelly raked many a chestnut out of the fire by one coup de main or another. Kelly became so sick of the big captain's insolence that he at last resolved to quit the ball field forever rather than play in the Spalding-Anson regime again. The Chicago club never won the pennant by clean fielding. It did so by tremendous batting, daring base running, and strategic work.

The happiest ball tosser in the country yesterday was Michael Joseph Kelly. Since the snow disappeared he has been waiting patiently for a chance to polish off Cap Anson and all that's left of the old guard. He played a prominent part in his club's performance and did his work with a will.

When the two great players were straining every nerve for the same nine it was a heat for the base ball lover but now Captain Kelly plays and kicks for one side and his ex-superior kicks and plays for the other. When the Chicagos play here you want to sit on the bleaching seats over back of first base, that's where the fun always is. Yesterday Kelly stood in the coacher's box by the first bag and kept up a volley of good-natured chaffing with Anson and occasionally fired a shot over to his old 'pard' Williamson. The crowd behind first had lots of innocent fun at Anson's expense. When he stepped off the bag to stop a poor throw from Burns and missed it anyway there were cries of, 'You're no good, Baby' and 'You ought to get Spalding to sell you too, Cap.'

Every time Kelly touched the ball with his bat or his hands there was a big yell. The work of the billiard expert and Grand Pooh-Bah of the White Stockings didn't hold a candle to the play of Boston's

prize beauty this day. The first time Anson stepped into the batsman's box there was warm, hearty applause. But the rest of the time he was guyed and shouted at just as he has always been. Anson didn't take very kindly to low balls and Rad found that out in a hurry. That's where Captain Mike has the advantage on the Chicago mogul, he can see a low ball now as well as a high one as Clarkson discovered when Kelly bashed the ball for two bags twice.

Daily got three strikes to begin the first inning, then Clarkson sent him to first on balls. Then Kelly came up and punched the ball for two bases sending Daily home with the first run of the game. Captain Mike stole third and then looked a little mad as he danced off the base with his cap in his hand. Billy Nash popped a little fly to right and Kelly took off. It was a short throw for Cahill and Mike saw that the ball would beat him. As a last resort he threw himself into the air and landed on the ground with his feet on the plate just as Myers stepped aside and the game was tied.

The next time Kelly batted there were two mates aboard. He sent a ball whizzing over third base and when he pulled into second base both of the base runners had scored. The Bostons won it 4-2."

On the 27th of May Radbourn put a muzzle on the croakers who had been belittling him by making monkeys of big Captain Anson and his satellites. The Windy City nine could muster only four hits. Kelly hit to Burns in the third and should have been out but Burns made a poor throw that let in two runs. In the sixth the game was delayed ten minutes when Burns hit a foul tip that smashed Daily's mask and cut his cheek severely. Kelly played doctor and treated the wound with a piece of court plaster. The Bostons scored two in the fifth, two in the seventh, and one in the eighth to emerge victorious by a count of 8-3.

After the warm-up for the June 2 game in Philadelphia Kelly had a chat with the Quakers' catcher Jack Clements, a rarity as a left-handed backstop.

"So folks are callin' you fellas Phillies now are they, Jack?"

"I suppose Quakers was starting to sound a bit too stuffy, we aren't

what you'd call a bunch of Puritans."

"How do you like the dressing-rooms here in your new palace?"

"The park's huge and so are the dressing-rooms ... and the closets for our clothes as well. You could have a game uv cards in them."

Clements looked around to see if his manager was within earshot. He wasn't.

He chuckled and told Mike, "After we lose a game Harry Wright will come to our dressing-room to read us a damned parable on life. When we hear him coming we hide in our closets and Wright comes in and wonders how we can get dressed so fast.

The bulk of the fielding was done by Kelly at second base. He astonished the natives, they'd never seen him play the infield. Two weeks before *The Globe* man wrote that "Kelly covers the second bag as though he has never played anywhere else. His double plays are things of beauty."

Ferguson fired the ball in and 87 of the 119 pitches he threw sailed across the plate. Kelly managed two hits off him, one a two-bagger down the right field line with men on second and third. His team-mates got just another five for two runs. Young Madden was even better, he shut out the Phillies on five hits.

On June 5 it was "authoritatively stated" in *The Detroit Free Press* that the Chicago players and the cup that cheers were "utter strangers" and Kelly hadn't looked at wine of any color since he joined the Boston team. "Heaven help him if the Triumvir get a chance to fine him. They'll take a big slice." *The Globe* believed the Triumvir "would have no occasion to fine Cap'n Kelly this season. He is a good deal of a man and when he says he won't do a thing there is nobody who can make him break his word. The Bostons are playing a rattling game of ball and are pulling victories through tight holes and loose ones. In Hornung, Johnston, and Kelly, Boston has an outfield that cannot be surpassed."

The Washington cranks had taken to calling their team "a bum nine" but Kelly and Nash combined for five errors that gave the Na-

tionals the majority of the runs they scored in a 7-7 tie on the sixth of June. The team was staying at The Metropolitan in Washington. Billings had chosen it because it had begun to show signs of age and the rooms went for $2 a night, half what they had been.

After dinner Mike went up to his room to change. He'd spilled soup on his chest and wouldn't be caught dead wearing a stained shirt around the capital. There was a knock on his door. Puzzled as to who it might be, Kelly went and opened the door, his shirt still open.

A woman who'd sat in a box seat that afternoon stood in the door.

"What a magnificent chest you have, Mr. Kelly," she said admiringly.

The handsomely dressed woman had luxurious blonde hair but her large, accommodating bosoms were certainly her best features.

"I could say the same uv you. I've just *had* dinner, could I take you somewhere for a drink?"

"Do you not have anything here?"

"I do, if whiskey will serve."

"It will."

Mike went to the dresser and poured three fingers of whiskey into two glasses. "I'm afraid I've no ice."

When he turned around the woman wore nothing but her high-heeled boots.

Mike marveled at the site before him. His tongue started on her mouth, drifted down to her perfect breasts and erect nipples, lingered there a while, moved down to her stomach, and then to her thighs. She moaned and shuddered and began undoing the buttons of Mike's trousers.

The Washingtons put young Gilmour in to pitch the next day and he "made money out of the Bostons." Mike wasn't alone in going hitless. The Nationals did a lot better at the bat against Radbourn and won 6-3. Connie Mack opened the sixth with a pop fly Kelly should have easily caught. He didn't go after it, he was too busy exchanging glances with the woman who'd visited his room the night before.

Mike muffed a high fly in the sixth on June 10 letting in two runs and his fumble in the eighth cost another. He was favoring his left hand. In affixing a spike to his shoe he'd run a knife blade clear through his thumb. Kelly partially redeemed himself with a three-baser - the longest ever hit at the grounds - that allowed O'Rourke and Wheelock to score. The Beaneaters took all three games from the Phillies but stayed a game and a half behind the start-studded Wolverines, who swept the Hoosiers in Detroit. The Beaneaters beat the Washingtons on the 13th and again the next day to pull within a half game of first place. They were taking Kelly's example and had improved wonderfully in sacrifice hitting. "The only" led in the competition for the N & S cigar prize with 20 chances on which he'd succeeded in moving the runners over 16 times.

In the first inning on June 16 Hornung made a nice single over second base. Kelly struck three fouls then smashed out a three bag roller to right center. Wise hit a little one to Keefe and while he was being put out Kelly tore home hellbent for leather, his legs churning like piston rods on a high engine. The crowd of 3,500 yelled with glee. In the fifth Kelly got three strikes then a wild pitch came. Kelly struck at it and got first base safely. Then Keefe made a series of gyrations and threw another wild one that bounded into the grand-stand. Kelly got around to third and would have scored had some unpatriotic citizen not passed the ball down to O'Rourke. Nash struck out.

Mike opened the seventh with a bounder that Buck Ewing deftly avoided as it would surely have done him injury. A passed ball let Kelly go to second. Nash hit to Keefe and Mike stood perfectly still, dead in the water between second and third. When Keefe ran to touch him festive Mike dodged about while Nash reached second. Ewing, Richardson, and Keefe managed to run Kel down. The patrons loved it.

"'T'was anuther grand performance, Kel," a euphoric crank called out.

"'You're a clever oyster, Michael," chuckled another.

In the eighth Kell delighted the crowd again, raising a perfect babel of sound with a drive over the left field fence.

333

"They couldn't touch you out *that* time, Kel," yelled a man who'd watched the ball soar over his head.

The Beaneaters' 12-5 win drew them to within a half game of the League-leading Wolverines.

"Half a game back, Kel," said Billy Nash as they took off their sodden uniforms. "Same time last year we were in fifth place and already seventeen games out of first. You've made quite the difference."

Goodwin & Co. looked to cash in on Mike's fame by producing posters and several different Old Judge and Gypsy Queen cigarettes cards featuring portraits of him, one with no cap, another with "$10,000 Kelly" holding his bat on right shoulder, and another with his hands cupped together awaiting a fly ball. There was a special "Smoke Four Base Hits" card of Kelly as well.

Two games were played at the South End grounds on Friday, June 17. Nearly 5,000 people saw the entertaining game the Bostons won and another 5,000 watched the tiresome afternoon one they lost. It was dollars to doughnuts no one would see another inning like the first one in the morning game. In all, nine men in succession hit safely, five singles, four doubles, one three-bagger, and a home run. Ten earned runs were scored. The crowd was in an uproar the entire time. William Harris, said "the wild scene beggared description." On the way to the dressing-room Kelly, who'd scored four of the Bostons' nineteen runs, told Sam Wise he could still see balls going out to center field.

Welch tied the Bostons up in knots in the afternoon game, a 6-1 win for the Giants. On his way out of the grounds Kelly smiled when he saw a large sign that read "The Only Kel cigar, 12 for $1 at Brock's old stand, 19 Water street. They're something fine." Then he focused on the sign next to it that read "E.W.D. WHISKEY Five years old, strictly pure at $3 per gallon. Orders by mail or express promptly attended to. DIXON BROS., 41 and 42 Commercial Wharf, Boston and the even more interesting one across the street that advertised Lilly Clay's Colossal Gaiety Company and their 30 DASHING LADIES culled from European Capitals at the Grand Opera House. He

didn't imagine his dowdy wife would be very keen to see that. He hoped he could catch one of their performances on the road.

The Beaneaters travelled to Indianapolis on the 21st of June. The Hoosiers cooked their egg 4-3 in the first game but the Bostons drubbed them 17-8 in the second. Kelly's thumb was healing but his leg was bothering him something awful. He was obliged to wrap yards of rubber bandage about his leg to run at all and sliding was absolutely out of the question. The trouble was a nasty Charley Horse. Mike had been the victim of it for two weeks now.

The ovation began at 1:30 the next day, at which hour Austin's military brass band made its appearance at the Leland House in Chicago and began a serenade in Kelly's honor, "See the Conquering Hero." The street was almost impassable so great was the crowd. Some 5,000 people jammed the north entrance of the hotel. Inside, the corridors were packed with Kelly's friends and acquaintances. He held a levee and a circle of admirers twenty deep craned their necks to see their handsome hero.

Shortly before 2 o'clock the White Stockings arrived in three carriages. They forced their way into the hotel and paid their respects to their old comrade. Anson and Kelly rode to the ball grounds in a large barouche drawn by four magnificent bays.

"You know what, Kel," said Anson on the way. "The official scorer robbed me of first place in the League batting list last year."

Kelly chuckled. "I robbed you out of it by doing more batting than you did. Baby shouldn't cry."

A male quartet sang a ditty composed for the occasion to the tune of Yankee Doodle Dandy,

> "Michael Kelly came to town,
>
> To sing a little chanson,
>
> He said, 'I've come with Boston beans
>
> To do up Baby Anson
>
> Oh, I come high but Yankee land

With its bright shekels bought me,
And though I didn't like to go,
Ten thousand dollars bought me.

Away with all the Bills and Jims
That grace the base ball cycle
It's devil take the whole of them
For I'm the only Michael

So here's to our only Mike
As handsome as he's handy
Three cheers for Kel and three as well
For the Hub has got our dandy."

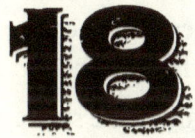

"For goodness sake, brace up."

Kelly's heart swelled with pride when he saw the multitude his popularity had drawn, a crowd of more than 12,000. Umpire Doescher called Kelly from the bench and amid a tempest of deafening cheers he was presented with a floral pyramid five feet tall composed of the choicest and rarest flowers. The simple inscription in red immortals read simply "Kel". Silver Flint came out of the grand-stand and presented Kelly with an even larger display, a six-foot tall floral emblem in the shape of a ball diamond. The base lines were marked with neil roses, the foul lines, bases, and pitcher's box were bunches of daisies and across the center was "Kelly" in white immortals. Blue flags fluttered at the end of the foul lines bearing the motto "He plays to win".

"There mustn't be a single flower left in town, Frank. How the devil am I supposed to get these on the train?" asked Kelly.

Flint shrugged and said, "You'll have to tell them to add another car."

Then Doescher handed Kelly a box. Mike opened it and found a red, white, and blue jockey cap composed of six pieces of silk bearing the letters **B O S T O N**.

"Put it on, Kel," a lean man with a jaw like a tolerant mastiff shouted from the stands.

He did, to the crowd's delight and he kept it on throughout the game.

The band played "Flowers that Bloom in the Spring" and the game began. Hornung drove a ball to Burns which he fumbled and the crowd erupted as Mike strode to the plate. Anticlimactically, Kelly was given first on balls and the crowd groaned.

It didn't take long for them to get excited again. On the first pitch he took off for second and the yell "Slide, Kelly, Slide!" swelled from the stands. His injury had cut his speed in half and Pfeffer was waiting for him with the ball when he arrived at second.

"Sorry to spoil your moment," he shrugged as he applied the touch.

Mike shrugged and patted Pfeffer on the back. "Not your fault, Fred, I shouldn't be playin' with the leg like this, just couldn't let folks down when they went to such a fuss."

"You never could."

A young man by the name of Wabash found himself seated beside a young girl with a blue and white striped parasol. She told him her name was Miss Breezy. "Are you an admirer of the national game, Miss Breezy?" he asked.

"I do not deem the influences surrounding base ball particularly elevating or refining, Mr. Wabash, though I occasionally witness a game."

She continued with rather more emphasis than the circumstances warranted and startled Mr. Wabash. "I can tell you one thing, in trying to win the pennant without Mike Kelly the Baby has bitten off more than he can chew."

Kelly hit an atmosphere burner to short his next chance with the willow. Burns gathered it into his hands and without stopping to let it cool fired the ball to Anson before Kelly, who was almost limping, could reach first base.

The crowd got another chance to cheer in the fifth when Kelly drove Hornung home with a base knock to left field and again when he gingerly trotted home when Wise hit the ball over the stone fence. He came to bat with the bases loaded in the ninth. The spectators stood up in anticipation of him coming through in a big spot as he so often did.

"Crack!" went his bat and the crowd gasped. The ball climbed and climbed and smacked hard into the fence a foot from the top.

"The dear soul," sighed a matron in the grand-stand who was

dressed like a peacock as Kelly, who normally would have had little trouble making it to third, hobbled lamely to first and stopped.

"The poor man should be laid up in bed, not trying to play a game of ball," said a man in front of her.

"And I'd like to be there to make him feel better," said a girl two seats over with a dimple she'd made in one cheek with the aid of an orange stick under her breath.

"What was that, dear?" asked the matron.

"I said I'd like to send him a letter," she answered.

John J. Drohan wrote of Kelly's big day in *The Boston Globe*, which had given more print to Kelly than anyone since Abraham Lincoln. "The 24th of June will be inscribed in the annals of the game as a red-letter day in the base ball history of Chicago. It will also be re-membered by one player as one of the proudest days of his life. That man is Michael J. Kelly. Never before has any man in the base ball profession been more highly honored than he was today. But all pleasure has its sting and Kelly, in spite of the magnificent ovation given him, is terribly discouraged and down-hearted.

In the first place he has severely suffered the past three days with 'Charley Horse' and was utterly unfit to play ball. Had it not been for the mammoth preparations made and his disinclination to dis-appoint the public Mike would not have donned his uniform. But he did and considering the circumstances he played a great game of ball. The effort was just too much for him. He was in great pain throughout the game and tonight is completely knocked out. It is hard to say when he will be able to play again. He leaves tomorrow for Mount Clemens, Michigan where he will rest until in condition. He hopes to join the team in Detroit but even that is in some doubt. To cap the climax of Kelly's misery the Bostons were defeated after having the game well in hand.

William Harris wrote of the state of the Beaneaters, "Even at this distance I can hear the wail of the croakers and faint-hearted. The team has been away from home for five games and have lost four of them. Not a cheerful record, but in most respects they have played better ball than at any time this year. Kelly has been doing vigorous work with the willow. He has made 11 safe hits in his last 24 at bats. Kelly leads the Bostons with 36 stolen bases and is a close second to Ray in the race for the Jordan, Marsh & Co. prize bicycle. He is two back of Johnston for the team lead in runs scored even though he has played fourteen fewer games. All the Bostons have excelled in base running. They have struggled for two simple reasons: umpires and the hardest kind of luck."

Kelly was staying at the Palmer House. On the way to his cab he heard a voice from behind him, a female one.

"Mr. Kelly."

Mike looked the woman up and down. She wore a tight-fitting blue and white calico dress and a peaked brim bonnet of wired buckram covered in silk taffeta and decorated with a band of feathers and ribbon. She had watery blue-gray eyes and looked to be in her early twenties. Kel didn't recognize her. He was sure he'd remember seeing such a lovely lass as she before. The girl left the friends she was with and came over to Kelly.

"Yes," said Mike. "That's me, Michael Joseph Kelly, at your service."

"My name is Hilary. Hilary Chalmers."

"Pleased ta meet ya, Hilary, what is it that I can do for you?"

"I wonder if you have any plans for tomorrow morning?"

"Well a shave and some breakfast are all I can think of off the top uv me head. Why do you ask?"

"I paint portraits, Mr. Kelly, rather good ones I've been told, and with your strikingly symmetrical features, I believe you would make an excellent subject. Would you sit for one?"

"How long would it take?"

"All I would do is make a detailed sketch. You wouldn't need to stay while I add the paint."

"And how much would I be paid? The Bostons paid three thousand for my picture."

Hilary looked horrified. "Three thousand *dollars*! Oh, my. Daddy is rather well off, but I couldn't ask him for …"

Mike took her hand. "I was just havin' a wee joke, young lady. I'd be glad to sit for you, and the presence uv your delightful company'd be the only pay I'd ask."

Hilary exhaled. "That's a relief." She opened her clutch purse and extracted a card. "Here is my address, please come as soon as you have had your breakfast."

"I'll see you at ten."

"Thank you, Mr. Kelly. Until tomorrow." She squeezed Mike's hand, gave him a dazzling smile, and left to join her friends, who'd been giggling the whole time.

As Mike turned to go he chuckled when he heard one of Hilary's friends tell her, "He's even more handsome up close," and the other say, "I might drop by your place tomorrow morning, Hilary, I think I left a pair of gloves there."

When Kelly arrived at Hilary's mansion the next morning a servant answered the door. Behind him stood Hilary. She took his hat, handed it to the butler and led Kelly out of the huge entrance hall and through a library and billiard room to the room where she painted. She indicated a chair by the window and Kelly sat down and made himself comfortable. Hilary worked quickly.

A woman who looked a lot like Hilary but older came in and looked at the sketch and then at Kelly. She had classic bone structure, delectable rosy lips, and serenely bright blue eyes that Kelly guessed made men quail before her gaze. She wore a fetching gown of green velvet with a tight bodice and a plunging neckline in which a diamond at the end of a chain rested snuggly—and happily Mike imagined.

"This is my mother, Mr. Kelly. Mrs. Phillip Chalmers …

"Felicity," the woman interrupted.

"Pleased ta meet ya, Mrs. Chalmers."

She cast him a dirty look.

"I mean Felicity. A pleasure it is ta make yer acquaintance." He looked her up and down. "I can certainly see where Hilary gets her looks."

Felicity smiled, then stepped forward and offered her hand. Mike thought of kissing it but shook it lightly instead. He could tell she thought it was a rather delicate handshake for a rugged ball player. He chuckled. Felicity looked confused.

"I got in trouble fer shakin' the president's hand too tight at the White House one time. They've never had me back."

She laughed. "Would you care for some whiskey, Mr. Kelly?"

Mike took an instant liking to Felicity, she wasn't the least bit ho-ity-toity like most women of her status. He looked into the parlor and saw a handsome liquor cabinet and guessed there was some awfully good stuff inside. "I certainly *would* care for a whiskey, but I've a game today and I wouldn't want the lads to smell anything on me breath. Coffee'd be grand if it's not too much trouble."

"Not at all." She turned and called out the door, "Jives, could you make coffee for our guest."

Jives, in a white jacket, arrived at the door, apparently he'd been hovering. In a clipped English accent he said, "Yes, ma'am," turned and left.

Mike sat in front of the huge bay window while Hilary, surrounded by several of her meticulously drawn portraits, worked away, replenished her supply of charcoal, frowned, erased, and sketched again. Her mother was never far away.

A wail came from Pittsburg, where the Beaneaters would play next, in the shape of a telegram from Horace Phillips, the owner of the Alleghenys. He was wild over the rumor that Boston's star attraction would not appear in Smoky City. Manager Morrill's reply was that Kelly would go to Pittsburg if he was allowed to have a substitute base-runner. He had no doubt his offer would be accepted.

Kelly played and *The Pittsburgh Daily Post* delighted in the home nine's success.

"The victory was a clean cut one right from the stick. The fact that the visitors had been paraded through the streets principally on Kelly's account made the victory more enjoyable than it would otherwise have been. Sires and sons, maids and matrons cheered their utmost and those who could safely throw their hats in the air delighted in doing so.

Kelly was the lion for a time. He made a two-base hit in the first inning that plated Hornung and Sutton, but that was his last. His fielding was mediocre, though there was an excuse for him as he was unable to play, his leg being so sore he couldn't run the bases. Tate ran for him. At any rate, 'Kel' was well received."

Mike sat out the last two games in Pittsburgh but was heartened to read a piece in *The Boston Globe* that took *The New York World* to task.

"When will The New York World learn to let the Boston club and Kelly alone? From the beginning of the season this sheet has been doing all it can to depreciate the Boston captain and his work. Its latest yarn is the assertion, false as false can be, that the men in the team are jealous of the attention paid Kelly. Why, you poor deluded thing, the boys all like Kelly and play under him as men never played for any other captain."

Judge and Jury.

Kelly sat out the three games in Detroit as well. *The Free Press* weighed in on what he meant to his team.

"There is one thing Detroiters deeply regret and that is the absence from the Bostons of Cappen Kelly. They are anxious to know if the Beaneaters, reinforced by the Unique Michael, can rise above the level of mediocrity that has distinguished the play of the club in the past. There is a suspicion that Kelly is the spinal cord that has kept the team upright thus far."

With Kelly out of the lineup the Bostons lost two of the three games in Detroit and tied the other. Mike was in Mount Clemens.

It had eleven mineral baths drawn from springs scattered through the town. In 1870 Dor Kellogg, a flour mill proprietor, had cured his severe case of eczema by bathing in the salty mineral water and a local physician had started prescribing bathing for his patients who suffered with rheumatism. Interest in the curative powers of the mineral waters grew and another doctor built the first bath house, "the Original", in 1873. It marked the beginning of the city's fabulous bath era and Mount Clemens was now known as "the Bath City of America."

The Fountain was the third bath house in Mount Clemens. It offered larger rooms and tubs for guests so crippled as to have difficulty bathing in the usual tubs. Mike stayed at the Fountain Hotel. It was connected to Bath House via a heated passageway. The Fountain had seventy bathrooms, forty cooling rooms, ladies' and gentlemen's parlors, a gymnasium, and a physician's office.

Mike used the gymnasium and he visited the physician's office. He thought the doctor helpful and quite pleasant, but he liked alluring Nurse Rebecca even more. She offered to give his afflicted area a massage after he had a mineral bath. Mike enjoyed both immensely. The massage resulted in a great deal of swelling which Nurse Rebecca treated in fine fashion.

On July 7 Kelly was back in uniform for the first home game against the Alleghenys. They were not. By some mishap the Smoky City nine arrived in Boston before their uniforms and had to play in their everyday clothes or in plumage borrowed from the Beaneaters. The crowd guyed them, especially James McCormick, who pitched in a tunic that had BOSTON across the chest. Indeed it looked as though he was pitching batting practice, he was "swiped" hard. Mike felt bad for him, he knew that in a loss to New York in May his friend had surrendered 28 hits and allowed 10 runs in the last two innings. James wasn't the same pitcher he'd been in the Chicagos, his arm was shot. In '88 he'd be tending bar at Dave Treado's.

Kelly was in good form after his baths and massages. His appearance electrified the crowd and energized his teammates. For a "Charley-horse" player Mike did some clever sprinting. He thrilled one

and all with two singles, a triple, and a home run in a 17-6 win.

Between innings Kelly told Burdock about his baths and massages in Mount Clemens. He told him about Nurse Rebecca too. When Jack asked for details Mike just told him the massages were quite therapeutic but added that she had wonderful hands ... and very willing lips.

After the game Tim Murnane jumped out of the press-box and hurried over to tell Mike something.

"What juicy tid-bit have you got for me this time, Tim?" Kelly asked with a grin.

Murnane smiled back. "Oh, it's a good one, Kel. What do you suppose the Chicagos did after their train got in from New York last night? After they'd checked into the hotel."

"Went for dinner?"

Murnane shook his head.

"Had a few beers and went looking for painted ladies?"

Murnane shook his head again.

"What then?" asked Kel, puzzled.

"They had a prayer meeting."

"Oh, me stars and garters! A *prayer meetin*?"

"I'm not fooling."

"Well I'll be damned. I don't seem ta recall there bein' too many uv those when James, Abner, George and I were in the Chicagos."

Kelly smashed three hot drives in his club's July 13 game against the Detroits. The first went by Shindle like a shot, the last one put a dent in the left field fence above the "B.L." sign. The finger that had been split open by Buck Ewing's spike hadn't fully healed and the pain caused him to muff a ball knocked out to right field. Some Detroit rooters jeered him and made sarcastic remarks but he smiled when a jolly soul from County Cork shouted, "Kape up yer heart, Michael, me sun, don't lave the beggars vex ye". The Bostons triumphed 12-4 in spite of Dimples Tate's five errors.

After beating his old club 3-0 then losing to them 7-6 Kelly was determined to best them in the closer on July 21. "Talk about ball playing, kicking, tricks, fun, and excitement," exclaimed *The Globe*, "there was more of all five than are generally condensed in any ten games and 7,500 souls shouted and applauded until their throats were hoarse and their hands raw.

Kelly scorched a grass-cutter to Williamson for an out his first time at the bat but made the Bostons' first hit in the third. Nash flied out, then "Kel made one of his wonderful steals and set the crowd by the ears."

He made a scratch hit his next time up by great running after a slow grounder to Williamson, who couldn't get him this time. Hornung, who'd been on second, ran to third and then home when Anson dropped Williamson's throw. He picked up the ball and fired it to second as Mike was already on his way there. The ball sailed over Fred Pfeffer's head. Anson fumed when he saw that novice Sullivan was standing stock-still in left field.

"That man is going to have to learn to back up his infielders or Ans'll have his head," Mike chuckled to himself as he raced in the general direction of third base. There was a good deal of bobbery in the stands as Kelly tore toward the plate. Jimmy Ryan had hustled over to get the ball Anson had overthrown and it was now on its way home. Kelly made a terrific slide.

"Safe!" shouted Phil Powers, with a little more enthusiasm than seemed appropriate.

Forgetting that Powers was armed, Anson charged at him. Kel wasn't sure he'd ever seen the big man run so fast.

"He missed third by thirty feet!" yelled Anson.

Mike looked sheepish. "Thirty, Cap? Come on. It was more like twenty."

Powers overruled himself and declared Mike out. The crowd cheered anyway.

"The only Mike never fails to put on a show," said a well-dressed gentleman in a box seat.

"And a good one at that, Charles," said the even better-dressed man next to him.

"You know, Farnsworth, I rarely bothered to attend a game until the Bean Chewers acquired Kelly for that princely sum," said Charles.

"Neither did most of *them*," said Farnsworth, pointing to a group of women who were staring and pointing at Mike.

Williamson and Burns were put out to start the Chicagos' half of the inning then Daly came to the plate. Mike knew that he'd batted out of turn his last time up but hadn't said anything because Daly had struck out. Kelly knew that Baldwin's name came eighth on the lineup card. Daly's was ninth.

When Daly reached base on a fumble by Nash and went to third on Tate's wild throw to catch him, Kelly yelled, "Time!"

Powers looked puzzled. "What is it, Mike?" he asked.

"Take a look at this lineup card," said Kelly. "Recognize the handwriting?"

"I do," said Powers. "It's Anson's."

"And who is supposed to bat after Burns?"

Powers looked again at the card. "Baldwin."

"That's right."

Powers hesitated a moment and then yelled to Anson. "Daly is out for batting out of turn."

Anson stared at him then pulled his own lineup card out of his back pocket.

"Shit!" he said loud enough that a lady who had just called a nearby male spectator boorish for smoking a cigar in her presence huffed, "Goodness gracious, such language." Anson ignored her.

Charles turned to Farnsworth and chuckled, "It looks as though Anson needs Kelly back to help him keep things straight."

Anson stormed, coaxed, and threatened Powers to no avail. "I'll pull my men off the field if Daly's out," he raged.

"No, you'll not," said Powers. "Now get back to your coaching box. He turned back toward the diamond and yelled, "Play!"

They did, with Anson sulking and muttering under his breath.

In the seventh inning Dimples Tate struck out. Hornung hit the ball hard to left field but Darling got under it. Then Kelly made his third single of the day, a liner Baldwin was more than happy to get out of the way of.

"Look, he's off *again*," said Farnsworth as Mike took off for second then made one of his patented slides.

"Three hits, three steals," said Charles.

"Another of his famous hook slides," pointed out Farnsworth. "Kelly always manages to juke the baseman into thinking he's going to come at the bag from a different angle than the one he'll actually take."

They chuckled as Kelly bounced up and held his hands apart to indicate to Powers by how much Williamson had missed him.

"Hey!" protested Williamson. "I didn't mind you doing that when it was *other* shortstops, but's not so damn funny when it's me you're doing it to."

"Sorry, Ned. But you know me, anything to win a game of baseball."

In the bottom of the ninth the Chicagos needed one run to tie and two to win. They didn't manage it and Mike Kelly was responsible for their failure. After Ryan and Darling fouled out Anson sent a two-bagger to left center. Then Pfeffer made good on his title of stayer by making a base hit to right field and Anson let loose those long legs of his and started at a 2.40 rate to tie the score.

"He would have done it too but for Kelly's line throw to the plate. The big captain bore down on Brother Tate. His flight was rapid but all the strength of Kelly's arm was in the ball and it came true as an arrow from the bow with a speed that left Anson in shock. Tate

squeezed it and touched Anson with time to spare and the wild howl that rose from the crowd proclaimed that fortune had not ceased to smile on Boston and that Anson and his men had been vanquished."

The crowd poured onto the field and a thousand people surrounded Kelly and cheered him in a wild ebullition of joy. Once Kel had freed himself from the enthusiasts Anson approached and pounded him on the back. "'Twas a helluva throw, Kel, I was sure I'd be safe by a country mile."

"I've still got a bit uv whip in me wing," chuckled Kelly.

The Globe's evening headline read,

ANSON vs.KELLY
The Great Chieftains Locked Horns

Captain Mike Downs Spalding's Right Bower in an Old-Time Kicking Game at the South Grounds

The Beaneaters arrived in Chicago on July 27 for a three-game series that would start the next day. They were not a happy lot having been swept in New York.

There was a note for Mike at the front desk the next morning. It smelled of lavender. In graceful calligraphy was the message *I should like to speak with you this evening.* It was signed Felicity Chalmers.

"What could *that* be about?" Kel said to himself. He put the note in his pocket and headed for breakfast.

Later, after he'd finished his dinner he crossed the street to Leroy Payne's livery.

"I'm goin' ta one uv the finest parts uv town, Mr. Payne. Could you set me up in somethin' grand?"

Payne looked around and scratched his balding head. "Let me think a wee minute now, what would a fine young man such as yourself want to pull up to a grand house in. A brougham? No, too large? A barouche perhaps? A cabriolet? A landau? No, you'd need a driver."

He spotted a wain-wright with a shock of red hair rubbing a final

coat of black lacquer onto a perch-high phaeton. "Joshua, hitch that new phaeton up to one of our best horses for Mr. Kelly."

The man looked up. "What about that frisky young, dappled gelding you bought last week, Mr. Payne? He'd be a perfect match for this carriage."

The gelding seemed pleased to be out on a jaunt in the cool night. He stepped out smartly, pulling the light rig at a thrilling clip, the shiny spokes of its high wheels buzzing.

A couple of well-dressed guests on their way out of the hotel to go to see "Davy Crocket" at Haverly's Theater stared as Mike flew past them.

"Isn't that the base ball player that's taken a room here, Charles?" asked the woman.

"He's Mike Kelly, Mildred. He's the new man in the Boston base ball team."

"Well *whoever* he is, he's liable to run someone over at that speed."

Kelly saw them, grinned, and tipped his hat, which was in danger of flying off his head.

"I shouldn't have thought a ball player could *afford* to stay at the Palmer," said Charles.

"Perhaps he spends his money the same way he drives," har-rumphed Mildred.

When Mike arrived at the Chalmers mansion he was surprised that Felicity answered the door herself. She could tell he hadn't expected her to.

"Come in, Mr. Kelly."

He stepped inside into the vestibule, taking in the mingling scents of lavender and furniture polish. He looked around, puzzled.

"I gave the servants the night off. My husband is in Brussels on business. Hilary is at her aunt's."

Felicity led Mike through the reception-room and into the library.

He looked around at the heavily carved black walnut walls lined with glass-fronted bookshelves and was a little taken aback to see a glass case containing a pair of silver dueling pistols on a richly polished sideboard.

He sat in a garnet *Bergère* chair beside the ornate marble fireplace, set his hat on the arm of it, and took out a cigarette.

Felicity picked up a heavy silver lighter from the table and lit Mike's cigarette, then looked down. "Your hands! What on earth happened to them?"

He looked at them, splaying his fingers apart. "That's what a fella gets takin' foul balls off his fingers a half dozen times a day year after year. I hardly notice anymore."

Felicity went to the cabinet and took out a bottle.

Mike read the label out loud. "Cassidy and Company Monasterevan Whiskey."

"I'm told it is rather smooth." She poured three fingers of the whiskey into a crystal class and handed it to Mike. Then she grasped his shoulder lightly, dragging her fingers lightly across it. Mike noticed that her nail polish matched her lipstick. He thought he heard her inhale a little. She lingered a beat before sitting down in a love seat. A normal chair would have not contained the bustle of her dress.

Mike took a sip of the whiskey.

"Do you approve?"

"Aye, that I do, I've never tasted the likes uv it."

Kelly looked at her, losing himself a little in her beautiful eyes. "What was it you wanted to talk about?"

She fluttered her long, lush eyelashes and ran the backs of the fingers of her right hand across Mike's strident mustache. "Nothing, really. I simply wanted the pleasure of your company … and to drink in your good looks again. Hilary is doing a wonderful job of capturing them. I know she's looking forward to showing you the painting when she's done."

"I'm lookin' forward ta seein' it. I'm sure it'll be a great deal better than what they put on the cigarette cards."

Felicity looked at him. "I'd like to have that handsome face between my breasts, Mr. Kelly."

Kelly wasn't sure what to say. Then he did. "I'm pretty sure I'd like that too. I'm thinking that skin uv yours is probably about as smooth as this whiskey."

She unclipped the clasp at the top of her gingham blouse. "You'll have to let me know."

Mike was about to pull Felicity toward him when she put her hands up to indicate he shouldn't.

"But I thought …"

"One minute," said Felicity.

"I'm ready," said Mike.

Felicity looked down between Mike's legs and smiled. "*That* is prodigiously apparent." She took off her jade earrings, claimed his mouth with a hot, blistering kiss, and pulled his head down into her bosoms.

When he woke up the next morning Mike knew it was going to be hard to think about baseball instead of Felicity's incredible body.

In the fourth inning Kelly sent the ball over the fence just in time to catch the train. It was a foul ball and up to foul doings so instead of boarding the train the proper way it went through the window without waiting for the sash to be raised. It travelled so fast the crash of the glass was mistaken by many for the echo of Kelly's bat.

Mike lay in bed all morning on Saturday the 30th. "I'd have to rally ta feel near death," he said to himself as he shivered beneath the covers.

He got up at noon to take some soup and ate a slice of beef, contrary to the orders of the physician who'd told him to eat nothing and drink nothing but milk.

"I can't play ball on milk," Mike had told the doctor.

"You should not be playing ball at all," he'd said.

Kelly went back to bed and shivered some more but when game time approached he donned his war paint and feathers and headed for the grounds.

There was a considerable delay in starting the game as the huge crowd encroached upon the right and left field gardens. It was delayed even more when a bench in the right wing gave way, throwing sixty Board of Trade brokers against a fence and smashing their fine hats.

The Bostons were absolutely faultless. As far as the League rules went two ghost hits, ones that were really bases on balls, were the only errors of the Hub team. Radbourn had several different curves secreted near his right elbow that the champions had never seen before. Kelly retired Williamson and then Burns by squeezing foul tips and the crowd cheered.

"Line her out, Kel!" yelled a man whose voice Mike recognized when he went to the plate in the first. Kelly blazed away at the ball, but he was far too weak to line them out today.

In the fourth Jimmy Ryan sent a high foul back of the plate straight at a nervous man in the front row. Instead of running for cover as he thought he should he crouched down upon Kelly's shout of "Don't move" and Mike made the catch for the third out.

When the clubs changed places for the next inning Kelly yelled to Pfeffer. "How's that fine sittin' with ya, Fred?"

Mike knew that Anson had fined him $25 for "a careless error" and Spalding had refused to rescind it. Incensed, Pfeffer had complicated matters by making incautious remarks to the press and the feud had dominated the sports pages for weeks.

"The two of them can go straight to Hell," Pfeffer yelled back.

The crowd was in a high state of excitement in the ninth when the White Stockings loaded the bases. Their team trailed by six runs but not after Darling drove the ball to the club house to clear the bags. The crowd howled like madmen and half of the spectators in the fifty

cent seats threw their five-cent cushions into the air ad libitum as Darling pulled into third base. General Dixwell's collar wilted like a hot-house plant. He smashed his umbrella into pieces against the back of the seat in front of him and yelled, "Damn it!"

Kelly determined to take a chance and let Darling score if he wanted to. To lessen Jimmy Ryan's chance to hit safe Kel didn't come up under his bat. Young Ryan was in such a hurry to knock the cover off the ball that he struck at the first one pitched. Mike smiled. He'd known Rad wouldn't give him anything he could hit until it was absolutely necessary. The ball went skyward and amid the horrible yells of the crowd Burdie hooked on to it and the Bostons had won their first game since leaving home and won it gloriously. Kel was braced up by the victory and said he thought the boys would play good ball the rest of the trip.

In the first inning of the August 1 game in Indianapolis the jubilee moderated when Kelly hit one on the conk and across second base for a bag. Billy Nash came out of the woods and brought his captain home by a liner to right field for two bags. The Bostons garnered four runs in the second, the last when Kelly's drive to right brought Wise home. Michael J. scored again in the fifth after being issued a ghost hit.

Madden collided with the Indianapolis third baseman in the Hoosiers' half of the fifth. The Kid was knocked silly for a few minutes and lay on the ground a wreck. Kelly ran in as players gathered around but did nothing but stare at their stricken comrade. Mike rubbed Madden's head and doused him with cold water and then helped him to the bench. The Beaneaters prevailed by a score of 16-3 but lost the last game of the series and headed to Detroit five games back of the Wolverines, who base ball cranks everywhere conceded were the best club in the League on any given day.

The Beaneaters were surprised when they saw the Detroits were putting Larry Twitchell between the points for the first game of the four-game series. He'd pitched just twice in '86 but it spoke volumes about the weighty batting of the Wolverines that he'd end '87 with an

11-1 record. The Bostons tore into Twitchell for sixteen hits and led 11-6 going into the ninth. Then the Wolverines made the Beaneaters weary and the crowd giddy by sending six men across the plate for a 12-11 win.

According to Tim Murnane, "the first four innings the next day were a travesty and the last five a farce in which Michael J. Kelly played the part of low comedian and brought down the house. The boys played about as bad a game for four innings as they could well put up. Kelly had been very lively in the first game of the series. He'd done a fair bit of chinning of the crowd, the players, and the umpire and he was roasted for it by the Detroit papers. As a result, the spectators yelled disagreeable and aggravating remarks and guyed him to an extent that would rattle anyone. Of course they had the opposite effect on Kelly.

The Wolverines seemed to show contempt for their guests by putting Henry Gruber in to pitch. The Beaneaters had never faced him and he was a complete mystery to everyone but Sam Wise who made four hits off the rookie. Detroit held an 8-0 lead after four innings. Knowing all was lost, Kelly went in to pitch an inning, just as a joke. The scheme worked so well he kept it up and to the surprise of the spectators and the disgust of the newsmen in the press box he made jays of the Wolverines. He pitched the rest of the game without a run being made by the League's best hitters. He turned the crowd completely over with remarks such as 'That was a wild pitch not a passed ball on my good friend Tate' and 'Tell the man from the Free Press to say that I am the boy wonder.' Umpire Sullivan was convulsed and laughed so hard he could hardly call balls and strikes.

About the only persons on the grounds that didn't extract any fun out of Kelly's monkey business were the Detroit directors. These gentlemen were hotly indignant and claimed that Kelly's actions would drive people away and cause them to lose precious gate money. I believe they are wrong, there will be three or four times as many people on hand tomorrow."

General Dixwell was blossomed out in a tall silk tile hat for the

third game of the set and the boys won. They went fishing the next morning and Dixwell went along. The gang made him wear the hat and they caught a hundred fish. The next day the general had his tile ironed and wore it to the game and the Bostons won again thanks to a home run by Kelly. Dixwell left the team at Detroit and went off to Saratoga. After Pittsburg pulverized the Beaneaters 23 to 3 the general telegraphed the team: "For goodness sake, brace up. If you want my hat I'll send it on."

Unfortunately, the Bostons did not brace up. They lost all three games in Pittsburg and two of three in New York to fall six games behind the Wolverines.

On Saturday, August 13 a magnificent attendance of 8,500 greeted the Beaneaters back home from the disastrous 5-10 road trip that had dealt a crippling blow to their hopes of a pennant. J.J. Drohan said, "People are saying that Kelly was a good man in Chicago where he was associated with such players as Gore, Williamson, Pfeffer, and Anson but the distribution of his brains among a lot of third-class players has not only proved disastrous to himself but to his nine as well. Because Kelly could cut across the diamond and play all manner of tricks on and off the diamond the rest of the Boston team think they can do the same, but they can't and many a run has been lost by some clodhopper attempting to mimic the performances of Kelly."

Mike covered second base in "hallelujah style", reaching base four times and scoring twice in the Beaneaters' 4-2 win. When the players got back to their dressing-room there was a letter to Manager Morrill from the directors of the Boston club pinned on the bulletin board below the words, "Have your road uniform cleaned this week. It read, "Manager Morrill, we the Directors of the Boston club offer $2,000 to be equally divided among the players should they win the pennant."

News from Quincy that the "only Mike" and a party of his friends had arrived at Hough's Neck brought hundreds to the seaside resort. "Women as well as men pressed forward to squeeze the hand of the $10,000 beauty, who smilingly received them all. Kelly is very fond of

sea bathing and was seen sporting in the surf with a female acquaintance in a revealing bathing costume."

Before his first at bat at home to the New Yorks on August 15 Kelly, who had just been voted the League's best base runner in a *Boston Herald* poll, was presented with a statuette of a ball player and a box of cigars. "Dimple" Tate made considerable fun and bugged the miniature player off the field.

In the Giants' at bats in the ninth inning Richardson hit a drive to left that yielded three bases. Keefe's hard grounder bounded over Wise's head and the New Yorkers won.

"There followed a scene the like of which has never been witnessed on the Boston grounds. Umpires have been hooted and guyed but no crowd has ever tried to do one harm. A mob of angry cranks surrounded Sullivan and he would have been handled very roughly but for the interference of Kelly, who, with the assistance of a policeman, escorted Sullivan to the dressing-room. The crowd was in a very bad humor, hallooing and putting on greatly, and nothing but Kelly's popularity saved him from being mobbed. A number of small boys threw stones and one struck Sullivan in the head. Three officers finally led Sullivan to the carriage of some New York friends and he was rapidly driven away.

Kelly never caught so well as he did against Pittsburg on August 27 and he was on base all afternoon in the Bostons' 28-14 beating of the Alleghenys.

The game was held up in the sixth inning. Kelly and a few of his new millionaire friends had been toasting one another in their box seats. "You have failed to make a hit but twice in the last twenty-five games, Kel," one of them told him. "In those games you made fifty-three hits."

Another man raised his glass to Mike and said, "Kelly always bobs up."

"Is there any chance you could join us, Mr. Kelly?" invited the umpire. "If your coterie of admirers can spare you that is. It seems I'm all alone behind the bat just now and I have no mitt."

Mike downed his drink, said to his friends, "It seems me services are required, gents. May you always have a clean shirt, a clear conscience, and enough coins in your pocket to buy a pint," and jumped on to the field.

The spectators around the millionaires roared.

Kelly hit for the cycle and scored six runs. In between, he had a few more drinks with his friends.

Mike went on a toot on the 1st of September and the next day, still recovering from his escapade, he sat on the bench. Tate was behind the bat when McGeachey popped up a foul fly. Mike could see that it was out of Tate's reach and that of Morrill as well. Quick as a flash he jumped up and ran for the ball.

"Kelly now catching for Boston!" he yelled to Powers, and then proceeded to catch the foul. Confused, Powers scratched his head and then put up his thumb. McGeachey and the rest of the Hoosiers screamed in disbelief at the call but Powers said there was nothing in the rule book about when a manager could replace a player.

"In fact, Rule 28 says any present, uniformed player may be substituted at any time by either club," Kelly told McGeachey. "I've as much right to replace Tate while a ball's in the air as at any other time during the progress of the game."

The League changed its substitution rule the next year.

The Elks held a benefit that night and Kelly's outrageous substitution for Tate was the man topic of jocularity. On Thursday night the team went to Nat Goodwin's opening at the Grand Opera House. After the play the actors drank champagne, the players temperance drinks - at least that's what J.J. Drohan told his readers. Mike had a word with Goodwin about Siobhan's aspirations.

On Friday, the Bostons entertained the Indianapolis club again after downing them 10-7 the day before with help from Kelly's latest trick. They intended to take all three scalps from the Hoosiers and were bound to have them. The Hoosiers sent 21-year old Lev Shreve to the pitching box and it proved a great miscalculation. The

Beaneaters rattled him terribly, scoring nineteen runs on thirty-one hits. Wise and Burdock had five each. Stemmyer was batted from pillar to post as well, surrendering eleven runs on fifteen hits. He didn't have enough speed to break a hen's egg at ten paces. Kelly was on base six times, three of them on hits, two on phantom ones, and once on a muff.

On September 8 all the cranks were talking about Radbourn's suspension for ineffective pitching. Neither Bill Harris nor Tim Murnane could understand it. They felt Old Hoss had pitched the best he knew how even when he was in poor condition. The directors were keeping their counsel as to why Radbourn had been laid off and he was frustrated. If he wouldn't be traveling with the team he wanted to go home.

"Hell, it should uv been my ass they suspended after the way I played yesterday against the Philadelphias," groaned Kelly. He'd ended the 3-2 loss by hitting a lazy fly ball into right field after four other futile trips to the plate.

The Michael Joseph battery was in the points on September 10. *The Globe* scribe found the two Mikes an interesting contrast, Kelly big, athletic, and good-humored and Madden small but nervy and determined. Little Michael Joseph Madden did the pitching and big Michael Joseph Kelly the catching and so well did they do the Bostons were enabled to close the home season by defeating the gilt-edged sluggers from New York. The contest was a great one and 6,500 people expressed their approbation of it by cheering nearly every play. Lewis Webber, the Boston fire department chief, was on the Beaneaters' bench. He distracted some of the players by talk of how his department needed new equipment to reach the upper flowers of the growing number of skyscrapers but he soon joined the chorus of cheers.

Madden was told by management that there would be an extra $50 in his pocket if he were to win and the boy pitcher earned his money gallantly. Kelly worked behind the bat without a single flaw and his throwing was superb. His feats of reaching Connor's foul,

catching a wild pitch behind George Gore's back, and picking off two base-runners in dreamland, one at first the other off third when there were three men on base, largely influenced the final result.

When Doescher called "Play" Welch faced Kelly wearing his usual confident smile. It grew by degrees as three strikes were called. His smile vanished when Kelly hit a low liner over Ward's head to right center. Gore could only get one hand on it and wasn't able to pull it down. Kelly tore around to third. Billy Nash lashed one out to left and Kelly trotted home with the game's first run. In the third, Kelly rapped a nice single and tried to steal second on Nash's fourth strike. Brown made a terribly high throw and the crowd went wild with joy when Kelly came home.

The players had no time to celebrate or say good-bye to their adoring boosters. They left for Detroit after the game over the Hoosac Tunnel & West Shore route.

Earlier that day every member of the Browns' starting nine players, with the exception of Charlie Comiskey, who'd been involved in the planning of a game against the Cuban Giants signed the following letter to owner Chris Von Der Ahe.

"We, the undersigned members of the St. Louis Baseball Club, do not agree to play against negroes tomorrow. We will cheerfully play against white people at any time and think that by refusing to play we are only doing what is right."

When Anson heard about it he was delighted.

The Globe announced that it would tender the members of the Boston base ball team a banquet at Young's Hotel on Saturday evening, October 15 at 8 o'clock. Colonel Charles Taylor would preside and after the dinner present the newspaper's base ball trophies to the winners of their competitions, Messrs. Wise and Kelly."

Of Kelly, *The Globe* said, "He is undoubtedly the best-natured man who plays ball for money, rarely losing his temper and seldom making an exhibition of it. He possesses a peculiar facility of sizing up a crowd and seems to know how much they can stand. In victory, he is jubilant but defeat, no matter how severe, cannot crush him. His base-running this year has been of the best order. Not only has he won The Globe medal, he outstripped every base-runner in the league save Ward and Fogarty in the number of bases stolen and considering his fewer chances has more than equaled either player. All in all, Kelly is beyond a doubt the best base-runner in the National League."

In November the Giants embarked on a postseason barnstorming tour of California. Although their roster boasted numerous future Hall of Famers, Ward, Ewing, Connor, and Keefe, the main draw was the appearance of "King" Kelly, who uncharacteristically neglected to stock up on whiskey and had nothing to drink until the train crossed into Nevada and the bar car re-opened.

In addition to Kelly's portrait, an advertisement for one of the teams' first games enthusiastically heralded his arrival in California:

**"Coming! Coming!!
MIKE KELLY - The $10,000 Beauty.
DON'T FAIL TO SEE HIM!"**

Kel enjoyed his time on "the Slope" as the West Coast was called, but not the poker game at which he dropped $1,500.

THE

$10,000

BEAUTY

"Stop teasing, you're driving me wild!"

On January 15, *The Cincinnati Express* reporter wrote that: "Michael Angelo Kelly, the famous $10,000 ball tosser, reached the city last evening with Mrs. Kelly, but minus the magnificent brunette mustache that formerly struck terror into the hearts of rival players. Mr. Kelly had just arrived from San Francisco and is in the city for just one night. He was clothed in royal purple and sported a $195 watch and diamond-studded sleeve buttons.

Kelly denied in the most Shakespearean twang that he was not compelled to sacrifice his mustache for criminal purposes with intent to dodge the officials of the glorious climate of California. He had merely tired of the gold coast and sighed for the sweet breezes from the cranberry swamps of New Jersey. He liked California, had been treated well there, but was content to eat codfish balls in the Garden State. He registered in a fine Spencerian-Bulwer-Eugene-Higgins hand and immediately sought the rest and quietude of the theatre over the Rhine with Mrs. Kelly. Then he is going back to Paterson to remain the rest of the winter.

'No minstrel business?' I asked him.

'Not for me. I am settling down to prepare for next season. Boston stock is showing up. I think we'll be in the fight more bitter than ever.'

The $10,000 man bowed and called to the elevator boy that he was ready to go up and the interview was over."

On February 19 *The Globe* ran reflections on base ball by Kelly. Asked about his propensity for kicking during a game he said, "be-

cause of being the $10,000 beauty and all that sort of thing there was more or less excitement regarding my appearance last season. In some towns they had an idea that I was a sort of Jumbo. Down in Hartford I remember playing ball just as good as I ever did before and keeping pretty quiet all the way through it. At the conclusion I heard a conversation between two men.

One said, 'so that is Kelly is it. Well what do you think of him?'

His partner replied, 'Well I firmly believe he is an overrated player. Why he didn't kick a bit. He can't play ball.'

You see he wanted more kicking and less ball playing. There wasn't much excitement in the game and it made him very sore indeed.

Asked to recount his early days Kel said, "I played my first games as a member of an organized team in Washington when I was 15 years old. I went with the Keystones and played in various positions. In '73 I began to play in Paterson, New Jersey. They were organizing a base ball team and asked if I would join. I replied that I'd be very happy to. The captain was William Purcell. He was a cranky sort of a boy but he could play great ball. The great Nolan was the pitcher. For several years we played together and won game after game from the amateur clubs of New Jersey. In '76 Nolan quit and my friend James McCormick went in to pitch and I to catch. That was where we first got the reputation as the Jersey battery that has stuck to us these many years. Sometimes we got $1 for the day's work, sometimes we got $4 but rarely more than $5. The best games were with the Stars of Covington, Kentucky and the Mutuals of Brooklyn. I'll wager they expected to slaughter our nine but we defeated them and the Buckeyes from Columbus as well.

It began to get cold and the winter came and like Othello a ball player had no occupation. My winter business in those days was to leave Paterson at 4 a.m. and go to New York and I would leave there at 6 o'clock with a big bundle of newspapers to sell back home. I did this for four years and finally got so tired of it I went into a factory to learn the silk weaver trade. I stuck at it until the opening of the ball season. My friends advised me to stick with it and leave base ball

alone but I was a crank of the game and couldn't leave it alone if I wanted to, so I went at it again.

I played several games with the Port Jervis team but I didn't care much for the place and jumped at an offer to go to the Buckeye club with Jim McCormick for my pitcher. Mike Dorgan and I led off and I made a base hit in the first game I played. I was so tickled I started to steal second but I was thrown out and the gang gave me the laugh. I didn't think I was such a great player after that. Chub Sullivan was the first baseman. He was a big-hearted fellow. The boys played good enough ball but we didn't seem to have the proper support from the patrons of the game and the club disbanded in September. I looked about me and didn't know just what I would do. I received a fine offer from the Cincinnati club and I was more than glad to get in with such an array of talent as they had.

A little thing occurred in the '79 season which convinced me that circumstances can make or break a man's future. Deacon White got discouraged at the business of being captain during our Eastern trip and resigned while we were in Troy and Cal McVey went into authority. We lost six of our nine games. Dickerson was drinking pretty hard and I was playing in rough luck. After the second Boston game was finished the record showed that out of the last 21 times at the bat I'd reached first base but once and that was by virtue of an error. McVey announced privately that he'd telegraphed Jack Leary who was then in Manchester to come the next day and play on the nine in the last game in Boston. He said he hadn't made up his mind whether to lay off Kelly or Dickerson but he thought I seemed to be so completely demoralized that I was the one to be relieved.

Much to Cal's disappointment Leary didn't show in time for the game and I was put in again to play right field. I was so desperate that I guess the ice was broken and I succeeded in scattering my ill-luck to the winds. I went to the bat five times that day and made two doubles, a triple, and a home run and Cal was delighted with my stick work. The team returned home and in the first game against the Chicagos I was very lucky and batted in every run made and won the game for my club. At the end of the season I stood among

the leading batters. What might have been the result if Leary had appeared on the grounds that day in Boston? I would have been laid off and returned to Paterson in disgrace. I might never have had nerve enough to play in a league club again … which moves me to repeat that sacred thought. Great God, on what a slender thread hang everlasting things."

On March 2 the National League refused to abandon its $2,000 salary limit while at the same time expanding its schedule from 126 to 140 games.

J. J. "Jack" Drohan, who was helping Mike write base ball's first autobiography, wrote that "Kelly is one of the busiest men in Boston. In the morning for a couple of hours he is at Winslow practicing for the baseball season; from 12 to 2 he has a stenographer at the Clarendon Hotel and discusses the closing chapters in his book; in the afternoon he practices again, sees his shorthand man; then goes to the theatre to play his part in the evening."

On March 21 Kelly made his Boston stage debut as Dusty Bob in Charles Hoyt's *A Rag Baby* at the Park Theatre. It was his first time acting as a character in a full-length play. He told the stage manager that as a young man he'd had a non-speaking role in a Paterson theater that required only that he be thrown through a window.

Despite poor weather and a play that was nearing four-years old, the theatre was full to overflowing. At his first appearance late in the final act the show was stopped for several minutes due to the large and loud reception he received just for stepping on stage. The Hoyt & Thomas Company enjoyed packed houses throughout the production's Boston run. Such attention hardly seemed fitting for a novice actor with only ten lines in the play but the acclaim surrounding Kelly was due less to his acting ability than it was to his status as Boston's biggest celebrity.

At 33, Old Hoss Radbourn really was old now, even though he'd pitched just 425 innings in '87 - nothing like the 632 he'd thrown in '83 or the 678 in his incredible 60-win season of '84. He would have the worst year of his career in 1888, winning just six games against

sixteen losses in spite of a quite respectable 2.87 ERA.

Astoundingly, in spite of seasons of 53-16, 36-17, and 38-21, Spalding sold 25-year old John Clarkson to the Beaneaters. Clarkson believed he was poorly paid and wanted to play closer to his home in Cambridge. The Boston magnates were prepared to go down deep into their pockets for Clarkson. They'd seen an increase of over $50,000 in gate receipts thanks to Kelly. It was a terrible mistake for the Chicagos. Clarkson would win 38 games in 1888 and 49 in '89.

A cold north wind blew in early April and the boys needed to wear several inside garments as well as wool sweaters. Kelly had worked himself down to 183 pounds and said he could easily lose another ten. He and John Burdock played a game of handball after practice one afternoon and several spectators looked on. The game went on hot and heavy and finally the beauty got the best of it. He was a curious sight in gray Knickerbockers, stockings to match, Indian moccasins he'd purchased in San Francisco, half a dozen flannel shirts, and an old gray coat. Around his Roman head was wound a white silk handkerchief.

The Bostons played an exhibition series in Baltimore in the middle of April. Asked why he'd kicked so strongly in the games, Oyster Burns said he did it to see if he could get Kelly rattled.

"Get Kelly rattled?" asked fellow outfielder Blondie Purcell in a voice of deep disgust. "It'd be as difficult to rattle a dead Baltimore mule as him. Kel wouldn't get rattled if a house fell on him."

The Beaneaters beat the Phillies 4-2 in the finely contested but frigid season opener on April 20. It was too cold for ball-playing and the spectators shivered in wraps and tightly buttoned overcoats. Kelly got a laugh from the people shivering in the box seats when he said, "I swear I'll never sign another contract that requires me to play ball before the First of May."

Mulvey and Kelly were responsible for the win. The former threw wildly to the home plate to cut off Kelly and "the Beauty", as he afterwards admitted to Umpire Daniels, hugged Clements to prevent him from securing the ball which allowed Wise to score. After that

ungentlemanly act Kelly further tantalized the crowd by facing the grandstand and shouting, "That's the soup."

In the opinion of Murnane, Mike Kelly was the hero of the Bostons' second game. "His two home hits were the prettiest seen for a long time and Colonel Rogers of the Philadelphia club said they were as long as any he had seen made on the grounds. Kelly sent in three runs ahead of him by his timely stick work and made three runs himself."

When a new ball was given to Casey in the eighth inning he prepared to strike Kelly out. Mike found Casey's first pitch to his liking and away it went - a long, beautiful drive over the "Boston Electric Lighting Company, lighting your way, every day" sign on the right field fence. Mr. Eben Jordan, Dr. Delaney, and several other Boston gentleman scattered about in the grand stand led the applause, which broke into cheers as Kelly came in on the home stretch.

"He cost Boston $10,000," said Colonel Rogers, "but he's worth every dollar of it and more. He cost our club $3.75 for new balls today."

After taking four straight in Philadelphia the team headed to Washington in a fine mood. In the first game the Nationals' batsmen fell one by one before Clarkson and when they didn't Kelly settled their individual and collective cases. Murnane wrote. "It is difficult to find language complimentary enough for the great work performed by Kelly. Not one man was allowed to steal a base and his clever throw in cutting off Irwin in the ninth inning saved the game for Boston. Michael made two desperate attempts to win the game, once in the eighth inning and again in the eleventh and he was successful on the second occasion."

It was getting pretty dark when Kelly went to the bat.

"Now Kel," shouted Ubbo from the coacher's box.

"I will if I can," answered Kelly.

After two strikes were called he rapped a weak one to O'Day. The feeble grounder would have been an out if hit by an ordinary

runner—in fact an ordinary runner wouldn't have even tried for the bag. But by a burst of speed rarely seen on a ball field Kelly got to first base.

He took his cap off and one could see his eyes gleam as he watched every movement of O'Day like a cat watches a mouse. The instant O'Day's shoulder moved, away went Kelly like the wind. The ball travelled over Myer's head and into center field where Dummy Hoy picked it up. He made a beautiful throw to third but Kelly slid ten feet to the bag and Umpire Lynch called "Safe!"

Honest Sam Wise accomplished the rest with the aid of his little stick. He caught an outcurver and banged it to center. Mike raced across the plate for a 1-0 win.

Kelly was terrific behind the bat in the first game in New York, a 4-3 win. He raised a tremendous shout from the large audience when with darkness settling in he drove the gray, haggard ball into the right field corner. Tiernan got the ball and whipped it to third but Kelly was already standing on the bag like a gladiator atop a slain lion when it arrived. Wise hit one to left and before it had a chance to roll to a stop Kelly had trod upon the plate with the winning run. The Boston boosters who'd made the trip to see their first-place team were frantic with delight.

When news that Kelly had knocked out a three-base hit in the last half of the tenth inning reached *The Globe*'s office a cheer went up from the newsroom that brought the whole work force to that part of the building. "Tick, tick" went the instrument. "Kelly scores on Wise's hit," sang out the operator, hardly able to contain his excitement. A shout went up that fairly shook the building.

In his hotel room after getting back from the Polo Grounds Tim Murnane sat at his typewriter and punched out, "Kelly is back to his old Chicago form and, free from a captain's responsibilities, is earning his salary and more. It is pretty safe to figure that the Bostons will win three and possibly four of every five games they play with Clarkson in the box and "the only Mike" behind the bat."

At that particular moment Kelly was being entertained by an acquaintance named Lydia, or so she claimed. She wore a tight-fitting mauve corset, light blue stockings held up by dark blue garters, and dark blue laced boots. Mike enjoyed the show she put on for him and what came after.

After nine straight wins to open the '88 season the Bostons lost their second game in New York the next day. The weather was cold and disagreeable and the players and spectators shivered and shook for an hour and 45 minutes.

Burdock led off the third by placing the ball in the gap between center and right. Clarkson hit to Tiernan and Kelly came to the plate. He let one bad ball go by. The next one was a beauty and Kelly made a tremendous whack. Gore sprinted after the ball and Burdock took off. Gore fished the ball out from under waiting buggies after assuring himself it hadn't rolled through any of the horse droppings. During the time Michael was making the circuit of the bases the crowd amused itself by cheering him vigorously. Kelly's home run was all the Beaneaters could manage against Ledell Titcombe and they lost again, 4-2 this time.

"We need ta get back to our winning ways," Kel told the team.

The Giants changed the general order of things on Thursday, going into the field instead of to the bat. Kelly was the first man to get a crack at the ball with the complexion of immaculate snow and he hit the first pitch into the audience foul. It was strange how the crowd would react when the leather lost itself among the rows of seats. If the visiting nine was at the bat the sphere would be returned promptly by an eager spectator. If the home club was batting and the ball shied off the diamond the chances were decidedly in favor of it remaining there.

Sure enough, the ball was quickly returned. Kelly drove it out to center field for a base and the crowd gave Michael plenty of applause for his beautiful hit. He went to second on Wise's base on balls and scored when Morrill rapped the still crisp ball hard with his new black bat.

Kelly began the sixth with a cracker to right field that raised his batting average to .500, a degree of that the modicum of phantoms.

Wise was hit by a pitched ball and he and Mike moved up a quarter. Morrill banged the ball over the right field fence and all three scored. Kelly made another pretty hit his next time at the bat. He raced around for three bases and scored on Wise's sacrifice to Slattery.

In the ninth the Giants got two men on base for Buck Ewing, their only .300 hitter. Clarkson got two strikes on Ewing then signaled to Mike that another good ball was coming. Ewing dug in as Clarkson wound up and let go the pitch.

"Look out!" screamed Kelly.

Thinking he was about to be hit, Ewing hit the dirt.

"Strike three," called Umpire Daniels as the ball sailed over the center of the plate waist high.

The crowd roared, some out of resentment, most in admiration of Kelly's clever subterfuge. They left the grounds unhappy. The visitors won 6-2 and headed to Grand Central station to board a New York Central train for Detroit. They would visit every city in the league before finally heading back to Boston on May 25. J.D. Rockefeller's luxurious Wagner Palace car was attached to their train in front of the caboose.

Kelly's brigade pulled into Pittsburg on May 10 a game out of first place with twelve wins and just three losses and checked into the Hotel Anderson at the corner of Penn avenue and Sixth street. Mr. Morris, the hotel manager, told them that William Jennings Bryan and his wife had just left and then instructed Patrick Doody, the head porter, to see to their bags as the players would be taking a tally-ho to the grounds directly.

Kelly had two hits and just missed getting two others in a come-from-behind 7-4 win over the Alleghenys, but it was a costly one. Morrill had put Clarkson in right field. The first ball hit his way went between his legs and two runs scored. When a fly was hit to him it

hurt his finger so badly it had to be put in a splint by a physician. Kel told Morrill it might not be wise to put his best pitcher in an unfamiliar spot again.

Two days later the Boston boys played one of the worst games of the season but still managed to pull it out of the fire. Tom Fullwood, *The Globe*'s correspondent in the Smoky City, wrote that, "They were decidedly off at the bat and in the field. Kelly, who kept on encouraging his men, was the exception. He seemed thoroughly posted as to Hardie Henderson and larruped two beauties off his deliveries." His sacrifice fly in the eighth brought in the winning run.

Kelly checked into the Palmer House when the Beaneaters arrived in Chicago that night. A reception had been planned for Clarkson and Kelly, the returning heroes. Many of the city's factories closed for the day and a large number of houses in the wholesale district dismissed their employees at 2 o'clock, at which time the Second Regiment band headed by a platoon of police marched to the Leland Hotel. A decorated arch had been erected over the Madison street bridge. Kelly and Clarkson rode in a carriage drawn by four white horses. Fullwood had been surprised when Spalding told him that "nothing was too good for Mike and John." It was quite a spectacle, the Chicago players wore opera "crush" hats, broadcloth full dress, swallow tail-coats, and alligator skin boots. The rotunda of the hotel was jammed with cranks trying to meet Kelly. Joe Hornung watched and said, "There is the greatest ball player on earth." The people who'd overheard nodded their agreement. "Hooray for Kelly!" one yelled.

The game was called after six innings. Anson had kicked to have it called after five. His club trailed 17-5. The Bostons tacked on another three in the sixth for good measure.

Mike was glad to be back the Palmer House. He got the best night's sleep he'd had in weeks after a midnight visit from green-eyed Colleen, his favorite chambermaid.

She pulled off her smock to reveal a baby blue French woven corset.

"I've missed this," Mike told her as she slipped in beside him under the covers. He put one hand around her and undid the string of

her corset with his other hand.

"I see you're still an expert at helping girls out uv their clothes, Michael Kelly. Have you been keeping in practice?"

"A wee bit," said Mike. He kissed her and she slid under him.

"I see you're ready to get started, Mr. Kelly," teased Colleen, feeling the familiar growth between his legs.

"I was ready a second after I heard your key turn in the lock."

Kelly got plenty of applause from the overflow West Side Park crowd the next day, though much of it was muffled as many of the ladies in attendance wore white gloves. He and Clarkson had been welcomed by musicians dressed in blue bullion and helmets decked with plumes, shrieking youngsters, and blaring horns. The Chicagos' black as night pantaloons and shirts were in sharp contrast to the gray and red raiment of the visitors' uniforms.

Mike still had a smile on his face from Colleen's visit. Before he went to bat several Chicago players sprinkled sawdust around the home plate, light rain had started to fall. Kelly swung his Western ash and drove the ball down to the RELIABLE TAILORS sign. It bounced all the way back to Fred Pfeffer at second. Kel was standing on the bag when Fred gobbled up the ball and turned to tag Kelly.

"You still get around the bags like a deer," said Pfeffer.

Sammy Wise tried his luck with his little bat and sent the ball into left center field.

"See you again soon, Fred," said Mike as he tore off for third.

"I imagine you will," said Pfeffer as he turned for a throw from Sullivan.

The yellers in the crowd yelled "Hurray, hurray, hurray" when Kelly scored the game's first run.

With Johnston and Brown on base in the third Kelly drifted the ball to center to score Johnston and send Brown to third. The crowd let out a hearty volley of cheers that were even louder this time.

"I wish he was still doing that for *our* side," groaned a man with

huge side-whiskers.

"Back again so soon, Kel?" Pfeffer chuckled as Mike pulled into second.

"I missed you is all, Fred," explained Kel.

Wise drove a ball to Williamson that was too hot to handle and Kelly made third. A minute later he winked at Sam Wise, who was taking his lead off first. Sam nodded and took off for second. Mike sprinted for home but stopped in his tracks when Pfeffer took Tom Daly's throw, ignored Wise, and fired the ball back to Daly.

"Playin' Chicago ball are ya, Tom?"

"Aye, that I am, Kel," said Daly as he whopped the ball to Burns at third.

Seeing that Wise was already heading there, Kel made a mad dash for home. He made a ten-foot dive for the plate but Burns' throw beat him and Umpire Lunch declared him out.

Kelly made another single his next time up, this one to right. The ball rolled past novice Bob Petit and under the seats Spalding had ordered set up. A man in a rumpled Alpaca sack suit reached under his seat and handed the ball to Petit but before he could throw it to the infield Kelly had run to second base to the amusement of the crowd and Fred Pfeffer.

"We really oughta stop meeting like this, Fred," said Mike.

The New York Sun said, "Capt. Mike Kelly has braced up wonderfully and is playing ball with the same vim and ability that won for him his enviable reputation. He is showing up strong in the field and at the bat and much of the success of the team is due to Sir Michael's efforts.

A little incident in Thursday's game will show how quickly he can see an advantage and act thereupon. Kelly raced from second base on a hit and happened to jump over the plate without touching it. The ball was close at his heels and he had no time to waste. Half a dozen Chicago players rushed in to back up the catcher and those

in the grand stand that had seen Kelly's omission were sure he was a goner. But Kel began to gesticulate wildly and accused Burns of intentionally blocking him at third and while the attention of the other players and the umpire were fixed on listening to Burns deny the charge Kelly cool as a cucumber sidled over to the plate and stepped on it. The crowd went crazy and so did the Chicagos when they realized what their former teammate had done."

By now a steady drizzle was drenching the players and the spectators who hadn't thought to bring umbrellas. The White Stockings kept trying to get Lynch to end the game before it became official, but he let things go on until the Bostons scored five runs and made it 20-5 after six innings. The win tied the Beaneaters for first place.

Now Tim Murnane was even more enthused about Kelly. "Everyone in Chicago is kicking tonight because Spalding was foolish enough to let Kelly go. The phenomenal all-round playing of Mike Kelly this season has never been equaled. His catching has been of the highest order and his batting and base running are ahead of any work that even this great player has accomplished in the past. In the first nineteen games he has made 40 safe hits while the rest of the team have combined for 126. He shows up still better when it comes to run-getting, having scored 23 while his comrades have managed to get around the bases just 67 times. In base-running he comes in just one behind the other fifteen men together. This is certainly a record to be proud of and Kelly is certainly to be congratulated. Colonel William C. Lyon, an originator of the White Stockings and vice-president under Hulbert, is said to be negotiating for Kelly's return to Chicago. He said he had taken Kelly's departure from the Windy City very much to heart and claimed that Anson's team would be pennant winners if Mike came back. The Colonel is sanguine in his hope for success."

Kelly had a sore arm and Joe Hornung and Ezra Sutton were afraid they had rheumatism. Clarkson had pitched the last two days so Morrill put Kentuckian Bill Sowders in the box the next afternoon. Sowders was wild and badly beaten up. A fine drizzle made the ball greasy and Kelly was dancing around the plate all afternoon

picking balls off the wet grass and catching others over his head.

"Kelly's still a corker," said Anson when Mike went to bat in the eighth to the merriment of the crowd. He rubbed his bat affectionately then batted the mushy ball for three bases. It was about all the Bostons could muster. They fell 9-2 and dropped to two games out of first. The last game in Chicago was a lot worse. They got Chicagoed 13-0. For once Mike was glad to leave the Windy City.

The Bostons won their first game in Indianapolis and lost the second. There was a smattering of applause when Kelly, who was leading the League in hits, runs, and batting average, went to bat in the first inning the next day.

"Yer a fine-lookin' tin thousand dollar beauty," yelled a grizzled old man in the stands.

Four called strikes went by him and Kelly's bat never budged from his shoulder.

"Guess I'm blind today," he told Sam Wise when he came to take his place.

The crowd whistled "The Rogue's March" the next time he went to the bat. He was jeered when he let two strikes go by then he drove the next one over the center field fence.

After he crossed the plate, a wide grin under his famous mustache, he yelled to the old man who'd guyed him. "Well I got the best of you, old man. I'm eatin' strawberries and ice cream on the salary I earn for performing in front uv suckers like you."

The crowd roared when the wily old Turk got the best of Kelly with, "And the bartenders get the rest."

On the train to Boston Tim Murnane talked to the *Indiana Tribune*'s base ball correspondent. The Hoosiers were heading out on their first Eastern swing of the season. It didn't take Murnane long to get around to his favorite subject, Mike Kelly. He'd just been reading what other sports columnists were writing about him.

"Kelly has been getting a lot of abuse from a certain Boston pa-

per—not mine of course—the Herald. We all know the game he's been putting up. He's helped the club out of many a hole and to be treated the way he has with a sore arm is dead wrong. The Boston club should know Kelly will always do as he did when he was with the Chicagos and could go out and take a drink and still play his great game. A good time now and then never hurt him when he was with old man Anson and it won't now if they don't make a storm in a teacup over it."

When he got back to his office Murnane wrote, "Kelly is covering the second bag as though he has never played anywhere else. His double plays are beauties and he made a miraculous one-handed stop of a hot grounder in the neighborhood of second base to choke off a rally on Saturday. He leads the League in batting with a percentage of .446 and if he had done his usual hitting the home side would probably not have been swept by the Phillies in their first games in front of their boosters."

It didn't help that the Beaneaters had sat for a team photograph on Friday. Sam Wise had told Kelly they never won a game on a day when they had their picture taken.

On Tuesday the Bostons lost 8-0. John Haggerty was the superintendent of the revamped grounds, now South End Grounds II. When a construction firm had built a new double-decked grandstand for the 1888 season John had used the old boards from the previous grandstand to build a one-story house on the edge of the property to provide a dressing-room for the ballplayers. Kelly was his favorite player, he said Mike was the foxiest man who ever wore a base ball suit. Haggerty was sure that the horseshoe that had been hung at the entrance to the grand stand was a Jonah. He took it down and it worked. The Beaneaters swept a rare Wednesday double header from the Hoosiers on May 30.

Kelly sat out the first game, huddling inside a thick red jersey, his throat wrapped. He wasn't needed as Clarkson tossed a 3-0 shutout with Tate behind the plate. In the afternoon Kel played "a wonderful game of ball" especially in light of his condition. His arm was fine

now and after he threw out Bassett and McGeachy only one of the men from Hoosierville assayed to steal a base. His only error was a muff of Bassett's foul fly that had no bearing on the 4-2 final score.

After the game he waved his teammates together and handed Morrill a small box. John looked confused but shrugged and opened it. Inside was a burnished red horseshoe decorated with bright ribbons.

"It's a beauty," said John.

"It's the gift of a lady from Palmer," explained Mike. "She hopes it'll bring the club the same luck you had in '83," explained Mike.

Then the players dressed for the show. The two teams had been invited to a performance of "Dawn" by the manager of the Hodis Street Theatre.

"You look terrible," Morrill said to Kelly before the game against Pittsburg on the fifth of June. "I can't tell if your skin is gray or green, but you've contracted something frightful. I'll understand if you're not up to playing today."

"No, John, we lost yesterday and the Chicagos had a cake walk over the Phillies. Now we're two and a half behind them. We have to win. I'll play."

For a man who was ill, Kelly did awfully well. He rapped out a double, a triple, and two singles and caught a magnificent game. Sam Wise led off the game with a two-bagger and Johnston tried to do the same, but Dalrymple made a very neat catch of his long fly. Kelly lined a couple of balls foul and Galvin objected to the position he took at the plate. Umpire Lynch thought Kelly was all right and Michael proved that he was when he drove the ball away to the right field corner. The hit allowed Wise to score and Kelly sprinted like a fiend to third base. A tumult of applause erupted from the stands.

A portly man in a Gondola hat far too small for his head stood up in the grand-stand and sang in a clear, low voice,

"All walks of life show one great man,

In poetry it's Shelley

In base ball too there's excellence

There's Mike, the only Kelly."

The crowd loved it. When the man beside him pounded him on the back the surprised baritone almost dropped the silver flask he was about to take another drink from.

In the fourth inning Dalrymple banged a beauty to right field for two bases. Maul sent the ball spinning along the ground to left field and Dalrymple tried to score, but Hornung's throw to Kelly killed him at the home plate. An inning later Kelly threw out Sunday when he tried to steal second base. "Yer not *that* fast, Billy," he yelled to him.

"Helluva throw, Kel," said Sunday as he smacked the dirt from his uniform.

The next pitch hit Kelly in the knee. Lynch was glad it hadn't hit him. "If any more come that way I'll catch them in me teeth and spit 'em down to second," he told Lynch.

In the sixth Mike sent Boston stock up several points when he belted the lop-sided ball to the skirting boards in the center field fence and reached second standing up. Nash gave it another jump, sending one to right for a base and Kel flew around third and just beat Miller's tag.

Clarkson laced a ball to center field in the eighth and Richard Johnstone followed with a liner to left field for three bases. The crowd shrieked for joy.

"One more is all we want, Michael," yelled a leather-lunged hat finisher several rows up in the stands.

Kelly gave him what he wanted, a fine drive to the left garden that scored Johnston.

The Smoky City boys scored three in their half of the eighth, but things were well in hand by then, the Bostons walking off with a 10-5 win.

As he boarded The Limited on his way out of Pittsburg on the

sixth of June Kelly told a reporter from *The Post-Gazette* that in his opinion there was no reason why a player should be hit by a pitched ball. He hadn't been hit by one all season. The reporter filed his story when he got back to the office.

"Tomorrow, the one, the only, the glittering gem of the Boston team, $10,000 Mike Kelly will catch for the All-American All-Stars against Anson's men in New York and return here on the evening train."

"Pretty big jump to play one game," Kelly told the reporter as he lounged against a pile of trunks, "but I am well paid for it. Honest John Kelly and I are opening up a saloon in New York next week or the one after and we need the funds to fit the place up."

"Will you play ball next season?"

"It depends on whether our little venture brings us wealth. If it does, Michael will sit in a comfortable chair, smoke cigars, and whistle Irish airs. If the thing fails, I presume you will find me doing the great act for Boston again. We're going to run a saloon and sporting headquarters and have twenty-eight rooms fitted up handsomely, a hotel on a small-scale."

"What would you be paid if you do play ball?"

Kelly chuckled and doffed his hat at a lady who was smiling at him and giving him the once over. "Billings told me it doesn't matter much whether they pay me a thousand or ten thousand, it will all be gone at the end of the year."

Things went South after that. Kelly was sick and it showed. At least he was doing better than Larry Corcoran. Mike had seen a piece in *The Sporting Life* about him. He'd been fined by the London Tecumsehs for drunkenness, then got into a fight with teammate Shorty Howe. He bit Howe's finger so hard the fingernail came off. Both players were released and Corcoran's baseball career was over. *The Sporting Life* noted, "Larry Corcoran has come to that dernier resort of decayed ball players - bar tending. He hands out drinks in a Newark saloon." George Gore wasn't a whole lot better off. He was being hissed every time he went to bat at the Polo Grounds.

On June 15 in Boston the Chicagos marched onto the field in white jersey suits and clawhammers galore.

"Get a load of those outfits," Sam Wise said to Kelly.

"They look too damn pretty to win a ball game," chuckled Mike.

He was right, the White Stockings managed just three hits off Clarkson. They poked their sticks at the ball gingerly as if they were afraid to hit it.

Kelly made a square meal of foul tips and played without a single miscue. After the Chicagos had opened with two runs Kelly's beautiful and timely three base-hit tied the score. He played with his usual animation and his running conversation with the patrons kept them in stitches.

On June 30 Kelly led the league in hits and total bases on clean hits. He ranked third in runs scored and trailed only Connors in AV. TB. with a .516 mark but he went without a hit against Buffinton and the Philadephias, who clubbed the Bostons 7-0. One of Kelly's fingers was broken in the preliminary practice but he insisted on playing anyway and he was in agonizing pain every time he swung the bat. He did smack one to deep center field in the sixth but Andrews sprinted for the ball and flagged it down. Kelly felt sorry for Johnston and Hornung, who spent the afternoon chasing the leather or watching balls soar over their heads. Only one ball came Kelly's way and Hornung ran in front of him and caught then dropped it.

Kelly picked up the ball and fired it into second base and then turned back to Johnston and said, "That muff there'll ruin your perfect record, Dick, you hadn't an error all season."

"I thought it'd hurt too much for you to catch it," explained Johnston.

"Well then, you won't mind cuttin' me steak for me tonight."

Johnston cocked his head to one side and gave him a curious look.

"I was just follin' with ya is all. I'm dinin' with a young lady tonight and she's mighty good with her hands."

The Beaneaters lost four games straight but took three of their

next four. Then the bottom fell out. They won just two of their next seventeen and fell to sixth place, a whopping sixteen games out of first. The four-balls rule had driven up averages across the League but it wasn't doing the Bostons much good.

Kelly was in his old position in right field on July 1 and went around in good shape, showing few effects of his charley horse. A gentleman in the reporters' gallery said Kel will no doubt get right down to playing seeing that he had bet on the wrong tip at the races last Saturday and got hit for a good round slice of American dough.

The Beaneaters were in Philadelpia. Early in the season they'd beaten the Phillies four straight times, but they were a lot stronger now. They'd shut the Beaneaters out in three of their last meetings and were hoping to knock the championship bee out of the Bostons' bonnet.

Casey and Clarkson were invincible and the score was 0-0 after seven innings but the visitors scored one in the top of the eighth. Kid Madden had bought a little brindle puppy for 15 cents at Gloucester on Sunday and the dog had immediately been christened the team's mascot. The players tied it to their bench and were delighted with him.

Fogarty, who'd been got out every time at the bat, kept glaring at the brindle. When the Phillies came off the field for their half of the eighth he went over to Trainer Tom Taylor and asked him for a knife. Then Fogarty snuck over to the Boston bench and cut the string holding the mascot. He chased the frightened puppy out the end of the pavilion. It came back but the charm had been broken. The Phillies scored twice and won the game.

A newspaper article the next day said, "The Bostons are one of the most superstitious sets of ball tossers in the land. They have implicit faith in hoodoos and mascots and Mike Kelly ascribes the club's ill-fortune to the fact that he did not bring his parrot on the trip.

After losing five of their first six games on the road at the end of June and the beginning of July the Beaneaters won their first two in Chicago on the 7th and the 9th. As usual, Kelly was staying at the

Palmer House. When he got back there was a note for him at the front desk. He recognized the flowing handwriting immediately and smiled. The note said:

> I've been reading the Sports page to see when you'd be
> back in town. My husband is in New York on business.
> I thought you might like to come by for a chat.

No one answered the door when Mike got to the Chalmers mansion. He tried the door and found it unlocked. He went inside and looked around.

"Felicity?" he called out.

"I'm in the library."

When Mike went to the library, he saw no one. Then he looked up. Felicity was on a ladder, apparently looking for a book on the top shelf. When he went over to the ladder and looked up at her shapely legs he was thrilled to see that she wore no underclothes.

As she descended toward him Mike unbuttoned his fly.

Felicity saw that he was ready, quite ready. She lowered herself and he grabbed the sides of the ladder and slowly entered her. She moaned. He pushed hard inside then pulled out. He pushed back inside and pulled out again.

"Stop teasing, you scoundrel," gasped Felicity. "You're driving me wild!"

THE
$10,000
BEAUTY

"The baseball business is a fickle one."

Morrill fined Kelly for keeping late hours and drunkenness after the July the Fourth double header in Indianapolis. Kelly pled guilty to staying out late but abjectly denied being intoxicated. It wasn't drink that kept Mike from playing when the Beaneaters went to Chicago, it was a sore finger. He was a spectator during the first game on Saturday and he wasn't seen until he came into the Leland on Monday. What he'd done and where he'd gone with friends wasn't known. When he found a note in his box informing him of the fine he wasn't that upset, he went to the races at the West Side Driving Park. That night he sat with the rest of the team in private boxes at Holey's and watched "The Corsair." Between acts he and some of the others went out for fresh air and suds.

Kelly didn't return to the hotel with his teammates. He and Ed Williamson and some others headed out for a late supper. He wasn't seen until 10'ocock the next morning. Morrill hadn't planned to use him that afternoon but Kelly donned a uniform and begged to go behind the bat, painful finger and all. Kelly's catching was about as bad as it could be. He had four passed balls and his conduct on the field was listless and nasty. The one time he reached base he made no attempt to steal second even though he had several opportunities. The Bostons lost 6-1.

A report on July 10 said, "Several members of the Boston team are drinking heavily and manager Morrill's bed has not been one of roses. Since last week at Indianapolis Mike Kelly has been guilty of breeches of discipline in staying out late and drinking. Morrill heard him coming in at 2 o'clock the other morning and fined him $25.

Kelly's conduct in Chicago has not been an improvement. Morrill intimated that Kelly would not be paid for time he has been enjoying himself when the club should be reaping the benefits of his services. Morrill is hurt that during the team's spell of weak hitting they are without their strongest batsman."

When the team got to Pittsburg Mike stayed behind to look after the luggage while the rest of the team headed to the park. After the team returned from an 8-6 loss Mike stood outside the hotel with Joe Hornung and Sam Wise.

"I intend to take the pledge tomorrow morning and not drink a drop of liquor for one year, boys. I have received an offer to go into business next year and I plan to accept. I have no desire to play under Morrill any longer."

In Boston, Soden told reporters who visited his office and found him busy signing checks, "Kelly may have taken unwarranted liberty in going off on a spree while his sore hand unfitted him for play but he is a fine fellow, a favorite throughout the land and an invaluable man to the Bostons. It would take a bigger check to buy Michael away from us than it took to secure his release from Chicago."

Things got worse in the Friday double header. The sixth place Alleghenys shut out the Beaneaters in both games. Kelly sat out the morning game and didn't get the ball out of the infield in the afternoon one. He took Brown's place in right field and made a miserable showing. He refused to try for a ball and folded his arms while Johnston covered his territory. Needless to say, Morrill didn't use Kelly on Saturday, or Monday, or Tuesday for that matter. Even though he led the team in runs, stolen bases, and batting percentage, it was the nadir of Mike's career.

The Bostons were in free fall. Losers of ten of their last eleven games, they arrived home on Thursday, July 26 to host the bottom dwelling Washingtons and lost 5-4. Their dormant bats finally awoke on Saturday and they overwhelmed the hapless Nationals 16-1 but then the Phillies came to town and dispatched the Beaneaters three straight, then the Giants did likewise. A lot of unkind things were

being said about Mike. It didn't matter to Kelly, who thought much of it was bosh. He believed there was only one thing worse than being talked about, and that was not being talked about.

At the beginning of August *The Chicago Tribune* sports editor wrote, "Kelly leads the Bostons in everything - base hits, doubles, runs, batting, stolen bases, and runners thrown out. And he could do it if his skin was full of imprisoned sunshine from now until December. Kelly is a ball-player and the ghouls who are gibbering at him should retire to the bone-yard."

On August 2 *The Globe* recounted Kelly's latest stunt.

"Boston came very near to losing Mike Kelly last night. Every time the club has visited Mike's old stamping grounds 'the only' has filled up with Chicago fluids and on the last Western trip he was off two days on a spree and as a result was fined two days' pay. Kelly fondly believed that the money he was fined would be remitted and great was his disappointment when the men were paid off and he found his little bundle $25 short.

He was full of wrath and gave expression to several impolite things. He declared that he was leaving the Boston club to its own fate; that he would shake the dust of the old town from his base ball sandals and go forth never to return.

He consulted the railway time-table and announced that at 11:30 in the evening he and Mrs. Kelly would depart for New York and then go to their home in Hyde Park. He packed up all of his belongings and made ready to depart. But the exercise of packing had worked off some of Michael J's bile and on sober second thought he concluded not to act rashly and decided to finish the season with the Beaneaters."

The Globe's William Sullivan was concerned about the clubs. Under the headline "Kelly Does Not Lose Two Days' Pay" he wrote, "What brought around the triumvir I do not know. I only know that they have set a premium on insubordination and completely overthrown all discipline in the team. How can this move be otherwise? Morrill was given full authority to run the nine as his judgment dictated. He did so and fined Kelly two days' pay which didn't go. The punishment of Hornung for insubordination goes, Kelly's don't. And yet we wonder why the nine don't win? At the beginning of the season almost every Boston player was given a liberal increase in salary. This seems to have swelled more than one head and has resulted in carelessness and indifference. Some of the men have had altogether too soft a snap.

The directors are considering the advisability of getting a manager. They have lost a great deal of confidence in Morrill and don't think he has been sufficiently energetic and firm. They have hired detectives to follow the players. Johnston has been drinking a great deal more than is good for him and has been enjoying himself more than is good for the team. He has been informed that he must stop or take the consequences. There is going to be discipline or else there will be mischief to pay."

The Triumvir took no action but the Beaneaters went on a tear anyway. They beat the Hoosiers, Wolverines, White Stockings and Phillies in two-game sets though it still left them 14 games behind the league-leading Giants.

On August 21 in Philadelphia, Kelly and the Phillies' rising star Ed Delahanty each made two hits and scored one run. In the sixth inning Tom Brown hit a slow roller to second. Charlie Bastian ran in, scooped it up, and fired the ball to Sid Farrar, the Philadelphias' captain. A broad stretch of daylight was visible between Brown and the bag when Farrar caught the ball.

"Not out," called Umpire Valentine.

The large crowd, which had been orderly in the main, let Valentine have it.

"The man was out, Valentine," yelled a leather-lunged man high in the stands. "You're the worst umpire in the game."

In the seventh, Ed Delahanty lined a ball directly over the first base bag good for one base at the very least. He was half-way to first when Umpire Valentine yelled, "Foul ball."

Delahanty trudged back to the plate, gave Valentine a dirty look, and picked up his big bat. "'Twas fair and you know it," said the brawny young Irishman.

"Get back in there and bat, busher," barked Valentine.

Fifty or more cranks yelled at him.

Frustrated, Delahanty struck out, but the ball skipped between Pop Tate's legs and Delahanty threw his bat away and took off for first. He beat Tate's throw but Valentine called "Out."

Now there was a perfect tempest in the stands. *The Times* reported that, "All of the 4,000 people in the stands stood up on their hind legs and howled their disapproval. Many of the spectators displayed a painful lack of breeding. One gray-haired base ball enthusiast stood up in his private box and yelled, 'You're a robber, Valentine, a rotten thief.' Bedlam broke loose and even pretty mouths hissed at the obnoxious umpire.

'It's a bare-faced theft,' said a well-known booster. 'Valentine should be run out of town.'

'I never in my life saw a game in which the umpire willfully gave one club the best of it on purpose until to-day,' declared the financial editor of a daily paper."

When Kelly came in from the field at the end of the inning he stopped at the water cooler. He filled the cup with ice water and turned to Harry Wright, who as usual wore a dark suit and a black top hat.

"You have a lot uv fanatical boosters in this town, Harry."

"Don't I know it," said Wright.

"You don't want to get on their bad side, that's for sure."

"Are you gonna pull any of your monkey shines to-day, Kelly?" called a crank in a sack suit.

"Wouldn't think uv it," said Mike.

"Well that would be a first, you following the rules for an entire ball game," answered back the rooter.

Mike went to answer back and decided against it. He turned his cup upside down and fired it the length of the bench.

As he crossed the plate with the winning run in the ninth Kelly looked up at the man. The man shook his head in disgust and tore up his score-card.

James McCormick's wife Jennie had been ill with consumption. She passed away in her sleep that night. When Cap Anson heard the news his stern and rigid mind became at once sympathetic in the extreme. He remarked, "That is the greatest loss poor Mac could suffer. God only knows what I would do were I to lose *my* wife."

Kelly left his Boston teammates and went to Paterson to console his old friend. Kelly had a local florist make a tremendous floral wreath and then served as a pallbearer at the funeral. McCormick was left to raise his son James and his daughter Francis on his own.

On August 23 the Boston team arrived in Washington after their ride on the Philadelphia Express train that had started running in June. Winners of nine straight they felt confident of another. There was little of note in the first five innings but Kelly put some life into the affair when he led off the sixth with a safe hit and stole second. Two hands were out when Morrill drove one out of Swampdoodle Grounds for a home run. Kelly led off the eighth with another hit, this one longer than Morrill's or any other home run hit at the park. He was on base in the ninth with the winning run when Billy Nash struck out on an inshoot that caught the handle of his bat. The winning streak was over.

The Beaneaters had already tried and sacked three second basemen, two of whom couldn't hit and one who'd fractured his skull falling off a tram so they signed Joe Quinn. He'd had an interesting career. In 1881, he'd played alongside Hoss Radbourn and Charlie Comiskey in the Dubuque Rabbits. He'd been on Henry Lucas' Union Association champions then worked as an apprentice to an undertaker in the Kerry Patch slum. In '88 Quinn signed with Des Moines of the Western Association to play second base for the Prohibitionists. The club didn't want to let him go but when they ran into

financial trouble they reluctantly let him go over to the Beaneaters. Kelly took to Joe immediately and took the teetotaler under his wing, guiding him through the minefield of life in the spotlight. Mike loved listening to him talk, Quinn was from Australia. Everyone thought Kelly and Quinn were base ball's most improbable pairing.

An August 24th 'Special Telegram' from Washington to *The Inter-Ocean* said: "the bean-eaters captured the game after a hard struggle. The visitors from Washington made it close but took their soap with the same old ladle. The 'Senators' tied the score in the fifth and again in the seventh but stupid base-running and two yellow decisions prevented them from forging ahead". Kelly settled matters in the eighth by landing the ball over the fence. The ball struck a telegraph wire then bounded out of sight. After the game Kel grinned and said, "That pitch hit the apple of the plate's eye."

Kelly had been feeling rough for a few days and on Friday he told Morrill he was too sick to play the next day. Morrill thought him well enough to play and put his name on the score-card but Kel didn't appear. When Morrill got back to Willard's Hotel he went straight to Mike's room and told him he was being fined $100 for insubordination.

Kelly left for New York that night to be sure he would be there in time for Monday's game. The rest of the team was taking an afternoon train the next afternoon. Tim Murnane wrote, "Kelly feels bad about the $100 fine that Morrill has put on him for not showing up at the grounds. He told your correspondent before he left, 'I suppose the Boston papers will jump on me. I went to Morrill at two o'clock and told him I felt sick and was going right to bed. He said he couldn't excuse me. I told him fair and square that I was going to bed and I did and remained there until seven this evening. I wouldn't have cared about the $100 fine if Morrill had kept it between us instead of telling all the reporters and embarrassing me to the other players."

Kelly's catching was extra fine in New York on August 28. It was the first game he'd played since Morrill's fine and he jumped right in and played for all he was worth. The Giants didn't care to run the

bases after he nailed Slattery, their fastest man, in the second inning. They didn't score a single run on Clarkson, whose proud wife and parents sat in the grand-stand. They were delighted when he crossed the plate with the only run he needed. The Beaneaters won all three games in New York but they were still a mile behind the Giants.

Mike looked through the New York Sun's Entertainment page the next morning to find something to do on his last night in town and was delighted to see that Lilly Clay's Colossal Gaiety Company was performing "The Beauty in Dreamland" at the Palmer Theater. The announcement noted that the company had been booked to play at the Union Square Theatre but it had burned to the ground.

The company promised a night of bawdy burlesque and "a coterie of charming and cultured English and American Lady Artists" and said the show would consist of Lady Comedians, Lady Vocalists, Lady Instrumental Soloists, Lady Musical Directors, Lady Ticket Sellers, Lady Doorkeepers, and Lady Ushers."

Mike was quite impressed with the show's stars, Emma Warde and Hilda La Porte but he didn't visit their dressing-rooms after the show. He'd been invited to the home shared by Hattie and Fannie, two of the lady ticket sellers. After the three had downed a bottle of fair-to-middling whiskey the 'ladies', who'd soon prove to be nothing of the sort, invited Kel to join them "in the boudoir." They took off everything but their shoes, then playfully undressed Mike.

"That's a lot of manhood for just one man," said Hattie when Mike was fully erect.

"Most certainly enough for two *women*," giggled Fannie.

"Let's find out," said Hattie.

She put Mike's mustache between her breasts while Fannie focused on his lower region, then they switched. Then Fannie guided Kelly's swollen member into Hattie's willing derriere. He didn't last long but they made sure he was ready to get back to business in short order.

As usual, General Dixwell was in Box #11 just behind the tele-

graph operators for the first game of a seven-game home stand on August 30. Dixwell had been despondent when his pets had dropped ten of eleven games in late July and early August to fall seventeen games out of first place but he was as chipper as a youngster with a new pair of Christmas skates when they followed that up with their 15-1 stretch. Kelly's good friend Nat Goodwin sat with Director Conant. Nat wore a white yacht suit with fine blue stripes and a shining buff shirt and waved his cane frantically whenever the New Yorks muffed one or Mike did something great. Treasurer Billings sat a few rows back as usual - a safe distance from foul balls.

Kelly's batting was splendid and he made some pretty throws to second base. With two out and Brown on base in the first Kelly smacked the shiny new ball hard, leaving a dent between OFFICIAL LEAGUE BALL and A.G. SPALDING & BROS. It rose high in the air and went booming out over O'Rourke's head. The New York left fielder got under the ball, juggled it a few seconds, then clumsily kicked it away when it dropped at his feet. Brown scored and Kelly tore around the bases, stirring up a cloud of dirt when he slid safe into third. He smiled as he brushed the dirt from the BOSTON letters on his chest and heard General Dixwell yell "Hi! Hi" over the cacophony from the stands. Nash sent one whistling between third and short and Kelly caused another roar from the crowd when he made it home. Then he went and sat on the bench and the giddy spectators hooted and howled until he got up, turned to the stands and raised his cap.

Johnston was the first to bat in the third. The fifth bad ball went close to his head and Dick ducked. The ball hit his bat and dribbled in front of the plate. Umpire Valentine gave him his base and after a delay while Ewing did his usual kick Brown bunted a slow one that Ward sent to first before Brown could arrive there. Quinn followed with a two-baser into the crowd and came home on Kelly's second long hit to left.

Kelly snuck a peek out to left field when he went to the bat in the fifth and saw that O'Rourke had moved back to shadow of the fence. Mike dropped one well in front of him, then stole second and

went to third on Ewing's slow fielding and poor throw to Richardson. Nash got his base on balls and then a signal from Kelly to go. He took off for second. Ewing looked Mike back to third then threw to second. This throw was worse than the last and as the ball headed out to O'Rourke Kelly sprinted home with another run. Nat Goodwin and General Dixwell left arm-in-arm together with matching grins a mile wide after the Bostons' narrow 3-2 win.

After making only seven hits in fifteen games Kelly had thirty in his last eighteen and was fast assuming his place among the leading batsmen. On the fifth of September he was "the star of the game" making four hits, stealing three bases, and scoring four runs to lead the Beaneaters to a four-game sweep of the Nationals. Tug Arundel got coltish around second base in the third inning and Mike threw him out. He threw out Dummy Hoy an inning later and there wasn't much stealing after that. Kelly's play was of the kind that cemented his reputation.

"Kelly's the prince of them all when he's out for the corn," an old codger who'd been coming to games since Spalding had been the Bostons' ace told his grandson.

Surprising news came from Detroit as to the goings-on of Honest John Kelly. "Umpire John Kelly has been on an extended spree here and night after night has been seen on the streets in a beastly state of intoxication. His umpiring in consequence has been outrageous-ly poor. Yesterday, as the result of a tear the night previous, he was unable to appear at the grounds to officiate. Then, in company with a Detroit tough, Kelly went out on a painting expedition, assaulted a woman, and is now in the Police Station on a charge of assault and battery preferred by the woman in question."

'Jasper' wrote the following piece on October 13. "Today will wit-ness the final appearances on the ball field of two of the brightest stars of the base ball world. Michael J. Kelly will play for the last time and John Kelly, regarded as the best umpire in the game, will umpire his last game of ball for the season if not for all time. The secret of the withdrawal from the base ball field of the two Kellys can be easily

told. They are going into business partnership and expect to do so well that neither will have the slightest use for base ball in the future.

During a series in Chicago Michael and John had a series of discussions about the future. John pointed out the advantage of living in New York, each would be closer to his home and family.

The umpire told the player, 'Mike, this business will not last forever. We will be getting older and will be pushed aside by younger men. The base ball business is a fickle one. Suppose you fall down and fracture a leg in the game tomorrow. The scheme is to get out while you're still a favorite and you can cash in on your big name in business. Let us strike while the iron is hot and success will surely follow us.' Mike thought over John's suggestion. As the Beaneaters were warming up the next day Mike told John, 'Go ahead, if you secure the proper sort of place I am with you.'

A few weeks ago the umpire selected a location at the corner of Thirty-first street and Sixth avenue. For two weeks it has been undergoing extensive renovations. The place has close to 30 rooms and will be run in the style of Clarke's Hotel on Washington street in this city.

What Michael Kelly has done for the game will be told later by some historian. They will tell that he was the first catcher to instruct his pitcher with signs and the first to back up first base. He has done a thousand things of which space will not permit the telling here. 'The Two Kells' will be the inscription over the door. May their shadows never grow smaller."

Kelly was broke by November and it would be some time before he'd see any money from 'The Two Kells." He met Billings for dinner at Clark's where he signed a contract for the '89 season and got an advance check for $2,000. Kelly looked at the check, patted his prominent belly, and told Billings, "I want to play every game next season ... to keep the fat off. I worked all I knew how last spring to get the club in good position. Then when I got hurt and couldn't play and I was fined for laying off. That was no way to encourage a player and I admit I never really put my heart into my work after that. On two occasions when the crowd got on me on the home grounds my

hands were in the worst possible condition and yet I remained in the games when I would have given considerable to be out and nursing them." As usual, Billings believed most of what Kelly said.

"Put the fork to O'Rourke."

In January, Kelly appeared in "A Tin Soldier" at the Fourteenth Street Theater in New York. A theater critic stated that "some evidence of his popularity may be gathered by the fact that the galleries of the house every evening last week looked like the grand-stand at the Polo Grounds on the occasion of a particularly notable game of ball. Yet the $10,000 ball tosser is by no means happy. He is on the stage only a few minutes and has but a half-dozen lines to speak but says he has a brilliantly colored case of stage fright."

After one of his performances Mike had a late supper with George Gore, who'd come to see the show, and told him about his experience in the theater.

"When I made my entrance the first night I was made up so tough me own mother wouldn't have known me. For an instant the audience didn't recognize me. I started in to speak my lines when suddenly I heard a noise as though the roof was falling in. I'd been recognized and the people in the front began to shake the house down. Of course the lines were knocked clean out of me head. I'd have been done for had Mrs. McKee not thrown the lines to me and saved me life. People who've seen me on the ball-field never suspected that I caught those lines a lot more eagerly than I ever caught line hit balls.

I've lost fifteen pounds and been perspiring like a fountain pen ever since my first appearance. If Frank McKee would come in and say we don't require your services after to-night I'd go away through that back door so quick he'd think I was spirited away."

Two weeks later came word that Kelly had given up liquor drink-

ing. He told a reporter who'd offered to buy him a drink, "Imbibe? No, sir, none for me. I am done with the booze … other than to sell it to the patrons of my saloon. I'm in training for the coming season's work. I run several miles through Central Park every morning and am feeling in fine form." He grabbed his belly. "Of course I still need to get rid of this."

"I found something out the other day," said the reporter. "Since the day the Triumvir paid $10,000 for your release from the Chicagos they've carried a $10,000 policy on your life."

Mike whistled. "Then I'd better not run in the park *at night*?"

John L. Sullivan went on a rampage and quarreled with Jerry Dunn at The Two Kells. Sullivan had already quarreled with another man who was going to stab him. Kelly managed to separate them but Dunn drew a revolver and threatened to shoot the Boston brawler dead if he hit him. Kelly told the man to leave or he'd call the police.

Kelly had a bad attack of the grippe and went to Florida to shake it. When he returned he went to the Polo Grounds where the New Yorks were practicing. George Dickson, a sports reporter, was surprised to see him in an unbecoming coat of foreign make though he saw that he had the familiar diamond in his cravat.

Dickson was talking to George Gore, who looked to have thrown back a few. Dasher Troy had the refreshment privilege at the Polo Grounds. He ran a bar under the grand-stand and another in the rear of the men's stand. Gore had clearly been indulging at one of them.

"You know, George," said Dickson, "Kelly can entertain a fellow better with stories of his experiences than anyone I know. Actually, you appear in several of them, though I could never share the details with my readers."

"It's hard for some people to make Kelly out," said Gore. "He's a mental jack-a-napes. Mike's blunt in his speech, but often he's in a kidding spurt and all he says doesn't go."

Dickson chuckled. "Kelly has considerable conceit but it's all par-

donable and oftentimes downright laughable. He can say more funny things in an hour than anyone else in base ball."

Kelly went to a vaudeville show that night with Nat Goodwin. The
third act was a magician named the Famous Keller.

"Never heard uv him," said Kelly.

Keller asked for a volunteer to come up on stage.

"Why don't you go?" suggested Goodwin.

Kelly laughed at the idea that the slight-of-hand man could do
anything with him. "*Me*? I don't put any stock in magic."

A man in front of them overheard him. He turned and said, "Say,
you're Mike Kelly. I'm sure Keller would love it if someone famous
like you went up."

Other people around them had heard.

"It's King Kelly!" shouted one.

"Where?"

"There."

"*Kelly, Kelly,*" people began to chant.

"You've no choice *now* I suppose," said Goodwin.

Kelly shrugged his shoulders and went up on the stage.

"I would like you to go inside this," said Keller, indicating a cabinet the size of a closet.

Kelly looked at the audience, shrugged again, smiled awkwardly,
and stepped inside.

He emerged a minute later. His coat was turned inside out and his
hat was on backwards. A sign hung from his neck that read, "MIKE
KELLY KING OF THE DIAMOND."

Kelly wore a stunned look on his face.

The audience laughed, then broke into applause. Keller bowed.

"I'm a true believer in spiritualism now," Kelly told the audience.

They laughed and applauded again.

Kelly, who was twenty pounds over his usual playing weight, was scheduled to be one of the big attractions at the Elks' benefit at the Boston Theatre the second week of March. He was to recite "Casey at the Bat" but decided to go with a Philadelphia combination to Jacksonville instead. Questioned about his decision, Mike said, "I want to go South to get in condition and show those friends of mine down East that I'm still in the game notwithstanding that I've drawn $2,200 of my next season's salary already."

The reporter went back to his office and wrote, "The more money Michael receives the more he gets to spend and the higher he flies. When he came here from Chicago he was willing to hustle for his side, but he soon lost heart when he found he was almost alone in the 'get up and get' style he had practiced for years alongside Anson, Burns, Williamson, and Pfeffer, and from then out played good ball only in streaks."

Director Conant was asked about the controversy over who would captain the Bostons in '89. "Why don't you boom Kelly a little," he asked the reporter. "He isn't a bad fellow and I would like to see him have another fair trial. He has made some enemies by stuffing some of the newspaper men but he's a good fellow at heart."

Asked to compare Morrill with Anson, Kelly said, "Say, I was taking some chances when I was with the Champs but you never heard of Old Ans putting up a few dollars fine on me, did you? Do you know it has cost me $200 in extra traveling expenses since I joined the Bostons? Why Morrill's always looking up some cheap hash foundry and most of the boys are dead sick on him for it. Last year we often struck towns on a Sunday morning when people were coming from church and were loaded in a horse-car with traveling bags big enough to put a ton of coal in just to save a couple of dollars for a club that was making $400,000. In New York we were always put up in the tenth story in danger of our lives if there was ever a fire. When we traveled under Old Ans every man had a lower berth on the train."

The Beaneaters played an exhibition game in Baltimore on April

15th. *The Baltimore Evening News* said, "Mike Kelly has a new silk hat which he is flashing around the streets of Baltimore. He has induced an epidemic of heart flutters among the pretty Oriole girls."

The Boston directors had opened the vault again. They'd lassoed catcher Charlie Bennett, infielder Hardy Richardson, and Dan Brouthers from the cash-starved Wolverines. The acquisition of Bennett would allow Kelly to avoid catching as often and go back to the outfield where he could play almost every game. Brouthers provided a monster upgrade over John Morrill at first base. After leading the league in strikeouts with an incredible 86 in 1887 and batting .198 in between quarrels with Kelly in '88, Morrill had been shipped off to Washington.

Kelly would take over as the Bostons' captain but it remained to be seen what he would do as a subordinate of Manager Hart. It was thought that "the saloon influence" had ruined him but in Philadelphia on April 23 he guarded the bases well and his two passed balls did not affect the result, a 3-1 win for the Bostons. He hit a vicious liner at Sid Farrar who dropped it like a hot potato and then tried to blow the sting from his hands.

The Boston Herald ran a piece about the The Two Kells the next morning. "Mike Kelly's New York saloon comes under the heading of all-night resorts which only pay as long as the police are disposed to look the other way. During the winter it has been the sanctuary of sporting men, actors, rounders, and the gang of non-producers who live in the shadow of the man who spends his money freely. The air breathed in such a place is not calculated to clear the lungs and harden the muscles of a ball player and the surroundings are not exactly such as cluster round the man who is appointed to maintain discipline in a ball team. Kelly has the most undesirable following of any field captain in the business."

The Bostons opened the '89 season by splitting their games in New York and Philadelphia but they came to life in Washington sweeping the three-game series in the nation's capital. Kelly had three hits and scored three runs in the last game, a 23-3 cakewalk in which Rad-

bourn made monkeys of the Nationals without exerting himself in the least. The team left at 7 a.m. the next morning for Trenton, where they would cross bats with the Cuban Giants. They expected a good stiff game from the dusky fellows. The Giants put up a good fight but the Bostons triumphed 5-2.

In the Beaneaters' first home game of the season Kelly made a neat catch of a long fly up against the fence in the first inning. With Brown on base in the sixth Mike squared himself for a little batting and ripped one that whizzed through Connor's legs. The ball rolled into the outfield and Kelly raced around the bases for a home run as the boosters on the bleaching-boards "volleyed and thundered." Mike was glad he'd worked as hard as he had to shed his superfluous flesh.

The Bostons swept a four-game series from Pittsburg to move themselves into first place. In their game against the Cleveland men on Friday, May 17 the Spiders, who got their nickname from the web design of their tunics, loaded the bases in the third inning but McKean popped a short fly for Nash and the baby's cake was all dough. Kelly singled his first time at the bat, opened the fifth with a double to left, and put in his third hit of the 14-4 win in the ninth.

The work Kelly did at the bat in the Bostons' 5-3 win over the Hosiers on May 25 was the hallmark of the game. Each of his hits, two doubles and two singles, came when he was leading off an inning. Murnane considered each of them "a gold karat put in according to the most graceful code." The Beaneaters swept a four-game series from the White Stockings to take a 3½ game lead over the surprising Philadelphias.

In an exhibition game in Worcester on the last day of May, Cudworth got his base on balls in the second but was thrown out trying to steal by Kelly, who was in his glory. He completely captivated the Worcester spectators who were delighted to see a League game after seven years of minor league ball. They howled in delight equally when he struck out or made a clever play.

"He's still as handsome as he was in '82," a woman in a box seat

nearby whispered to her friend in hopes her husband wouldn't hear.

"Didn't you step out with him a time or two when the Chicagos came here, Gertrude?"

"Shhh! Stanley can't know I spent time with a man like Mike Kelly."

"Do you often think of him?"

Gertrude sighed. "I'm afraid I do, Phyllis. A man like him is hard to forget."

There was a roar the next inning when Kelly threw out Meister when he tried to steal second. Two innings later a Worcester batter scraped the ball in front of the plate. It plowed a furrow in the hard clay and Kelly dug it out of the hole with his hands and threw the man out at first.

Johnston struck for two bases in the eighth and came home on Kelly's hit, which the right fielder fumbled, allowing Kelly to run to second without a throw. He drew a throw when he made a wild attempt to steal third and got caught between the bases. The crowd roared their approval anyway.

On June 7 Kelly's publisher released a second edition of "Play Ball." He wouldn't have much chance to promote the book, the Beaneaters didn't have a single open date until the close of the season.

Keefe was at his best on June 11 and pitched his finest game of the year. His work saved the day for the New Yorks who played poorly. If the Boston club had had even ordinary luck they would have made a dozen or more runs. Kelly played with his usual dash and tried to get his boys in winning form but without base hits they could do little.

"Drive their man Keefe up on a reef," he called to his men when they went to bat in the first. "Let's be Ewing's undoing. Put the sword to Ward. Put the fork to O'Rourke."

His remarks caused no small amount of amusement.

When Hardy Richardson popped up to Roger Connor in the fifth Kelly turned to the grand-stand and yelled, "Is anyone up there any good with the old Hickory?"

When Whitney made a fine catch of Dick Johnson's hard grounder on the third base line in the seventh he yelled, "Art, could you not let a couple uv those get by? I'll have a word with the scorer and make sure they aren't errors."

When Keefe struck out Dan Brouthers in the eighth Mike yelled, "Sir Timothy, it looks as though you could use a shave and a haircut. I know just the place, they've got a chair for you now if you hurry."

On June 13 Morrill sent up a heaven-kissing fly that finally thudded into the dark recesses of Kelly's big new glove. He'd missed an easy one the previous inning. After the 7-1 victory in which he'd gone hitless he told Manager Hart, "If I'd missed that fly that Morrill sent out to me I'd uv had to sneak out through the right field gate."

The Globe believed that: "Ladies are growing more interested in the game every day. This is as it should be. Their presence in the grand-stand lends a charm to the surroundings and the men on the field play better ball to impress them. Many of the fair ones score the games and talk intelligently on the points of play."

Several barrelfuls of sawdust were scattered around the home plate before the morning game of the June 17th double header. Kelly laughed every time the Senators' captain Arthur Irwin yelled at Dummy Hoy to do something. The whole crowd laughed when he ran right up to Hoy and yelled even louder what he wanted of him.

Kelly got his base on balls in the first inning and went to second on Brouthers' one-baser. Richardson cracked a beauty sending them both home.

The Senators scored three in the fourth to take a one-run lead but the Bostons had a chance to tie things up in the seventh. Brown reached first and could have stolen second but Johnston ignored Kelly's signal to take a couple of pitches so Brown could go. He swung at the first ball and grounded into a double play.

"Sorry, Kel, that was stupid of me," said Johnston.

"Don't beat yerself up about it, Dick," said Mike. "Just don't do it again."

On June 19 Kelly accepted five chances in right field that in Tom Fullwood's consideration were "simply perfection"; three of them were made after hard runs. He got his base on balls in the third and made "a beautiful steal" of second. Brouthers hit one safe then Richardson sent one to the pitcher and while the ball was going to first and back home Kelly scored by a fine slide. He corked a double his next chance but expired there when big Dan was a victim of Smith at first. The Beaneaters' three runs in each of the first and third innings were all they needed, Clarkson held the Pittsburgs to just one.

In Indianapolis on the 21st the Beaneaters, who held a five and a half game lead over Cleveland, sent Clarkson to the mound even though his arm was lame and he could throw nothing but slow balls. It almost worked. Kelly was given his base in the first, stole second in great style, and scored on a passed ball and Brouthers' run-out. Kelly singled his next time at bat, stole second again and scored on Richardson's two-bagger up against the right field fence.

Con Daily hit one to right in the seventh. Kelly, who'd make a fine step-ladder catch of a liner the inning before, raced in to gather it and threw him out at first. Daily was shocked, he was as sure as he was born he'd hit safe. When Kelly batted to Bassett in the bottom of the inning it was his turn to be called out at first on a close play. He kicked and the crowd guyed him.

There was some anxiety before the July 4 double header in Cleveland for fear that Clarkson would not be able to play. He'd gone through a painful operation to remove a coal cinder from his eye. The crowd of 5,659 was the largest that ever attended a game in the Forest City and the seating capacity was intended for half that number. The spectators lined around the field ten deep and some were right behind the umpire. The players couldn't use their bench as the crowd was roped in ten feet in front of it. The size of the turnout seemed to make the home players nervous, they managed just three safe hits, while it braced up the first-place visitors. The first game started at 10:10 and was a whitewash after five innings.

At 1 o'clock the Boston team went out and "gave an open-air matinee full of 'old gold' ball." O'Brien was in the box for the Spiders and

Boston found him a cake full of raisins. The fifth was the inning that did the business. 'Rad' tossed the ball up and it looked as big as a sunflower to the babies and how those kids did nurse the dew drops. The Boston men who howled at the morning game were shamed out of their boots." Kelly made three hits and scored twice in the hour and forty-minute 11-7 Cleveland win.

The Beaneaters got back home on July 7. After the promising start to their trip, a sweep in Pittsburg, they 'd won just three of their last dozen games on the road and they'd fallen out of first place. Soden asserted that certain of the men looked as though they had been imbibing. Director Conant chose not to believe him and Hart told the directors that not a single man was drinking on the Western trip.

Kelly was given a cordial greeting by the South End Grounds crowd of 6,084. Many of them had come to see the Clevelands, who'd overtaken their club.

"What curious shirts they wear," a woman in a hat adorned with ribbons, flowers, and feathers remarked. "It looks as though their veins are sticking out for Heaven's sake."

"They're a rather light-bodied lot," said her husband, "but I hear they are wonderful fielders."

"The one that looks like an Indian is about the only *big* fellow in the nine," said a young man in a split braid straw boater. "They say McAleer's the *liveliest* spider in the web."

The admirers of the home team anxiously watched every movement by Kelly to see if he'd grown slower since the last time they'd seen him.

"He looked fine to *me* the last time we came," Annie Clarke, an ardent Boston booster who wore a navy blue cap edged with a pink lace scalloped border, told her father.

Everyone was thrilled when Kelly pasted one through the infielders as if they were made of tissue paper but they groaned when he was thrown out trying to steal. The throw that nailed him was not a particularly swift one.

The Bostons scored all their runs in the second inning and coasted to a 6-1 win that put them back into the lead.

An east wind made a light overcoat a must the next day. The youngsters from Cleveland had their ace Cinders O'Brien in the box. He hadn't exactly been a puzzle to the Bostons thus far and he was quite wild on this occasion. The home team did a little duffing. Joe Quinn couldn't have picked up a $10 gold piece if it was offered to him on a silver salver. Kelly was rather lethargic. He couldn't hit the ball out of the infield and his throwing from behind the bat was "a strange and curious thing."

A small boy in a newspaper cap ran off with a foul ball but a big cop captured the boy *and* the ball.

"It appears they haven't *all* got flat feet," chuckled Kelly.

Ganzel had three of the Bostons' fourteen hits in an easy 15-5 win.

Kelly had just his second hit of the series the next day and his club fell to the Spiders 5-3.

John Drohan thoroughly enjoyed the tilt with the Alleghenys on July 12. He wrote, "All the boys had on their clean clothes and they played good ball. The day was ideal for outdoor sports, the mackerel sky being the players' favorite. The real pleasure of the day was the brace taken by Johnston and Kelly. They seemed like new men and livened up the entire multitude. Umpire Curry did not appear so Weeden was fished out of the stands and came up behind the bat in his usual voice, low and sweetly suggestive of the cooing of doves. The crowd was unusually small but if the boys keep playing as they did today there will be no fear of empty chairs. If you wish to see how things look from a balloon take a seat at the top of the grand-stand, it will take you some time to get used to it but every word spoken by the players can be heard just as clearly as from the press-box."

When Kelly walked up to the plate in the first inning a lady in the grand-stand wearing a blaring red shawl mistook his sliding pads for bunches of muscle and said, "What remarkably muscular thighs."

He got second base when Fields misjudged his short fly to left field

the next day. His steal of third was a thing of beauty. The Boston's 6-4 triumph ran their record against the Pittsbugs to 10-0. Kelly told Bill Conant it was too bad the Beaneaters had to play other clubs too.

On July 14, Bastille Day coincidentally, the players voted on a secret manifesto. John Ward, the president of the Players Brotherhood, told a group of astonished reporters, "We have determined to play next season under different management."

Kel was in stitches the next morning when he read the account of the Chicagos' loss in New York while getting his shave. The barber had to keep asking him to sit still. "Listen to this," he told him. "Anson's hop-skip-and-jumpers were crushed to earth today by two girls. They were young, pretty, and vivacious. They sat just back of the Chicago players' bench and the way they hoodooed the lavender-clad men was a caution. One glance into their captivating eyes was sufficient. The victimized player would stagger to the plate and all he could discern of the ball Mickey Welch shot across the turkey was a blue-eyed streak or a black-eyed inshoot.

There were brunette fly balls and red-haired grounders and all during the game the girls sat looking like two Galateas done up in ice cream. Poor Fred Pfeffer was especially hoodooed, he couldn't hit within a foot of the ball. Even Papa Anson felt the witchery. His best effort was a long hazel-eyed fly which fell into Gore's hands. With the girls' help, Welch put up a great game and afterwards told the young ladies he would gladly pay their way into the game the next time he pitched against the Chicagos."

Heavy thunder at noon kept a lot of rooters away from the July 17 double header. Radbourn was considered the greatest twirler on earth with a moist ball and it was a pleasure to see the old master between the points. Brown came home on Kelly's safe hit past Denny in the third inning. Murnane enjoyed Kelly's next stunt. "Mike stole second and pulled the bag off the corner and tobogganed with it several feet past its original location. The merriment was not lessened when Kel crawled upon the bag and sunned himself like a frog on a lily pad then meandered back to the second corner with the base under his arm.

Kelly was as lively as a cat on the bases. He has a tantalizing way of standing with his foot close to a base but not on it till the baseman thinks he can catch him napping.

The game was getting too one-sided to be interesting when Jerry Denny calmly and with malice aforethought lambasted one of Rad's twisters over the railroad tracks and two men trotted in before him.

The Hoosiers had to leave early so the first game was stopped at the end of the sixth. Kel sailed the ball over the fence to label himself for an uninterrupted passage around the bases in the fourth inning of the late game. General Dixwell thought he was in Box 13 in Pittsburg and let out a 'Hi! Hi!' that made Kelly prick up his ears as he flew around the bases."

After the game Dixwell invited Kelly to a garden party at his home on Lime street in the suburb of Beacon Hill. When Mike arrived the general was talking with some friends from the Boston Bowling Club, of which he was the president. When one of them called him Arthur, Kel was confused for a second until he realized that General was of course not his host's actual name. As Mike looked around the room he saw that everyone was dressed in accordance with the Boston Braham dress code he'd heard talked about at the Elks Club. Mike felt a little uncomfortable and was a bit surprised Dixwell had invited him, the Brahmins had no love for the Irish immigrants who'd arrived on famine ships.

John Lowell Gardner Jr. was the first person Kelly recognized. He'd seen a photograph of him addressing a board meeting in the newspaper. It was a rarity. According to the Brahmin code, you must only be mentioned in the newspaper when you are born, marry, and die.

Gardner, who liked people to call him Jack, had abandoned his wife Isabella and was talking with some other men about his business endeavors, his prodigious art collection, and his philanthropic pursuits.

The men next to Gardner's group were all members of the Somerset Club. They were talking about the fascinating demonstration

of Philip W. Pratt's 6-cell electric automobile that had taken place at Winthrop Square.

Mike walked by another group and heard one of the men tell the portly gentleman beside him that his son's marks had tumbled because he was too busy staging a play with other members of Harvard's Hasty Pudding Club. The other man said, "Harvard's prime function is not educational, my good man, it is to serve as a vestibule through which young men enter society."

Some bejeweled women were talking about what the Cabots, Coolidges, Lodges, Parkmans, and Perkins were doing. Jack Gardner's wife Isabella was in the middle of a cluster of older women. Mike overheard her tell them, "It is a rather curious thing that the mind cure craze has captivated the Boston fancy so. Apparently when a patient visits the mind curer, a Christian scientist, she sits in a comfortable chair and is requested to think of nothing at all while the operator sitting opposite puts her vigorous mind to work for half an hour …"

Kelly was suddenly aware of a woman he hadn't noticed, a young one. He certainly noticed her now. Her dress was an ivory confection with point lace and pale green and ivory satin ribbons cunningly formed into a garden of roses across the fitted bodice and down the back of the trailing skirt. She had spectacular shimmering eyes, perfect cheekbones, and a radiant complexion.

Mike hated to tear the General away from his friends but he simply had to get Dixwell to introduce him to the girl.

"Josephine, I should like to introduce you to the man that is usually most responsible when my beloved Beaneaters win a game of base ball. This is Michael J. Kelly."

"Mike, this is Josephine Henderson. She has just completed her studies at Bowdoin Finishing School, where I understand she place first in her class."

Josephine shook Mike's hand and said, "We've never met but I feel as though I've seen you before. Downtown I believe."

"Were you watching a street-car go by?" asked the General.

"I believe I ... Wait, your picture was on the side."

"His handsome visage is on a great many of the city's street-cars. The Boston club paid Mr. Kelly a king's ransom to use his image in advertisements."

"How clever of them."

"What are you plannin' ta do now that you're done with school, Josephine?" asked Kelly.

"Well I shall certainly not do what my parents wish me to."

"What's that?"

"Marry a boy from one of the finest families on town."

"So what *will* you do?"

"I am heading off to Austria to study music and art. But before I do, I should enjoy learning a bit about our national pastime. I've never been to a game." She looked Mike up and down. "But I believe I would enjoy seeing *you* play." She turned to Dixell. "Do you think you could arrange it?"

"Why of course, Josephine. You can join me in my private box. I'll explain the rules and point out when Michael bends them."

Josephine went to the game the next day and she had dinner with Kel that night. Of course she didn't tell her parents.

Tim Murnane wore a new suit to the game on July 20. He wrote that: "Gumbert pitched for Chicago. His delivery was easy and the ball he sent up for the Bostons looked as big as a toy balloon and as full of good nature as the boss lady at a strawberry festival. The Beaneaters managed nine hits but could send not one man across the plate.

Kelly should have been declared safe in the first inning at the initial bag. He did a good bit of sprinting and reached there a trifle ahead of the ball but Powers said 'Out'. A howl of disappointment came from the bleaching-boards. A plump matron in the grand-stand set down her ear trumpet and told her startled husband she'd like to scratch Powers' eyes out.

Kelly hit to right field in the fourth. When Duffy threw the ball in to first Kelly put up his arms as if frightened and let the ball of yarn hit him on the shoulder. As Anson, who was in a good mood because Kelly had made him a present of a big bat the old man had been longing for ever since Mike had told him about it, scrambled to get the ball Kelly raced to second. He was just about to third on Richardson's ground ball but heard 'Out' and turned to see that Richardson hadn't beaten the throw to first.

'You ought to buy a new pair of legs for Hardie,' yelled a crank wearing steel-framed spectacles of smoked glass from the bleaching-boards.

In the sixth Richardson was on first when Pop Smith grounded to Anson. He might have prevented a double play if he had slowed up, but it would take a Kelly to work *that* trick. The loss cut the Bostons' lead over the New Yorks in half. If all the men would wake up and play as well as Kelly has the last few games we would be scoring victories instead of defeats."

After beating the Washingtons handily in the last two games of their home stand the first place Beaneaters were in high spirits when they arrived in Philadelphia the night of July 24. The next afternoon they played with a dash that was much appreciated by their supporters, who of course included General Dixwell as well as J.B. Billings, who'd made the trip to see them. A party of Hardie Richardson's friends had come from Gloucester to root for him.

The Phillies were a much stronger club than the one the Beaneaters had defeated so easily in Boston two months ago. They'd just swept Mutrie's Giants by tallying 32 runs in the three games and had 96 hits in their last six.

Under the headline "BIG DAN'S BAT AND KEL'S BASE-RUN-NING WIN THE GAME" Tim Murnane described the ending for his anxious readers in his own inimitable style. "When the Quakers went up for their last chance the crowd was as quiet as a midnight poker sitting. Mulvey hit weakly and went out and one big sigh went

across the field. Clarkson wiped his forehead and twisted the ball for Jimmy Fogarty. Jimmy is a waiter and John shot them over to make him hit. He met the ball and was safe on first and it took an ugly bound to Nash. This was a life and the blood came back to the cheeks of the ladies in the boxes.

Sid Farrar from Melrose, Mass. came up with a smile. 'Our John' fired one over the pan and before you could wink the ball was tearing down the pasture and before Dick Johnston could get it back Fogarty had crossed the plate and Smiling Sid was alone on the second bag. Things were getting serious and Clarkson pulled up his belt and blazed one over for Schriver and to the delight of the Quaker crowd Farrar scored on the hit. Every, man, woman, and child stood up in their seats and waved their hands and handkerchiefs and put the question back and forth. 'Say, what do you think of our Phillies? Ain't they just dandies.'

A run meant the game for Boston and Kelly was at the bat. The captain got first as his hard grounder went over Myers' head. Clarkson was on the coaching lines. 'Now, Billy, old man,' said he to Sir William Nash of Virginia. Almost before the batsman had taken his position two balls went by him with a swish. Both would have taken the button off his shirt if he hadn't jumped back.

'Play ball!' sang out Kelly from first base as stealing second now would be taking a foolish chance. Sanders was rattled and the next ball went high. 'Make him put it over,' called Michael J. The next pitch was inside. 'Too close,' announced Powers who was officiating his first game in the city, and Nash took his base sending Kelly down to second.

'Now then, Dan,' sang out the Boston boys in chorus as Brouthers squeezed his bat. He tried to bunt to advance the runners but the ball rolled foul and he changed his mind and straightened his tall frame up for the next pitch. It was a fast one and Dan cracked it plumb on the nose straight at Fogarty in center where he picked it up on the second bound and lined it to the plate. Kelly had been playing well off second. He made a wide turn at third and came down the path toward home in great style. A long, low slide just as Schriver swung

around at him with the ball and Kelly was safe and the game was won for Boston."

Kelly coached from the bench the next day with a lame leg. With the visitors holding a 3-0 lead Powers called the game on account of darkness after seven innings. A happy General Dixwell handed the players a "Sleeper's Eye" cigar as they got on the omnibus for their hotel. Kelly took a cab to the train station. He was heading to New York to spend Saturday night there, Fannie and Hattie were in need of his services again.

Mike rejoined the team for Monday's game back in Boston with the Phillies, which was "of the sensational order" according to Murnane. Patrons were overheard to say, "Wasn't that a dandy stop?" and "Isn't Farrar getting cocky?" and "I tell yer what, old Kel can still hit 'em" and "I just saw the horridest-looking sailor" and "Oh, her bustle is all askew."

With Hallman and Myers on base in the fifth Gentle Sam Thompson picked out one he liked and hit the sphere up against the pickets over the high slats of the right field fence and as the runners thought it was a home run they were taking things very easy and jogging around the bases. Hallman had scored, Myers was rounding third, and Thompson was heading to second. Umpire Powers was struggling to see but in the fog he couldn't follow the flight of the ball. Kelly was playing right field. He had a ball hidden in the long grass near the fence and when Thompson made his hit Kel never looked at the ball in play at all. Instead he dove for one he'd hidden in the grass. He fumbled around a bit as though he was looking for the one Thompson had hit then threw the one he'd hidden on a line to home to nab Myers.

Myers returned to third. Neither he nor Thompson had seen what Kelly had done but Captain Farrar and the other Phillies ran in around Umpire Powers and claimed that Kelly'd had a ball concealed on his person and had thrown it up against the fence. The umpire saw nothing of that kind and would not allow it."

Thompson was sure the ball had cleared the fence. He roared like

414

a lion and called down the vengeance of high heaven on Powers. While he was ranting and roaring, Kelly, with an injured and innocent air, calmly assured Powers that the ball never went near the fence at all. Powers believed Kelly and Thompson, close to crying with rage, was fined for kicking.

The Philadelphia Press described it as "the four-bagger the umpire would not see." The controversial call soon became the talk of the baseball world and several days later the *Pittsburg Telegraph* noted that this was not the first time that Kelly had resorted to the trick. "Kelly used the extra ball trick at Boston Monday. The press reports all agreed that Thompson's hit went over the fence. The players and spectators saw it, but Powers did not. Ground Superintendent Hebrank said Kelly had played the same trick two seasons before.

The Bostons scored a pair of runs to tie things up in the eighth. "Ladies waved handkerchiefs, old men danced jigs, and young men yelled until they were red in the face."

Kelly came to the plate with one out in the tenth. "He was given a hearty cheer as he squared away for business. He hit one sharp and hard between third and short that Mulvey, who can cover ground with any infielder in the league, reached but allowed to get away from him.

By a wonderful slide after a fine start Kelly reached second. Nash was out for the stuff. He cracked one safe to right and Thompson fell over it in his anxiety to get it home to head off Kelly. Nash's hit and the captain's run were cheered for fully three minutes. A man on top of the grand-stand made such an effort to howl he burst his collar button hole and then began to say words with big D's which would not sound proper in a parlor."

There was an abundance of good old-fashioned Hoosier campaign yells at the August 7 game in Indianapolis. Tim Murnane said it was "a slaughtering match and the Boston men were the victims." Rad was in the box and he pitched one of his old-gold games. The Hoosiers feasted on his slow curves. Base hits followed one another like dried apples on a string until thirteen runs were chalked on the

blackboard for Glasscock's "Indians." The final was 13-7 Indianapolis. The loss dropped the Boston's lead over New York to one game.

Kelly hit a two-baser in the fourth on August 9 and flustered John Tener from County Tyrone, Ireland, the tallest of Chicagos' unusual four-man rotation, so badly in the seventh that he committed a balk. Then he kicked over a call by Powers and got him to award first base on balls to Brouthers. Kelly singled in the ninth but it was for naught as the Bostons failed to make hits again and went down 9-0.

They were as glum as a lobster when it was over. "Nine nuthin'. Hell, we might just as well uv spent the day at the pub and forfeited," groaned Kelly.

Kelly put a ball down among the weeds in right center for two bases in the first inning of the August 12 game in Pittsburg and went to third by an error of Fields. Nash was so anxious to bring him in he hit a heavenly dewdrop that fell with a thud into Carroll's big fat glove, stranding Kel.

With the score 2-2 Hardie Richardson started the seventh with a single.

"Throw me that heavy club," Mike called to the bench as he walked in from the coacher's line.

Nash went and got it out of Kelly's leather bag.

Mike looked at Richardson, he was no more than a foot off the bag.

"Get a damn lead will ya then, Hardy, yer clinging ta that thing like you were ivy on an old ruin."

The people in the grand-stands laughed at that one.

A minute later Morris let one go and Kel met it square, steering it toward the left field fence.

"Hi! Hi!" yelled diminutive General Dixwell.

"Does it have enough steam power to make it over, General?" asked Tim Murnane.

"You're the ex-ball tosser, Tim, you tell me."

BANG went the gray ball against the wall.

"Six inches more was all it needed," groaned Dixwell.

"Look at Kelly," said Murnane. Richardson had scored and Mike was going for two even though the ball had bounced through the daisies back toward the infield.

He made it and raced home a minute later. Nash came through this time and sent one to deep center. The Boston rooters in private box No.11 cheered and it was like the rasping of a saw to the spectators around them.

"Hi! Hi!" yelled General Dixwell again.

He was startled when a police officer came over to his box and towered over him. "You'll have to stop that noise or go out on the bleaching boards," demanded the gruff cop.

"Well, I've made the noise a hundred times before this year and I don't believe I'll stop it now," the General replied with a scornful smile. Is my cheering likely to keep the policeman on your beat awake?"

Several fans in the crowd sympathized with the General and started up a solid defense with a chorus of "hi hi's" that sent the deflated cop away.

Pud Galvin's shoots had never been swifter than they were the next day.

"We're like a culled gemman with ninety cents on the outside uv a poker game today, boys," Mike told the others after Galvin had shut them down in order in the sixth. "We've as much chance uv winning this game as you'd have tryin' to get Old man Anson to crack a smile."

The Alleghenys trampled the stunned Beaneaters 9-0. Word came over the wire that New York had made four runs to Cleveland's one in the fifteenth inning. Tim Murnane sent out for a quarter's worth of bunting and proceeded to write his account for the morning paper.

The Boston club arrived in Cleveland at 2 o'clock on the 14th of August. Their train was more than an hour late. After a light lunch they had a brief practice. Radbourn was to be between the points but told Hart he was too ill so Madden, the plucky little Portland boy,

was put in. The Bostons had all of their top batsmen in their nine and not a man would have given a chew of tobacco for the Clevelands' chances with the likes of Kelly, Nash, and Brouthers in their lineup. The Cleveland babies had lost their grip with the willow of late but they would not have any trouble in hitting Madden.

After he had pitched a few balls it was plain that he had precious little speed; each ball came wandering up to the plate in a trance with a tag attached to it which read: "Hit me or let me go by." Kelly, who ranked third in the League in stolen bases and led the Bostons in home runs and sacrifice hits, offered to go in for Madden but Hart opted to let the kid stay in and absorb a terrible leather pounding. The Spiders made 26 base hits and would have scored more than their 19 runs had Kelly not thrown out seven base runners.

Ed Beatin, a lefty from Baltimore, was badly beaten on Friday. The Boston sluggers trounced the Clevelands 13-0. On Saturday, runs were a lot harder to come by, hits too, a combined total of just eleven. The Beaneaters notched a run in the seventh to eke out an hour and 25 minutes 2-1 decision that put them a game and a half ahead of the Giants, whom they were going home to face.

The first game of the August 19 to 21 three-game series resulted in a 4-4 tie. The second game ended in a 12-2 rout of the visitors, who wore white suits, black caps, and black stockings. "The home team got down to business in the second and were never rushed afterwards, giving the Giants one of the most crushing defeats ever suffered by a first-class team playing a blood game," reported Tim Murnane. The double umpire system was tried again and gave splendid satisfaction to the large weekday crowd of 9,097.

"At the start Kelly was presented with a massive blackthorn stick brought over from Cork, Ireland by his friend George Floyd in appreciation for his love for the old country. Mike lifted his cap in acknowledgment of the gift. When play began and Kelly came to the plate a suppressed murmur of 'Will he hit it?' passed among the spectators, who were on the tip-toe of expectation.

'Bet your life he will,' was the reply as Kelly cracked the crisp ball

to the left field fence for two bases. After the third out of the Giants' ninth landed in Richardson's hands the march to their carriages in waiting was not according to the latest military code. Capt. Ewing and his privates trailed along in twos or threes. 'There will be no joy in Harlem, Barney Brogan has closed up shop!' sang out George Floyd as the last slump-shouldered Gothamite disappeared through the gate.

Charlie Bennett hit one over the fence in the seventh in the last game of the important series. Kelly said something to him as he followed him at the bat.

"Did Kelly chide Bennett for losing the ball, Papa?" asked a lad in a newsboy cap.

"No, son."

"Why not?"

"Because Mike feels in his bones that he is about to become a sinner himself."

Kelly earned a box of Sleeper's Eyes cigars by shunting one of Crane's drops over the left field fence into the railway car shops.

"I think that went to Ireland," chuckled the father.

"Kelly isn't going to Ireland is he?"

"No son, he's not."

The Bostons scored four times in the sixth to put the game out of reach and added icing to the cake with another brace of runs in the ninth for a 10-4 win that boosted them to a 3½ game lead over the Giants. "We'll get even when you lot come to New York," Buck Ewing snarled at Kelly.

Things looked rosy, the eighth place Washingtons were coming to town.

THE
$10,000
BEAUTY

"No one sells newspapers like he does."

Kelly was stymied at the bat in the first game but his team held on for a 7-5 win. The Nationals made a comeback in the second game as well. Trailing 5-0 they scored six in the sixth to take the lead. Mike lined the ball into the seats in left center for two bases allowing Ganzel to score the go-ahead run in the top of the tenth but the pesky visitors plated a pair in the bottom of the inning to win 8-7.

Kelly had a single and a double and worked Keefe for a base on balls in the last game on Saturday and stole four bases. He and the other men headed to the train station in a good mood after a 9-3 win.

Kelly went from Boston to Philadelphia on his own hook on Monday, August 21. On the train ride he read a note on the sports page that said Phillies' shortstop Arthur Irwin had moved his family from Philadelphia to South Boston, his old home. Kel didn't think much about it.

The opening game of the series would go down as one of the most exciting and stubbornly-fought contests ever witnessed on the Philadelphia ball grounds. It required twelve innings to decide the victors but the game wasn't over even then. Kelly crossed the plate with the winning run on a line hit into the seats by Dick Johnston that was good for four bases but Johnston failed to touch first base.

Phillies' captain Sid Farrar saw that as soon as the ball rolled into the outfield Johnston had turned and walked to the players' bench. Kelly, who was legging it around third, yelled at him to go to touch first base.

After Kelly scored Farrar yelled to his catcher Jack Clements, "Throw me the ball!"

"*I'm* the winning captain," said Mike and Clements tossed *him* the ball.

Farrar rushed at Kelly and demanded it. Mike shook his head. "Nuthin' doin'," he said.

Farrar reached to grab the ball and Mike put it behind his back. A burly policeman hurried over and shouted, "Give it up, Kelly," but bold Michael would not.

Now the crowd surged onto the field. Two hundred or so men and boys surrounded Mike, Sid, and the officer. A moment later the entire crowd joined the mob and Mike's head could be scene bobbing around like a cork on an ocean wave.

Big Dan Brouthers pushed his way to his captain's side. "Leave him alone," he yelled.

Soon thereafter players from both clubs arrived on the scene. Some members of the crowd didn't quite understand what had happened but the hard core base ball enthusiasts were explaining to them that for Kelly's run to count Johnston was required to touch first base and he had not so Farrar wanted the ball so he could tag him out.

"Oh, I thought it was just Kelly cutting up some of his monkey shines," said a man in a brown mixed suit. "Remember how he substituted another ball for the game one in Boston and robbed Sam Thompson of a home run."

With great effort and the help of the policeman and another officer who joined him the Boston players pushed Mike toward the cellar door under the right field pavilion. Arms flew wildly and a few base ball bats could be seen but the crowd around the players was too tightly packed for any damage to be done.

Suddenly a dozen new policeman with menacing clubs emerged from the door. Kelly made a mad dash for it but was grabbed and held back. Joe Quinn got two resounding punches in the face. Johnston attempted to pounce on Quinn's assailant and

got smashed to the ground.

The melee continued, the police swinging their clubs left and right, then they stopped. Someone was yelling, "I got the ball from Kelly!" It was big Ed Delahanty, who'd grabbed the ball from Mike's hand while he was distracted. Now he held it over his head so his teammates could see it.

Everyone stared at Delahanty as he ran to the first base bag and stepped on it emphatically. The riot subsided and Delahanty went with Farrar to look for the umpires to witness his triumph but should have known they'd be hiding. They were finally found under the pavilion. Umpire Curry was so badly shaken he couldn't remember whether he'd been behind the plate or on the bases when Johnston had made his hit.

"You were behind second base," his partner McQuaid told him.

"Well I didn't see anything," said Curry. "I suppose I was watching the ball. Yes, that's right I was watching the ball."

"Well I didn't see what Johnston did either," said McQuaid. "I was too busy watching Kelly to make sure he touched third base."

On that basis the Bostons were awarded the victory.

On August 27 the visitors, winners by a score of 13-6, made their last run in the eighth on a three-baser to the flagpole by Kelly, who ran home on Clements' wild throw to get him at third.

Kelly had been afraid to go to the grounds in the players' omnibus. He hired a coupe at the Girard House and went in style. He missed the coupe after the game and was compelled to ride back to the Continental in a street-car. He got a lot of looks from the other passengers and a couple of men behind him were mumbling about what he'd done the day before.

Red-faced Colonel Rogers was still in a lather when Kelly went to the bat in the eighth inning. "Boston has a lot of men who are a disgrace to their profession," he told another lawyer as they sat in the owner's private box. Just as he said, "Kelly there should be expelled from the league," Mike cracked out the three-baser and one of the

traveling correspondents remarked, "There's nothing wrong with *that* old boy."

Gleason made a hit in the ninth but was put out by Kelly's sharp throw to Smith. Delahanty flew out to Johnston and Clements closed the game on a long fly to Kelly.

The much-anticipated series between the two front runners in New York was anti-climatic. Each club won a game and they tied the other. The Bostons hoped to put some breathing room between themselves and the Giants when they got home to take on the Hoosiers. They took both ends of the Monday double header from the Indianapolis club but Kelly had little to do with it, making just one hit the whole day.

The scoreboard read 7-1 Boston after three innings on September 3. The Beaneaters had scored three runs in the first and four in the third mostly by luck as baby soft fly balls kept landing in all the right places. After that the Boston men went down before young speed-baller Rusie like yellow leaves before a strong wind. Richardson's single and Kelly's long drive to the seats in right field that McGeachey pulled down after a long run were the sole occasions where a ball was hit hard and over the infield.

The Indians arose in their might in the ninth and tomahawked Kelly's gang. It was a terrible slaughter and the crowd departed the grounds in gloom.

Yellow fielding by the home team was the order of the day on Wednesday. Tom Brown was laid up so Kelly put Hardie Richardson in left field and Quinn in his place at second. That meant Pop Smith had to play shortstop and it did not go well. His three errors led to four of the Hoosiers' runs. They jumped out to a 2-0 lead in the first inning. Andrews put in a single and Denny hit a ball to the right of Smith that he scooped up beautifully. Quinn ran to second for the double play starting catch but for reasons known only to him Smith let it go to first instead and the ball may still be going as it shot by Brouthers' head "like a meadow lark over a salt marsh" and landed in the lap of a startled woman in a white felt hat. Two runs came in and

the crowd moaned just as they had the day before.

The home side tied things in the third. Kelly reached on a force out. Two pitches later he took off for second and reached it by a terrific slide. Wanting to be able to score on a fly ball, Mike made a mad dash for third. Buckley was on the lookout for him but a desperate slide saved Kelly's bacon. Unfortunately he twisted his ankle badly. Brouthers sent a high one to center and Kelly limped home. He'd occupy the right garden for the rest of the game.

Glasscock started the trouble in the fourth with a grounder full of English to Quinn. Denny sent one hopping along the ground to Smith that rolled between his widespread feet. Nash picked up the ball, touched his base, then snapped it smartly over against the bleaching boards. The gentleman it landed beside tried to laugh it off but his expression changed when McGeachy singled both runners home. Boyle held the Beaneaters to one run the rest of the way and they lost one they knew they should have had. It would come back to haunt them a month later.

The telegraph transmitted word of the Giants making short work of the Pittsburgs at the Polo Grounds. The Giants and Beaneaters were now tied atop the heap. The Alleghenys were next up for the Bostons. Kelly thought of playing the next day but knew his ankle needed at least a full day to recuperate.

"He reminds me of a mechanical toy with a sick mainspring," General Dixwell told Nat Goodwin after Radbourn had lobbed another one to the plate on Thursday.

The jovial actor looked at the sullen faces around him. "It's as quiet as a trout brook beneath a weeping willow in here."

"The Pittsburgs were putty in their hands all year," groaned Dixwell.

"Another bad day for the Australian. Quinn's not getting his dickey bird assists today."

"We could sure use your friend Michael."

They both groaned when Rowe picked out one of Radbourn's juicy offerings and drove it through a hole between the slats in the

fence in right field for a home run.

At the welcomed termination of the brutal game the spectators slouched their way to the exits after a third straight loss.

"We were never even in that one," a disgusted rooter told his brother.

"Old Hoss really needs to be put out to pasture."

Kelly put himself back in the lineup on Friday but he wasn't in his usual good humor. He batted two fouls into the side seats when he led off the seventh then lined the next offering into the seats beyond center field. It was good for three bases but Kel took his time and settled for two. He was glad when Billy Nash cracked the ball to almost the same spot and there was no need for him to sprint home, he made it easily. The Pittsburg batters couldn't do a thing with Clarkson's shoots. After Radbourn's slow ones the day before they looked like rockets. The Bostons got a much-needed win and were heartened by the score board which showed the pesky Hoosiers had beaten the Giants.

With darkness enveloping the grounds in the seventh inning on Saturday Kelly went up to face Galvin, who'd been shooting the ball over the pan with great speed. Pud was startled when Kelly gladdened all hearts by lifting one over the left field fence. After a 5-3 win Murnane chuckled, "You're a big man, Michael. Had you seen the bunch of beauties that applauded your long drive it would have driven you to drink."

G. Waldon Smith, the well-known photographer, took a wonderful picture of the Bostons on the grounds. The team looked as natural as life, the picture was expected to have a wide sale.

The Beaneaters took both ends of a September 12 double header from the Spiders but very nearly lost both games the next day. The Clevelands were on the verge of winning the morning one when Radbourn hit his first home run of the season to tie things in the ninth. The captains got together and agreed to call it a draw so there'd be time for the second game. The Spiders won the afternoon tilt 3-0. Kelly was on base three times but he was stranded on each occasion. The Bostons couldn't afford to lose games to the likes of the Clevelands.

The New York World didn't disclose its sources when it told its readers that, "Mike Kelly is likely to captain the Cleveland team in the Brotherhood League next season. Al Johnson, the head of the Cleveland trolley car operation, has made him a splendid offer. When Kelly retires from active work on the diamond he will probably start a baseball factory. He learned the trade from Spalding when he was in Chicago."

Great hitting and superb fielding enabled the Boston team to defeat their most troublesome opponents in Indianapolis on September 26 and climb back into a tie with the New Yorks in the race for the championship banner. Henry Boyle started in to pitch but got all he wanted for the day in the third inning when the Beaneaters made nine hits and scored eight runs. Kelly did some lively leather hunting. He made three catches in deep right field, two of them magnificent.

He came up with the bases full in the second and pushed his bat against the third ball he saw for a sacrifice. The ball shot past Hines however for a clean single and two runs came in. Kel hit safe again in the eighth and scored on Brouthers' two-baser to double up the home side 12-6.

Indianapolis put Kentuckian Lev Shreve, who'd wind up with an 0-3 record for the year, between the points on Friday the 27th and the Boston men pummeled his pitches with reckless abandon. Kelly larupped a ball off the right field fence in the middle of the five-run first inning. The Hoosiers had proven tough customers for the Beaneaters so Kelly kept the boys down to hard work. The day was cold but clear and the players needed to keep moving to stay warm.

By the eighth inning it was so dark the fielders couldn't see line balls and several hits were made on that account. General Dixwell was in the press box squinting.

"Hang a lantern on the ball so we can see it," he yelled to Umpire McQuaid.

"He wants to see what it looks like by moonlight," called out a crank a few rows below.

The game was won to all intents and purposes with the score at 15-3 and the crowd began to depart the grounds. It had been a good day for Kelly. He'd made three hits, stolen two bases, and scored three times. He wished there was some place in Indianapolis to celebrate. The Spencer House where the club was staying had no saloon. The Temperance movement in Indiana had made it difficult for any kind of drinking establishment to operate and Kel didn't fancy taking in a minstrel or variety show or an operetta. Luckily, one of the inn's chambermaids was anxious to do more than clean his room. She wasn't as comely as Colleen but she was a lot more experienced in the art of pleasuring a man. Mike wished the Hoosiers weren't on the verge of folding, he was a much bigger fan of the Spencer House now.

Charlie Radbourn was down to pitch on Saturday but he begged off so Clarkson, who was in uniform, went between the points. He'd pitched so often on the trip he had no speed. Kelly homered in the eighth but by then the game was out of reach, the Hoosiers had scored six runs in the fifth inning.

When the Boston men arrived at National League Park on September 30 the grounds still looked unplayable. It had poured rain until noon so a small army of workers was scraping up the mud and laying sawdust down around the bases. The visitors put in a run in the first inning when Richardson scored on Nash's double. He tallied again on a pretty drive by Kelly and two sacrifice hits.

The Bostons trailed the Clevelands 3-2 after six innings when Captain Faatz asked to have the game, claiming it was to dark to see the ball.

"We can see to play," Kelly called out. "I'll show you." With that he walked up to the plate to do business. He cracked the first ball sent to him down the right field line for two bases and yelled to the bench, "Now then, boys, let's tie this game right now."

Nash hit to first and Kelly was on third with Brouthers at the bat and one run needed. Dan was given his base and Dick Johnston was

equal to the emergency for he spanked one past short that sent Kelly and big Dan home. Quinn hit safe and Johnston scored. The Cleveland fielders swore they couldn't see but McQuaid was unmoved. He signaled for Smith to bat. He hit to the pitcher and when he threw wide to third Quinn ran home with another run.

The Bostons guyed Faatz who said, "We have to finish it out now."

His men were shut out and that was enough for Faatz, he told McQuaid to call the damn game and stormed off into the darkness.

More rumors leaked out of New York, where members of the Brotherhood had apparently leased a park for a team to use in the 1890 season.

On the first of October the Beaneaters, who'd won five of their last seven, had a record of 81 wins and 43 losses. The New Yorks' record was 79 and 43. A cold wind whistled across the grounds, picking up and carrying discarded scorecards and empty peanut bags. Kelly's hands stung when he clouted a ball far down the right field line in the first but spritely Stricker pulled it down after a long sprint. The visitors got three men across the plate in the third on a red-whiskered muff by Twitchell and singles by Richardson, Kelly, and Brouthers but the Spiders regained the lead in their half of the frame just as the score of the Giants' game against Pittsburg went up and the crowd mocked the Boston men with shouts that the New Yorks were ahead and would win the pennant.

In the seventh inning Kelly pointed to the scoreboard. The other Beaneaters turned and saw that the Alleghenys had scored twice in the sixth to tie the game and at that point it was called due to rain. Bennett got his base on balls and Kelly went to the coaching line next to him. "Come on boys," he yelled to the bench, "we're out for the money, let's give 'em a Garrison finish."

Clarkson tried to bunt and failed. Then he took a full swing and sent the ball humming past short for a single.

"Go!" Mike yelled at Bennett.

Richardson went to the plate. He motioned to Kelly and the two

huddled together. "Should I sacrifice or hit out, Kel?" he asked.

Mike smiled. "Suit yerself, Hardie, whatever tickles yer fancy."

Richardson nodded, went back to the plate, and sent the first ball he saw spinning just inside third base. Bennett scored and Richardson and Clarkson were now lodged on third and second. Kelly slammed an inshoot that Grumber managed to knock down. Clarkson was halfway home and started back when he saw the ball heading to third. He changed his course and legged it for home when he realized Tebeau had thrown high and John was safe. Kelly was already at second base and Hardie was at third. Nash cracked a beauty over second base. Both runners scored and the Bostons won 8-5. The ride back to the Hollenden was a high-spirited one.

Mike was enjoying an Admiral cigarette in front of the hotel after dinner when three local base ball cranks came up to him.

"Mike Kelly," said the tallest of them. "Great game today."

"Yes, indeed," said another. "Just what you'd expect from the greatest ball tosser in the land."

"We'd like to buy you a drink," said the third. "There's a new place a block from here that just got in some ten-year old rye."

"Sorry, fellas, I've a big game tomorrow."

"Just a couple of quick shots then."

"I suppose a *couple* wouldn't hurt."

Five hours and three bottles later the cranks, who'd encouraged other patrons to tell Kelly they could drink him under the table, had accomplished their mission. He'd be in no condition to play the next day.

The Globe laid out the disturbing details of what transpired in Cleveland the next afternoon.

"Mike Kelly, the high-priced star in the Boston club, created a scene at the League Park. It is claimed that he was intoxicated and that whiskey was the cause of the disgrace which came up on him at the beginning of the seventh inning. Kelly was in uniform but too

indisposed to play, having spent last night and this morning in jol-lification with theatrical friends. He attempted to warm up but discovered that his hand had lost its cunning and fly balls were a deep mystery to him. He sat muffed up in an overcoat on the bench and made profane comments on the game as it progressed.

'You never win, when I don't play,' he yelled to his teammates. 'King is King. I am king.'

After a couple of calls went against his club Kelly made a vigorous kick against the umpire, shaking his finger at McQuaid and yelling, 'You're bound to do the Bostons out of the championship, McQuaid.

Several of his teammates collected around Kelly and asked him to desist but he refused."

In Boston's half of the 6th Richardson was touched out at the plate. Kelly took exception to Umpire McQuaid's latest call and when the inning was over he stormed over to him with eyes blazing and yelled in the umpire's face. "You came West to rob the Bostons of the pennant, McQuaid. You roasted the life out of us at Indianapolis and here you are again fixed to give us the worst of it!"

He drew back his fist to slug McQuaid but two burly police-men grabbed him. Kelly broke free of their grasp and made for McQuaid again. One of the policemen put his hands around Kelly's neck and started to choke him. He and his partner dragged Kelly away from McQuaid and out through the gate. Outside, they reluctantly let him loose. Kelly lit an Admiral and strode into the street with a dejected air. He tried to re-enter the grounds but the stalwart policemen had locked the gate. He thought about hopping the fence but it was too high.

The Clevelands scored three runs in the fourth, two in the sixth, and another pair in the eighth for a 7-1 win. After the game Dan Brouthers said, "There is no man in the business that gets along bet-ter with umpires than Mike Kelly, but Mike made a bad break going on the field when he wasn't in the game."

On October 4, *The Pittsburg Dispatch* reported that, "The big, tough Boston men landed and they are determined to allow nothing

to get away from them that's within gunshot. They're working as if they are in a life and death struggle. The usually jolly Mike Kelly was on hand in earnest, as penitent as a little truant in the presence of a dominie's rod but was sadly out of form. He made one glaring mistake in the field—a bad fumble—and another running the bases but it was not so bad, the Bostons could have made a boatload of mistakes and still won. Galvin was no match for Clarkson, the great twirler from the East."

The paper also reported that the Giants had beaten the Spiders 9-0 and that President Young had decreed that if the Bostons and New Yorks ended the season in a tie they would play a series of three games to determine the championship. Pop Smith had joined the Brotherhood but when asked a question about it he said, "I'm not at liberty to say a word on the matter."

The October 4 game was a back-and-forth nail biter in which the two sides fought like wildcats. Harry Staley, the Pittsburg pitcher was determined to win. If he lost he'd lead the League in that category. The Beaneaters got to him for a pair of runs in the third but the Alleghenys put three on the score-board the next inning. Boston tied it up with a run in the sixth and it stayed that way until the ninth.

The home team went wild when Billy Sunday made a successful bunt to Nash who threw wild to first. Sunday, now completely reformed but let go by the Chicagos anyway, ran around to third. Dunlap tried to drop one into right field but hit four foul flies just out of Bennett's reach instead. Then he lined one between third and short and Nash leapt into the air and hauled it down. Sunday had started running and was an easy out. Staley hit hard, but Richardson caught it after some hard running.

Bennett opened the Bostons' half of the ninth with a crisp single to center. Madden put in a little bunt to Beckley and beat the ball in a race to first. Kelly hit to Rowe, who threw wide to third in hopes of getting Bennett. Nash was hit in the finger by a pitch and the member was badly bruised, but Powers refused to give him his base. Kelly figured he didn't want the Bostons to win that way. Nash was more than a little bit warm under the collar. He made a big kick, then struck out and everything rested on Brouthers' big shoulders. He cracked the ball to third base and it went right past 41-year-old Deacon White on a jump. Bennett crossed the plate and Kelly yelled "Touch first!" Dan ran there and stomped on the bag.

Kelly smiled and turned to look at the special bulletin board that had been hung on the left field fence to show the news from Cleveland. "Shite!" he exclaimed. The Giants had beaten the Spiders again. There was still a tie for first with one game to play.

The first inning of the Beaneaters' final game of the season on October 5th was a disaster. When Rowe put a little fly over second base Kelly, Quinn, and Johnston all raced for it and no one got it. On the ball's first bound Quinn reached for it and ended up knocking it right past Kelly. Miller drove one to center, then White got first on Pop Smith's bad fumble. Fields flew out to Bennett then Smith threw wild to first on Hanlon's grounder. The Pittsburgs had a 6-1 lead after six and that's the way it ended. Kelly had three hits off Pud Galvin but it didn't matter a damn, the Giants had won again in Cleveland. Mike knew there would be a lot of long faces back in Boston. The Beaneaters had come so close it was heart-breaking. It was the first time in big league history the championship was decided on the last day of the season.

Kelly was disappointed with his own season. He'd led the League in doubles and stood fifth in Extra Base Hits, but he wasn't even among the top ten in batting average or On Base Percentage. He didn't know if he'd have another chance for a championship. Would there even be a league next year? A lot had been going on behind the scenes.

Two days later *The New York Evening World* reported that Mike Kelly still had many admirers and friends in Beantown even if he did fail to bring the pennant to the Hub. Steward Bickford of the Boston Tavern, a warm friend of Kelly's, sent him an invitation to drop into the tavern in the course of the evening. The invitation was accepted and in one of the private dining-rooms of the tavern Kelly sat down to as fine a spread as ever tickled the palate. He had to smile when the charlotte russe was brought to him. It was shaped in the form of a soup tureen and on the cover was the inscription "Slide, Kelly, Slide".

At the end of October General Dixwell, the bewhiskered warrior, made a warm speech in the clubhouse congratulating the Boston men on their work over the season and presented each of the sixteen players with a handsome scarf-pin.

"I'm sorry we let you down," said Kel when he was given his. "I know how much a championship would have meant to you."

"Perhaps next year, Michael."

"You can be sure uv it, General."

The Boston Globe heralded A.G. Spalding's mission across the Pacific to the Sandwich Islands and Australia to advertise base ball "an idea that in its scope and boldness exceeded anything ever attempted in the world of sports." What they didn't know was that Spalding had a hidden agenda. It was no coincidence that the leadership of the Professional Base Ball Players Brotherhood and the most influential players in baseball were with him across the world when the National League owners were meeting to finalize a new pay structure. Players would now be judged on their performance, special qualifications, personal habits, earnestness, and adherence to team rules and paid accordingly. There would be five rungs on the new ladder with an increase of $250 for each rung. The highest salary was to be $2,500. When they returned to the States and heard about it, Ward and the others were livid.

On November 4 the first meeting of the Base Ball Brotherhood was held at the Fifth Avenue Hotel in New York. The entire base ball world centered its attention on the gathering. As usual, Kelly was the height of fashion. He wore a tall, shining silk hat, a handsome chinchilla overcoat thrown back to reveal his tight-fitting Prince Albert, an English check pair of tight-fitting trousers, and a beaver overcoat. He stopped to talk to the press outside the hotel.

"What do you have to say to the owners of the Beaneaters, Kel?" asked the reporter from *The New York Times*.

Kelly thought for a second and got a little smile on his face. "I would say to them, if the three uv yas want a job next season, I'll give you one." He paused for effect ... "taking tickets at the turnstiles."

Everyone roared.

"Well, a good beginning's half the work and you have to crack the nuts before you can eat the kernel," said Mike.

The reporters chuckled and scribbled that one down.

"Slán go fóill, fellows, I'm goin' inside to manipulate the wires that'll startle the livin' hell out uv the baseball world."

The reporter had heard his Irish parents use the expression and explained to the puzzled others. "Slán go fóill. It just means, goodbye for now."

"What a character!" said the man from *The Daily Mail*. "There's never been a player easier to write a story on than Michael J. Kelly."

"And no one sells newspapers like he does," said the reporter from *The Times*.

The big guns of the seceders' ranks were present in full force: James O'Rourke from New York, Ed Hanlon of Pittsburg, Arthur Irwin from Washington, Dan Brouthers, and Fred Pfeffer. There was nothing but silence from their council chamber until 7 p.m. when Kelly stepped into the chilly evening air in front of a crowd of reporters, pencils at the ready, to make a declaration.

"Gentlemen, there was a time when the League stood for integrity and fair dealing, but today it stands only for dollars and cents. Once, it looked to the elevation of the game, now all eyes are upon the turnstile. Men have come into the game with no other motive than to exploit it. Measures originally intended for the good of the game have been perverted into instruments for wrong. The reserve rule gave the managers the power and they didn't hesitate to use it. We players are bought, sold, and exchanged as though we are sheep. Even the disbandment of a team doesn't release its players from the octopus grasp of the owners. We mean to tolerate it no longer. We've resolved to meet with the owners and persuade them to accede to our requests or …"

"Or *what*, Kel?" asked the man from *The Times*.

"You'll see, Harry. If the league wants to fight, we'll be ready."

With that he turned and went inside.

"These boys mean business," said *The Philadelphia Inquirer* reporter.

"No, George, I think these boys are in business."

Tim Murnane, who was firmly on the players' side, wrote, "Some base ball enthusiasts say the star players will change their minds at the last moment, but they have taken the bit between their teeth and nothing can change their course. The legal threats sent by Colonel Rogers and other league magnates have had about as much effect as water on a duck's back."

A week later the Brotherhood leaders got together for another meeting at the Fifth Avenue, but a secret one this time. At 7 p.m. they released a statement that said, "When we made a strong effort last spring to reach an understanding with the League we were told the matter was not of sufficient importance to warrant a meeting. When they refused to meet with us in October we began to organize ourselves and form our own league to play next season. We look forward to the support of the base ball public."

O'Rourke nudged Kelly and pointed to something on a piece of paper.

"Thank you, Jim." He turned back to the reporters who wondered what it was that Kelly might have left out.

"Our committee has passed a resolution that no professional gambler can have a stake in any of the new league's clubs."

Their other decisions - to charge 50 cents for admission, ban alcohol sales, and play no games on Sunday - would cost the new league the support of its natural constituency of sympathetic working-class laborers.

"Can your league make money for its investors?" asked the man from *The Evening World*.

"Every authority has it that our venture'll be a paying one. We figure ta clear $240,000, $50,000 in each of New York and Boston alone."

Kelly said that the Brotherhood had nearly all of the League and Association star players lined up and he was going to get the rest of them. He said Soden had offered him $5,000 plus $5,000 a season for three years to stay with the Beaneaters but he'd told him, "I'll stick by Johnson even if I have to pull the bell-rope on a horse-car. There isn't enough money in all uv Boston to make me a traitor."

On November 17 *The Buffalo Morning Express* reported that the Boston directors had signed Arthur Shelhassie of Syracuse to replace Mike Kelly. Shelhassie had never played a major league game and was such an unknown commodity they got his name wrong. "What sort of figure will he cut as compared with Michael Kelly now of the Players' League?" *The Express* wondered. Schellhasie would play nine games for the Beaneaters and post a sparkling .138 batting average.

Ed Delahanty had signed with the Brotherhood league's Cleveland club and Ed Williamson and Jimmy Ryan were reported to have signed on with the new league as well.

"Well, Mike, are you going to sign back on with the Beaneaters?" asked the youngest of the reporters that tracked Mike down outside a watering hole.

Kelly looked at him as if he had lost his mind. "Do you suppose I want to die? Do you think I want to be caught in the streets of Boston late one dark and foggy night by some of the Knights of Labor fellows and disappear from the face of the Earth like poor Dr. Cronin? I've signed a Bruterhood agreement and with them I'll win or lose."

On November 27th *The New York Times* confirmed it. "Michael J. Kelly, Captain of the Boston Baseball Club, better known as the "Ten-Thousand-Dollar Beauty" or "the King of the Diamond," attached his signature to a Brotherhood contract this morning shortly after midnight.

The next night, which was Thanksgiving, the audience at Hooley's Theater in Chicago was enjoying a performance of Hoyt's play "A Brass Monkey" when one of the stage boxes was occupied by Kelly and the author of the piece. When the curtain rose on the auction room scene the two went on stage. Hoyt asked the young actor

playing the auctioneer for his pen and ink and said to Mike, "I have brought you here to sign a Brotherhood contract."

The audience howled.

"I am with you," said Kelly, "all the best men have signed with us, Ewing, Ward, Hanlon, Pfeffer, Williamson …"

"What about Anson?" asked Hoyt.

"Not yet, but if you let me alone with him I'll bet a hundred dollars to one I'll have his name to a contract."

The audience roared again. Mike made a show of signing the paper and Hoyt said, "Now come outside and I'll pay you whatever advance money you need."

Kelly turned to the audience and said, "I'm one of the bosses now, ladies and gentlemen. Next year we players'll be in charge and the National League owners … he paused for dramatic effect … will be drivin' horse cars for a livin'."

The two linked arms and left the stage to hoots and howls.

John Ward told reporters the next morning, "It's been decided that in the best interests of the Players' League Mike Kelly will leave to-night for San Francisco where the majority of last season's Boston League club are at present giving exhibitions of ball-playing. None of them has as yet signed a Brotherhood contract and it will be his purpose to obtain their signatures. This morning Al Johnson, the primary backer of the Brotherhood's Cleveland club, and Ned Hanlon visited the bank and drew a thousand dollars to be used by Kelly for his expenses. Kel is at home packing for his trip."

Before Kelly left for San Francisco he told a *New York World* reporter, "I will sign all the Boston players or jump off the Long Wharf" and showed him them the contract he'd signed. It was with Al Johnson. It contained a provision that Kelly "shall abstain from drinking alcohol during the 1890, '91, and '92 seasons."

The next day the paper's baseball news column listed the salaries the stars of the new league would receive - if the league got off the ground: Ward $4,200, Ewing $5,000, Welch $2,500, and Kelly $4,500.

438

After telling the readers about the abstinence clause in Kelly's contract the columnist editorialized, "That settles it. The 'only Mike' will not play good ball next season. Kelly without rye? Great Scott! He's a goner, to be sure."

On December 3 *The San Francisco Examiner* announced that, "King Kelly, the greatest of a ball-players, was in town, having come in on the overland train yesterday morning. The King's mission on this side of the Rocky Mountains is in the interests of the Players' League and he brought with him a bunch of contracts and will endeavor to secure the signatures of the members of the Boston club to Brotherhood contracts. He was authorized to offer Clarkson the same money he received last season. Kelly told a reporter he'd offered to add another $500 from his own pocket but Clarkson wanted more.

The reporter asked if the Players' League would succeed and Mike said, "It's a go for sure. You can bet $1,000 to a penny on it. The King wouldn't be in on it if it wasn't."

Asked what he thought of the defection of Denny, Boyle, and Glasscock he thought a moment then said, "Well, I had rather not express my opinion. The language wouldn't look too good in print."

Did you hear what Anson said about your new league, Kel?"

"No I've not."

He said the Brotherhood is nothing but a labor union just like the bomb throwers from Haymarket. We hang communists in Chicago. They'll probably play ball on Sundays, sell beer, charge a quarter, and let darkies in."

A *San Francisco Chronicle* man sat down across from Kelly while he ate breakfast the next morning in the white and gold trimmed American Dining Room adjacent to the enormous lobby of the Palace Hotel. He looked around in awe of the ornate furnishing.

"Al Johnson gave me a big check so I could travel in style."

"Have you made much on your games here, Mr. Kelly?"

"We have. And we netted a handsome profit on the games we played on our way *out here*."

A waiter brought the reporter a coffee, offered a menu that was declined, and left. The reporter asked Kelly if he was leaving the League because he'd been mistreated.

Kelly pushed away his plate and lit a cigarette. "Some uv us have no grievance. Ward, Ewing, Pfeffer, and meself are satisfied with our treatment. It was only to help the other poor slaves that we went into the brotherhood. I was offered five years at $10,000 a season, $50,000 but I said I wouldn't quit the boys for half a million. Hell, I'd uv signed with the brotherhood for ten dollars."

"I just spoke with Billy Nash. He told me he had his mind on holding out for an increase from the Triumvir but when you got here and swooped down on him he found himself utterly unable to refuse you and without a word put his name on a Brotherhood contract."

"I have Nash, Daly, Brouthers, Richardson, Radbourn, and Madden."

"So pretty well the whole club."

"Pretty well."

"Al Johnson will be glad the expense money he gave you is being well spent."

"We've no game today, I think I'll take lunch at the Northstar Café, their beer's as cold as a banker's heart."

"And tonight?"

"I'll probably go back to the Old Ship Saloon. There's a comely bar-maid that's taken a shine to me."

"What about the new place that's opened in the Irish neighborhood?"

"Where?"

"On Lincoln Way … just off Ninth avenue."

"What's it called?"

"The Little Shamrock."

"Sounds as though I might have some luck there too."

"What's your opinion of the deserters, Mike?" Tim Murnane asked Kelly as he sat at the Two Kelly's two weeks later. The doors

swung in and a cold blast of air swept inside. Murnane put his coat back on. Kelly wiped a beer glass and set it down on the bar.

"When the brotherhood scheme was first talked of Ganzel and Clarkson were among our most enthusiastic supporters, Tim. Or so it *seemed*. They attended all our star chamber meetings and Clarkson was one of the first signers of the agreement we made under oath and signed at the Sherman House. He asked for one of the biggest blocks of stock in the new enterprise and uv course we were led to believe he was with us heart and soul."

"And?" asked Murnane.

"And all that time they were in the employ of the League and acting as their spies. So, my opinion uv those two rats is that I'm one uv a bunch uv brotherhood men that'd like to see those two scoundrels strung up."

"Henry Chadwick, who does not share my opinion of what the brotherhood is doing, is writing some pretty nasty things about your gang."

"And what would you expect from the editor of Spalding's Official Base Ball Guide? Of course he sided with the League. What's the father uv base ball sayin' now?"

He says Al Johnson rattles on and on about the misery and hardships the poor, oppressed members of the brotherhood have had to endure under the League despots who paid them $20 to $50 an hour salary and then turns around and pays his streetcar drivers a dollar a week."

"And can us overpaid under-worked ball tossers work until we're seventy years old like his drivers? We have to make hay while the sun shines and damn it that's exactly what we mean ta do."

"Well, I had better get home before Martha sends a Pinkerton after me."

Kelly said, "Wait, Tim."

"What is it?"

"The other brotherhood leaders."

"What about them?

"They asked me to thank you for the support the Globe is givin' our cause."

"Well it isn't only me ..."

"It's *mostly* you, and we're mighty grateful uv it we are."

"Tell them it's my pleasure. I wasn't very well treated when I played for the Beaneaters and Grays."

"I didn't help that you booted more balls than Mike Kelly."

"I suppose not."

"What? You don't want the $25,000?"

On January 18, 1890 *The Chicago Daily News* said that "Charlie Comiskey, star first baseman of the St. Louis Browns, came to town yesterday morning and at 4 o'clock signed for three years to serve as captain and manager of the Players' League Pirates; the contract is said to be worth $5,000 per annum. When A.G. Spalding was asked for his reaction he said he could care less, he doubted the Pirates would ever play a game."

On January 28 a court ruled against the New York Giants in their attempt to keep John Montgomery Ward from playing for any other team, citing that his contract lacked mutuality and pointing out that the contract was completely one-sided and as a result unenforceable. The Justice wrote, "In particular, the ten-day notice clause allows the League to set a player adrift at the beginning or middle of the season at home or two thousand miles away, sick or well, at the mere arbitrary discretion of the plaintiffs." The League persisted but ten days later a New York Court ruled against the Giants' attempt to keep Buck Ewing from jumping to the Brotherhood League.

In New York, Kelly gathered with Johnny Ward, George Gore, Edward Talcott, the Director of New York's Brotherhood club, actor Nick Engel, and several others at the large parlor over Engle's place on 27th street to celebrate the decisions. Ward read a telegram from Al Johnson that said he and opera star DeWolf Hopper, whom his co-star in "Boccaccio" had called the biggest baseball crank that ever lived, were beyond the skies with joy over their great victories and encouraged them to drink a bottle with him.

Talcott stood up and invited the entire party to a supper at Delmonico's, where Ward proposed the health of Mike Kelly who had "traveled farther and worked harder than any player in the land to sign his old comrades who'd failed to keep their promises."

At the first corporate meeting of the Players' League its stockholders elected Charles Porter as president, Frederick E. Long as treasurer, and Julian B. Hart as secretary; on the board of directors were four stockholders and four ballplayers, Dan Brouthers, Arthur Irwin, Hardie Richardson, and Mike Kelly.

On March 24 Tim Murnane wrote that "the Boston Players' League team will prove to be one of the greatest batting combinations ever gotten together. In Brouthers, Kelly, Nash, Stovey, Kilroy, Richardson, and Irwin the team will pull out many an up-hill game by dint of their willows."

The National League tried to intimidate the University of Virginia into refusing to recognize the Players' League and preventing its team from playing exhibitions against Brotherhood clubs. The team's manager said, "We will allow no one to dictate to us whom we will play. We recognize the Players' League as being run on principle and fair play.

The Reds arrived in Charlottesville at 2 p.m. on the 25th of March. A crowd of 1,800 roused up people, close to a third of the city's population, gave them a hearty college cheer as they walked onto the field, smiling and raising their caps as they did.

"My, but there are some beautiful women here, Mike," Arthur Irwin said to Kelly.

"A few too many, I think, Art," replied Kelly as an especially lovely girl waved at him.

Kelly had three hits and scored a pair of runs in the Red Stockings' 14-4 win. Like whiskey and cheese, he was improving with age and running better than he had in years. That night the players went to a show at the Tremont Theatre. Kelly picked up several telegrams at the Omni Homestead where the Reds were staying from other teams that wanted to play his club, but he decided to stay in Charlottesville

a while longer. The scenery was too good.

The lovely girl from the game had sent a message to the hotel. Mike smiled when he read it.

> **Dear Mr. Kelly,**
>
> **I thoroughly enjoyed your ball-playing this afternoon and would very much like for you to visit our home at 17 Ashley avenue tomorrow evening after dinner.**
>
> **Looking forward to seeing you then,**
>
> **Blanche Calhoun**

Kelly had his men up bright and early for a run across the countryside the next morning. All were in uniform except Daily and Murphy who weren't feeling right. Two hours practice was taken on the college grounds. Richardson, Stovey, and Kelly borrowed a couple of guns and went hunting for a couple of hours after the practice. Kelly saw a rabbit at the foot of a mountain and took aim but the gun failed and the rabbit scampered off unharmed. Mike didn't mind, he was thinking about his upcoming visit to 17 Ashley avenue.

He was surprised when he got there and Blanche was the only one home.

"The family is in Europe … on vacation," she explained. "I gave the servants the night off. It's just the two of us."

At the game Blanche had worn a Victorian hoop skirt with drop shoulder sleeves, a high neckline, and voluminous skirt, grandly embellished with ribbons and bows and held out by layers of petticoats, crinolines, and hoops. It was unseemly for a woman to show skin before late afternoon.

Blanche, whose neckline was much more revealing tonight, motioned for Kelly to sit on the settee on the large veranda. "I am drinking mint juleps this evening. I believe I've had four already, I was nervous about whether you'd come. I'll get you some of my daddy's excellent bourbon for you."

With that she swept up her skirts and went inside.

The bourbon was delicious. It was clear that Blanche had indeed been imbibing for quite some time. A southern belle was supposed to be fragile and flirtatious while also sexually innocent. Mike thought Blanche was beautiful but risky to touch, like porcelain. She got out of her chair and sat beside Mike.

He kissed her. "I've been wantin' to do that since I got here. Did you mind very much?"

"I'll show you how much I minded." She grabbed his face and kissed him as hard as he'd ever been kissed. Fifteen minutes later they were in Blanche's bedroom.

The team moved to Savannah and the men enjoyed it almost as much as Charlottesville. The attitude there was all for the comfort and enjoyment of the players and the kindness shown them by the leading citizens was more than they could have imagined. They received several invitations to club rooms and private dinner parties. Kelly accepted as many as he could but he was careful about how much he ate and drink.

Murnane reported that, "Captain Kelly was never in such condition as he is this season. He is besieged with letters from all sorts of cranks. From the number of people who are striking him for loans, you would judge the general impression that he is a banker."

The Globe devoted two columns to Murnane's account of the Red Stockings' exhibition game against the Brooklyn Ward's Wonders on April 3. "The base ball Brotherhood was baptized in the rays of the sun of Austerity which, kissing the swift foot of the Only Kelly and the massive brow of the Bismarkian Ward, caused the grass to shoot forth from its prison of cinders in the new Congress street grounds and called out a greater mass of people than ever surrounded a Boston diamond.

As they stood in front of the Tremont House at 1 o'clock John Graham's procession of 15 tally-ho coaches quickly summoned a large and interested crowd. The whips found their tasks a slow one in the welter of horse cars, cabs, and barges. Bacon street and Commonwealth avenue were merrily awakened by the bugler who halted

at the Huntington avenue station as the teams of Kelly and Ward alighted from the Worcester special.

Hundreds of people loitered about the neighborhood and the scene was a lively one. When the procession re-formed there were fifteen carriages behind the tally-hos, a number sufficient to make a triumphal pageant. A chain of sidewalk spectators stood on either side all the way down and through town. Each of the approaching horse cars was overflowing and the cabs and barges that ran from the post office every ten minutes were thick. There was such a jam in Congress street as to make every one of Kelly's men feel like a millionaire. Several times the procession met or passed the old league's team in its circus barge of faded glory but there was no bloodshed.

The players finally jumped from their carriages and wended their way afoot to and through the side gate. Bursting his winter shell, the indelible base ball crank walked abroad once again in all his bounding enthusiasm, fairly rolling in the novel luxury of two games and two leagues to choose between.

The ticket-buying line extended almost to the bridge and thriving scalpers rose rapidly in their price to a dollar. A gate gave way before the eagerness of the crowd which had been gathering since 10 o'clock and many made a display of coin and waved treasury notes in a vain endeavor to pay their way in. All around were hawkers of every kind of ware and the entire spectacle was an enlarged view of a country cattle show.

Men with climbers ran like squirrels up a line of new telegraph poles skirting the further side of the grounds and perched themselves amid the wires. Others arrived with their own ladders and gained the tallest view-points to which they could climb. Some on-lookers could be seen in the distance clinging to the masts of vessels on the three sides of the peninsula. Those in the still unfinished grand stand beseeched those below to "Sit down" so they could see. Most fell to their knees in the cinders and those who did not were showered with all sizes of carpenters' scraps.

Before the games Murray & Murphy's Irish Brass Band played

447

"Auld Lang Syne."

Three sections in the grand stand were reserved for ladies and there was netting in front of it to shield them from foul balls. Smoking wasn't permitted around the ladies and male cranks were encouraged to curb their tongues or risk a severe and embarrassing beating with a parasol.

The crowd seemed heightened by the thought that the old league had not such great attendance up at the South End, a sample remark being, "I'll bet a frost has struck 'em over there today." The appearance of the candy butchers who generally frequented the rival league's grounds seemed to confirm the jollifiers in their conviction that the Brotherhood was on top and their trays were patronized in reckless good nature.

Suddenly Kelly appeared and a chorus of "Kelly, Kelly" swept through the throng. There was in this cry something childlike, innocent and prattling. He assisted the police in driving back an army of cranks who had inhabited the diamond. They fell back before him with such meek, gaping awe that he needed not apply any physical force, although the breasts upon which he laid his urging hands are no doubt all the prouder for their contact with the Only.

The game was entirely subordinate among the attractions of the day and it proceeded among unbounded good cheer but with less than the usual attention to detail. The people had come to see a housewarming rather than a contest. The grand stand enjoyed seeing the ball knock off a policeman's helmet as much as any run that was made and even when defeat came to the home nine there was nothing like the usual outbreak of disappointment and when the great crowd poured homeward it was not easy to determine from their bearing which side had won. The Players' League is alive, on with the dance and let the soda water sizzle."

It was a regular Fourth of July in Fitchburg, Massachusetts on April 14. The announcement that the Boston Brotherhood team was to play an exhibition game against the town nine was enough for shops and offices to close for the afternoon. The weather was perfect and ladies in their colorful Easter bonnets were out in force.

Kelly's men arrived on the 11 o'clock train and were met by a large and curious crowd. The players were packed into a tallyho and heralded by a bugler on their way down the main street to the Fitchburg hotel a mile away. Heads were pushed out of every door and faces flattened against every window on the route. The locals howled with delight when Kelly threw a complete somersault while going for a foul fly over the low rail that encircled the race track around the ball field.

"It's a miracle he wasn't hurt," the mayor said to his wife.

Murnane's summary of the Reds' preparation for the 1890 season read, "Fresh from a hard week's practice at the foot of the Blue mountains of Virginia the Reds put the Giants to sleep in one round. They toured New England cities where they received unprecedented attention and played to crowds that were remarkable for the time of year. Every player has worked hard and taken interest in the success of the club. Much doubt has been expressed about Michael Kelly's ability to handle them. In this I must say I once agreed but thought the only way to find out was to give him a good fair trial. So far he has taken a great deal of interest in the general affairs of the club as wells as its team work. He was more than willing to set a good example for the other players as his work in games in Savannah, Charlottesville, and in other ones nearer to home has shown.

Last year Kelly was disgruntled when the management of the Bostons was taken away from him. He is a different person this spring, fifteen pounds lighter and fit to play for a kingdom. Madden and Radbourn are in extra fine fix and Gumbert has made a good impression as a talented, all-round player and a heady pitcher and good batsman. Matt Kilroy didn't go South with the team and has let himself out but once at Providence last Saturday. He has great speed, all the curves, and perfect control of the ball. Arthur Irwin is a heady player who will do much toward bringing bunting to Boston. Harry Stovey is full of life and a fighter. As a hitting team there is no equal in the game, *The Globe* writer wishes the boys a prosperous season both in victories and patronage."

On April 17 *The Fall River Daily Evening News* printed a feature entitled, "KNIGHTS OF THE BAT AND BALL." The first player described was Mike Kelly. "Pluck, endurance, grit, ambition, and foxiness are the principal characteristics necessary to the baseball player of the present time. Michael J. Kelly, the premier among ball players, the $10,000 beauty and the hero of many adventures on and off the field, is admittedly the greatest trickster in the profession. As a base runner he has few superiors. In a recent game he made a hit that to an ordinary player would have been a solid single but Kelly wanted more. Quinn, the second baseman, was waiting with the ball in his hands but Kelly threw his body out and shot his hand in, grabbing the bag as he went by. It was a remarkable slide and no one but the king of base runners could have accomplished the move.

He is a ball player from his feet up and always wants to win. As a batter he is a daisy. He bats together with his wrists and strikes at anything, often jumping two feet across the plate in his eagerness to knock the leather out of sight."

When Kelly and Ward marched their Brotherhood men at the Congress Street Grounds for the official home opener on April 19 escorted by Reeve's band and a tally-ho coaching party over 10,000 people gave them a hearty welcome. Later the crowd swelled to more than 12,000. After the exciting game the Boston players were fairly mobbed by admirers. Only 3,000 people went to see the Beaneaters' opener. In New York, 13,000 turned out to see the Brotherhood Giants and only 5,000 attended the National League Giants' game. In Pittsburgh 9,000 attended the Players' League Burghers' opener. Only 712 showed up to see the Alleghenys. The League teams featured only a couple of players anyone had ever seen before. "Maybe they should put their names on their backs," one crank joked.

"Radbourn's twirling of the leather sphere against the champions of the world was as damaging as a mowing machine and as graceful as the dropping of a lotus blossom," according to *The New York Times*.

In the fourth inning Brouthers drove a liner to center and Ir-

win laid down a clever bunt along the third base line. Kelly sent the Keefe-B ball flying to left center and by a daring piece of running got second as both runners scored.

He did phenomenal base-running in the sixth. He got first on a clean hit and second on Radbourn's sacrifice. Richardson got in a single to left but O'Rourke fielded it swiftly and fired the ball home on a line. Kelly saved himself with one of the finest slides base ball boosters had ever seen.

On April 24 the Giants left the United States hotel and traveled in carriages to the Congress Street Grounds. They wished later they had stayed at the hotel. Kelly made base stealing completely out of the question for the speedy Giants and they fell 6-1. A couple of times he deliberately muffed a pitch and when the runner took off for second Kelly gunned him down. The Reds already had four runs on the scoreboard when Kelly went to bat in the sixth.

"Come on, boys, he yelled to his mates. "Let's put a clincher on this one."

Melodious-voiced Con Murphy put on one of his seductive smiles and worked the Reds' captain for two strikes. But Kelly had a bigger smile when he lined Murphy's next pitch into center field and Irwin scored the Bostons' fifth run.

That night Kelly and George Gore played poker in Johnson's sixth floor hotel room. Mike told Johnson what Anson had said about the Brotherhood.

"He told a bunch uv reporters we are nuthin' but a labor union no better than the bomb throwers at the Haymarket and that communists in Chicago get hung. He said we'll probably play ball on Sunday, sell beer, and let niggers inta the league."

Gore consumed five or six large glasses of whiskey and when he was half primed and found himself down close to fifty dollars he threw his cards on the table and got up. He headed toward the open window.

"Are ya needin' a bit uf fresh air ta change yer luck, George?"

451

asked Kelly.

But George didn't stick his head out the window. He climbed *out of* it.

"George!" shrieked Kelly.

Johnson was closer. He ran to the window and looked down to the street in horror. He saw nothing but a couple of carriages passing by. Hanging by his fingertips from the ledge was Gore. It took all of his might but Johnson grabbed Gore by the wrists and pulled the quickly sobering and terrified 195-pounder back up onto the ledge where Kelly helped pull him back inside.

When Johnson had caught his breath he said to Gore, "Forget about the fifty dollars."

The Reds traveled in a special car named "The Shaughram". It was named for the play by Irish playwright Dion Bousicault. The seats were richly and thickly upholstered. Kelly liked to say "were on velvet, boys."

On April 30 the largest crowd that had ever witnessed a game in the City of Brotherly Love "saw the Boston and Philadelphia teams baptize the new Brotherhood Park. At 2:30 twelve members of each club set out in open barouches. Besides the players there were three carriages for the newspaper men, the Players' League was getting a lot of ink. At the big locomotive works the workers crowded to the open windows and cheered and waved for the Brotherhood men with whom they felt a new connection.

"Three cheers for the Brotherhood," let out one of the workers.

The Boston players came out of the visitors' club house on the opposite side of the pavilion dressed in their new dark blue uniforms with white stockings. During their preliminary practice the band played "Over the Garden Wall" while the players danced the sphere around the diamond.

Kelly didn't score any runs in their 9-6 win but he made two hits and he drove his men like a redshank. He played his third straight game behind the bat without error and stopped all at-

tempts at base stealing.

The audience showed no hard feelings for the visitors' triumph. The managers of the Walnut Street Theatre and Keith's Bijou Theatre gave Kelly and his men pressing invitations to see the shows at their houses.

The Reds were staying at the Continental. John L. Sullivan had supper at a table across the dining room from the team's table that night.

"I'm real anxious for the Reds to win the pennant," the champ told the guests he was sitting with. "My friend Kelly is the greatest ball player in the world."

As he said it Kelly spotted Sullivan and went over to his table. It wasn't long before the two most recognizable and famous men in the sporting world attracted a crowd of gawkers.

"As I live and breathe, if it isn't Michael Joseph Kelly himself in the flesh," Sullivan boomed. He looked Kelly up and down, taking in his tight-fitting, expensive suit with violets in the buttonholes. He looked as athletic as he had ten years ago in Spalding's tight-fitting uniforms. "And a lot less flesh there is to him than the last time I laid eyes on him."

"I'm layin' off the beer and potatoes, champ," said Mike.

"I'm on a diet meself, Kel," said Sullivan, "I got anuther match comin' up soon."

"They look pretty fit," a man with bushy grayish-brown sideburns in a frock coat said to his handsome wife. "I'm told they are interested in stage careers when they retire."

"I would certainly pay to see Kelly perform," said his wife.

Her husband gave her a disapproving look.

"Well, I hope ta see you again while we're in town, John, maybe get ta yer fight, but I got someone waitin' for me just now."

Sully grinned. "What's she look like, Kel?" chuckled the champ.

She's a fine lookin' woman, a wealthy widow and a base ball en-

thusiast. I think she may be interested in gettin' a piece of the club."

Sully leaned over, "Or in letting *you* have a piece."

Kelly thought about punching Sullivan in the shoulder but thought better of it.

A week later the team arrived in the City of Churches and changed into their uniforms at the Pierrepoint House, a fine, six-story hotel on Montague street in the center of Brooklyn Heights' cultural district. They ate breakfast in the fine dining room then headed out to the long veranda that ran along the back of the hotel. Johnny Ward was there with some businessmen. He was stroking his pencil-thin mustache and discussing the Players' League's financial status. Kelly lit a cigarette and listened in.

"What shape are the Reds in, Kel?" asked Ward.

"I leave such things to the partners, Monte. I tried doin' the numbers at the start and found I had no head for it. What about the uther teams?"

"Considering we're never the only game in town, not too badly. Both leagues would be drawing more if they would have agreed to play on different dates."

"You told us a couple of the teams were struggling, John, said a distinguished looking man smoking a huge cigar.

"True, Buffalo especially."

Mike knocked some ashes off his sleeve and lit another cigarette. "The players who put in money last winter will be lookin' for a piece uv the pie in October, Monte."

"Well then let's hope there are pies to slice."

On May 5, Tim Murnane, wrote that, "Kelly's work behind the bat has been first class in every respect. He has caught in eight games without an error. He was never in better condition for his work than he is this season and there is no player living who can inspire his men as he does and the reason is palpable ... he can hit and run the bases and work all the fine points as well."

On the 8th of May Kelly's men struck a snag. He kept his men around the hotel until 2:30. From the veranda they watched pretty girls partaking in the craze that had captivated Brooklyn's young people - roller skating. Kelly spent his time telephoning the ball park to see if the game would be played. Rain threatened. Finally, he was told the grounds would be wet but the game would be played and he rounded up the team and they headed to Eastern Park.

With one out in the fourth inning Jack McGeachey and Emmett and Seery, outfielders who'd jumped from the Indianapolis Hoosiers, reached base, Mac going to third on Seery's safe hit. Seery tried to steal second but Kelly shot the ball to Quinn who sent it back to him and McGeachey was caught out at the plate. Kelly and Quinn had practiced the play over and over in Charlottesville. Kelly and Irwin caught Joyce the same way in the sixth.

Kelly sent two runners home in the seventh but the Brooklyns had scored eight runs in the first five innings, three more in the sixth, and another four in the 7th. The run they scored the next inning proved to be the winner.

After the game some of the players who'd never see it went to look at the Brooklyn Bridge.

Mike Kelly was the hero of the May 19 game at the Congress st. grounds. The Boston men, smarting from four losses in succession, two at the hands of the babies from Cleveland, gave the westerners "a trimming such as they will not forget for many a day." Dan Brouthers had his batting togs on, the veteran wielder of the bat lined the ball out for singles or two-baggers almost every time he came to bat.

With Pete Browning on second and Stricker on third in the opening frame Larkin bounded a grounder to Brouthers who threw to Kelly and Mike ran Stricker out between third and home. The 'only' was loaded with ginger. Larkin held first base, not daring to go down to second against Kelly's arm. He got there anyway, Daley was so erratic he walked the bases full. A hit would put Cleveland on earth. Two strikes were called on Twitchell by Umpire Jones. Kelly, who was watching the baserunners like a hawk, threw to Quinn and Brown-

ing made a dash for the plate. Quick as a flash the ball was back in Kelly's hands and Pete was touched out to end the inning.

Kelly opened the third for the home nine by a base on balls. He made a dash for second and Sutcliff threw wild to Stricker. The ball went into Radford's territory and Kelly sped for third. Radford threw badly to Tebeau and Kelly scored.

Daly opened the seventh by a line fly to Delahanty and Brown flew out to Browning. Kelly got his base on balls, stole second handily, and soon after glided into third. The spectators went berserk. Stovey got a free ticket to first and kept right on running toward second. Sutcliff threw to Stricker and Kelly made a break for the plate. Sutcliffe looked to see if he was going and the ball dropped out of his hands. The king was cheered to the heavens.

Boston began the ninth with the top of their batting list. Brown made out to Twitchell then Kel was given life when Delahanty tripped over the ditch in left field and missed his fly. After Stovey was retired Delahanty to Larkin Nash made a hit then started for second. Sutcliff shrugged and threw to Stricker. Sure enough, Kelly took off for home. Ball and man reached the plate at the same instant but the throw was in the dirt and Mike was safe yet again.

It ended 14-3 Boston and they were now tied with Wards' Wonders, whose mascot "Whistling Joe" was said to be "as black as the National League's blacklist," for first place.

Capt. Kelly, who gave his team a quiet curtain lecture before the game, covered first in the 10:30 game on May 30. His wife and his pretty young niece occupied a box in the pavilion. Mike was presented with a massive horseshoe of flowers when he came to the bat. Kelly put himself at first base in the morning game and played "out of sight, setting a record by throwing out five base runners. "Even Anson never did that," he said later. Dummy Hoy reached first on Billy Nash's low throw to Kelly but Hoy was nipped trying to make second when Kelly took the ball as it came off the low fence and fired it to Quinn.

The Reds trailed by a run in the ninth and with two out they were

ready to start to lunch and put their jackets on but Stovey hit a drive that would have been a home run on any ground in the land. Each team scored a run in the eleventh then Kelly came to the front in the twelfth with a hit hard to left, stole second on a clever slide, and scored what proved to be the winning run. His niece clapped her white-gloved hands together vigorously and looked around proudly. The Bostons remained at the grounds for their lunch, the visitors, who didn't mind spending a little money because their share of the receipts was over $3,200, went back to their hotel.

Kelly took Irwin's accustomed place in the short field in the second game, which didn't start until after 4. In the fourth inning he hit safe to left for two bases to send Nash home. Two innings later, after Brouthers had sent one into the center field bleachers for two bases Kelly hit one on the trade-mark into the hurricane deck of the grand stand for a home run to cheers from the handsomely dressed audience. Every lady attending the game had received an elegantly engraved schedule and boys had been encouraged to bring their best girl to the game so she could show off her prettiest new gown.

Secretary Hart invited the newspaper men to partake of a bounteous dinner at the United States Hotel that night. To no one's surprise, not one of them declined.

The Reds were in the Big Apple on June 2nd. It took some time to reach Brotherhood Park but once inside the big fence the view of the field and the surrounding scenery were enough to compensate for the three-quarter hour ride on the elevated cars. Buck Ewing wanted a new hat and bet Kel that his nine would come out on top. Gore started things off for the New Yorks by striking out but Kelly dropped the third strike. "Catch me if you can," he told Mike as he took off for first. Gore could still fly but Kel's throw beat him anyway. Kelly made three hits and was on base four times but scored just once. He was the object of repeated cheers from a bevy of lovely female admirers in the balcony boxes.

The New Yorks' mascot was a lady with shiny black skin. On her head was a bluish white lace cap and around her neck a white silk handkerchief.

The visitors held a 5-4 lead after seven but the Giants tallied three times in the eighth and another three times in the ninth to win it 10-7. Mike headed to a store in Manhattan and came back with a fine new dicer for Ewing.

Kelly's catching of Radbourn the next day was "perfection personified." Not one pitch got away from him and he worked like a beaver all through the game. He got little chance to swing the willow, the Giants were afraid of Kelly and sent nothing reachable his way. He got his base on balls four times. After one of them he was picked off first. He'd been admiring a young woman in the grand stand. The Bostons won 14-5.

W.I. Harris was impressed with Kelly's steely eyes on June 11 in the game against the Brooklyn Wonders. "Kelly came on the grounds knowing no such word as lose and showed grim determination and perfect confidence that he would win. Once he was hit with a foul tip and another time Dave Orr's bat kissed him and not lovingly. He donned his inflated breastworks, buckled on his mask, and started in again. When the ball struck him in the knee and a bat nailed him in the chest made him see stars he cried out, 'You can put a Gatling gun on me. If any more balls come me way I'll catch 'em with me teeth and spit 'em over to second.'

It got so warm that Ward lost his head and informed Kelly that if he tried to rattle him he would hit him in the head with the ball. Kelly told Ward that if he tried anything so foolish he would chase him all over the lot and when he caught him he would break him in two."

Joyce stole second in the Wonders' first at bats. Kelly wasn't at fault, his throw was lightning-like, but Irwin who received it allowed the runner to get away from him. He was just the second man in twenty games to steal second on Kelly, who was playing the game of his life. The Wonders had the bases loaded in the second when Kelly and Brouthers executed a pretty double play on Kinslow's little hit to the box, Kelly catching Seery at the plate with his old trick of throwing to Quinn at second and getting it right back. The Reds won it 5-2 to move three games ahead of the second place Brooklyns.

At 12 tonight the boys will leave for Boston over the Shore line. In light of their 9-3 record in their past dozen games they should receive a rousing reception when they face the Quakers on Saturday."

The Boston players received an invitation from the one of the team's directors, Charles A. Prince, the general counsel for the New York & New England Railroad, to go bluefishing on his new yacht, which was named Helen after his society wife. He'd arranged for the building of the Congress street ball park. Prince had made a lot of money by speculative stock investments in railroads and baseball teams with money it would turn out later he'd embezzled from friends, family, and the railroad. The boys were thrilled and orders for an early call the next morning were left with the hotel clerk.

Ten players, Harris and Murnane, and General Dixwell started for Larchmont in search of the yacht but without avail, the number 13 turned out to be unlucky.

"I guess he forgot his promise," grumbled Kelly. "Damn lawyers."

The yacht had already sailed for Boston.

Dixwell made the day a pleasant one for the players anyway. He hired three carriages to take them to New Rochelle where he hired two catboats and an afternoon of bobbing for eels and blackfish was enjoyed.

John Kelly in a dark suit and a Fauntleroy cap appeared in the role of umpire for the Reds' June 14 game. Mike had seen Tom Gunning around town and when he'd asked him why he wasn't umpiring any more Gunning had told him that Ward had driven him out of the game. The Reds were back home hosting the Giants after going 6-4 in Philadelphia, Brooklyn, and New York. He was "as emphatic in his decisions as a Maine judge on a liquor seizure case. But Kel and justice went hand in hand."

The Reds and Athletics split their double header on the 16th. Kelly had four hits. In the past week he'd raised his average from .213 to .330. Tim Murnane wrote: "The Boston club would be in fourth position but for the head work of Mike Kelly. He is a captain that works

off the field as well as on, and he has the social qualifications to work his points most successfully."

Several barrels of sawdust were scattered around the home plate before the morning game of the June 17th Boston-Philadelphia double header. The teams had played one the day before. The Athletics took the opener 13-11 and lost the afternoon tilt 12-2. Kelly had five hits including a home run and a double that were the longest drives seen at the grounds with the exception of Dave Orr's drive in the first Brooklyn series. Besides hitting like a battering ram the captain caught both games until the score stood 22 to 4 in the second one and he gave way to Swett.

In the pavilion Harvey Cobb, his derby hauled down to the tops of his ear, kept score and explained the points of the game to an elderly gentleman who had yet to see a game of ball before.

"That's Kelly," Cobb said to the old man when Mike went to the plate. "He's the most famous player in the game. The rooters can't take their eyes off him."

The man could understand why by the end of the game, it seemed as though Kelly was running the bases or coaching his men from behind the bat or the coaching lines the entire time.

An appetizing lunch was set out in the club house for the players. *The Globe*'s newspaper boys were invited and they were thrilled when Murnane introduced them to their hero Mike Kelly.

"That was a grand game you had, Mike," said a freckle-faced twelve-year-old. "You had more hits than a lot of players get in a week."

Mike chuckled and looked at his bat. "Me pet was good to me this morning, me sun."

"Can I get your signature?" asked another lad.

"Yes you can." He grabbed a piece of paper. "And what might your name be?"

"Johnny."

Kelly wrote "To my good friend Johnny, signed Michael J. Kelly

of the Bostons."

Johnny looked at it. "Wait 'til I show this to my father, he's one of your biggest boosters."

The diamond was still wet when Curry called "Play" again at 2:30. The pavilion was full, one-third being members of the fair sex and two-thirds of the sterner one. Kelly spent a lot of time talking to the contingent from the fairer sex which resulted in his being caught off base on two occasions.

He got his base on balls in the first inning and went to second on Brouthers' one-baser. Richardson cracked a beauty sending two runs home.

Johnston was called out on strikes to start the fifth. Kelly clipped one that had the proper ring past Sandy Irwin and then stole second, but he was stranded there by Brothers and Nash. Wiping his wet hands on his sides as he ran Mike made a fine catch of Wilmot's line fly close to the ground a few minutes later.

The Reds' pitching had been so dismal they'd split the two double headers even though they scored 57 runs in the four games.

On June 25 Spalding had Kelly up to his penthouse suite at the Astor House at Broadway and Vesey, New York's finest luxury hotel. He poured whiskey into a crystal glass and handed it to him. Kelly sat down in a chair in front of the window and lit a cigarette.

"I'll come right to the point," said Spalding. "All of the Players' League teams are losing money. I'm sorry to say so, but starting your own league was a foolish blunder."

He reached into his pocket and took out an envelope. He handed it to Kelly, who set down his drink and took it. Inside were bills, thousand dollar bills.

"There are twenty-five of them, Mike."

Kelly stared at the money. "Twenty-five thousand dollars!"

"That's for three years. What do you think?"

"I think it's quite a lot uv money."

"Is it enough to bring you back?"

Kelly got up. He headed for the door.

Spalding was confused. "Where are you going?"

"Fer a walk. I'll take me a bit uv time to think it over."

A half an hour later there was a knock on Spalding's door. It was Kelly.

"I've decided not to accept."

"What? You don't want the $25,000?"

"Aw, I want it bad enough, but I've thought the matter over and even for all the money in Chicago I cannot break me word and go back on the boys?"

"I heard you're in quite a lot of debt."

"You heard right."

Spalding gave Kelly one of the bills.

"Maybe that will tie you over."

"Thank you. I appreciate it, Mr. Spalding"

"After all these years ... call me Albert. Best of luck to you, it's no secret we still miss you here in the Windy City."

"Kelly's Last Slide."

On the 27th Pirate captain Charlie Comiskey sent Charles "Silver" King between the points. King was a rugged specimen, 6 feet tall and 180 pounds. According to sportswriter Edgar G. Brands, King "possessed wide shoulders, a barrel chest, long brawny arms, and hands so big they could completely surround and hide the ball." Notwithstanding his muscular physique, honed while learning the brick trade from his father, King's most distinguishing characteristic was his "tow-headed" shock of silver hair and light skin tone.

King was credited as one of the first pitchers to use a crossfire delivery. According to one description, King began his delivery in the back left corner of the pitcher's box and stepped to the right, releasing the ball as his hand flew over his shoulder."

On the 21st King had tossed an eight-inning no-hitter against Brooklyn at Chicago's South Side Park, yet lost 1-0. Brooklyn tallied its run by an error. His opponent, Radbourn, was one of his heroes.

When Capt. Kelly went to the bat the first time he was presented with a handsome gold-headed cane. Mike smiled from his forehead to his collar-bone and turned toward the grandstand. In his usual loud clear voice he said, "I have always followed the example set by the illustrious General Grant and accepted all presents."

The crowd laughed, then roared.

Kel handed the cane to the batboy and stepped to the plate and cracked out a fine base hit which drew another cheer. It was one of only four hits the Bostons could muster against King. After the sec-

ond inning Kelly complained the ball didn't have the usual ring and believed that a couple of dead ones had been rung in on him.

On June 30 Sullivan wrote that, "Better ball was never witnessed and the hitting was freer, more timely, and harder than any club has shown during the season." Kelly, who was batting .363, three points behind league-leading Carroll, caught wonderfully well and never let the men's spirits lag at any time in the game. He also played a part in a triple play. With runners on first and second Ned Hanlon popped a ball to shallow right field. It looked as though it would fall safe so the runners took off, but Quinn ran hard, caught the ball, and fired to Kelly, who touched the oncoming runner and threw to Brouthers for the third out.

On the tally-ho ride back to the hotel after the game Kelly read a telegram that had come for him that morning to the other players.

"Listen up, boys. It's from Secretary Hart. Have made arrangements for the July the Fourth double-header to be played in Boston instead of at Buffalo's home grounds."

"That's great news, Kel," said Dan Brouthers.

"We'll have three times the crowd in Boston," said Arthur Irwin.

"Which will mean a lot more dollars in our pockets," said Kel. "Ain't it grand that all the proceeds don't go to the owners like they do in our old league."

The club celebrated on Sunday and paid the price on Monday, losing 17-9 in Pittsburg.

On July 2 in Pittsburg Kelly thought he would give Gumbert a chance to win a little glory in his native place and the gentlemanly player never worked harder for victory. Uncle Jim Galvin pitched for the Burghers but met with a cannonading that made him retire in the eighth inning. When Kelly struck out without turning a hair in the first inning he got a laugh from seven little Galvins in the stand. In the last half of the sixth Brouthers worked Galvin for his base and Kelly sent him gamboling all the way around the circuit by a drive to the fence in right field for three bases. He scored and so did Nash

but that was all the visitors could muster until one in the eighth that left them two short.

In his account of the Red's game the next day W.I. Harris wrote, "The 'only' Mike cannot be downed more than temporarily. There isn't another like him in the baseball business. After 'Kel' was made the mold was broken. He is an original of originals, a handsome, dashing fellow who plays with his brains as well as his body. His wit is as quick as a flash and he has invented about half of the tricks of the game that are now in general use. One of his famous ones is to wait for his base on balls and tantalize and worry a pitcher and exhaust his strength and patience by bunting every good ball into foul ground and so earn a needed run.

Few better all-round players ever donned a uniform. His batting record does not show his full worth because he always plays for his side not himself, taking his base on balls when the team needs a runner and sacrificing when a teammate needs to be moved into scoring position. Kelly is a great run-getter and as a base stealer he has few equals when it comes to stealing one when success means victory.

In private life Kelly is his own worst enemy as he has a whole-souled, generous nature that has a tendency to keep him poor. Michael Kelly is very popular with the public. He has a personality that seldom fails to enliven any game in which he participates.

As a captain, Kelly was not a success in '89. The main reason was that he was often dissipated, and his example was not conducive to discipline. This year he has stayed on the water wagon and kept himself in condition and his men in line. He is dictatorial when the occasion requires him to be but jolly when his men do good work. His handling of the team has stamped him as one of the greatest of base ball generals, at least in the eyes of Bostonians. It looks now as if he ought to win the Players' League pennant."

Harris added that Mike still had the watch he won for base running land and keeps it running slow because he's always in fast company.

The Reds downed the Cleveland Infants 16-8 on the 9th. Once

again Kelly led the way with a single, a double, and three runs scored. The Burghers came to town and had their hats handed to them by scores of 12-6, 12-5, and 15-3. None of the games counted, however. Due to an injury to Arthur Irwin, Manager Hart had arranged to 'borrow' the New Yorks' change shortstop Gil Hatfield for the series. When John Ward, whose Wonders were in a dogfight with the Giants each four games behind the Reds, saw Hatfield's name in the box scores he hit the roof and had the three wins disallowed.

Boston and Chicago played a battle of the giants on July 18, the last game of the Reds' homestand. It was "by long odds worth going miles to see. First one team was ahead, then the other, but the men stuck to their work without a break until victory hung in the balance."

Kelly hit one on to the seats above right field in his first time at the bat but was touched out at third on Boyle's liner to Latham. Umpire Knight missed two calls on the bases but Kelly couldn't convince him to change his mind or come out from behind the catcher so he could see better. Knight wouldn't budge. The Bostons scored twice in the seventh on a home run by Nash and a lucky hit by Brown that sent Gumbert home.

Gumbert was first to bat in the ninth and struck out. Brown hit to Comiskey, Stovey drove one past short for a single then stole second and third, and Kelly came to the plate.

"Crack one, Mike" came a yell from the grand stand.

"Just like the old days, Kel," called another voice.

Kelly smiled, tipped his hat to the crowd and sent the first ball like a shot between Williamson and the second bag. Stovey jogged home as the crowd yelled, "Three cheers for Kelly!"

The Chicagos still had an inning to score one run to tie the game or two to win it but Gumbert was as steady as an old vet. He retired the Pirates in order and one of the greatest fighting games of the year was over. The two teams departed for Chicago via the Fitchburg road at 7 that night.

After the Bostons arrived and checked into the Grand Pacific Kelly realized he was thirsty. An hour later, after stopping to watch the mayhem caused when a wagon full of logs collided with a streetcar, he and Charlie and Dave, a couple of reporters from the Trib were sweating and drinking beer on the patio in front of a Chicago saloon.

One of them was looking at the Sports page. "Say, Kel, here's some good news for you. For the all-important Independence Day games the Brotherhood teams attracted 45,700 boosters to the National League's 32,244."

"That is good news, Charlie. You know, there are a lot of men in the Pirates I know … Latham and O'Neill and Comiskey from the Browns, and Fred Pfeffer, Jimmy Ryan, and my pal Ned Williamson from the old club."

"I hear Pfeffer raised $20,00o for contracts, it's no wonder he was able to sign so many top players. That's why they're giving your Reds a go."

"That they are," said Mike, pulling at his collar and signaling inside for another round. "But there's hardly a man in the Colts I could pick out of a crowd. Hell, Burns and Cap are the only ones I can think of."

"Oh, I've got a corker, for you, Kel," said Charlie. "You know how Pete Browning hit .250 for the Colonels last year and his drinking got so bad the team was thinking of hiring someone to run around the bases in front of him with a glass of whiskey to speed him up. He's right around .400 for the Clevelands now."

"Aye, he looks five years younger and the ball's rocketing off that Louisville Slugger of his."

"Well a reporter for the Philadelphia Press ran into him on Chestnut street the other night. A bunch of Cleveland National League men came up and invited Pete to go for a drink with them."

"What uv it?"

"Seems old Pete told them, 'No thank you, boys, you can't get me inside a saloon. I've stopped for good and I don't want to be seen in front of a saloon. I never knew what it was to go to bed sober until

the 14th of last August and if I live another month it'll be a year since I touched liquor. Some men know when they've had plenty; I never did. Since I stopped I feel like a new man. I sleep better, have an awful appetite and when pay day comes I have more to my credit than ever before. A player cannot drink and play ball."

"Good for Pete," said Kel.

The reporters looked at one another and back at Kelly.

The waiter set a tray of beers on the table.

Mike took one and held it up in the air, licked his lips, announced, "Here's to Temperance Pete Browning" and took a big swig.

On July 21 Johnny Ward's Wonders beat the Infants 5-4. If the Reds lost to the Prates in Chicago the Brooklyns would be just a half game back. *The Tribune* reported that, "Lady Baldwin had great speed and shot them over the plate for all he was worth. The score was 1-0 Boston in the six inning and the crowd was making more noise than a band of comanches after capturing a keg of whiskey. They roared after the home nine captured their first run when Nash threw O'Neil's grounder low to Brouthers. Ryan hit one to left field. Richardson got the ball and threw it to second but there was no one there.

"What the hell was that?" yelled Kelly.

While Radbourn was batting Kelly ran from his coaching box to the pitcher's box. Baldwin straightened up and stepped back.

He pointed at the dirt in front of the box. "Do you see this?" he called to the base umpire. "He's been stepping over the line every pitch."

"You're the best kicker in the land, Kelly, always were," shouted a tipsy crank from the bleaching boards.

The home plate umpire walked out from behind the plate and saw the incriminating marks Baldwin's spikes had made. He turned around. "Go to first on illegal delivery, Radbourn."

"Satisfied, Mike went back to the coaching box. On his way he called to the crank, "Good uv you ta say so."

That got a rise from the cranks.

In the seventh Latham rolled a bunt up the first base line. Brouthers ran in and scooped it up. He turned to throw to Radbourn but he was still in his box.

"Had it occurred to you to cover first, Hoss?" yelled Kelly, who was playing shortstop.

Radbourn just shrugged.

"That's one reason you got released last year," Kelly muttered under his breath.

Williamson flew out to right field for what should have closed out the inning. Baldwin hit a hot grounder that deflected off a stone and bounced over Kelly's head. Duffy bunted down the third base line and Latham scored the winning run.

Kelly knew they needed to win the next two in Chicago. He stayed in the hotel that night. The second game was a 2-1 nail-biter. The Chicagos kept getting men on base but whenever they tried to steal Kelly gunned them down. According to the *Tribune*, "Captain Kelly was behind the bat and the way he nailed the fleet-footed Pirates as they went for second was grand to behold."

A crank who was enjoying the contents of his flask yelled, 'Bring on your other catchers. Our man Kelly'll give them cards and spades.

Tim Murnane wrote, "Comiskey and Kelly worked the lines for all they were worth. Both generals knew that a slip-up might lose the game and each was anxious to add another victory to his nine's winning string.

Sharp fielding by Kelly, Quinn, and Tom Brown in the sixth kept the game scoreless. With one out in the Boston half Stovey, whose grim expression makes him look like a convicted killer, cracked one safe to right and went around to the three-quarters post on Kelly's perfectly placed bunt. Brouthers hit an ugly grounder that Comiskey smothered and threw to first as Stovey scored the first run of the game.

With one out in the seventh Jimmy Ryan hit a home run to knot

the score at ones. The next two Chicagos went out then Farrell hit a daisy cutter to short. Kelly made a clever pickup and a sharp throw to first to get him and end the threat.

Kelly took up his favorite stick in the ninth. With the score still tied the crowd was at a fever pitch. He tightened his belt, and pulled down his cap.

"Now, Kel," sang out Harry Stovey from the lines and his captain responded with a ringing old single past short. Brouthers got his base on balls and Kelly signaled to Hardy Richardson to hit to right to avoid a double play. He went after an out curve, met it with an easy wrist motion, and shot the sphere between Pfeffer and Comiskey. Duffy came in for it on a dead run as Kelly legged it from second. He rounded third with a wide swing like a cutter going around a stake boat and thundered down the home stretch and was under the wire by a length and one of the finest games ever seen in Chicago was won by the Boston men. Where all played well it would be unjust to single out any one man, but Kelly's all-round work was great and worth more than a passing mention. His hitting was timely and his fielding brilliant and he worked his team every minute the game lasted. The boys headed to dinner with a spring in their step tonight.

The third game was just the opposite, the Reds had a regular walkover, bludgeoning the Pirates 22-5. Kelly hit a double and three singles. He drove in Brown in the first, stole second, and came all the way home on Farrell's wild drive. He scored his second run of the game the next inning on Richardson's sharp single with the bases loaded. The game was held up in the fourth while Latham went to the clubhouse to change his breeches which he had torn sliding into second. Kelly made another hit his next time up and after stealing third scored again on a sharp single by Richardson. The Boston captain belted a ball to right for a double in the seventh and two more runs were added to the visitors' string.

Anson and his wife were in a box seat. He wore a seersucker coat, she a mauve bombazine and a large calico bonnet.

"It looks as though your batting eye still works, Kel," said Anson

as Mike passed the grand stand after scoring for the fifth time.

Mike tipped his hat to Mrs. Anson and said, "That's not Corcoran or Clarkson in the box, Cap, we need ta make hay while the sun shines. The damn Brooklyns are right on our tail."

"My boys were in the thick of it 'til the middle of June. Since then we've played like old nags not young colts."

"I'm sorry, Cap, but I read your club's box scores. Malachi Kitridge behind the bat, Bob Glenalvin at second, and Walt Wilmot in center? It's a wonder you win at all."

"Well I did not expect you could pull yourself together and lead a club after what happened with the Beaneaters but you're proving a lot of people myself included wrong."

"I still luv the game."

"And you can still play it."

"Pleasure to see you again, Virginia I hope this old bugger's a lot more pleasant at home than he is on a ball field."

Virginia's mouth curved into a smile. "A little bit, Mike, just a little. It is good to see you in such good condition and doing so wonderfully on the field. I know my husband wishes you were still in his nine."

The Bostons had spent a long time racking up all those runs. They were to catch a train for Pittsburg at 5:50 so they went from the grounds to the station in uniform, grips in hand.

In Hartford the players weren't having supper that night. The city's nine was playing a team from Baltimore under electric lights.

Kelly was in excellent condition and playing first-rate ball. While several of his teammates were struggling at the plate his batting wasn't a problem, he was among the league leaders as usual. But the batters behind him weren't hitting and he wasn't scoring runs at his normal rate.

Rumors had circulated for months that Cap Anson and A.G. Spalding were up to a plan of getting the ear of certain Players' League men into which they would sing a siren song. Buck Ewing had been

meeting secretly with Spalding and Anson in order to break up the Brotherhood. John Day developed an elaborate scheme with Spalding to attempt again to get Kelly to defect. The two owners began by asking him to meet with Anson, in Youngstown, Ohio, and told him that Buck Ewing would also be attending the meeting. Kelly saw through the ruse and invited the magnates to confer among themselves in a warmer climate.

Mike heard that Ewing and Hardy Richardson had been seen whispering at a corner table in a dimly-lit cigar store in Philadelphia called Keffer's. When he questioned Richardson about it Hardy flat out denied it. Regardless, the two had been unable to persuade a single player to jump back to the National League.

Kelly's batting was grand on Friday, August 1. Gumbert and Buffalo's George Keefe sent the ball over the plate for all they were worth and the batters sent it flying to every quarter of Olympic Park. Tom Brown led off the first inning with a base on balls, went to second on a wild pitch, and scored on Kelly's single. The first two men up for Boston in the fourth went out on liners right at Clark and Twitchell. Stovey worked Keefe for a base on balls, Kelly and Brouthers hit safe, and by the time the side was retired the Reds had scored four runs. Kelly made his third hit of the day the next inning as the Bostons tacked on five more runs and knocked Keefe out of the box. Mike got his fourth hit in the sixth and the Reds added another five runs to the heap. Gumbert got bombarded with eighteen hits but the league-leaders triumphed by a tidy score of 21-13.

Tim Murnane telephoned his wife from the lobby of the Richmond Hotel in Buffalo that night.

"I thought you told me the Richmond had burned down a couple of years back," she told her husband.

"It did, Martha. This hotel was rebuilt on the site of the original Richmond. It burned to the ground in March of '87. It was one of the most horrific blazes in Buffalo history. It killed fifteen employees and guests even though there were many heroic rescues of women and children. Nearby hotels and taverns threw their doors open to pro-

vide makeshift hospitals for the survivors, many of whom had leapt from their windows. Neighbors claimed they'd never heard anything as haunting as the sounds of their shrieks as they plummeted to the street. Much of the blame for the fire fell on the telegram companies."

Martha was puzzled. "The *telegraph* companies. Why them?"

"They'd strewn a dense web of overhead wires and cables that impeded the rescue attempts. The city ordered them to string their cables underground."

"I've been reading your articles. The team's still doing well."

"They've won six of nine so far."

"Are they still being followed?"

"By the rest of the league? Of course. They *are* in first place."

"No, silly. By detectives."

"Oh? Them. Yes, they're still on their … on *our* trail."

"Have Kelly and Hornung been behaving themselves?"

"Better than usual. Not when they give the sleuth hounds the slip though. Kelly's pretty good at that."

"So you've told me."

"One particular man, a short fellow with a mysterious air about him has been eyeing the boys very sharply. They got together and put up a job to see if he was one of the private eyes. Brown and Madden walked out the front door and up Chestnut street. Dick Johnston was to follow the fellow if he went after them."

"Did he?"

"Sure enough, as soon as Brown and Madden left the hotel the man lit out after them, shading his face with his hands. Brown and Madden walked four squares and then shot up an alleyway over to Spruce street but the man was right after them and Johnston right behind him."

"What were Kelly and Hornung doing while all this was going on?"

"They were having a couple of drinks."

"How do you know?"

"I was with them."

"Tim, I don't think the Globe sent you west to drink liquor."

"What would you have me do? Drink, sarsaparilla with them drinking rye."

"Well …"

"Kelly always tells his best stories after a few whiskeys, I've told you that. They helped get me that raise, didn't they? Boss says every time they print one of them they sell more papers."

"You don't try to out drink Kelly do you?"

Murnane laughed and other hotel guests looked over at him. "Out drink Mike Kelly? Have you taken leave of your senses, dear. *No one out drinks Kelly.*"

The clerk from the front desk came over. "I am sorry, Mr. Murnane, but your time is up."

"We're hopping on the New York Central on Wednesday morning, Martha. Should be home in time for dinner."

"I love you, Tim, don't let Mike Kelly lead you to any dens of iniquities."

"Dens of iniquities? I hadn't thought to ask Kel to take me to *them.*"

"*Good bye*, Timothy Murnane."

"Love you."

The next day *The Buffalo Morning Express* reported that, "King Kelly was in a rage last night and the object of his wrath was one of his own men, Ad Gumbert who was kind enough to umpire in Gaffney's place yesterday. Ad undoubtedly went in with the intention of doing what was right and started in by calling Daly safe on first when nine of ten people thought Wise had thrown him out. Later he called his captain out at third on a close play at a critical stage of the game. When Cunningham caught Quinn napping in the sixth Kelly raved because Gumbert called him out. Kelly tore his hair out and threw his club twenty feet. When the Buffalos made the winning runs in

the eighth on Connie Mack's drive onto the cupola the crowd got up and yelled like demons. Kelly scared the home side boosters. With two out and Swett on first he knocked the ball over the fence but the hit was foul by ten feet and the crowd sighed in relief. Kelly hit the next pitch to Wise who retired Swett at second to end the game."

On August 8 *The Globe* had a merry account of the home team's win the previous afternoon. "Buck Ewing and Mike Kelly handled their forces right through nine innings of one of the best games seen in Boston this year. There were plenty of witty remarks sent out by the captains. Everyone seemed to be 'Wally Gibbs' with Kelly. 'Long John' Ewing, who figures to fare better than his six and thirty record in Louisville last year, was firing them over the plate like mustard seeds. Brother John is something like six feet four in height and built on the fishpole plan."

Kelly nailed Johnston when he tried to steal second base in the fourth and picked Whitney off first in the fifth. In the seventh Gil Hatfield sent a ball to deep right. Kelly unfurled his wings, soared three feet into the atmosphere and came down with the ball to the chagrin of Hatfield.

The game went along with a rush for six innings and Kelly and Ewing were both on the lines giving orders every chance they got.

'We've got you know, old man,' sang out Kelly.

'We Giants are bound to cut loose and pile up the runs yet,' answered Buck."

The Bostons scored three in the eighth to win it 4-2.

On August 12 Kelly was presented with a house and lot valued at $10,000 and furnishings worth $3,000 more. The estate was on the Main street of the aristocratic town of Hingham, one of the most beautiful townships in the old Bay state.

The estate, which was located a mile from the railroad station, contained five and a half acres of land, a two and a half story house, a stable in keeping with the style of the house, and other outbuildings including, one outfitted as a bowling-alley. A shaded piazza extend-

ed across the entire frontage. One entered the residence by a flight of wide granite steps into a large hallway from which rose a broad, circling staircase. Doors led to a library with bow windows. Next was a spacious dining-room with high ceilings and a French glass door that opened onto the south piazza. Beneath, a large double cellar, cool and dry, contained airy arrangements and bins for coal to supply the great furnace. On the second floor were a modern bathroom and six sleeping rooms, large and high with many windows looking out onto the sumptuous grounds.

When Kelly took the train for Hingham he was followed to the Cushing House by close to fifty personal friends in a special car. Host Cushing welcomed the party and Arthur Dixwell paid the captain a high compliment and said that should he succeed in bringing in the championship to Boston he and the other members of the team would be well remembered. Dr. Galvin presented the deed for the house to Kelly, who thanked one and all, including his friends in San Francisco, Chicago, and Boston who had contributed to the wonderful gift and promised a small bottle on ice to anyone who might call during the winter months. Then the party sat down to a tremendous spread and many magnums of champagne.

At 8:30 two barge loads left the Cushing House for "the king's" new residence. The house was illuminated by electric lights and looked beautiful set back from the road at the end of a spacious lawn with a well-shaded driveway. Kelly was on the porch to welcome the guests having preceded them in his new horse and wagonette. Mrs. Kelly with several friends brightened up the parlors and the party was not long in making themselves at home.

Arthur Irwin was among the few guests still there as the grandfather clock ticked toward midnight. Kel was dying to ask him about the woman on his arm.. He found the two of them alone in the dining room admiring the expensive new silverware cabinet and called Irwin over.

"Who's your escort, Arthur?" Kel asked.

"Her name is May. She's from Philadelphia. Isn't she grand?"

"Aye, that she is ta be sure. Quite luvly. If you don't mind me askin', how old is she?"

"Eighteen."

"Eighteen! And you're what? Thirty."

"Thirty-two. May's from Brookline. She's a big booster of the team, comes to all our games. We're to be married in a few months."

Kel was in the middle of taking a sip of wine. He nearly spat it all over the new white rug.

"Married?"

"Yes, Kel, married."

"But you have a wife and four children in Philadelphia.

"I do. But May and I will live here in Boston."

"Oh well then, why didn't you say so?"

Kel walked away and left the lovebirds alone. He looked at his wine glass. "I need somethin' a lot stronger than this," he said to himself.

Soon there was talk of giving John L. Sullivan a residence in Hingham to equal King Kelly's. The Hinghamites didn't take kindly to the idea of having the brawler as a neighbor. Sullivan was notorious for having recently hit up a Boston bar and boasted he could kick the ass of anyone in the place. When a drunk took took him up on his wild boast, Sullivan took him out into the alley behind the pub, thrashed him senseless, and threw his unconscious body into a dumpster. The problem was that there was nothing to the rumor.

The Players' League race was excruciatingly tight. Boston led with a record of 54-37, Brooklyn was still second, 2 ½ games behind, Chicago was three back, New York four behind, and Philadelphia was five games out.

Captain Kelly, who made four of his team's fourteen hits, came in for a twirling act on the 16th at Brotherhood Park in New York. Gumbert got roughed up again so Mike put himself in to pitch when the Giants had scored four times in the seventh to tie the score 13-13. He gave up just one run the rest of the way and the Bostons got

two in the closing frame to win a wild one 16-15.

The Reds and the Chicagos played two on August 27. Capt. Kelly was again the "white-haired boy" of the day. With two out and runners on second and third and one run to tie and two to win in the ninth inning of the first game Kelly, who'd made six catches, one a terrific running one in the right field corner, came to the bat full of confidence. The spectators knew that Boston's most timely hitter was up and watched every movement with an eager eye. For years Kelly had proven himself a great batsman in such an occasion.

Mike got ready, splaying his hands a few inches on his bat as always and squeezing it just a little. "I'd give me eye teeth for a baser here," he said to himself. He straightened himself up with his heels close together standing as erect as a town pump.

Baldwin was in the points for Chicago and was pitching for his reputation. He went into his premeditated pantomime and managed to work in two strikes on his man.

"Hit her out, old man," called Irwin from the coaching box.

The next ball came over the plate with a rush but was met on the trade mark and away it went spinning down over second base while Gilbert and Brown came home with their runs. Kelly doffed his cap to the crowd as the crowd cheered for fully two minutes.

"Give him another house," someone yelled with the roar subsided. The crowd cheered again.

Kelly's four hits in the second game were all clean ones. The rest of the Reds combined for four. The Chicagos prevailed 8-2 and hurried for their coach. They had a 7 O'clock train to catch. On their way out of the park Comiskey sang out to Kelly, "Those Pittsburgs are likely to make it warm for you during the rest of the week."

"We'll be with 'em, Commy," was Kelly's response.

The Reds routed the Burghers 18-0 on August 2 and had a "cinch" on Friday with 16-4 and 5-2 wins. After sweeping the double header the Bostons' drew 2,390 to the Saturday morning game at the Congress Street Grounds. Brown opened things with a fine hit and Kelly

put in a double and scored on Brouthers' single. Kilroy was in the box for the home nine but Kelly replaced him with Gumbert after he'd surrendered seven runs in five innings. It looked like an uphill job to pull the game out of the fire but Kelly's men got there in great form. With the score 7-2 in the fifth Kelly hit safe and scored on singles by Richardson and Nash. Kelly's men got in there in great form with four runs in the eighth then four more in the ninth. It was accomplished by some of the prettiest hitting ever seen in a ball game according to Murnane. Kelly sent home two runs in the eighth, stole second, and tied the score on Big Dan's single. Gumbert sent home the winning run by driving the ball on a line over the left field fence. Kel singled again in the ninth, his fourth hit of the morning. The visitors scored a blank and Gen. Dixwell leaned over his box and called for three cheers for Gumbert who'd so skilfully issued blanks to the Spiders over the last four innings. The Bostons won it 11-7. Their captain had led the way once again with three runs and four hits. With his club well ahead in the afternoon game Kelly retired in the sixth after a hit in two tries for a .714 average for the day's work. His club didn't need him much, winning 7-2. Four wins in two days, Kelly felt good. He felt even better when the Reds beat Cleveland 18-9 on Tuesday and 12-6 on Wednesday to open up a three-game lead on the Brooklyns.

A steady rain Saturday, September 8 forced the club to return "silver-halves" to nearly 2,000 loyal cranks when the game was called off. Some of the players headed home for the weekend. Murnane told his readers that Captain Kelly was making things lively in Paterson but left the details to their imaginations. The silver bat he'd been given by the *Enquirer* was still on display in a store window.

Kelly had caught the last five games without an error, a first for him, and stood out as the best thrower to bases in the three major leagues. It was a rare occurrence to see a man even try to steal a base on him. He told Manager Hart that he was going behind the bat for every game until the Reds clinched the pennant.

On 10 the *New York World* said: "If King Kelly wants any more houses he can have them. The number of happy cranks in Boston is

equal to its population. The only unhappy men in town are the Giants, who fell five games behind the Beaneaters."

The Boston Herald reported that some of the Chicago players had been accused of a brutal and unwarrantable attack upon an Old Colony brakeman on Wednesday evening last while the man was in the performance of his duties. He was insulted and pummeled and two bruised eyes show that the punishment was not slight. Captain Comiskey was on the train but declined to interfere. It was said that the players implicated were under the influence of liquor.

The headline on the Globe's base ball column on September 26 read:

"KELLY'S GREAT TEAM CAN'T BE CAUGHT."

Captain Kelly has shown himself a master mind in handling a great ball team and to his head work as well as good playing belongs no small share of the credit."

Mike's team was not caught and the city loved him all the more for bringing them a championship. Kelly played a few games for an American Association team the next year but he batted badly and drank too much. He decided to return to the theater.

On November 9, 1894 the headlines read, "At 9:55 last night "King Kelly" heard the decision of the Great Umpire from which there is no appeal.

The slight cold, aided by the east wind and murky chill was too much for the player. He was taken to the emergency hospital. About five o'clock he was given the last sacraments of the church after which he rallied a little. But he soon began to sink and at the hour stated he said, "This is my last slide," and he was called out for the last time. His wife was sent for but she did not arrive in time to say goodbye.

Kelly was loved for the unyielding pluck and courage with which he did his work. Among his mates and his profession he left behind not a single enemy.

Kelly could not pass a mendicant and keep his hands in his pock-

ets, and it can be truly said of him, he would share his last dollar with anyone who approached him and was in need.

He was the single most important reason that women became attracted to baseball. Before Kelly, very few females could be found at baseball games, the beau ideal of a ball player, shrewd, skillful, and so quick-witted that his work was always a wonder and a delight to all who watched him. He will be missed by all of the baseball public."

John Montgomery Ward was asked to name the most essential attribute of ball-playing. He described a somewhat occult one that is found among a handful of players – the faculty of being able to do the right thing at the right time. Some men, he said, no matter what their other faults have that faculty and such players are heroes.

If a man can be depended on in a pinch he is rated a first-class player and the public learn to condone his errors. The late Mike Kelly he said was a good example. No one ever accused "Kel" of being much of a fielder and he could drop a fly or two and fumble a grounder with the greatest finish, but if there ever came a chance to win and it fell to him to do the work, he could be depended upon to come through.

Also by
W. G. Braund

———

Rube Waddell :King of the Hall of Flakes

—

Babe Ruth & the 1927 Yankees have the Best Summer Ever

—

The Only Del: The Greatest Batsman in the Land

About the Author

After completing *"The $10,000 Beauty"* and the screenplay based upon it, Will Braund headed in a whole new direction, he's now writing Children's Books.

The series is called Cat Tales. The first one, *"Mocha: The Fluffy Pants Kid"* will be followed by *"Katie Loves Marbles"*, and *"Mocha's Forest Friends."*

OUT OF THE PARK